CRIME AND DEVIANCE

SKILLS-BASED SOCIOLOGY

Series Editors: Tony Lawson and Tim Heaton

The *Skills-based Sociology* series is designed to cover all the key concepts, issues and debates in Sociology. The books take a critical look at contemporary developments in sociological knowledge as well as essential social theories. Each title examines a key topic area within sociology, offering relevant examples and student-focused pedagogical features to aid learning and develop essential study skills.

Published

THEORY AND METHOD (*second edition*)
Mel Churton and Anne Brown

RELIGION AND BELIEF
Joan Garrod and Marsha Jones

CULTURE AND IDENTITY
Warren Kidd

POLITICS AND POWER
Warren Kidd, Philippe Harari and Karen Legge

STRATIFICATION AND DIFFERENCE
Mark Kirby

CRIME AND DEVIANCE (*second edition*)
Tony Lawson and Tim Heaton

EDUCATION AND TRAINING (*second edition*)
Tony Lawson, Tim Heaton and Anne Brown

HEALTH AND ILLNESS
Michael Senior and Bruce Viveash

Forthcoming

THE MEDIA (*second edition*)
Marsha Jones, Emma Jones and Andy Jones

THE FAMILY (*second edition*)
Liz Steel, Warren Kidd and Anne Brown

Skills-based Sociology
Series Standing Order ISBN 0–333–69350–7
(*outside North America only*)

You can receive future titles in this series as they are published. To place a standing order please contact your bookseller or, in the case of difficulty, write to us at the address below with your name and address, the title of the series and the ISBN quoted above.

Customer Service Department, Macmillan Distribution Ltd, Houndmills, Basingstoke, Hampshire RG21 6XS, England

Crime and Deviance

Second Edition

Tony Lawson

and

Tim Heaton

First edition 2000
Second edition 2010

Published by
PALGRAVE MACMILLAN

Palgrave Macmillan in the UK is an imprint of Macmillan Publishers Limited, registered in England, company number 785998, of Houndmills, Basingstoke, Hampshire RG21 6XS.

Palgrave Macmillan in the US is a division of St Martin's Press LLC, 175 Fifth Avenue, New York, NY 10010.

Palgrave Macmillan is the global academic imprint of the above companies and has companies and representatives throughout the world.

Palgrave® and Macmillan® are registered trademarks in the United States, the United Kingdom, Europe and other countries.

ISBN 978–0–230–21782–9

This book is printed on paper suitable for recycling and made from fully managed and sustained forest sources. Logging, pulping and manufacturing processes are expected to conform to the environmental regulations of the country of origin.

A catalogue record for this book is available from the British Library.

A catalog record for this book is available from the Library of Congress.

10   9   8   7   6   5   4   3   2   1
19 18 17 16 15 14 13 12 11 10

Printed and bound in Great Britain by
CPI Antony Rowe, Chippenham and Eastbourne

Contents

Acknowledgements

The authors would like to thank Emily Salz and Anna Marie Reeve for their editorial help on this book and others in the series. The authors and the publishers would like to thank the following for permission to reproduce copyright material in the form of extracts, figures and tables: Blackwell Publishers; Guardian Media Group plc; the Home Office; McGraw-Hill Ryerson; the Labour Party; the Law Society; the *New Statesman*; the Office for National Statistics; Pearson Education Ltd; Stanley Thornes; The General Council of the Bar; and Thomas Nelson & Sons Ltd. Every effort has been made to trace all the copyright-holders, but if any have been inadvertently overlooked the publishers will be pleased to make the necessary arrangement at the earliest opportunity.

Chapter 1

Introducing the Sociology of Crime and Deviance

After studying this chapter, you should:

- understand the philosophy underpinning this book
- recognize the problematic nature of the terms 'crime' and 'deviance'
- have reflected on whether there is such a thing as the sociology of deviance and criminology
- be aware of the subject matter of the subsequent chapters in this book

THE PHILOSOPHY BEHIND THE BOOK

We have three aims in writing this book. We wish firstly for you to take an active part in your own education. *Interpretation, application, analysis and evaluation* are the central skills that new sociologists must demonstrate in any examination. Interpretation means that you should be able to look at different types of information, such as that presented in tables and text, and be able to communicate your understanding of them. Application is being able to take sociological and non-sociological material and use it in relevant ways to answer set questions. Analysis means to break down debates and arguments into their constituent parts. Evaluation means being able to assess sociological debates and arguments by examining and evaluating relevant evidence. We are also concerned with providing you with a good solid understanding of sociological knowledge.

The best way of developing these skills is to practise them yourself. Hence we have designed a series of exercises that are tied to these four skills, and if you carry them out you should be able to improve your performance in these areas. You will be able to identify the skills that each question is designed to develop by looking out for the following symbols: [I] for interpretation, [A] for application, [An] for analysis and [E] for evaluation. However, we also want you to understand the interconnections between all the information in this book, so you will also find that there are *link exercises* for you to do. These will not only help you to perform skilfully, but will also increase the sophistication of your understanding of the sociology of crime and deviance.

Our second aim is to present you with sociological knowledge that is appropriate and useful for your examination performance. We decided that we did not want to present knowledge that you can glean from other textbooks as it would be pointless to try to cover ground that is more than adequately covered elsewhere. But, we do want you to be as up to date as possible with topics that are familiar to you, so that you can apply the relevant material in your examination. We have therefore focused on developments in sociology during the 1980s, 1990s and 2000s.

We have not attempted to tell you all there is to know about sociology in this period, because to develop your sociological skills you should be finding out for yourself what has been happening in society and sociology during this time. We have, however, tried to give you an overview of the debates that have been going on and the sociologists who have been writing about crime and deviance in this period. You will find that much of the material concerns the theories and ideas of the new right and of the postmodernists, and how other sociologists have responded to these developments. To help you consolidate your knowledge and understanding, activities that test these are included in the exercises. Questions that require you to demonstrate sociological knowledge and/or understanding use the symbols [K] and/or [U].

Our third aim is to help you to pass your examinations in sociology. We have therefore included a series of exam questions for you to do, with some key concepts and critical thinking questions. We believe that if you carry out the activities connected to the questions you will help yourself to pass any examination. You may prefer to conduct the activities with a teacher or lecturer, and she or he may be able to build upon the ideas and activities in order to improve your performance. However, you could also use the examination activities as supplements to your other work in sociology, as you go through your course, or as a revision aid as you near your examination.

The important thing to remember is that we cannot do it all for you. You will gain most from this book if you approach it in an active way and are prepared to apply the information and skills in the examination itself. If you just read the text and miss out the exercises, you will only be doing half of what is necessary to pass any sociology examination.

WHAT IS DEVIANCE?

Traditionally, sociology has seen deviance as some sort of opposition to the societal consensus on the proper way to behave and think. In the *Rules of Sociological Method*, Durkheim (1973) describes a complex relationship between crime, deviance and difference. He sees these three phenomena as degrees of divergence from the norms (rules) of society, in which crime attracts social censure of an official kind, while deviance is more lightly censured by a social rather than a necessarily official reaction. On the other hand, individual difference is to be celebrated as the essence of human society. Deviance therefore stands between crime and difference, whereby individuals live their lives at the edge of 'normal' society without always attracting legal sanctions. Crime and deviance are therefore inevitable consequences of the range of individual differences that exist in any society. The greater the differences, the greater is the need for the concept of deviance. The definition of what is deviant and what is criminal relies on the scientific analysis of a given set of social circumstances. The need for analysis stems from the fact that what is deviant is not always obvious (see Exercise 1.1 to explore one such distinction). Sensibilities – that is, judgements about what is acceptable and what is not – vary from society to society, and what may be condemned in a traditional society as unacceptable difference (for example homosexuality) may be celebrated in postmodern societies as a lifestyle choice, or at least one to be tolerated because of its difference.

ⓘⒶ

Exercise 1.1

A useful distinction is made in sociology between legal and illegal deviance. Legal deviance refers to behaviour that breaks social norms or standards but remains within the law. Illegal deviance (crime) refers to behaviour that contravenes the law and is subject to formal punishment. Bearing this distinction in mind, draw up an extended version of the chart below and classify the following deviant acts into either legal or illegal rule breaking. We have provided two examples to get you started.

Deviant acts

- Murder
- Homosexuality
- Rioting
- Suicide
- Euthanasia
- Rape within marriage
- Smoking marijuana
- Terrorism
- Killing in wartime
- Prostitution
- Alcoholism
- Having a tattoo
- Speeding in a car
- Busking
- Divorce
- Tax evasion
- Vandalism
- Nude sunbathing

- Road rage
- Mental illness
- Environmental pollution
- Farting
- Single parenthood
- Street begging

- Drinking alcohol
- Smoking in a pub
- Bigamy
- Child abuse
- Transvestism
- Joy riding

Legal deviance	Illegal deviance
Mental illness	Rape within marriage

You may have found it difficult to allocate some of the deviant acts in Exercise 1.1. You may have ended up saying that it depends on the country in which you live, the time period in question or the circumstances in which some of the acts take place. If such thoughts came into your head you were right, because there is no absolute or universal way of defining a deviant act. Rather, deviance is a social construct. It is something that is relative to time, place and social situation.

Moreover the definition of deviance is interwoven with the issue of power, that is, who in society is able to impose their view of what is acceptable and what is not. For example Sumner (1994) argues that it is those who benefit most from the prevailing system who have the means to create ideological censures, that is, the dominant notions of right and wrong in society. It is the activities of the media and the education system that are crucial in determining which behaviours are accepted by the majority as 'normal' and which are considered 'deviant'. Yet the acceptance of social acts as non-deviant can also be determined by society at large, regardless of what the 'official' definitions are.

ⒾⒶ
Exercise 1.2

To illustrate the way in which deviance is a relative concept, draw up a chart like the one below and use the list of deviant acts in Exercise 1.1 to provide four examples of legal or illegal behaviours that vary according to time, place or social situation.

Relative nature of deviance	Example of deviant act
Time	1. Rape within marriage
	2.
	3.
	4.
Place	1. Bigamy
	2.
	3.
	4.

Social situation	1. Nude sunbathing
	2.
	3.
	4.

WHAT IS CRIME?

At first glance the definition of crime seems to be deceptively simple, that is, it is what the law declares to be illegal. However, postmodernists such as Henry and Milovanovic (1994) argue that this is just a tautology (saying exactly the same thing in a different way) and does not encompass the complexity of what is meant by crime. For example interactionists have pointed out that an individual act can be defined as crime or not-crime, depending on the circumstances in which it is carried out (see Chapter 4). But a whole range of other factors are neglected in the tautological definition, such as the role of the law enforcement agencies, what the perpetrator and the victim contribute to an action being defined (or not defined) as a crime, and what has been omitted or exaggerated by participants in coming to a definition of an act as a crime or not a crime.

While this is to insist that crime is a socially constructed phenomenon, it is not to accept, as some critics suggest, that crime is somehow not real and that violent behaviour is merely fictional. Henry and Milovanovic argue that crime is about the exercise of power, the inflicting of pain and hurt on individuals caught in an unequal relationship at a particular moment (see Chapter 5). This power may be expressed by denying something to others, by inflicting real pain on others or by making victims out of those with less power. However, the law can only cover some of the ways in which harm is inflicted in the exercise of power. What is also criminal are those governmental and business practices or family interactions that are not formally illegal but result in harm to others. This of course is a very radical position, in that it criminalizes many of the activities of the state that have usually been seen as the normal and legitimate exercise of power.

THE RELATIONSHIP BETWEEN CRIME AND DEVIANCE

The ways in which crime and deviance are conceptualized in sociology are varied, and it is oversimplistic to treat them as the only two possible categories for activities that lie outside the social consensus of 'normal'. Hagan (1994), following Sutherland (1949), argues that there is a continuum of activities ranging from those formally proscribed by the law, to those whose legal situation is less rigid to those seen as conformist. This would include behaviour that is actually or potentially subject to punishment by society, depending on the contingent circumstances in which the behaviour occurs. A crucial contingent condition for classifying behaviour is the seriousness with which it is viewed, taking into account that not all groups will see the same behaviour as serious to the same extent, and that the social response to any behaviour in terms of penalty will vary (Figure 1.1).

Relatively infrequent but serious crimes such as murder are generally agreed to be very harmful. Other activities may attract some censure from some groups, but there is little consensus about the seriousness or even the normality of the behaviour. This suggests that there is room for movement as the social response to activities changes over time or according to culture. For example the social attitude towards homosexuality has changed from legal censure to relative acceptance during the second half of the twentieth century. We can thus make a distinction between consensus crimes, which are generally seen as truly unacceptable; conflict crimes, which while illegal are not always viewed as such by society and are often seen as ways in which some social groups may establish some advantage by manipulating the law; social deviations, which are activities that are not actually illegal but are subject to some sort of regulation, usually by the state, such as mental illness; and social

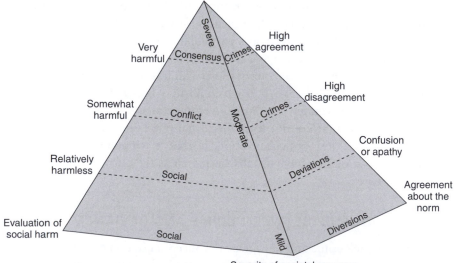

Figure 1.1 Kinds of crime and disrepute
Source: Hagan (1977).

diversions, which are the variations in fashion and lifestyle that frequently occur in society.

IS THERE SUCH A THING AS THE SOCIOLOGY OF DEVIANCE?

Sumner (1994) argues that the sociology of deviance has collapsed under the impact of new social conditions and under the weight of its own contradictions. He draws upon the work of Foucault (1967) and others to suggest that the sociology of deviance is intimately connected to the world of modernity and has no resonance in late modernity (or, as some would have it, postmodernity). The argument rests on the belief that the concept of deviance emerged as part of the scientific search for ways to control populations, leading to the creation of new categories of people such as the insane or the deviant. These new concepts were developed as an attempt to manage social problems and potentially disruptive social behaviours in ways that avoided authoritarian oppression. They were ways in which liberal democracies in the West attempted to establish order through increased surveillance and self-surveillance and without recourse to state violence of the most immediate type.

The development of industrial society resulted in an increase in the numbers of people who were unemployed, sick or mentally unstable, and the elites in liberal democracies sought to manage these problem groups by means of increased administration, with the voluntary consent of the 'victims' of social development. Concepts such as homosexuality, prostitution and illegal drug use, therefore, did not refer to some absolute categories of abnormal behaviour, but were developed through scientific discourse (the ideas, concepts and language used to carry out the activities of science) as elites established new ways of dominating the population. These discourses established that groups such as the unemployed were 'not like we normal people' but were characterized as 'other'. This was an important step in achieving a new hegemony or dominance over the mass of the population without reliance on repression.

The concept of deviance was therefore developed as part of the modernist project, defining as inherently deviant those activities which ran counter to a supposed societal consensus. As the forces of postmodernity gained pace, Sumner argues, the concept of deviance lost all scientific credibility, especially as the consensus that deviance supposedly violated could not be empirically shown to exist. As the boundaries between categories of behaviours blurred, as scientific 'metanarratives' (science as an all-encompassing explanation for everything) began to be rejected, and as the importance of individual difference rather than strict social categories grew, so the concept of deviance was increasingly abandoned. By the mid-1970s hardly any sociologist employed the concept of deviance to define actions beyond the social consensus – because such a consensus did not exist.

From the 1970s onwards sociologists increasingly turned to the concepts of crime and law, rather than what they saw as a romanticized 'deviance', which had been stripped of its scientific usefulness by its adoption by various political positions, from the right to the left. Rather than being scientific, the concept had now become ideological and therefore of little scientific use. The development of approaches by the new right to crime and disorder hastened the demise of the concept of deviance as the new right rediscovered harsher social censures and attitudes towards criminal behaviour (see Chapter 6). The new right's overtly ideological approach to social order has been paralleled by the left in that they have turned away from their attempt to establish overarching theories of crime and moved towards the development of pragmatic strategies for the management of antisocial behaviour.

Rather than the concept of deviance, Sykes (1992) suggests that the concept of the victim is now the defining idea in the field of social difference. Concern for the victim arose from the interest that left realists (see Chapter 6) and feminists (see Chapter 8) began to show in populations of people who most experienced crime, often in an invisible way. In the postmodern world the dominant majorities feel increasingly threatened by a society that is seemingly out of control – previously quiet minorities are now asserting their rights as full citizens; immigration seems to be undermining the 'way of life'; the traditional moral order seems to be breaking down.

In these uncertain circumstances, citizens are increasingly resorting to litigation to resolve their grievances, real or imagined – or, as Sykes puts it, 'the National Anthem has become The Whine' (ibid.). Postmodern societies are characterized by an aggressive individualism, which fancies itself the victim of discrimination and constantly complains about its lot. Sykes calls this the privatization of discipline, which has produced a new social grouping of those who profit from the litigatory instincts of the victims – counsellors, lawyers, antidiscrimination advisers, human rights experts, and so on. The result, as Sumner (1994) puts it, is that 'the politics of blaming has now become a very big business'.

IS THERE SUCH A THING AS CRIMINOLOGY?

During the 1990s a heated debate took place within the field of criminology (the study of crime, criminals and victims from a variety of approaches, including sociology) as to whether such a discipline can be said to exist in the conditions of postmodernity. This was not just a dispute between different perspectives on crime – or a fundamental division between those criminologists who adopted a theoretical approach and tried to produce a general theory of crime and deviance and those who saw themselves as agents of the criminal law agencies with a practical focus, producing policies to control the criminal population – but was a condition of most academic disciplines in the 1990s. Part of the problem lay in the fact that many criminologists came from other academic disciplines. For example many sociologists became interested in crime, and some claimed that it is the sociological input that was most fruitful in the examination of crime (see, for example, Hagan, 1989).

But the influence of external factors on criminology was much wider than just other academic disciplines. Crime is still a matter of great concern to the public and to institutions such as the media and the police. These institutions generate 'discourses' that reflect the knowledge, activities and social, cultural and economic relations within those institutions. Discourses are therefore 'ways of speaking' about something that create a 'reality' about it. For example media discourses about social security fraud often deploy an image of the 'scrounger' and apply it to all claimants, whether legitimate or not. The discourses of the claimants themselves, which might present a different reality, are not given the same prominence.

There are many discourses that seek to influence the course of criminal justice, ranging from the criminal law agencies themselves, to the world of medicine – which offers input into the theoretical causes of criminal behaviour (for example the category of 'criminally insane') – to the media, whose output is the main way in which most people 'experience' crime (for example see Sparks, 1992). Clearly, many political organizations seek to influence the public debate on crime, and Gusfield (1989) suggests that for some organizations the control and regulation of 'crime' is the very reason for their existence, for example the opposing sides in the abortion debate. An interesting discourse that has permeated law enforcement is the military discourse, with the army-like organization of the police and the adoption of warlike metaphors such as the 'fight against drugs' (see McGaw, 1991). This 'militarization' came into its own after the hijacking of aeroplanes by al-Qaeda terrorists and their crashing them into the World Trade Center in New York. President Bush declared a 'War on Terror', which is carried out not just by the military. Cottle (2006) has argued that control of information (the 'image war') is a crucial issue in the fight against terrorism, as politicians and terror groups seek to have their own discourses dominate an increasingly diverse media.

Exercise 1.3

Ⓐ 1. Suggest two sources other than those mentioned above that shape the public perception of crime.

ⒾⒶ 2. Identify two factual and two fictitious television programmes that inform the public about crime. Write down any similarities and differences in the ways in which the factual and fictitious programmes depict crime.

Ⓘ 3. Newspaper reports on crime are a major means by which the public perception of crime is formed. To get you to appreciate the types of message that newspapers convey about crime we would like you to carry out a small content analysis. To do this, observe the following instructions and record your findings in a similar chart to the one shown below.

   (a) Read the same daily newspaper over a five-day period.
   (b) Cut out any stories to do with crime.
   (c) For each story, make a note of the crime committed and the social profile of the offender(s) and victim(s) (age, ethnicity, sex, and so on).
   (d) Record any other relevant points, for example the locality in which the crimes were committed and the column inches devoted to each story.

Day	Crime committed	Social background of offender	Social background of victim	Other relevant points
1				
2				
3				
4				
5				

4. Some sociologists argue that the media present a distorted or selective picture of crime.

ⒶⒺ   (a) In the light of your content analysis results, to what extent do you agree with this viewpoint?

Ⓐ   (b) Suggest one reason why the media might present crime in a distorted or selective way.

More fundamental is the fragmentation that has occurred in all forms of knowledge under the impact of the changes that we call postmodernism. Foucault (1972) argues that human sciences such as sociology and criminology are in a precarious position because they exist 'in the shadow of science' (Lawson, 1986). This position beneath 'proper' sciences, such as economics and biology, leads to a blurring of the boundaries between the human sciences as they search for explanations of the phenomena under study. The result of this is disciplines that no longer have firm boundaries but are influenced by other disciplines, and which in turn influence others. This is not just a temporary situation, awaiting some unifying theory, but a chronic state of fragmentation, which Ericson and Carriere (1994) argue ought to be celebrated rather than bemoaned. Acceptance of the fragmentation would allow pluralism to flourish, rather than difference being seen as some sort of intellectual crisis. The loss of solid boundaries around the field of criminology also allows new ideas and influences to penetrate criminological discourses (see Exercise 1.4). In the twenty-first century, for example, an increasing interest in the impact of human rights is evident, not only in terms of the legal framework that forms the backdrop for criminology, but also the way that a concern for human rights impacts on criminological theory (Silvestri and Crowther-Dowey 2008).

(K)(A)

Exercise 1.4

Identify six academic disciplines that have a contribution to make to the understanding of crime, criminals and victims.

Another critique of the idea of criminology as a discrete subject is that, by establishing finite limits to what might properly be investigated as 'crime', many social phenomena that could be of interest to criminologists become 'invisible'. Hillyard and Tombs (2004) argue that the focus of criminologists should shift from 'crime' to the wider concept of 'social harm'. This would divert attention away from the many petty events that are 'criminal', but which do not cause social harm, towards much more harmful activities such as tax evasion that are not traditionally seen as the legitimate objective of criminological investigation.

CONTENT OF THE BOOK

Having introduced you to the sociology of crime and deviance, let us now establish what is to come in the rest of this book. Chapter 2 presents statistical data on crime, offenders and victimization. The usefulness of different types of crime data are discussed. Chapter 3 explores a range of early and recent sociocultural explanations of crime and deviance. In Chapter 4 we address interactionist thought on crime and deviance, and reflect on labelling and phenomenological, ethnomethodological and postmodernist views. Chapter 5 examines conflict explanations of crime and deviance. The chapter adds to the debate on white-collar crime introduced in Chapter 2. Realist explanations of crime and deviance are dealt with in Chapter 6. Both right and left realist theories are explored, as well as other realist approaches such as routine activities theory and lifestyles theory. Postmodern developments out of realism are also explained. Chapters 7 and 8 draw on recent theoretical developments alongside more established ideas to account for the relationships that exist between ethnicity and crime and gender and crime. Issues regarding victimization are raised in both chapters. Finally, in Chapter 9 we consider a range of theoretical views on the workings of various aspects of the criminal justice system. We then examine different schools of thought in the field of victimology.

Important concepts

Crime • Deviance • Difference • Modernity • Politics of blaming
• Fragmentation of knowledge

Critical thinking

1. What is the distinctive contribution that sociology can make to an understanding of crime and deviance?
2. Is it possible to have an agreed definition of deviance when, as individuals, we hold ethical and moral ideas about the proper way to be behave that may or may not be shared with others? Does holding religious beliefs help or hinder reaching such an agreed definition?
3. Is the proper role of criminology to understand crime, to explain crime or to combat crime? Are criminologists just agents of the state?

Chapter 2

Crime Statistics

After studying this chapter, you should:

- be able to identify and begin to explain patterns of crime, offending and victimization
- appreciate the advantages of using official crime statistics
- understand the limitations of using official crime statistics
- have an understanding of alternative measures of crime and recognize their relative merits

Official statistics on crime and offenders are gathered by the police, the courts and other criminal justice agencies, such as prisons and the probation service. The information recorded is published annually by the state. In this chapter we will begin by presenting official statistical data on crime. We will then reflect on the advantages and limitations of such statistics. Finally we will critically consider two alternative survey techniques that have been used by sociologists and criminologists to supplement the official crime data.

OFFICIAL STATISTICS ON CRIME

Official statistics on crime provide valuable information on trends in law breaking, the nature and extent of offending in any given year, the geographical distribution of crime and the social make-up of criminals. According to official statistics, crime rates in England and Wales rose significantly from the mid-1980s to the early 1990s (the so-called 'crime explosion') but declined thereafter, though there were small increases in some forms of crime between 1997 and 2004, due to changes in accounting procedures by the police (see Item A).

This exercise is designed to establish how much you know about crime in Britain.

(K)(U) 1. Read each of the following statements and fill in the gaps with a logical guess.

- Crime reached a peak in England and Wales in . . . . . . (year).
- In England and Wales . . . . . . million offences were committed in 2006/7.
- Crime is most likely to be committed by . . . . . . (state 'males' or 'females').
- For males, criminal activity peaks at the age of . . . . . .
- For females, criminal activity peaks at the age of . . . . . .
- The . . . . . . are over-represented in the prison population (state 'working class' or 'middle class').
- More crime is committed in . . . . . . areas (state either 'urban' or 'rural').
- The ethnic group that tends to be over-represented in the prison population, given their proportion in the population, is . . . . . .

(I) 2. Now that you have made your guesses, compare your answers with the official statistical data in Items A, B, C, D, E and F.

Item A

Table 2.1 Crimes recorded by police, by type of offence 2006/7

United Kingdom	Percentages		
	England & Wales	Scotland	Northern Ireland
Theft and handling stolen goods	36	33	23
Theft from vehicles	9	5	3
Theft of vehicles	4	4	3
Criminal damage	22	31	30
Violence against the person	19	3	26
Burglary	11	7	10
Fraud and forgery	4	3	4
Drugs offences	4	10	2
Robbery	2	1	1
Sexual offences	1	1	1
Other offences	1	11	3
All notifiable offences (= 100%) (thousands)	5,428	419	121

Source: Self (2008).

Table 2.2 Incidents of crime by type of offence

England & Wales	Millions					
	1981	1991	1995	2001/2	2003/4	2005/6
Vandalism	2.7	2.8	3.4	2.6	2.5	2.7
All vehicle thefts	1.8	3.8	4.4	2.5	2.1	1.7
Minor injuries	1.4	1.8	2.9	1.7	1.7	1.5
Other household theft	1.5	1.9	2.3	1.4	1.3	1.2
Other thefts of personal property	1.6	1.7	2.1	1.4	1.3	1.2
Burglary	0.7	1.4	1.8	1.0	0.9	0.7
Theft from the person	0.4	0.4	0.7	0.6	0.6	0.6
Wounding	0.5	0.6	0.9	0.6	0.7	0.5
Bicycle theft	0.2	0.6	0.7	0.4	0.4	0.4
Robbery	0.2	0.2	0.3	0.4	0.3	0.3
All violence reported to BCS	2.2	2.6	4.3	2.8	2.7	2.4
All household crime	6.9	10.4	12.4	7.9	7.2	6.8
All personal crime	4.1	4.7	6.9	4.7	4.5	4.1
All crimes reported to BCS	11.0	15.1	19.4	12.6	11.7	10.9

Source: Self and Zealey (2007).

Exercise 2.2

Study Item A and answer the following questions.

Ⓚ 1. What is meant precisely by 'crimes recorded by the police'?
Ⓘ 2. Which was the largest category of offence in Northern Ireland in 2006/7?
Ⓘ 3. Describe the patterns of offences in Great Britain.

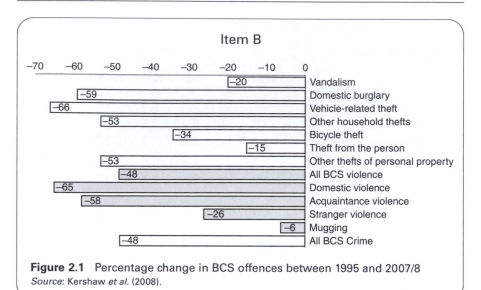

Figure 2.1   Percentage change in BCS offences between 1995 and 2007/8
Source: Kershaw *et al.* (2008).

Exercise 2.3

Refer to Item B and answer the following questions.

1. Which type of recorded offence has shown the greatest decline?
2. For which category of offence was the smallest drop in offences recorded?
3. According to the chart, has violent crime fallen faster or slower than all crimes?
4. What do you think is meant by 'acquaintance violence'?
5. Suggest two reasons why crime has been falling in this period?

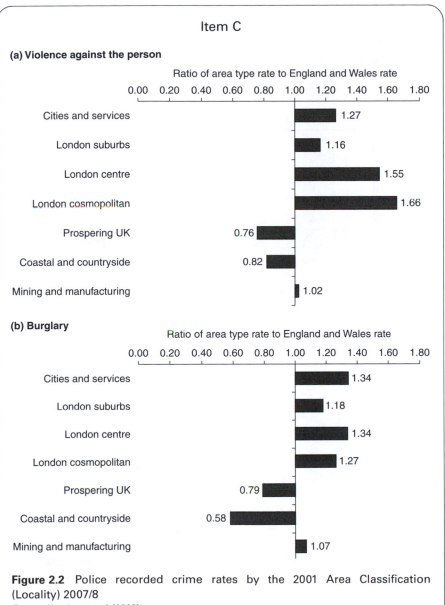

Figure 2.2 Police recorded crime rates by the 2001 Area Classification (Locality) 2007/8
Source: Kershaw *et al.* (2008).

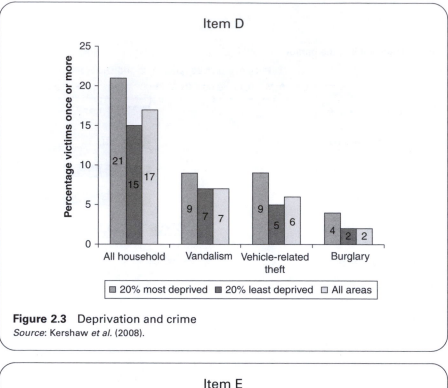

Figure 2.3   Deprivation and crime
Source: Kershaw *et al.* (2008).

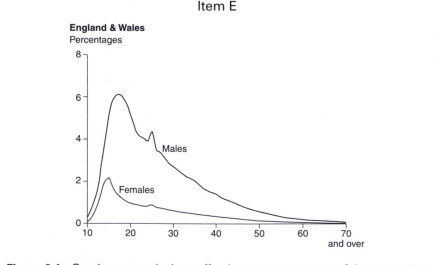

Figure 2.4   Gender, age and crime: offenders as a percentage of the population of England and Wales, 2006
Note: People found guilty or cautioned for indictable offences in 2006; excludes those whose age was not known.
Source: Self (2008) – data supplied by Ministry of Justice.

Item F

Table 2.3 Ethnicity, gender and crime: prison population of British nationals by sex and ethnic group, 2006

England & Wales	Percentages		
	Males	**Females**	**All**
White	80.8	82.7	80.9
Mixed	2.7	4.1	2.8
Asian or Asian British	4.9	2.0	4.8
Black or Black British	10.6	10.0	10.6
Chinese or Other ethnic group	0.2	0.4	0.2
Total (= 100%) (thousands)	62.7	3.4	66.2

Source: Self (2008) data supplied by Ministry of Justice.

Exercise 2.4

① 1. Using the data in Items C, D, E and F, in no more than 200 words describe the social distribution of criminality in England and Wales.
Ⓐ 2. Suggest two reasons why crime rates appear to be higher in urban areas than in rural areas, as shown in Item C.
Ⓐ 3. The social-class background of offenders is not routinely recorded in official crime statistics. Suggest one reason why such data may not be recorded.

①Ⓐ

Exercise 2.5

Official statistics can go out of date quickly. Try to update the statistics we have presented in Items A to F. You could start your search for data by referring to the most recent edition of *Social Trends*. You can also gain access to current statistics through the Home Office website on the internet. When you have completed your search, devise a set of questions – based on the data you have found – for another sociology student to answer (your questions should be of a similar style to the ones we have set for Exercises 2.2 to 2.4).

The advantages of using official crime statistics

Official statistics on crime and criminals are widely used by sociologists, criminologists, the police, the media and political parties. This is because they have a number of advantages and uses (see, for example, Sanderson, 1994). The exercise below encourages you to reflect on some of the potential benefits of using such official data.

Ⓐ Ⓔ

Exercise 2.6

Listed below are five advantages of using official crime statistics. Make your own list of five other possible benefits. (Hint: if you get stuck on this exercise think about some of the general methodological advantages of using official statistics.)

1. They offer the opportunity to identify rising or falling trends in crime by comparing crime rates over time.
2. They provide useful information on the social make-up of offenders.
3. It is possible to use the statistics to generate and test sociological explanations of crime.
4. They help governments to shape and evaluate their policies on law and order.
5. They are easily accessible.

The limitations of using official crime statistics

Social constructionists question the validity and reliability of official crime data. Cook (1997) argues that the process of recording offences involves various decisions that may lead to the inclusion or exclusion of individual crimes. It is often suggested, then, that the official statistics exclude a large number of crimes and criminals and therefore fail to present an accurate picture of the extent of law breaking in society. Crime statistics are said to underestimate the phenomena they are trying to measure because of the underreporting of known crimes, the invisibility of certain crimes and systematic bias entering into police practice. Thus crime statistics are said to be socially constructed (Morrison, 1995), that is, they are the final product of a complex process of decision-making by those involved in the reporting and classifying of criminal acts. Some consider that the end result is that the statistics tell us less about crime and criminal behaviour and more about the process of reporting by victims and the way the police go about their work. However, Newburn (2007,

p. 69) argues that there is 'a degree of acceptance that official data do provide an indication of general trends in crime'.

THE UNDERREPORTING OF KNOWN CRIMES

The most common means by which offences become known to the police is for the victims of crime to report them. However, not all victims report the crimes that have happened to them. The 2008 British Crime Survey (BCS) estimates that only 39.3 per cent of all offences were reported to the police in 2006/7 (Kershaw *et al.*, 2008). Comparable figures for previous years are shown in Item G. The extent to which crimes are or are not reported varies according to the type of offence. For example burglaries and vehicle thefts are frequently reported, yet cases of domestic violence and the theft of household property are vastly underreported. Reporting rates for different types of crime are shown in Items K and L.

Item G

Table 2.4 Trends in reporting to the police, BCS percentage estimates

	1981	1991	1997	2001/2	2005/6	2007/8
All BCS offences	31.0	43.0	38.8	39.6	39.8	39.3

Source: Kershaw *et al.* (2008).

Exercise 2.7

① 1. According to Item G, what was the increase in the percentage of offences reported to the police between 1981 and 2007/8?
Ⓐ 2. Suggest one reason for the trend in crime reporting between 1981 and 1991.

Item H

Table 2.5 Reasons for not reporting crime, England and Wales, 2007/8

Percentages		2007/8 BCS						
	Vandalism	Burglary	Thefts from vehicles & attempts	Other household theft	Other personal theft	BCS violence	Comparable subset	All BCS crime
Trivial/no loss/police would not/could not do anything	85	68	85	84	71	52	75	76
Private/dealt with ourselves	9	22	7	10	10	35	16	15
Inconvenient to report	4	3	5	5	6	6	5	5
Reported to other authorities	2	1	2	1	12	6	3	4
Common occurrence	2	0	2	1	2	3	2	2
Fear or reprisal	2	5	0	2	0	5	2	2
Dislike or fear of the police previous bad experience with the police or courts	2	3	2	1	0	2	2	2
Other	3	5	3	4	6	10	6	6

Note: Percentage of those who experienced a crime and did not report it to the police. Occasions where more than one reason could be given.
Source: Kershaw *et al.* (2008).

Exercise 2.8

Ⓘ 1. What does Item H suggest is the main reason for not reporting crime?
Ⓘ 2. According to Item H, what percentage of the public do not report crime because they dealt with the issue themselves?

Exercise 2.9

The following chart lists eight reasons why victims do not report crime (2007/8 BCS findings). We would like you to extend the chart and complete the blank spaces by copying it onto paper and carrying out the following tasks.

ⒾⒶ 1. Provide examples of offences that may apply to each of the reasons for not reporting. Two examples are given to get you started.
Ⓐ 2. Give four other reasons why victims may not report crime. In each case, offer suitable examples of offences.

Reasons for not reporting crime	Examples of offences
Too trivial/no loss	Vandalism
Common occurrence	
Police would not be interested	Noisy neighbours
Dealt with matter ourselves	
Reported to other authorities	
Inconvenient to report	
Fear of reprisals	
Fear/dislike of police	

THE INVISIBILITY OF CRIME

Because of the nature of certain types of crime they are either unlikely to be reported to the police or difficult for the police to observe. Examples are computer fraud, overcharging, illegal abortion, child abuse, fraud, illegal dumping of hazardous waste and drug offences. Such crimes are said to be invisible because either the victims are unaware a crime has been committed or there are no identifiable victims.

One of the biggest and in financial terms the most costly areas of invisible crime is white-collar crime (see Item I). Sutherland (1949) defined white-collar crime as crime committed by people of respectability and high social status in the course of their employment. Sutherland's definition is not without its problems though. Croall (1992) suggests that his definition is too narrow as it only includes offending by those in high-status occupational positions. She therefore offers a broader definition: 'crime committed in the course of legitimate employment involving the abuse of an occupational role'.

A further problem with Sutherland's definition is that 'it does not distinguish crimes committed for an organisation or business from those carried out at its expense' (Nelken, 1994b, quoted in Taylor et al., 1995). As Taylor et al. point out, this has led sociologists to make a distinction between corporate crime (committed on behalf of an organization) and occupational crime (committed at the expense of an organization). Corporate crimes (sometimes called organizational crime) often result in consumers and workers being exploited in some way, for example when organizations or corporations offer misleading descriptions of their products or when employers break health and safety laws. Occupational crimes can involve both lower-level workers and senior managers offending against the organization or business for which they work. Examples of occupational crime include false allowance claims and embezzlement. Also largely invisible in the official crime statistics are those crimes committed by the state in pursuit of political ends. (See pp. 149–62 for a fuller explanation of white-collar crime.)

The fact that much white-collar crime goes unnoticed has important implications for the validity of the official crime statistics and any sociological theories that take the statistics at face value. This is because the extent and importance of crimes committed by the powerful are underestimated (Box, 1983). The underestimation of white-collar crime may be all the more significant as we witness a shift in Britain from a manufacturing to a service economy. As O'Donnell (1997) observes, the nature of crime may be changing with the decline of the working class and the growth of the white-collar class. He points to the increase of white-collar crimes such as fraud and computer crime alongside blue-collar crimes such as burglary and car-related theft.

Item I

The impact of white-collar and technology crime.

The impact of fraud:

- In 2003/04, the cost of fraud to Customs and Excise alone was estimated to be between £4.8 billion and £5.4 billion.
- Losses through fraud on plastic cards have been on an upward trend until 2004, when £504.8 million was lost by illegal use. The introduction of chip-and-pin cards has reversed this trend.
- In 2003/04, 52 percent of people who bought over the Internet using their credit and debit cards reported that they were worried about doing so, yet only 3 per cent of users had been an actual victim of credit card fraud over the Internet.
- Benefits fraud for 2004/05 was estimated to be at £0.9 billion, a reduction from the £1.4 billion of the previous year.

Technology crimes:

- Of home Internet users, 27 per cent reported that their computers had been infected with a virus in 2003/04, which was an increase on the previous year's total (18 per cent).
- Only 2 per cent of computer users reported any hacking invasion of their home computers.
- Of 10–25 year olds, 25 per cent admitted that they had illegally downloaded software, music or films in 2003/04.

Global white-collar and organized crime:

- In 2003, it was estimated by the Organisation of Economic Co-operation and Development (OECD) that the illegal drug trade cost its members $120 billion. It is estimated that up to half a trillion dollars are laundered through the world's legal financial system each year (Galeotti, 2005).
- In the US, the most commonly reported technology crime is Internet auction fraud (44.9 per cent), where users are conned into believing that the auction site they are using is a legitimate one, leading to an average loss of $724.
- The contraceptive Depo-Provera was banned in the USA because it caused malignant tumours in animals that it was tested on. However, Upjohn Co. continued to sell the product in 70 other countries, and it was widely used in US-sponsored population control programmes abroad (cited in Simon and Eitzen, 1993).

White-collar crime affects all of us either directly or indirectly:

- All employee crimes create 'shrinkage' which affects profits, share returns and price levels.
- Tax evasion leads to large losses of revenue to the government, which has to increase general taxation to cover that loss.

- Consumer fraud is widespread and has a wide range of effects, from illness brought on by cheap and contaminated foodstuffs, to being sold shoddy goods or those of an inferior quality to what is described, to goods being sold in a dangerous state.

- Unsafe working conditions account for most industrial 'accidents'. In 2006–07, large sections of the rail network were found to have been neglected in terms of safety measures and were potentially unsafe. A number of train accidents brought this systematic neglect into the open.

Source: Wilson *et al.* (2006).

Exercise 2.10

Read Item I and answer the following questions.

1. What was the total loss on plastic card fraud in 2004?
2. Item I gives an indication of the global nature of white-collar crime. Using the item to illustrate your answer, explain the meaning of the term 'globalization'.
3. What percentage of 10–25 year olds admitted to illegal downloads?

4. It has been argued that white-collar crime is less serious than 'street crime' because victimization is often indirect.

   (a) Give an example of indirect victimization.
   (b) Explain how white-collar crime can affect victims directly.

Exercise 2.11

There have been a number of alleged cases of white-collar crime in the 2000s. From your own knowledge, make a note of any individuals or businesses that have been found guilty of a white-collar crime. For each case, briefly describe the nature of the offence and classify it either as a corporate or as an occupational crime. You might want to record your findings in a three-column chart with the following headings: 'Case', 'Nature of Crime', 'Type of crime (corporate or occupational)'. If you find this exercise difficult to complete because of lack of knowledge, refer to the Internet. The name 'Enron' might be a useful starting point, but do not limit yourself to American examples.

Exercise 2.12

Because of the relative invisibility of white-collar crimes they often do not come to the notice of the law enforcement agencies (note that many white-collar crimes are not investigated by the police, but by authorities such as HMRC and the Health and Safety Executive.

Ⓐ 1. Apart from the invisibility factor, give three other reasons why white-collar crimes may not come to the attention of criminal justice agencies.

Ⓐ 2. What are the possible implications for the official crime statistics of the police not being involved in the investigation of all areas of white-collar crime?

POLICE PRACTICES

The police as a formal agency of social control are said to create a systematic bias in the official crime statistics. Two main sources of bias are evident from the organizational practices of the police.

First, the police do not have to report all crimes to the government, only those that are classified as 'notifiable' (Newburn, 2007). In addition, the police may not record all the crimes known to them (Williams, 1997). It would be impractical for the police to record every minor crime as it would place a severe strain on the criminal justice system. Therefore judgments have to be made about which crimes to record, based on professional expertise, Home Office guidelines and even public and media opinion. This discretionary decision-making obviously has an important effect on the total number of crimes recorded in the official crime statistics. Croall (1998) argues that the reliability of the official statistics is reduced when one considers that recording practices vary between police force areas. In making decisions about whether to record a crime, the police follow Home Office guidelines. The 2002 National Crime Recording Standard revised these guidelines to prioritize the victim's perception of whether a crime had been committed or not, rather than using an evidential model for recording, which demands that there should be a basic level of evidence for any recording of an action as a crime (Reiner, 2007). The effect of this change is that recorded crimes are likely to show an increase from 2002.

Second, the police arguably operate a policy of selective law enforcement. Because the police do not have infinite resources they have to decide which types of crime to focus on, where resources should be deployed and who they should arrest, caution and charge. Some sociologists argue that such decisions are based on the police's perception of the nature of the 'crime problem', where most crime is likely to take place and who is most likely to be a criminal (Holdaway, 1983). Because police officers' perceptions about crime and offenders are often based on media reports and crime statistics there is a tendency for them to concentrate their efforts on 'street crimes', to deploy more officers in working-class and inner city areas and to be more suspicious of certain groups, for example the young, the working class, males and blacks. As Cook (1997) states: 'in practice, police resources are targeted at the poor and disadvantaged areas which are seen to "breed" crime, and not at middle-class suburbs and office blocks'. Such selective decision-making has an important effect on the types of crime and offenders represented in the official crime statistics, which in turn can influence our views about what constitutes the 'crime problem'. Cook believes that a self-fulfilling prophecy is set in motion, whereby police strategies (and the statistics that follow) add weight in the public's (including the police's) mind that a crime–poverty connection exists.

In the twenty-first century, the increasing sophistication of the crime statistics collected by the police and other agencies of the state have allowed a much finer analysis of crime, which in turn has led to new police practices on the street. This is often characterized as 'intelligence-led policing'. Since 2005, the National Intelligence Model has attempted to identify, at local levels, significant groups of law-breakers, areas of high criminality and new emerging patterns of offending, so that resources can be specifically targeted on them (Maguire and John, 2006). Let us explore these sources of bias in more detail.

The police may not record all the crimes known to them

Because the police have power of discretion when recording crime (Morrison, 1995), not all the crimes reported to them, or observed or detected by them, are necessarily recorded. The 2008 BCS estimated that, for those BCS offences that could be compared with police figures, only 42 per cent were reported and recorded by the police in 2007/8 (Kershaw *et al.*, 2008). However, it should be stressed that, as with the reporting of crime, the extent to which crimes are or are not recorded varies according to the type of offence (see Items K and L).

①Ⓐ

Exercise 2.13

There are a number of reasons why the police may not record all the crimes known to them. Some of these reasons are listed below. For each of the reasons, try to provide examples of offences that might apply.

1. The police may not agree that a crime has actually been committed. Although a victim may perceive that an offence has taken place the police may decide that a crime, as legally defined, has not been committed or they may believe that there is insufficient evidence that a crime has taken place. However, new 'counting rules' from 2002 have increased the weight given to the victim's perception of a crime.
2. The police may make the judgement that an incident is not serious enough to be recorded as a notifiable offence.
3. The police may agree with the victim's decision not to proceed with the prosecution.
4 Some offences are recorded but later written off if subsequent investigations show that an offence has not actually been committed or if the police believe that there were errors in the reporting of the crime. This process is called 'no-criming'.

Selective law enforcement

Box (1981) argues that the police operate in such a way that they are more likely to concentrate on offenders from the least powerful sections of society. However, he does not see police bias as a crude conspiracy against disadvantaged groups. Rather he sees it as a product of the occupational constraints under which the police work, for example their ideological views about crime and criminals, and their concern about invading privacy and damaging career prospects.

Whether police bias is conscious or not, the effect can be to increase the likelihood of powerless groups finding their way into the official crime statistics. Coleman and Moynihan (1996) cite some studies that suggest class bias may be present within the criminal justice system. It is worth quoting their review of evidence on class discrimination at length:

Research has found that the unemployed (... we can take employment status to be one rough indication of class position) are more likely to be stopped by the police (Smith, 1983), stopped and searched (Kinsey, 1984) and to receive a custodial sentence (Crow and Simon, 1987; Crow et al., 1989). Some of these differences, however, can be attributed to behaviour, offence seriousness and frequency of offending. The police's treatment of juvenile offenders has been shown to be affected by the perceived class of the offender; Bennett (1979) found that middle-class juvenile offenders were more likely to receive a caution than working-class offenders when arrested for the same kind of offence. Landau and Nathan (1983) found the police more readily prosecuting so-called 'latchkey' children.

At this point we should pause to express concern about those views which claim that the social make-up evident in the official crime statistics is the product of police discrimination. Moore and Sinclair (1995) argue that the effect of police bias on the official crime statistics is unlikely to be that great because only 8 per cent of arrests are initiated by the police, the other 92 per cent being the result of complaints. This point is reinforced by Sanderson (1994): 'the prospect of police practices making a major contribution to biases in official data is not that great when one considers how little crime is discovered by the police'. Perhaps, then, bias is brought into the system through those who complain to the police. Certainly Box (1981) acknowledges that the role of complainants can be crucial because they can influence the way in which the police respond to an incident. Coleman and Moynihan (1996) refer to an article by Shah and Pease (1992), who claim that there is evidence to suggest that victims are more likely to report an incident if the person who commits the act is black. However, we should stress that there is limited evidence of victim bias in the reporting of crime and therefore no firm conclusions can be drawn on this issue.

PROBLEMS INTERPRETING TRENDS IN CRIME

Interpreting trends in crime over time is a problematic activity. This is because crime rates can rise or fall for reasons other than increases or reductions in law breaking. On the most basic level, legislation changes the definition of what is a criminal act and can either create new categories of offences (anti-discrimination laws in the early twenty-first century in the UK) or eliminate others as laws are repealed (homosexual acts in the 1960s; see Newburn, 2007). Developments in technology can also lead to new forms of crime emerging. As the Internet has become commonplace, it has been used as a new vehicle for old crimes, as well as developing its own forms called cybercrimes. Wall (2001) identifies four types of cybercrime; trespass, such as hacking, spreading viruses and malware; cybertheft, such as the many scams that offer the unwary a chance to make money for a little invest-ment; cyberpornography, with child pornography in particular leading to new categories of offences; and cyberviolence, such as cyberstalking (Yar, 2006), which, though at a distance, is no less threatening than more direct forms of stalking.

Fattah (1997) points out that the official statistics are also prone to arti-ficial fluctuations and even intentional manipulation, suggesting that crime rates are affected by levels of reporting, police resources and recording prac-tices, the degree of public tolerance to particular crimes, demographic factors, and so on. Maguire (2007) counsels caution in interpreting short-term fluc-tuations in crime, as these may occur for many reasons other than real changes in the incidence of crime, such as changes in the counting rules or changes in the demographic characteristics of populations at risk, such as old people living on their own. The fact that crime rates can fluctuate for artificial reasons has important social implications. As Morrison (1995) sug-gests, crime statistics can be seized upon for political reasons, for example to declare a 'war on crime' when the statistics rise. Moreover he notes that social reactions to law and order crises can instil a fear of crime that is greater than the actual risk of crime. Commenting on crime statistics, Mor-rison states that 'our pursuit of a moral barometer produces an ambiguous instrument. What was meant to be an instrument of security ends up causing insecurity'.

Another difficulty in establishing reliable trends in the rates of crime is that there are several factors, such as what gets counted and how actions are recorded, that make comparisons over time difficult. For example, in 1998/9, the 'counting rules', that is the procedures and guidelines for includ-ing or not including actions in the criminal statistics, were changed. As a result, there was a 'rise' in the amount of crime recorded under the new rules and then a drop in subsequent years. Overall, both the official statis-tics and the British Crime Survey suggest that crime 'peaked' in the early 1990s and has been falling since. Nevertheless, this overall picture might mask increases in particular categories of crime, especially those of violence. On the trends in violent crime, the official statistics, subject to the new 1998/9 rules that included more minor acts of violence, showed an increase from 2000 onwards, while the BCS continued to show a decline. New counting rules under the National Crime Recording Standard, introduced in 2002, increased the weighting of the victim's perception of whether an offence had been com-mitted, rather than a police officer's view of the incident (Newburn, 2007). This would likely increase the number of crimes that get recorded in the official statistics.

Item J

The rates of crime

The Government was jubilant when announcing a fall in the official crime rates for the second year running in 1995. The number of annual recorded crimes fell by 570,000 over the 1993–5 period – the largest reduction since records began in the middle of the last century. The 5.1 million offences reported to the police in England and Wales included the first fall in violent crimes since 1946, down by about 5,000 to 301,400. There was a small reduction in the number of reported rapes, down to 4,800 a year. Sexual offences, overall, were down by 9 per cent. Murders, however, were up from 668 to 729 over the year.

Most of the police forces in England and Wales were affected – 35 of the 43 reported a reduction in notifiable crimes. It would seem, therefore, to be a nationwide trend, though we should be aware that the figures do not relate to Scotland and Northern Ireland.

The most influential factor affecting the overall reduction in crime rates is the large-scale reduction in property offences. These account for about 93 per cent of all crimes that get reported to the police, so a fairly small percentage cut in these figures will have a fairly large effect on the absolute numbers of offences recorded. Among property offences, vehicle crime saw the largest fall – down by 130,000 to 1.3 million over the year. Burglaries also appeared to be in decline – down 69,000 to 1.2 million cases. Again, though, caution needs to be exercised about these apparent reductions. A lot of people do not report burglaries or car crimes where (a) they see little prospect of retrieving goods or getting compensation for damage; (b) they are not insured; or (c) the loss of a no-claims bonus or the threat of higher premiums on insurance deter the victims from pursuing a claim.

However, the fall in crime continued under the Labour government elected in 1997, with a 10 per cent drop in total recorded crime between 1995 and 1999, and an 8 per cent drop in Scotland. Similarly, in the EU there was a drop of 1 per cent over the same period, and the biggest falls were recorded in the USA (down 16 per cent) and in Canada (down 11 per cent). In 2000, the rates fell markedly by 12 per cent from the previous year to the lowest level in 20 years.

- Violent offences were down by 19 per cent;
- Domestic burglary fell by 17 per cent;
- Vehicle-related thefts declined by 11 per cent.

However, overall drops can hide rises in individual types of crime. For example, homicides in 2002 rose to 858 from 849 in the previous year and from 735 in 1997. There were also significant increases in gun crime in 2002 (35 per cent from 2001), drug offences (12.3 per cent) and sex offences (18 per cent).

Source: Adapted from Denscombe (1996).

Exercise 2.14

(An)(K)
(U)(I) 1. Drawing on information in Item J and other sources, identify and explain five
(A)   factors that might create artificial increases or decreases in the official crime
(An)(K)   rates.
(U)(I) 2. With reference to Item J and other sociological evidence, assess the view
(A)(E)   that crime statistics serve an important ideological function.

A SUMMARY OF THE SOCIAL CONSTRUCTION OF CRIME STATISTICS

When considering the limitations of the official crime statistics we have shown that it may be unwise to take the figures at face value. Before we move on to consider alternative ways of measuring crime we would like you to consolidate your understanding of the social processes involved in the construction of crime statistics by completing Exercises 2.15 and 2.16.

(I)(A) ## Exercise 2.15

The way that crime statistics are socially constructed is illustrated well by McNeill and Townley (1989). An adapted version of their flow diagram is presented in Figure 2.5 (see overleaf). We have deleted some of the words from the diagram and your task is to find those words in the list provided.

Missing words

- Court appearance • Acquitted • Not defined as criminal • Arrest made
- Taken seriously by police, and recorded • Unobserved

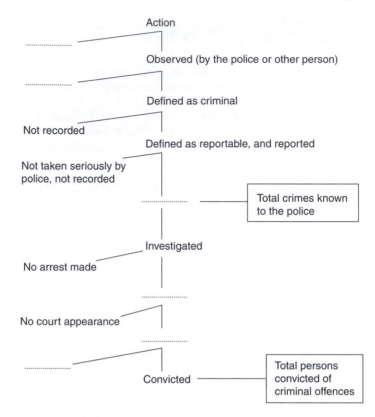

Figure 2.5 The social construction of criminal statistics
Source: Adapted from McNeill and Townley (1989).

Exercise 2.16

Bilton *et al.* (2002) convey the problematic nature of official crime statistics. Reproduced below is an extract from their book; but as with the previous exercise we have deleted certain key words. We would like you to complete the paragraph by choosing appropriate words from the alternatives offered to you.

Missing words

- social constructs • prosecution • social interaction • data collection
- policing • objective

The status of official statistics ... as facts begins to look shaky when one considers all the factors that have prevailed during the long process of ... Just who, for example, counts as a criminal in crime statistics depends on the law and its implementation, local ... policy, the capacity to defend oneself against a criminal charge and and so on. In this sense, statistics are not ... figures that tell the real story, but the end result of a complex process of ... Sociologists who are especially critical of statistics see them as merely ... that have to be deconstructed and demystified.

ALTERNATIVE MEASURES OF CRIME: SELF-REPORT STUDIES AND VICTIM SURVEYS

Given the limitations of the official crime statistics, sociologists and criminologists have devised other ways of quantifying crime in society. These alternative measures are self-report studies and victimization surveys. Both highlight the problems with the official statistics and aptly illustrate a 'dark figure' of unrecorded crime.

Exercise 2.17

Official statistics, self-report studies and victim surveys provide quantitative data on crime, and which has been the main focus of the exercises in this chapter. However, sociologists should not neglect qualitative methodology, which seeks to capture, among other things, the social meanings behind human behaviour.

(K)(U) 1. Explain what is meant by quantitative and qualitative methodology.
(A) 2. Identify two primary and two secondary qualitative research methods that could be used to gain a deeper understanding of crime and victimization in society.

Self-report studies

Self-report studies involve respondents answering questions about particular deviant acts they have committed over a given period of time (see Exercise 2.18). Surveys of this kind pledge absolute confidentiality and are administered in questionnaire or structured interview format. The sample populations are also often asked to give details of their social background (for example class, ethnicity, gender, religion, age, and so on) as one of the main aims of self-report studies is to acquire information on the social characteristics of offenders so as to facilitate a sociological explanation of crime.

The results of self-report studies are revealing. Not only do they indicate higher levels of offending than recorded in the official statistics, but they also show that deviancy, if often relatively minor, is spread throughout all sections of society. As Bilton *et al.* (1987) state in their review of self-report studies: 'various studies reveal that anything between 50 and 90 per cent of people admit some kind of illegal behaviour, whether trivial or serious, that could result in a court appearance'. Early studies suggested that whereas the official statistics indicated a working-class to middle-class crime ratio of approximately 5:1, self-report studies indicated that the ratio was closer to 1.5:1 (see, for example, Gold, 1966). Other studies noted similar changes in ratios with regard to gender (Johnson, 1979) and ethnicity (Chambliss and Nagasawa, 1969).

The kind of discrepancies identified between the official crime data and early self-report studies led some sociologists and criminologists to question the validity of official measures and those theories of crime which relied on them. However, it is important to note that many of the early self-report studies suffered from a number of methodological problems (see evaluation points below, and Coleman and Moynihan, 1996) and therefore the results of such studies have to be treated with care. Hindelang *et al.* (1979) claimed that inconsistencies between official and self-reported data were overestimated, if not an illusion. It is certainly worth noting the findings of the more methodologically advanced studies presented in Coleman and Moynihan (1996). Elliott and Ageton (1980) discovered significant ethnic and class differences with regard to self-reported offending. Farnworth *et al.* (1994) claim to have found a strong association between the underclass and non-trivial 'street crimes'. Bowling *et al.* (1994) found that with respect to gender the patterns of self-reported offending are broadly in line with the official data. Following their overview of crime data findings, Coleman and Moynihan (1996) conclude: 'perhaps the official statistics are not so bad after all. Their validity, as far as the characteristics of offenders are concerned, can be broadly corroborated by alternative data sources'. However, they note that 'many self-report studies sample the very groups most likely to be known offenders (young lower-class boys)...Little wonder, then, that such studies reflect the official picture.'

An advantage of self-report studies is that they can be used to explore areas of anti-social behaviour that can spill over into criminal activity, but which are often under the radar of the official statistics. The Offending, Crime and Justice Survey (OCJS), a Home Office survey, has led to several reports on young people's activities, such as under-age drinking (Matthews *et al.*, 2006) and crimes that involve fraudulent use of technology (Wilson *et al.*, 2006).

Exercise 2.18

Study the following self-report questionnaire and complete the tasks set out below.

Self-report questionnaire

1. I have ridden a bicycle without lights after dark.
2. I have driven a car or motor bike/scooter under 16.
3. I have been with a group who go round together making a row and sometimes getting into fights and causing a disturbance.
4. I have played truant from school.
5. I have travelled on a train or bus without a ticket or deliberately paid the wrong fare.
6. I have let off fireworks in the street.
7. I have taken money from home without returning it.
8. I have taken someone else's car or motor bike for a joy ride then taken it back afterwards.
9. I have broken or smashed things in public places like on the streets, cinemas, dance halls, trains or buses.
10. I have insulted people on the street or got them angry and fought with them.
11. I have broken into a big store or garage or warehouse.
12. I have broken into a little shop even though I may not have taken anything.
13. I have taken something out of a car.
14. I have taken a weapon (like a knife) out with me in case I needed it in a fight.
15. I have fought with someone in a public place like in the street or at a dance.
16. I have broken the window of an empty house.
17. I have used a weapon in a fight, like a knife or a razor or a broken bottle.
18. I have drunk alcoholic drinks in a pub under 16.
19. I have been in a pub when I was under 16.
20. I have taken things from big stores or supermarkets when the shop was open.
21. I have taken things from little shops when the shop was open.
22. I have dropped things in the street like litter or broken bottles.
23. I have bought something cheap or accepted as a present something I knew was stolen.
24. I have planned well in advance to get into a house to take things.
25. I have got into a house and taken things even though I didn't plan it in advance.

26. I have taken a bicycle belonging to someone else and kept it.
27. I have struggled or fought to get away from a policeman.
28. I have struggled or fought with a policeman who was trying to arrest someone.
29. I have stolen school property worth more than about 5p.
30. I have stolen goods from someone I worked for worth more than about 5p.
31. I have had sex with a boy when I was under 16.
32. I have trespassed somewhere I was not supposed to go, like empty houses, railway lines or private gardens.
33. I have been to an 'X' film under age.
34. I have spent money on gambling under 16.
35. I have smoked cigarettes under 15.
36. I have had sex with someone for money.
37. I have taken money from slot machines or telephones.
38. I have taken money from someone's clothes hanging up somewhere.
39. I have got money from someone by pretending to be someone else or lying about why I needed it.
40. I have taken someone's clothing hanging up somewhere.
41. I have smoked dope or taken pills (LSD, mandies, sleepers).
42. I have got money/drink/cigarettes by saying I would have sex with someone, even though I didn't.
43. I have run away from home.

Source: Campbell (1981).

1. If you wish, complete the questionnaire yourself. As with all survey data, the answers should be kept confidential.
2. Amend any questions that you think would benefit from improvement.
3. Add three other questions that you feel would be appropriate for a survey on juvenile delinquency.
4. This self-report study is from the early 1980s. Are there any changes you could make so that the self-report questionnaire asked more appropriate questions for the twenty-first century teenager? (Hint: what moral panics about teenagers and weapons have been in the news?)

Self-report studies: an evaluation

Self-report studies offer sociologists a useful alternative measure of crime. However, like official statistics they do provide sociologists with problems. Some of the uses of and problems with self-report studies are explained in Williams (1997), and we shall draw on her ideas to evaluate their usefulness. For a fuller assessment of such studies see Coleman and Moynihan (1996).

The uses of self-report studies:

1. They shed new light on the extent and nature of crime and the social characteristics of offenders.
2. Self-report studies can be used to test theories of crime.
3. They call into question the accuracy of official measures of crime.

The problems with self-report studies:

1. The results of self-report studies often lack validity. There is always a danger that people may exaggerate their criminality and admit to more crimes than they have actually committed – the so-called 'bragging factor'. Conversely some people may not admit to the full range of crimes they have committed because they may not trust the researcher to maintain confidentiality.
2. Self-report studies have often been criticized for selecting unrepresentative samples. There can be a number of factors that affect the representativeness of a sample, but perhaps most significant for self-report studies is the age of the respondents. A number of studies have been criticized for confining their samples to adolescents. As a consequence we have few findings on adult law breaking, in particular white-collar crime, domestic violence and child abuse.

Ⓘ Ⓔ

Exercise 2.19

In the light of your examination of the self-report questionnaire in Exercise 2.18, suggest at least one other possible problem with self-report studies.

Victim surveys

Victim surveys involve asking individuals about their experiences and perceptions of certain types of crime, including those which are not reported to or recorded by the police. Morrison (1995) maintains that victim surveys therefore offer a very useful tool for the criminologist. He states that:

> victimization studies shed a great deal of light on matters not reported and on discrepancies between the reports of crime, and the figures recorded by the police. These surveys may also ask questions about police behaviour, and the attitude of the respondents to police practices. They can also provide

information as to why victims have not reported crime, and highlight which offences are more likely to be reported.

In Britain both local and national victimization surveys have been carried out. Local studies are geographically focused and have been administered in a number of areas, for example Nottingham (Farrington and Dowds, 1985), Islington (Jones *et al.*, 1986; Crawford *et al.*, 1990) and Glasgow (Hartless *et al.*, 1995). Perhaps the best examples of national victim surveys are the state-sponsored British Crime Surveys of 1982, 1984, 1988, 1992, 1994 and 1996, 1998, 2000 and annually thereafter, each of which measured crime in the previous year. Until 1994 these surveys were based on representative samples of 10,000 people aged 16 and over living in England and Wales; but in 2001 the sample was increased to 40,000. International victim surveys have also been conducted to compare aspects of crime on a global scale. For example the 1996 International Crime Victimisation Survey showed that, with the exception of the Netherlands, England and Wales had the highest number of reported crimes per 100 population in the 'developed' world (see Mayhew and Van Dijk, 1997, for further findings).

Victim surveys not only provide us with a more realistic picture of the amount of crime in society but also illustrate how crime affects the lives of victims (Croall, 1998). We will now introduce you to some of the findings of the 1996 and 2006/7 British Crime Surveys by way of a number of exercises. (Further coverage of some of the debates on victimization and victimology can be found in Chapter 9.)

THE REPORTING AND RECORDING OF CRIME

Item K provides information on crimes reported to the police and the proportion of crimes surveyed by the BCS that were recorded or not recorded by the police in 1996 and in 2007/8. Exercise 2.20 is designed to get you to interpret this data, to suggest reasons for differing levels of reporting according to offence type, and to use the data to explain the analogy that is often made between the official crime statistics and an iceberg (see for example Kirby *et al.*, 1997).

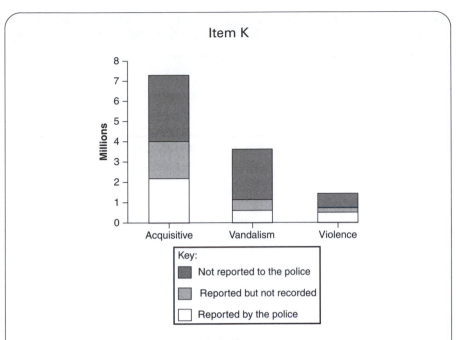

Figure 2.6   Recorded and unrecorded crime
Note: 'Acquisitive': burglary, theft of/from motor vehicles, bicycle theft, theft from the person; 'vandalism': incidents against household, property and vehicles; 'violence': wounding, robbery. *Source*: Mirrlees-Black *et al.* (1996).

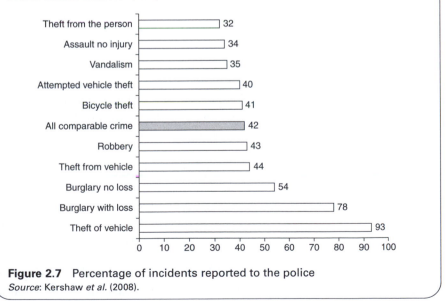

Figure 2.7   Percentage of incidents reported to the police
Source: Kershaw *et al.* (2008).

Study Item K and answer the following questions.

1. Give an example of the following:

   (a) Acquisitive crime.
   (b) Violent crime.

2. What percentage of robberies was reported to the police in 2007/08?
3. How many bicycle thefts went unreported?
4. According to Item K, 97 per cent of motor vehicle thefts were reported to the police in 2007/8. Give two possible reasons for this high rate of reporting.
5. Suggest one reason why 66 per cent of assaults with injury were not reported to the police.
6. 'Crimes recorded as known to the police only represent the tip of the iceberg.' Use Item K to explain this statement.

Comparing BCS and police statistics

Maguire *et al.* (2002, 2007) have argued that the BCS and police statistics are not directly comparable, but represent alternative pictures of the level of crime in Great Britain. This is mainly because they do not use the same categories of criminal offences when gathering their evidence. Moreover, neither approach captures the full extent of crime in the UK. However, the BCS does establish that there is a great deal of crime committed that never enters official statistics and yet the broad picture of the shape of criminal activity in roughly similar in both sets of statistics. The important thing to remember is that, although the BCS reveals that there is a 'dark figure' of crime, it still does not reveal the full extent of crime for two reasons. Firstly, there are limitations with the sampling used by the BCS: it does not include people under 16, those not in households, such as the homeless or those in prison, and it does not cover victimless crimes or the victims of commercial crime (Newburn, 2007). Secondly, what respondents are able and prepared to report to interviewers might not cover the whole spectrum of crime committed against them: they may misremember or forget episodes where they were victims; or they may wish to conceal deliberately crimes committed against them for personal or family reasons and so on (Hope, 2005).

Item L allows comparisons to be made between BCS data and police statistics in 1995. Exercise 2.21 encourages you to draw out the differences

Item L

Table 2.6 Comparison of BCS and notifiable offences recorded by the police

	1995 Police (thousands)	1995 BCS	% reported	% recorded of number	% recorded of all reported	% change 1993–5		% change 1981–95	
						Police	BCS	Police	BCS
Comparable with recorded offences									
Acquisitive crime	2 098	7 397	55	52	28	–11	1	80	135
Vandalism	461	3 415	29	47	13	0	0	130	26
Violence	235	1 173	44	46	20	6	17	129	75
TOTAL	2 794	11 986	46	50	23	–8	2	91	83
Vandalism									
Vehicle vandalism	–	1 851	25	–	–	–	3	–	19
Vandalism to other property	–	1 564	34	–	–	–	–2	–	35
Burglary	644	1 754	66	55	37	–11	–1	84	134
Attempts and no loss	169	975	52	33	17	–9	2	130	160
Burglary with loss	474	779	84	72	61	–12	–5	72	108
All vehicle thefts	1 209	4 312	51	55	28	–13	–1	85	146
Theft from motor vehicles	657	2 522	50	52	26	–13	–2	94	96
Theft of motor vehicles	402	499	97	83	81	–18	–8	41	75

Table 2.6 (Continued)

	1995 Police (thousands)	1995 BCS	% reported	% recorded of number	% recorded of all reported	% change 1993–5		% change 1981–95	
						Police	BCS	Police	BCS
Attempted thefts of and from motor vehicles	150	1 291	36	32	12	13	4	432	618
Bicycle theft	183	660	63	44	28	–11	10	45	205
Wounding	174	860	39	51	20	3	13	106	70
Robbery and theft from the person	123	984	46	27	13	21	17	132	65
Other BCS offences									
Other household theft	–	2 266	30	–	–	–	–4	–	49
Common assault	–	2 820	34	–	–	–	11	–	101
Other personal theft	–	2 075	30	–	–	–	8	–	31
All BCS offences	–	19 147	41	–	–	–	4	–	73

Source: Mirrlees-Black et al. (1996).

Methodological note on the 1996 survey

The survey had a nationally representative 'core' sample of 16,348 adults aged 16 or over. Face-to-face interviews were carried out mainly between January and April 1996. The sample was drawn from the Postcode Address File – a listing of all postal delivery points. The response rate was 83 per cent.

between the two datasets and to reflect on how the BCS data can be used to criticize police statistics. You are also given the opportunity to apply your knowledge and understanding of research methodology.

<hr>

Exercise 2.21

Study Item L and answer the following questions.

(K)(U) 1. Briefly explain what is meant by a representative sample.
(A) 2. The 1996 BCS was conducted using face-to-face interviews and had a response rate of 83 per cent. Suggest two reasons why this method of carrying out surveys has a higher response rate than postal question-naires.
(I) 3. What was the total number of all BCS offences in 1995?
(I) 4. Identify two ways in which the BCS findings differ from the police records.
(I)(E) 5. How might sociologists use the information in Item L to criticize the official crime statistics?

<hr>

WHO IS AT RISK OF CRIME?

The BCS provides information on the proportion of victims of different types of crime. Such data also identifies who is most at risk of crime in

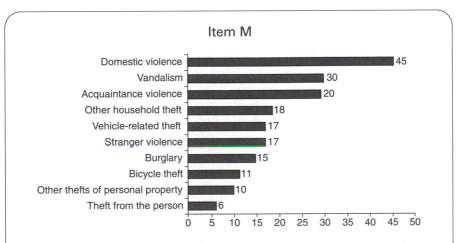

Item M

Offence	Value
Domestic violence	45
Vandalism	30
Acquaintance violence	20
Other household theft	18
Vehicle-related theft	17
Stranger violence	17
Burglary	15
Bicycle theft	11
Other thefts of personal property	10
Theft from the person	6

Figure 2.8 Proportion of victims who were victimized more than once in past 12 months, by offence, 2007/8
Source: Kershaw *et al.* (2008).

Table 2.7 Proportion of victims who were victimized more than once in the past 12 months by main offence groups, 1981 to 2007/8, percentages, BCS

	1961	1991	2001/2 Ints	2003/4 Ints	2005/6 Ints	2006/7 Ints	2007/8 Ints
Vandalism	33	31	32	29	30	32	30
Burglary	13	16	15	16	16	13	15
Vehicle-related theft	21	25	21	19	18	16	17
All BCS violence	27	32	34	27	27	28	27

Note: Ints = interviews.
Source: Kershaw *et al.* (2008).

Table 2.8   Victims of violent crime, by sex and age, 2005/6

England & Wales	Percentages				
	Domestic	Mugging	Stranger	Acquaintance	All violence
Males					
16–24	0.3	3.0	6.5	4.2	12.6
25–34	0.2	1.1	2.9	1.5	5.5
35–44	0.3	0.7	1.8	1.3	3.9
45–54	0.3	0.4	1.3	1.2	3.1
55–64	–	0.2	0.6	0.3	1.1
65–74	–	0.2	0.2	0.2	0.5
75 and over	–	0.2	0.1	–	0.3
All aged 16 and over	0.2	0.9	2.1	1.4	4.3
Females					
16–24	1.4	2.1	2.0	2.3	7.0
25–34	0.6	0.4	1.3	0.5	2.8
35–44	1.1	0.4	0.6	1.2	3.0
45–54	0.6	0.2	0.5	0.9	2.2
55–64	0.2	0.3	0.2	0.3	1.0
65–74	–	0.2	0.2	0.1	0.5
75 and over	–	0.3	–	–	0.4
All aged 16 and over	0.6	0.5	0.7	0.8	2.5

Source: Self and Zealey (2007).

terms of factors such as age and place of residence. The fact that certain groups of people are at greater risk than others led early victimologists to argue that crime may be precipitated by the victims and/or their lifestyle (see for example Wolfgang, 1958; Hindelang *et al.*, 1978). Such thinking has been subject to heavy criticism, notably for its tendency to blame the victim (Walklate, 1994). Whether crime is precipitated or not, victims of crime may face physical, material and emotional damage (Croall, 1998) and seek help from victim support groups. Complete Exercise 2.22, based on Item M to explore in greater detail the issue of who is at risk.

Exercise 2.22

(I) 1. In 1995, what proportion of victims were victimized more than once in incidents of burglary?
(I) 2. In 2007/8, which two crimes had equal levels of repeat victimization?
(A) 3. Suggest two reasons why acquaintance violence should have a high level of repeat victimization.
(A) 4. Describe the patterns of repeat victimization between 1981 and 2007/8.
(I)(An) 5. What are the relationships between violent crime, age and gender, as shown
(A) in the Item?
(A) 6. Briefly describe the ways in which crime may have a practical and emotional impact on victims.
(A) 7. Identify two relevant agencies and explain how they help to support the victims of crime.
(An)(E) 8. 'Crime is precipitated by the victim and/or their lifestyle' – explain and evaluate this view.

THE FEAR OF CRIME

The producers of the British Crime Survey argue that measuring people's fear of crime is important as it acts as an indicator of the pervasiveness of the crime problem and the degree of public concern about crime. Item N presents findings from the 2006/7 to 2007/8 survey on worries and anxieties about crime according to such factors as age, sex and locality. By completing Exercise 2.23 you will gain an understanding of such variations. You will be asked to reflect on possible reasons why measuring people's worries and anxieties about crime is important, and to identify direct and indirect relationships between people's fear of crime and their actual experience of it. When you work on Exercise 2.23 you should be aware that the BCS has in the past used the terms 'anxiety', 'fear' and 'worry' interchangeably as concepts that measure people's emotional reaction to crime. However, Croall (1998) expressed concern about the use of such terms, as 'worry' may encompass a variety of feelings and crime instils a range of reactions that may not necessarily include fear. Croall draws on Kinsey and Anderson (1992) to point out that victims of crime also experience emotions such as shock, anger and annoyance.

One of the criticisms levelled at the first BCS was its assertion that people's fear of crime was somewhat excessive in the light of the national average risk. The problem here is that national (and international) survey data averages people's experience of crime, and therefore disguises significant differences in the level of crime in different localities (Williams, 1998). Thus the intense fear felt by living in high-crime areas may be seen as quite realistic (Croall, 1998). One of the purposes of Exercise 2.24 is to develop your understanding of which social groups are most likely to fear crime and why people in general fear crime. You will also be asked to consider some of the precautions that individuals take to avoid crime.

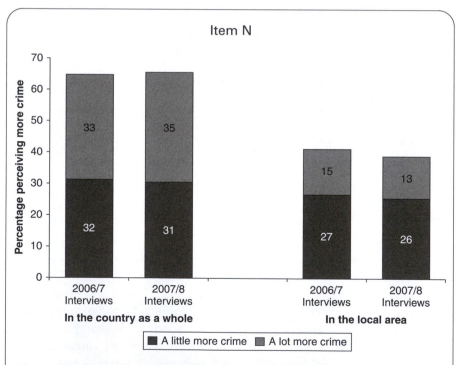

Figure 2.9 Perceptions of changing crime levels, 2006/7 to 2007/8
Source: Kershaw *et al.* (2008).

Perceptions of crime rates varied with demographic and socio-economic factors. In general, older people, women and those who read national 'tabloids' were more likely to think that the crime rate in the country as a whole had increased 'a lot' in the previous two years. People with educational qualifications at degree or diploma level and those in private-rented accommodation were less likely to think it had increased 'a lot'. For example:

- Fifty-one per cent of women aged 65 to 74 and 49 per cent of women aged 75 and over thought national crime levels had risen 'a lot' compared with 26 per cent of women aged 16 to 24.
- Readers of national 'tabloids' were nearly twice as likely as those who read national 'broadsheets' to think the crime rate nationally had increased 'a lot' (44 and 24 per cent respectively).

Perceptions of the local crime rate appear to be more strongly influenced by personal experience and area characteristics, while perceptions of the national crime rate are more influenced by general socio-demographic characteristics such as age.

People living in Hard Pressed and Moderate Means ACORN areas, in urban areas and in areas where physical disorder was assessed as high were considerably more likely to think that crime in the local area had increased 'a lot'. Those who had experienced crime in the past 12 months were also more likely to perceive crime levels locally to have risen 'a lot'. For example:

- Those living in Hard Pressed and Moderate Means ACORN areas were more than twice as likely to think crime locally had increased 'a lot' (19 and 18 per cent respectively) than those in Wealthy Achievers areas (8 per cent).
- Twenty-six per cent of those who had been both a victim and a witness thought crime in the local area had risen 'a lot', compared with 10 per cent of those who had not experienced crime in the previous 12 months.

Source: Kershaw *et al*. (2008).

Exercise 2.23

① 1. According to Figure 2.9, has the fear of crime in the local area increased or decreased between 2006/7 and 2007/8?
① 2. Describe the ways in which the 'fear of crime' varies according to social characteristics.
①Ⓐ 3. With reference to Items M and N, identify a direct and indirect relationship between people's fear of crime and their actual experience of it.

Ⓐ 4. Item N identifies various patterns with regard to people's fear of crime. Give one reason why it is important to measure people's worries and anxieties about crime.

Item O

Explaining patterns of fear of crime

Hough's (1995) analysis of the 1994 BCS results showed what factors best explain who is most anxious about crime, using multivariate analysis. Different factors played a greater or lesser part in explaining the different facets of anxiety about crime, but some main findings were:

- Those who worried about *non-criminal* misfortunes were most likely to worry about crime (but this was *not so* in relation to being out alone at night).
- Worry about mugging and 'feeling unsafe' was *not* related to having been a victim of street crime, although those who knew other victims were more anxious. But for other crimes (such as burglary), having been a victim oneself did increase worry.
- After taking other factors into account, the elderly were *less* anxious than others about burglary and car crime, but older women were much more likely to feel unsafe out at night, and older men were also more concerned than younger men.

- Being on a lower income was associated with most measures of fear, net of other factors likely to be associated with income, such as living in less salubrious areas.
- Local disorder (such as noisy neighbours, poor street lighting and teenagers hanging around) was predictive of virtually all measures of fear. However, the *supportiveness* of the neighbourhood was related only to worry about burglary and feeling unsafe in the area.
- People most fearful of street crime were those who:

  ○ judged their risks to be highest;
  ○ were in lower income groups;
  ○ lived in disorderly neighbourhoods with lower levels of social support;
  ○ were more vulnerable in terms of physical size, health and confidence in their self-defence abilities. This test of physical vulnerability as a predictor of anxiety was a new one and helps to confirm why the elderly are more fearful about street safety.

Irrational fears?

BCS results have sometimes been used to argue that fear of crime is excessive in the light of national average risks over a year. In our view, this is misplaced.

- Experience in the past year is only one indicator of risk; victimization prior to this will influence worry too.
- The consistent message of BCS results is that fear is highest in areas where the chances of victimization are greatest, and among those with most direct and indirect experience of crime. In other words, those who worry most generally have more grounds for doing so.

- Fear of crime is not just about the *chances* of being victimized, it is also about the perceived *consequences*. Thus, the most fearful groups are those who would be more socially and physically vulnerable to the consequences of crime if it occurred.
- Aligning any given level of fear of crime to any given level of objective risk misses the point that people can worry about something which may be very unlikely to happen but would be extremely distressing if it did.
- Finally, as Hough has persuasively argued, even if the 'right' people worry, to say they worry too much is a question of value rather than fact.

Source: Mirrlees-Black *et al.* (1996).

Exercise 2.24

1. Study Item O and identify which group of people are most likely to fear crime.
2. Using information in Item O and elsewhere, outline some of the possible factors that make people fearful of crime.
3. To what extent do the authors of the 1996 BCS (Mirrlees-Black *et al.*, 1996) believe that the fear of crime is excessive in the light of national average risks. Use the information in Item O as the basis of your response.
4. Identify two precautions that individuals may take to avoid crime.

Ⓘ Ⓐ

For this exercise we would like you to design a victim survey to glean information on various aspects of victimization. We have provided two sample questions based on questions that the British Crime Survey has asked in the past to get you started. You might find the guidelines below helpful when devising your survey, or you could also ask your teacher or lecturer for help. For ethical reasons we do not advise you to conduct your survey.

Guidelines for constructing a victim survey

1. Provide a clear title for the survey.
2. Provide an introductory statement explaining who you are and the purpose of the survey. You should also clarify any ethical issues; for example you may want to stress that the answers will be kept confidential and that the person completing the survey is welcome to read the findings of the survey.
3. Devise some relevant biographical questions. This will allow you to examine the way in which victimization varies according to social and demographic factors such as age, social class, gender, ethnicity and locality.
4. Construct key questions on victimization. Try to use different types of question, for example, Likert, ranking, factual, knowledge, opinion, motivation, open and closed.
5. Make sure you have a polite ending to the survey. You should always thank those who have taken the time to complete the survey.

Sample questions

1. How safe do you feel (or would you feel) walking alone in this area after dark?
   Very unsafe [ ]   A bit unsafe [ ]
2. How worried are you about each of the following crimes?

   Burglary: Very worried [ ] Fairly worried [ ] Not worried at all [ ]
   Mugging: Very worried [ ] Fairly worried [ ] Not worried at all [ ]
   Rape: Very worried [ ] Fairly worried [ ] Not worried at all [ ]
   Theft of cars: Very worried [ ] Fairly worried [ ] Not worried at all [ ]
   Theft from cars: Very worried [ ] Fairly worried [ ] Not worried at all [ ]

VICTIM SURVEYS: AN EVALUATION

Earlier on we drew your attention to what Morrison (1995) believes are some of the uses of victim surveys. However, victim surveys have their limitations as well. Some of the earlier British Crime Surveys were subject to criticism by left realists who favoured smaller-scale, local victim surveys. The Islington Survey (Jones *et al.*, 1986) adopted a more sensitive approach to potential victims and a more open type of questioning that allowed the respondents some leeway in reporting their experiences of crime and harassment. By taking a more open approach the survey found a greater level of crime than that depicted in the British Crime Surveys. Further criticisms of victim surveys are offered by Morrison (1995) in Item P (for more details on the problems with and uses of victim surveys, see Coleman and Moynihan, 1996; Croall, 1998).

The uses of victim surveys

Exercise 2.26

(I)(A) 1. Read the quote from Morrison (1995) on pp. 39–40. Identify the uses of victim surveys put forward by Morrison.

(A)(E) 2. Identify three other uses of victim surveys, other than those suggested by Morrison.

The problems with victim surveys

Exercise 2.27

(E) In Item P, Morrison (1995) identifies nine problems with victim surveys. Try to rank what you consider to be the four most important ones. Justify your ranking to another sociology student.

Item P

The problem with victim surveys is that:

- They cannot give a true picture of crimes which do not have any clearly identifiable victims, such as pollution.
- They have limited information concerning serious offences.
- Corporate crimes are difficult to cover.
- Feminists have been critical of the survey methodology noting that the assaults which women receive are underestimated, since they are often unprepared to report them to the interviewer as their assailant may be in the same room at the time of the interview.
- Victims forget about crime.
- Victims may not know that they have been victimized.
- They may invent offences to impress the interviewer.
- They omit offences to speed up the process.
- Evidence has revealed that many respondents are quite ready to define certain events as not crime which could actually be called crimes.

Source: Morrison (1995).

Link Exercise 2.1

This exercise is designed to get you to appreciate the different theoretical responses to the official crime statistics. We have provided a number of alternative responses to official crime data. Your task is to identify which of these views is held by the theories of crime listed in the sample chart below. When you have made your choices, copy the chart and place the appropriate letter codes in the empty boxes. It may be better to attempt this exercise when you have covered theories of crime in your course and/or read the relevant chapters in this book.

Alternative responses to official crime statistics

(a) The statistics provide a fairly accurate representation of crime in society.
(b) The statistics can be useful to explain crime.
(c) The statistics are socially constructed and therefore problematic.
(d) The statistics are not very useful for explaining crime.
(e) The statistics should be treated as an object of study. Thus sociologists should look at the decision-making processes involved in the construction of crime data.
(f) The statistics are a source of ideological conditioning.
(g) Alternative quantitative methods should be used to supplement the official statistics, for example self-report studies and victim surveys.

(h) Alternative qualitative methods should be used to supplement the official statistics, for example unstructured interviews and observation.

(i) Qualitative methods such as unstructured interviews and observation should be used instead of official statistics to facilitate a deeper understanding of crime.

Sample chart

Theories	Response to official crime statistics
Sociocultural and subcultural	
Interactionist	
Conflict	
Realist	
Feminist	

Exam focus

Try the following questions on your own, using the information and skills you have acquired while reading this chapter. Answer the questions under examination conditions, that is, take no more than an hour and do not use your notes or a textbook, having first learned your material.

1. Evaluate the usefulness of official statistics to a sociological understanding of crime.
2. 'Changing counting rules and changing laws mean that official statistics do not give a valid picture of how much crime is committed in the UK.' In the light of this statement, to what extent do you think that ANY statistics about crime can be reliable or valid?

Important concepts

Social construction • Under-reporting • Invisibility • Counting rules • Self-report studies • Victimization surveys • Fear of crime

Critical thinking

1. Why does the state put so much effort and money into the collection of crime statistics when the main effect seems to be to make the public fearful?
2. How truthful are respondents in self-report and victimization surveys? Does the former lead to underestimation and the latter to overestimation of the amount of crime in society?
3. If the official crime statistics are collected by non-sociologists, analysed by non-sociologists and presented by non-sociologists, should sociologists abandon them and just collect their own crime statistics?

Chapter 3

Sociocultural Explanations of Crime and Deviance

After studying this chapter, you should:

- understand the importance of culture in explaining crime
- have developed a critical understanding of the origins of sociocultural explanations of crime and deviance
- understand cultural explanations of crime and deviance
- be familiar with various forms of Control Theory
- be able to evaluate subcultural and control theories
- be aware of recent developments in Sociocultural Theory, including post-modernist views on the city and the underclass

Sociologists have long recognized the centrality of the idea of culture when approaching the issues of crime and deviance. The implicit contrast here is between sociological explanations, which rely on culture as their basis, and the biological emphasis that influenced the development of criminology as a discipline. The emergence of criminology in the early part of the twentieth century was affected by the dominant biological beliefs of the time, that is, that different populations of the human race have different (and sometimes pathological) biological characteristics. The study of crime at that time was affected by the interest of natural scientists such as zoologists in the subject of criminality, or, as Foucault (1977) puts it, criminology consists of a 'zoology of social sub-species' in which criminal populations are identified by their biological traits.

Item A

Biology and crime: the search for a 'natural' solution

Traditional biological explanations for crime looked at identifying either physical or psychological traits that would allow scientists (and, by implication, the authorities) to identify potential criminals and deal with them appropriately. While crude 'biologism' was largely discredited when the eugenics movement imploded after its adoption by the Nazis during the 1920s and 1930s, the idea of a biological basis for criminal activity has not gone away. A more modern approach looks to genetics, not to identify some 'gene for crime', but to understand how individuals may be predisposed to respond in particular ways to circumstances like a disordered family. The aim remains the same – to lead to more effective ways of preventing crime.

This is not without controversy, as opponents suggest that this is still a form of 'biological determinism', in which our behaviour is seen as being controlled by forces beyond our ability to act independently. This is the route that leads to eugenics – the selective breeding of human beings – to the separation of those deemed to be deviant from 'normal' folk. This stigmatization of individuals is immoral and unacceptable to many scientists.

Geneticists interested in crime do present a complex case and do not offer simplistic solutions in the way that is often portrayed. They argue that it is both genes and environmental factors that are involved in the causation of crime. A person's genes may lead to a leaning more towards some forms of action than others (disposition towards risk-taking, for example), which will then operate within the social environment in either legal or criminal ways. There is thus a complicated interaction between nature on the one hand and nurture on the other in looking at criminal behaviour, and it is this interplay that is important. Michael Rutter (2007) argues that there are certain types of crime that are more open to genetic influences than others. Petty crime is more susceptible than violent crime to genetic influence, as shown by studies of twins and adopted children.

Critics of this approach argue that genes can play only a small part in any causation of crime, precisely because there are so many fluctuations in the amount of crime committed from generation to generation. Increases in crime of the magnitude seen since the 1950s cannot have a genetic origin. Rather, criminologists should look to social practices to explain the differential crime rate amongst different social groups. It is much more likely that social factors are important in explaining the differing incarceration rate amongst blacks and whites in the United States.

Exercise 3.1

Debates on the possible biological causes of crime still go on today. However, few are willing to link crime solely to biological factors. As mentioned in Item A, some of those who suggest a possible genetic basis to crime also acknowledge the interplay of environmental factors. Carefully read Item A and answer the following questions.

ⒾⓀⓊ 1. Give a brief definition of the concept of biological determinism.
Ⓘ 2. For what types of crime are the influence of genetic factors thought to be important?
ⒾⒶ 3. Item A suggests that genetic research into human behaviour can lead to 'ethical problems'. Identify three such ethical problems.

If culture is defined as all the ideas, values, emotions and attitudes that shape and constrain individual behaviour in a society, then it can be seen that the culture of that society will be important in defining which activities are acceptable and which are not. From a traditional functionalist point of view, culture is a necessary prerequisite for the existence of a social system. The functionalists argue that, given the huge range of possible behaviours that an individual might adopt, culture is necessary to set out rules and norms for the limitation of that variation. Only by introducing such constraints is living together made possible (see for example Spiro, 1968).

For many sociologists, therefore, crime is a result of culture in some way. Sellin (1938) argued that social differentiation, the division of people into separate groups, is a product of the development of modern (as opposed to postmodern) societies, and this leads to cultural conflict, which is the main cause of crime. This cultural conflict takes two main forms. Primary cultural conflict takes place where the values of two different cultures, for example between a host and an immigrant community, clash. Though Sellin was concerned here with the United States and its experiences with successive waves of immigrants with their own specific cultures, this concept has obvious implications for ethnic minority communities in Britain (see Chapter 7).

Secondary culture conflict is the result of increasing social differentiation in modernity, where numerous groups, all with their own values and, in Sellin's terms, 'conduct norms', may clash with the dominant culture over the appropriate way to behave. Criminals are therefore seen as responding to values and norms that are different from the dominant culture in society. It is this concept of secondary culture conflict that has led many sociologists to examine the subcultural characteristics of criminals and deviants.

Other sociologists, such as Gartner (1990), have looked to sociocultural and socio-economic features, such as levels of unemployment, material deprivation and family dissolution, to explain differential levels of homicide in different societies. Similarly Braithwaite (1989) has established a statistical link between levels of economic inequality, especially unemployment, in society and the extent of property crime.

The biological explanations of crime were dominant during the nineteenth and early twentieth centuries, but the emergence of a social tradition in the study of crime during the early part of the twentieth century in the United States was an important development. Two main social traditions emerged – the Chicago School and Strain Theory, associated with the work of Merton (1938) – both of which rejected individualistic explanations of crime, turning instead to social explanations. In the case of the Chicago School, the focus was on inner-city, working-class, usually young males; while the latter focused on the wider structural relationships in American society as a whole.

THE CHICAGO SCHOOL

Item B

The geographical distribution of crime

In general, those police force areas that include large urban conurbations have higher rates of recorded crime than those in more rural locations. In 2006/7 all the metropolitan police areas had higher rates of crime nearing or over 100 crimes per 1000 population. London had the highest rate of all the police force areas in England and Wales, at 116 crimes per 1000 population, while the East of England had the lowest at 75. East of England was also the area with the least number of violent acts against the person per 1000 population, at 13, compared with 23 in London which had the highest rate. The Yorkshire and Humber area had the highest rate for burglary with 15 per 1000 population compared with a rate of just 9 in the South West.

Source: Kershaw *et al.* (2008).

Exercise 3.2

The Chicago School helps us to understand the relationship between crime and locality. To familiarize yourself with the geographical distribution of crime in England and Wales, study Item B and answer the following questions.

1. Which police force area had the highest rate of crime in 2006/7?
2. Item B suggests that the east of England had the lowest rate of crime in 2006/7. What was the crime rate (for all crimes) per 1000 of the population in the East of England?
3. By how much was the rate of burglary in the Yorkshire and Humber area greater than in the South West?
4. Item B states that 'those police force areas that include large urban conurbations have higher rates of recorded crime than those in more rural locations'. Making use of Item B, support this statement.

Starting from the assumption that the environment influences the way that the poor in society behave, the Chicago School focused on the urban situation when searching for an explanation of the incidence of crime. The sociologists associated with the Chicago School argued that the development of urban areas is not haphazard, but shaped by social processes in a patterned way. The urban environment can therefore be examined in a scientific way, through the careful and detailed observation of social life in different parts of the city. By comparing the results of such observations, causal explanations of phenomena such as crime can be established. Drawing on the work of Park and Burgess (1927) on the development and structure of cities, Shaw and McKay (1942) argued that the social organization in zones of transition largely account for the high incidence of juvenile delinquency to be found there. (The zone of transition is the central area of cities in which the poorest housing is located and to which immigrants into cities are first drawn. The social organization of an area refers to family structure, level of employment, the extent of community links, and so on.) By examining statistics on juvenile justice over a period of time they were able to establish that zones of transition exhibit high rates of delinquency, regardless of the movement of ethnic groups in and out of such zones. It is therefore the degree of neighbourhood organization in allowing or condemning juvenile delinquency that is important.

Shaw and McKay (1942) carried out a number of in-depth interviews with delinquent youths in such areas and argued that social disorganization, such as lack of community support and censure, lead to the establishment of traditions of crime that are passed down from generation to generation in the same way that other cultural traditions are transmitted. They were thus the first proponents of subcultural theories of crime.

In the 1980s and 1990s there was a revival of interest in the work of the Chicago School, especially the work of Shaw and McKay, and a number of sociologists have attempted to verify empirically the effects of social disorganization on crime rates. For example Reiss (1986), among others, began to look at how community stability and changes to urban areas – for example through urban renewal programmes – affect crime rates. The variables examined by these sociologists are those identified by Shaw and McKay, particularly the density of local community networks and the participation of community members in formal and informal organizations. For example, it has been shown, that where network density is high (that is, many members of a community are connected through direct relationships) there is a greater potential for social control of potential delinquents. This is because the transgression of social norms invokes the hostility of a large number of people and acts as a brake on delinquency.

Another dimension of this argument is associated with the work of Stark (1987), among others. Stark argues that social disorganization is related to incivility, that is, lack of interest in the locality. This leads to an intensification of the fear of crime, weakened social control and an increase in delinquency. Stark is therefore arguing that it is location, rather than the kind of people who live there, that provides the better explanation of crime rates.

Sampson and Groves (1989), in a large-scale survey of different communities, found that those with weak social networks, little participation in organized groups and unsupervised teenagers are characterized by high rates of crime and delinquency. This supports one of Shaw and McKay's central contentions, that social disorganization is the prime explanation of crime. However, other studies of residential areas suggest that housing areas with very similar patterns of social disorganization have very different concentrations of offenders (see Bottoms et al., 1992). The suggestion here is that housing allocation policy is important, especially when the local authority concentrates those with the most pressing housing needs in the same social housing area.

Sampson in the 1990s and 2000s developed a new way of looking at urban communities and the differential incidence of crime in different localities. He argued that some urban areas had more 'collective efficacy' than others and this was influential in deciding the amount of crime within them. Collective efficacy exists where members of a community are proactive in dealing with low level crime and antisocial behaviour. For example, where there is sufficient trust amongst neighbours – so that they are prepared to report crime to the police, deal with noisy youths amongst themselves or assist each other when there is trouble on the street – then there is collective efficacy, which exerts a downward pressure on the level of crime. Areas of high instability (or social disorganization) are therefore unlikely to develop collective efficacy easily (see Sampson 2006).

Evaluation of the Chicago School

Ⓘ Ⓔ

Exercise 3.3

Listed below are a number of evaluations of the Chicago School. Identify which are strengths and which are weaknesses. Record your answers in a two-column table that clearly separates the strengths from the weaknesses. When you record your answers, rank them in order of importance. Justify your ranking to another sociology student.

1. The ideas of the Chicago School have helped to shape social policies on crime. A number of community projects to combat crime and delinquency have been based on their theory of social disorganization.
2. The theory is difficult to prove empirically, for example in counting the number of contacts with positive and negative views of crime (see for example Pfohl, 1985).
3. The approach fails to explain the origins of the criminal subculture that is transmitted; it just assumes that it exists.
4. The Chicago School's ideas provide a more plausible explanation of crime than individualistic explanations. This is because the Chicago School recognizes the importance of environmental influences on crime.
5. The approach is not as total as it claims. For example, it fails to explain crimes of passion.
6. The concept of social disorganization has a powerful correlation with the high incidence of crime in certain areas.
7. As a theory it assumes that the growth of cities occurs in a 'natural' way, ignoring processes of power and inequality that shape the emergence of different urban areas.
8. The theory's validity has to be questioned, as it takes statistics at face value.
9. The approach has been influential in the development of empirical work on subcultures of crime.
10. It assumes that crime is committed by groups.
11. The concept of social disorganization can be vague and hides a disapproving value system that looks down on what could be seen as highly organized but different social arrangements.

DIFFERENTIAL ASSOCIATION THEORY

Sutherland's work on differential association (see for example Sutherland, 1942) built upon the insights of Shaw and McKay and others of the Chicago School, but sought to broaden the explanatory power of their theories by drawing up propositions that could explain a wider range of crimes than just the juvenile delinquency focused upon by Shaw and McKay. Sutherland argued that social groups are characterized by different attitudes towards criminal activity. If an area has a preponderance of attitudes that do not condemn criminality, then it is likely to exhibit high rates of criminal activity. Conversely, those with a predominance of unfavourable attitudes towards criminality are likely to be low-crime areas. This difference he termed differential social organization.

Related to the concept of differential social organization is the idea of differential association, whereby individuals engage in crime when they have been influenced by people with favourable attitudes towards criminality. Sutherland therefore had a structural (differential social organization) and an individual (differential association) strand to his explanation of crime. More controversially, he argued that this holds true at all levels of the class system, and can be used to explain the phenomenon of white-collar crime as much as lower-class crime (see Chapters 2 and 5). McCarthy (1996) argues that, while Sutherland did focus on the importance of attitudes in the development of a criminal career, he also recognized the importance of behaviour in this process, as budding criminals learn the skills of illegal activity. So while tutelage in the skills of crime is not a necessary precondition, most criminal activity does require some form of training.

Differential Association Theory was extended by Glaser in the 1960s and 1970s (see, for example, Glaser, 1978) to incorporate a more individualistic aspect into the theory. He proposed a theory of differential identification in addition to differential association. He argued that the intensity of the identification (a feeling of affinity or closeness) of one person with another is an important factor in the transmission of attitudes and values. The stronger the identification, the more likely that transmission will occur. Identification is not just a feature of personal relationships, but could be a characteristic of public media figures as well. This means that those in the public eye could influence the behaviour of those who identify with them.

Another offshoot from Differential Association Theory is Social Learning Theory, although there are other influences here as well. The development of the theory began with an attempt by Jeffrey (1965) to combine biological, psychological and sociological factors as an explanation of crime. The importance of his work was his insistence that criminal behaviour is learned, but that it can be independent of other people and be the product of specific biological and psychological traits that can cause certain forms of behaviour. He thus downplayed the social forces behind crime.

Akers (1985) has developed a more sociological form of Social Learning Theory, in which deviant behaviour is learned by individuals through the processes of reinforcement and punishment. Individuals learn deviant behaviour mainly by interacting with others. It can be direct, as in social conditioning, or indirect, through modelling behaviour on that of others. The learned deviance can then be reinforced or punished, and thus strengthened or weakened. Empirical support for the effects of Social Learning Theory has been quite extensive (see Pratt et al., 2006 for a meta-analysis of studies that showed support for social learning). Hence Glaser (1978) concludes that a crime is committed when an individual's expected gains outweigh the expected punishment (try this for yourself in Exercise 3.4). These expectations are based on past experiences and are learned from the social environment in which individuals live. As everybody's experiences differ and therefore learning differs, the propensity of any individual to commit crime also differs.

Ⓐ
Exercise 3.4

For this exercise we would like you to work with a partner. You are required to do a cost–benefit analysis of crime. This will involve you establishing the costs (expected punishments) and the benefits (expected gains) of crime. Record your analysis in a chart like the one shown below.

Costs	Benefits
1.	1.
2.	2.
3.	3.
4.	4.

Ⓔ
Exercise 3.5

Evaluate Differential Association Theory in terms of the theory's strengths and weaknesses. You should try to come up with at least three strengths and three weaknesses.

STRAIN THEORY

Merton (1949) departed from the main focus of the Chicago School by arguing that the existence of crime and deviance is the product of the nature of American society as a whole, with its emphasis on the 'American Dream'. He argued that those at the bottom of society are not socialized to accept their lot as in many other societies, but instead are taught to aspire to the highest position in society they can achieve according to their efforts and their talent. However, access to the material and status rewards to be had in American society through legitimate means, such as education, is restricted, and this inevitably leads to the emergence of illegitimate routes to success. This 'strain' between the goals of society and the legitimate means of achieving them – that is, a state of anomie – leads to different reactions, ranging from conformity to a variety of different types of deviant reaction, such as retreatism, rebellion, ritualism and innovation.

Merton was not necessarily arguing that, where strain exists, the majority of individuals turn to illegitimate solutions to resolve the strain. On the contrary, most people continue to conform. However, innovation – where the goals of society are accepted but legitimate means are blocked – will tempt some individuals into criminal activity. In societies where anomie exists – and Merton argued that societies that place great value on economic success are likely to be anomic – standards of right and wrong tend to be side-stepped in the rush to acquire material success. Merton therefore located the origins of deviance in the social structure of American society itself, rejecting individualistic theories that blame human nature.

Exercise 3.6

(K)(U) 1. What do you think is meant by the phrase the 'American Dream'? (Hint: it is to do with success.)

(A)(E) 2. Jot down what your 'British Dream' is. Think about what you would like to be doing by the time you reach the age of 35. What possessions would you like to own? Do you want to be married? Do you want to have children? Have your ambitions changed since the 'credit crunch' crisis of 2008? Compare your answers with those of other members of your sociology group.

Exercise 3.7

①Ⓐ 1. For this exercise there is a chart identifying Merton's five-point scale of reactions to the state of anomie. Your task is to copy the chart on a larger scale and fill in the blank spaces with appropriate paragraphs from the alternatives provided below. This will require you to think about what each of Merton's concepts means (if necessary, look up the words in an English dictionary) and then to choose the paragraph that best describes each term. Ask your teacher or lecturer to check your answers or refer to the book where the descriptions come from.

Merton's five-point scale of responses

Response	Description of response
1. Conformity	
2. Innovation	
3. Ritualism	
4. Retreatism	
5. Rebellion	

Description of responses

- This response involves giving up or losing sight of both means and goals by opting out or dropping out of conventional society, for example living a 'down-and-out' life of oblivion through drink or drug abuse. Such behaviour can occur in any social class, possibly giving rise to the 'tramp-who-was-once-a-duke' stereotype.
- This is the response of the majority, the stereotypical 'law-abiding citizen' who uses conventional means such as a job to pursue the approved goals of success, which may never be reached.
- Both goals and means are rejected, but *alternatives* are constructed. An example is the political revolutionary who rejects conventional society and strives to create a new society by means of violent revolution.
- Socially acceptable means, such as a job, are rejected, but the goals of success are still pursued. So a person might resort to crime to become rich, as in the case of gangsters such as Al Capone. Another way could be gambling or trying your luck in the National Lottery.
- This is where the means to the goals are accepted and conformed to, but the person loses sight of the goals. The person therefore goes through the motions but has no real interest in the outcome. An example might be the student who lavishes attention on the presentation of an essay but does not answer the question that has been set (adapted from Jorgensen *et al.*, 1997).

①Ⓐ 2. Now that you understand Merton's five-point scale of response to anomie, copy and complete the chart below, which makes use of a coding scheme (see notes at the bottom of the chart) to represent various reactions to the goals and means that capitalist societies set. As you can see, we have started the chart off for you. To complete the chart assign one of the codes in the means and goal columns for each of the responses to anomie.

Merton's responses to anomie

Responses	Means	Goals
Conformity		+
Innovation		
Ritualism		
Retreatism	−	
Rebellion		+−

Notes:

+ Acceptance of the goals or means
− Rejection of the goals or means
+− Rejection of the goals and means and substitution of new ones

(Adapted from Moore, 1996a)

Merton's work was extremely influential in prompting other sociologists to look at the wider social context of deviant behaviour. In the 1990s Strain Theory turned towards a more general explanation. Merton focused on the strain between societal goals, as expressed in material terms, and the legitimate means of achieving such goals. Agnew (1992) argued that the notion of strain needs to be expanded beyond the primarily economic towards other circumstances in which strain might lead to criminality. For example Agnew argued that the loss of a valued circumstance can lead to strain and therefore delinquency. The classic example of this is the death of a loved one or perhaps the end of a love affair, which may lead to illegal use of drugs or unusual behaviour. Agnew also sought to generalize the concept of strain to produce a more explanatory theory, for example by showing that certain types of strain were more likely to lead to crime and delinquency, such as when an individual sees the strain as linked to injustice, then anger and delinquency is more likely to follow. Similarly when strain is connected to low informal social control, such as when a young person gets thrown out of home, then this also is more crimogenic (Agnew, 2001).

Alternatively strain may be induced by the existence of danger or abuse, such as violence within the family or harassment by superiors at work. While there may be legitimate ways of handling such situations, Agnew argued that the resulting strain may lead to deviant behaviour such as running away or taking revenge on the abuser. A good example of this is young people running away from 'noxious circumstances', living on the streets and turning to pilfering or prostitution in order to keep going (McCarthy and Hagan, 1992).

While traditional Strain Theory tended to focus on lower-class individuals and their blocked aspirations, studies of adolescents generally suggest that present goals, not just future ones, have the potential for being blocked. For example, analysis of young people's goals suggests that they are just as concerned about immediate goals as about future economic success. So doing well in school, being popular, having good friends and being successful in sport are equally important goals for the average teenager (see for example Elliott et al., 1985).

In a further development of Strain Theory, Messner and Rosenfeld (2001) focused on the structural aspects of Strain Theory, noting that the United States had a much greater level of crime than other industrialized capitalist societies. They investigated what it is about US society that has led to this situation. They argued that, unlike in other industrialized countries that are not dominated by the 'American Dream', US society was dominated by the economy, with all other social institutions subordinated to it. So education was primarily seen as a mechanism whereby individuals could gain the skills needed to perform in the economic sphere. Other industrialized societies have social institutions that promote other ideas, such as civic responsibility, altruism (putting others first), self-sacrifice, and so on. It was thus the primacy of the economic in US society that encourages a situation of anomie, where it is each person for her- or himself in a competitive market place, and this resulted in higher levels of crime. Research by Downes and Hansen (2006) supports this interpretation as they show that those countries that spend more on welfare and social provision have lower imprisonment rates than the United States, with its emphasis on individualism and materialism.

In the twenty-first century, Strain Theory has re-emerged in new forms through the works of Young (2007) and Reiner (2007). Young argues that the conditions of late modernity led to 'social bulimia'. This is where those at the bottom of society are *included* within a strong cultural imperative to be materially successful, as evidenced by designer labels dominating the fashion choices of the underclass, while simultaneously they are being *excluded* from the potential to realize the material success by which status in late modernity is measured. The key elements in the inclusion/exclusion of the underclass are the ideas of meritocracy and recognition. While meritocracy suggests that all can achieve according to their talents, and recognition that all receive respect for their social worth, the acceptance of these social norms by the underclass contrasts strongly with the way that society practices exclusion of the underclass by labelling them as the 'other', denying them access to legitimate means of succeeding and attributing to them low social worth. In turn, this leads the underclass to feelings of relative deprivation and that mainstream society offers them no respect. As a reaction to this intense sense of frustration, some of the underclass turn to crime and violence, often amongst themselves. In emphasizing the humiliation that many of the criminal underclass feel, Young is moving Strain Theory beyond the economic constraints that the traditional Mertonian school rested on, and introduces a strong element of agency through the equation of strong cultural inclusion combined with structural exclusion.

Reiner focused on the domination of neoliberalism in post-Second World War societies, in which material increases for the mass of the population are combined with growing inequalities and an acceptance of an aggressive individualism, in which people no longer accepted responsibility towards others outside their immediate family and friends. The problem is that materialism in the form of goods and possessions is no longer sufficient to garner respect. Monetary success becomes its own reward and there is no natural limit to what individuals aspire to. As Reiner puts it, 'there is no terminal point for monetary aspirations and success breeds desire rather than satisfaction' (2007, p. 84). As a result, there is an imperative towards deviance, as institutionalized means can never fulfil the cultural goal of monetary success, and this feeds into increases in crime during the last half of the twentieth century.

Another development of Strain Theory focuses on contemporary societies that are in extreme circumstances of strain, to the point of disintegration (see Bayart et al., 1999). The notion of the 'failed state' is deployed to describe some societies where low but constant levels of civil war or political conflict lead to endemic criminality. Indeed in such states it is impossible to disentangle the activities of the agents of the state from criminal enterprises.

Evaluation of Strain Theory

ⓘⒶ
Ⓔ

Exercise 3.8

Listed below are a number of partly completed statements relating to the strengths and weaknesses of Strain Theory. Your task is to complete the statements by selecting appropriate finishing clauses from those provided.

Strengths

1. The theory clearly focuses...
2. It offers a useful typology...
3. The approach links the increase...
4. Strain Theory has led to many programmes...
5. Strain Theory can be adapted to new situations...

Finishing strengths clauses

- in deviant behaviour to the ideologies of societies.
- on the social when explaining crime and delinquency.
- such as the emergence of failed states in the late twentieth century.
- attempting to improve opportunities for the disadvantaged, for example Project Headstart.
- for different types of reaction to frustration.

Weaknesses

1. It offers a liberal rather than a radical critique of American society,...
2. It assumes that every American...
3. Delinquent subcultures might also be characterized...
4. It is not totally clear why one individual...
5. The more emotional aspects of Strain Theory...

Finishing weaknesses clauses

- are difficult to research and measure.
- and tends to accept that the structure of the United States is legitimate in itself.
- by low aspirations rather than frustrated ambition.
- opts for a particular mode of adaption.
- is socialized into the American Dream.

THE CULTURAL TRADITION EMERGING FROM THE CHICAGO SCHOOL AND STRAIN THEORY

Albert K. Cohen (1955): status frustration

Influenced by the Chicago School and Merton's Strain Theory, Cohen went further than both in presenting the delinquent subculture of the slums as not only supportive of criminality, but also malicious and hedonistic of itself. The delinquent behaviour exhibited by those socialized into the subculture reflects contempt for authority and opposition to mainstream society. For Cohen, it is status frustration in the pursuit of mainstream values that turns delinquent boys towards an alternative macho subculture in which they can gain status in the eyes of their peers. By status frustration, Cohen means that boys socialized into working-class culture are ill-equipped to compete with middle-class boys in a society that is dominated by middle-class values. However, it is not inevitable that all working-class boys will end up as delinquents. There are three options open to them. The first is adaption, where the boys make the best of their circumstances, but this might involve them in mild forms of delinquency. The second is to move outside their class, usually through education. The third is to develop a delinquent subculture in which alternative avenues to status are created. What seems to be an irrational reaction if viewed from the mainstream is perfectly rational from the viewpoint of the inhabitants of the slums.

Link Exercise 3.1

This exercise is designed to get you to apply material from the field of education and training. A number of research studies on schooling have noted that students who belong to antischool cultures are able to gain status among their peers by being deviant. Drawing on any material with which you are familiar, summarize the findings of one research study that has come to such conclusions. Make sure you make a note of the sociologist(s) who carried out the research and the year in which the research findings were published.

Item C

Running on empty

National television news gave brief coverage last month to the horrific road crash in Crumpsall, north Manchester, in which five teenagers lost their lives. A few days later, in Bury, less than six miles away, another such crash resulted in the loss of three young lives.

Police figures indicate that car theft in the 10 boroughs of Greater Manchester declined from 55,850 in 1993 to 45,953 in the year to March 1996, a drop of nearly 18 per cent. But in Salford, the home base of the five young men who died last month and one of those who died in the second crash, there was a 9.3 per cent rise during the same period.

This increase was recorded against all the best efforts of an impressive range of local authority/police crime prevention programmes in local schools and in inner-city areas, including a programme (Gears) specifically targeting the dangers and heartbreak of a car theft.

Some commentary from police sources has tried to identify these incidents as car thefts, resulting from widespread problems with drugs – implying that the cars were stolen by heroin addicts and sold on to raise money for a daily drug habit.

Criminological research into joy-riding and car theft has always highlighted the different attractions for severely disadvantaged young men of the car itself, of speed, and especially the chase, in an attempt to kick against the unravelling destiny of a lifetime of poverty and little opportunity.

Some researchers have favoured psychoanalytic interpretations of the relationship between the car and the male psyche wanting to undertake 'depth analysis' of the different types of car acquired more or less legitimately by affluent or upwardly mobile men, as well as the kinds of car acquired illegitimately by joy riders and car thieves.

What most of this research has glimpsed – though rarely commented on at length – is the significance of car theft and joy-riding as a momentary escape for young men from the constraints of their own narrow household and neighbourhood, the almost non-existent local labour markets, and constant self-denial involved in everyday poverty.

It is not only the speed which is a thrill, but the momentary sense of transcending the personal destiny of deindustrialization, of joblessness and poverty, and the meanness of inner-city living. In this specific respect, car theft can be a more effective way of 'getting away from it all' for the day than drug or alcohol abuse at home.

None of this, of course, makes the joy-riders and car thieves any more lovable. Local crime research suggests that young men who engage in these activities in inner-city areas such as Salford tend also to engage in robberies and burglaries in their own areas (as well as in outer boroughs), in general affrays in public space, and also in assaults on local people – especially women, students, and anyone identifiable as a 'foreigner', whether to the country or the area. There is little evidence at present of any reduction in the numbers of young men engaging in these different forms of angry and aggressive 'protest masculinity'.

Source: Taylor (1997).

Exercise 3.9

Study Items C and D, both of which relate to car theft. We would like you to use material from both of the items to lend support to Cohen's Status Frustration Theory. You should also identify in the items any arguments for car theft that are not adequately explained in terms of status frustration.

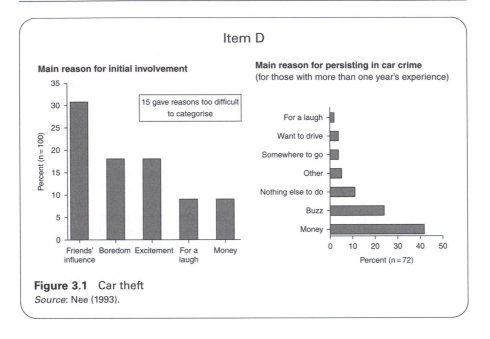

Figure 3.1 Car theft
Source: Nee (1993).

Cloward and Ohlin (1960): illegitimate opportunity structures

Drawing on Merton's theory of blocked opportunities, Cloward and Ohlin argue that in certain neighbourhoods there are limited opportunities for individual economic advancement, either in terms of further education or low-paid but stable employment. The young men who inhabit these areas could be caught up in different delinquent subcultures depending on the existence or non-existence of organized adult criminal 'enterprises'. The important feature is that the illegitimate enterprises are stable and offer a recruitment route for those whose opportunities are blocked. Entry into juvenile *criminal subcultures* is the first step towards acceptance into neighbourhood criminal employment, through the execution of criminal activities such as theft and burglary.

However, where adult criminal opportunities do not exist – the disorganized slum – the young disaffected tend to move into gang-type activity, of which defence of territory and violence are the principal features. This is the *conflict subculture*. The primary focus in this subculture is the gaining of respect, although it is gained by causing trouble, not only for the conforming members of the community but for the criminal subculture itself. It is the unpredictability of the gangs, in terms of where they might cause property damage or engage in violence, that makes them such a threat.

Those denied access to the opportunities offered by the criminal or conflict subcultures tend to move into *retreatist subcultures* based on drug and alcohol use. These are 'double failures' in that they are unable to succeed through either legitimate or illegitimate opportunity structures. Their reluctance to engage in violent, criminal or deviant activity may be because they have an internalized prohibition against violence, or because they cannot gain the reputation needed to join the other two types of subculture.

Item E

Drugs

The global drugs trade is big business. Estimates suggest that the illegal global drugs trade could be worth around £800 billion, second only in size to the world arms trade. The profits from drugs-related crime in the UK have been estimated at between £800 million and £4,000 million annually, with further millions spent on policing, customs work and prison for drugs offenders.

Opinion is divided on whether decriminalizing or legalizing some or all proscribed drugs would reduce drugs crime or cut the risks associated with taking some drugs – by improving the purity of some substances, for example. Certainly, a number of senior police officers in Britain have called for a serious rethink on dealing with drug users. What we do know is that more young people are *trying* drugs and that the range of drugs being taken by the young is also extending. By 16 years of age most youngsters are believed to have tried some illegal drug and that by that age almost one-quarter have tried a Class A drug such as LSD.

Home Office estimates suggest that there are around 30,000 drug *addicts* in the UK, but some pressure groups put the real figure at ten times this estimate, with Glasgow alone accounting for 8,500 injecting heroin addicts. This is the desperate, *Trainspotting* end of the drugs spectrum.

With between an estimated 500,000 and 1 million weekend Ecstasy users in Britain, the popular market for so-called 'leisure' drugs is booming. The 'blanket' enforcement policies on drugs threaten to criminalize thousands of otherwise law-abiding citizens from both sexes and across the social classes.

Table 3.1 Persons found guilty of, or cautioned for, drug offences, by type of drug

England & Wales

Thousands

	1990	1992	1994	1995	1996	1997	1998	1999	2000	2001	2002	2003	2004
Cocaine (excluding crack)	0.9	0.9	1.6	1.8	2.2	2.9	4.0	4.6	4.2	4.7	5.8	7.0	8.1
Heroin	1.6	1.4	2.7	3.9	5.7	8.2	10.1	10.8	10.7	11.1	10.7	10.5	10.1
LSD	0.9	1.4	1.7	1.1	0.8	0.7	0.5	0.4	0.2	0.2	0.1	0.1	0.1
Ecstasy type	0.3	1.5	1.8	3.1	3.7	3.7	2.7	3.8	5.9	6.8	6.1	5.5	5.2
Amphetamines	2.3	5.7	7.8	9.6	12.3	12.4	13.2	10.6	5.9	4.6	5.6	5.9	5.8
Cannabis[1]	40.2	41.4	67.2	72.0	69.1	80.9	90.5	81.1	70.2	66.4	78.1	82.1	49.8
All drugs[2]	44.9	48.9	82.9	90.6	91.2	107.5	122.4	112.8	99.1	96.5	106.6	110.4	82.8

1 Cannabis was reclassified on 29 January 2004 from Class B to Class C. Data for 2004 does not include police formal warnings.
2 Individual components do not sum to the total because each person may appear in more than one category. The total includes all drugs but not all drug offences.
Source: Babb *et al.* (2006).

Exercise 3.10

ⓘ 1. Carefully study Item E. Which two drugs are responsible for the largest increases in use between 1990 and 2004?

ⓘⒶ 2. Use material from Item E and elsewhere to construct an argument that
ⓀⓊ   the three types of subculture to which Cloward and Ohlin refer are interlinked.

ⓘⒶ

Exercise 3.11

Listed below are a number of deviant acts that members of deviant subcultures may commit. Your task is to identify which acts may be committed by members of criminal subcultures, which by members of conflict subcultures and which by members of retreatist subcultures. Record your answers in a chart like the one we have started off for you. You will find that some of the acts cannot simply be associated with one distinct type of subculture. This is because the act may be committed by people who span the different types of subculture. For these acts, record your answer in the 'combined' section of the chart.

Deviant acts

- Rioting
- Taking ecstasy
- Vandalism
- Sniffing glue
- Taking crack cocaine
- Burglary
- Football hooliganism
- Drug dealing
- 'Taxing' (theft with violence)
- Ram raiding
- Illegal possession of a hand gun
- Murder

Type of subculture	Deviant acts committed
Criminal	1. Burglary
	2.
	3.
	4.
Conflict	1.
	2.
	3.
	4.

Retreatist | 1. Sniffing glue
| 2.
| 3.
| 4.
Combined | 1.
| 2.
| 3.
| 4.

Criticism of Cloward and Ohlin's work has focused on whether the three types of subculture actually exist, and, if they do, how young people are recruited into them. Empey (1982) argues that delinquent boys tend to cross between the different activities that characterize the criminal, conflict and retreatist subcultures with ease and without any apparent contradiction. They also ignore the existence of delinquent behaviour that is not negative and hedonistic, for example drug taking, but consumption-oriented, such as trading in the black economy. From the new right comes the argument that, in the free market economy of the late twentieth century, there are few blocked opportunities and therefore little cause for the development of subcultures in the way described by Cloward and Ohlin. Feminists are also critical of Cloward and Ohlin's neglect of the experience of girls in their neighbourhoods and their response to blocked opportunities.

A further criticism has been the lack of empirical support for Cloward and Ohlin's ideas. For example their work implies that all delinquents have a high aspiration to succeed, but Agnew (1985) suggests that delinquency is highest where aspiration is lowest. He therefore argues that the relationship between aspiration and delinquency is much more complex, with aspiration declining when opportunities are blocked, which in turn leads to delinquency.

Miller, 1962: the exaggeration of focal concerns

Miller rejects the idea that subcultures within the working class are responsible for much of the criminal activity in urban areas. Rather, he suggests that there is a distinctive lower-class culture whose 'focal concerns' are oriented towards criminality, in contrast with the focal concerns of middle-class youths, which are connected to education and the gaining of qualifications. However, these middle-class focal concerns can also prepare middle-class individuals for criminal activities such as embezzlement or tax avoidance. The stress in lower-class culture is on physical prowess, excitement and street life, and young people exposed to these focal concerns can be led into law-breaking

activities associated with them, such as robbery and assault. Miller also identified the existence of lone parent families, where the father is absent, as a factor
in the learning of these focal concerns. Gangs offer a route for young males in
this position to learn 'masculine' behaviours, as well as providing a sense of
identity and belonging. The six focal concerns identified by Miller as characteristic of the unskilled working class are excitement, fate, smartness, trouble,
toughness and autonomy.

Exercise 3.12

The chart below pairs Miller's six focal concerns with examples of characteristics that might be associated with them. We would like you to copy the chart
and complete it by identifying one other characteristic for each of the six focal
concerns.

Miller's six focal concerns of the unskilled working class

Focal concerns	Characteristics associated with the focal concerns
Excitement	Taking risks
Fate	Luck
Smartness	Cunning
Trouble	Breaking the rules
Toughness	Machismo
Autonomy	Self-reliance

Item F

Theorizing hooliganism

Media coverage may help to
shape aspects of the hooligan phenomenon and to condition our
responses to it, but it does not
explain the allure of disorder and
fighting to some fans. Debates
about the deeper 'causes' of hooliganism have divided sociologists
and other academics for some
time. Most students will know of
the work of psychologists Peter
Marsh and his colleagues (1978)
at Oxford. They focused on largely
non-violent and ritualistic 'aggro'
at football and on the terraces'
own 'rules of disorder' which break
down into 'real' violence only by
accident or as a result of inappropriate intervention, for example
by the police. But, what happened
next?

Sociological approaches

Sociologists at Leicester (Dunning
et al., 1988) criticized Marsh
et al. not for arguing that ter-
race behaviour was ritualistic or

rule-governed, but rather for understating the amount of 'real' violence which occurred at matches. Their own account lays emphasis on the long, if patchy, history of hooliganism at football and the generation and reproduction of a particular form of aggressive masculinity, especially in lower-class communities. In these 'rough' neighbourhoods young males are socialized (at home, at work, in peer group gangs, etc.) into standards that value and reward publicly assertive, openly aggressive and violent expressions of masculinity. Young men are expected to be able to 'look after themselves'. Fights can be anticipated and enjoyed, not just because of the challenges they offer, but also because of how they make the protagonists *feel*. (Some fighters describe the football action as being 'better than sex'.) Such groups also have strong spatial and locational attachments (to neighbourhood, town, region, nation, etc.), which are 'activated' on the basis of the nature and level of external challenges.

Club football, as the site for symbolic struggles between representatives of 'rival' working-class communities, is an appropriate and attractive venue for testing masculine identities, particularly at the level of town or city affiliation. Young men like these 'defend' their own, their 'firm's' and their town's reputation against similar intruders who are out to 'turn over' their hosts.

A network of spectator rivalries, with its own traditions and folk memories, has grown up around football and especially around the ritual of travelling away. Much of this engagement is about 'running' opposing fans, but core hooligans also enjoy a fight when they can get one. Some fights are pre-arranged. As well as the status rewards involved in such activities, the camaraderie, loyalty and 'entertainment' value of hooligan involvement is prized by young men whose opportunities for status and excitement through other channels is relatively limited. Heavy drinking, for example, is often a key element in a 'good day out' and figures strongly in arrest statistics.

The lower-class 'aggressive masculinity' thesis has been criticized on a number of counts. The sociologist Ian Taylor (1987) returns to some of the themes about 'Englishness' and hooliganism mentioned above. He argues that the class fraction identified by the Leicester research as the production ground for hooliganism cannot account for the rise of the high-spending and fashionable soccer 'casual' who is at the heart of English hooliganism in Europe in the 1990s. He claims that the recent violence by English fans abroad is the specific product of an upwardly mobile and 'detached' fraction of the 'Thatcherised' working class, which has a certain residual solidarity born of neighbourhood and gender but is generally individualistic, chauvinistic and racist.

Taylor favours the troubled state of English *masculinity* rather than class as the key to the hooligan problem. These are hooligans with no real class affiliation or tradition; they, instead, express the values of a contemporary and unregulated kind of masculine brutishness of England in the 1980s and 1990s.

Anthropology and psychology

From anthropology Armstrong (1994) argues, too, that the stress on social class is overdone in the Leicester work, but he is also less interested than Taylor in gender. He asserts that members of 'The Blades' firm at Sheffield United – Armstrong is from Sheffield and his research focuses on a group he knows well – come from a range of locations and backgrounds and are involved in hooliganism because of its attractions as 'social drama' and the opportunity it provides for a sense of belonging, for competition, achieving 'honour' and inflicting shame.

For Armstrong, hooligan groups are diverse in their make-up (they can include staunch non-racists, for example), they exhibit negligible levels of organization and, *pace* Marsh, they enjoy confrontation rather than violence. For Armstrong, hooliganism is best understood through anthropology (the study of humankind) and biography rather than through sociology and structure. The social dramas enacted by 'The Blades' achieve 'communion between disparate individuals pursuing achievement and selfhood' (1994, p. 322).

Social–psychological perspectives offer different explanations but, like Armstrong, their focus is more directly on the *meaning* of the activity itself, rather than on the background of those involved. Finn (1994) sees hooliganism as an example of the search for a 'flow' or 'peak' experience: an intense, emotional experience not usually encountered in everyday life. Flow experiences allow for an open expression of shared, collective emotionality: an outpouring of joy or sadness, strengthening a common social identity. Hooligans, like other fans, seek peak or flow experiences through their involvement in football; unlike other fans, however, they reject the vicarious role of a football supporter in favour of a more active and rewarding role as a direct participant in spectator confrontations.

Kerr (1994) argues, in a similar fashion, that hooliganism, like some other sorts of crimes (e.g. joyriding), reflects the search for high levels of emotional arousal through risk-taking against a general background of long periods of boredom. Although most hooligan activities occur within a collective frame which limits the dangers involved (memories, again, of Marsh et al.), some fans can become 'addicted' to hooliganism, which leads them into ever more violent activities in order to achieve the kind of arousal they increasingly seek. These are the so-called 'super-hooligans', who may be older than conventional ideas allow.

Source: Williams (1996b).

Exercise 3.13

An(E) 1. In Item F Williams summarizes some of the established explanations for football hooliganism. We would like you to draw up a more spacious version of the chart below and complete it by summarizing in your own words the possible explanations for football hooliganism, as suggested by the various theorists mentioned in the item. We would also like you to describe how the different explanations offered could be used to support or refute Miller's theoretical ideas on juvenile delinquency.

We would like you to finish off this part of the exercise by writing a conclusion. We suggest that you approach this from two angles. First, weigh up the applicability of Miller's theoretical ideas to a sociological understanding of football hooliganism. Second, try to assess whether the sociological or non-sociological explanations in the item offer the most convincing explanations of football hooliganism. If you track down the article written by Williams you could compare your conclusion with Williams's discussion later in the article.

Explanations of football hooliganism

Theorists	Explanation offered	Level of fit with Miller
Marsh et al. (1978)		
Dunning et al. (1988)		
Taylor (1987)		
Armstrong (1994)		
Finn (1994)		
Kerr (1994)		

A① 2. Further on in his article Williams considers possible explanations for the decline in football hooliganism. Identify and explain three reasons why football hooliganism may be on the decline in the UK. You could again compare your answers with Williams's later observations in the original article.

Wolfgang and Ferracuti, 1982: a subculture of violence

Wolfgang and Ferracuti argue that there has developed in urban slums in particular a subculture that condones the use of violence as a solution to both social and personal problems. Acceptance of violence as a legitimate form of social expression leads to a process of differential association, which perpetuates the subculture of violence in those areas. This is conceptualized by Anderson (1999) as the 'code of the street', which he identified from a longitudinal study of minority youth in Philadelphia. The code is developed by marginalized young people, whose only concern becomes 'respect' from others in the locality. The code is an informal set of rules that prescribe violent reactions when an individual is disrespected, however slightly. The reaction encompasses all youth in the area, so that even those disinclined to violence are drawn into it in order to prevent their victimization by those who are quick to turn to violent acts. The idea of a code has some resonance in the UK where knife attacks by the young on the young have become a moral panic in the late 2000s.

Schwendinger and Schwendinger, 1985: towards an integrated approach

The Schwendingers have attempted to develop an integrated theory of delinquency, allying Subcultural Theory with Conflict Theory (see Chapter 5). Their starting point is the lack of focus in Subcultural Theory on middle-class delinquency, and they use Control Theory (see pp. 87–102) to help explain why middle-class delinquents commit crime. They begin with the capitalist mode of production, with its tendency to emphasize individualistic rather than collective values. This leads to a morality based on indifference to the fate of others. For young people, this means that their main interest is self-gratification, which involves indifference to potential victims. But because society is stratified into classes, the subcultures that grow up in each class differ in terms of values and types of delinquency. 'Socialites' who tend to be involved in higher education, 'street corner youths' who are more likely to hang around the streets and 'intermediaries' who occasionally move between the two former subcultures are therefore on a continuum of delinquent behaviour ranging from the traditional violence of the street corner youth to the date rape and car insurance fraud of the socialites.

Network analysis

Developed by Bartol and Bartol (1989), network analysis is an attempt to bring together many aspects of work on subcultures and the community. Bartol and Bartol argue that the conformity of young people to conventional patterns of behaviour relies in part on the strength of their links to society through personal networks. The important dimensions of human networks are (i) their multiplexity (that is, the number of situations in which the same people interact) and (ii) their density (the extent to which members of a network interact with each other). In neighbourhoods with dense multiplex networks (that is, the inhabitants interact with each other a great deal and in many contexts) delinquency is likely to be rare because of the capacity of the community to control and influence the members.

Friday and Hage (1976), among others, identify the family, the community, school, work and peer group as important networks. As the multiplexity of relationships increases across these five networks, the frequency of delinquency diminishes. The capacity of a neighbourhood to construct and maintain these networks can change over time. Under the impact of deindustrialization and disinvestment, low-income areas lose the density and multiplexity that militates against delinquent behaviour. This is because the unemployment that follows in the wake of industry leaving an area undermines the financial and social resources of those in the locality to maintain networks.

Bartol and Bartol (1989) consider it possible that socialization into narrow networks may lead to conflict with the broader society, as attachment to the immediate group prevents experience of the wider world. However, the individual in this situation does not experience any conflict, as the larger world has little salience (or importance) for him or her. Conflict arises only when the wider society attempts to control or label the narrower network.

Cultural criminology

Another development in the area of culture and crime has been to explore the connections between these two phenomena in a more systematic and reciprocal way (see for example Ferrell, 1995). The central idea here is to examine the interactions between images, symbols and subcultural styles and the legal authorities that define some of these as criminal or deviant. For example Lowney (1995) shows how a young Satanist group has used subcultural styles such as an upside-down cross dyed into the hair to signify their difference from the mainstream Christian culture of the southern United States. But the relationship between crime and culture is seen as a two-way street, in which some subcultural styles become demonized through the activities of moral entrepreneurs such as media commentators and local church leaders, who deploy symbolic imagery and cultural references to encourage the criminalization of the activities. In the case of the young Satanists, traditional Christian symbolism was used to persuade the law enforcement agencies to police their activities.

Cultural activity can itself become subject to the criminalizing process of the political and legal authorities. Thus the issue of 'style' is the main focus of cultural criminology, that is, the ways in which an 'aesthetic' (a particular way of walking, talking, dressing, and so on) becomes representative of a particular criminal activity. (Exercise 3.14 will deepen your knowledge of subcultural styles.) Consider for example how the image of the 'skinhead' is associated with violence and racism.

(A)

Exercise 3.14

Copy the following chart and complete it by identifying the 'aesthetic styles' associated with the deviant cultures listed.

Deviant culture	Aesthetic styles
Football hooligans	
Ravers	
New age travellers	
Bikers	
Green activists	

In order to bring about the criminalization of deviant images, symbols and styles, moral entrepreneurs and the legal/political authorities operate as cultural enterprises, manipulating mass-media images, the news and public opinion in order to create 'folk devils', that is, groups of people who are generally reviled and seen as outside the mainstream (see Chapter 4). Moreover, much of the focus of the activities of the moral entrepreneurs is on cultural expression itself, such as art, photography, music, architecture, and so on, as they seek to define the boundaries of good taste and decency. Consider the controversy that the photography of Robert Mapplethorpe aroused (see, for example, Boulton, 1990), or the attempt by the authorities to disrupt rap artists' careers.

Ferrell (1995) argues that these activities also show a clear bias against marginalized groups, especially blacks and gays, and that this necessarily embroils the legal authorities in a mass of contradictions. He quotes Strossen (1992), who describes how the United States Supreme Court banned nude dancing in bars but not nude dancing in high-culture entertainment such as opera. However, Ferrel comes to argue that the meaning of crime is highly contested between criminals, the mass media, politicians and the police and is not just a straightforward attack on marginal groups (Ferrel, 2005). As the police and authorities and criminals jostle to create images of crime through a media that are either more or less favourable to the criminal (the threat of crime versus the romance of crime), crime control becomes a 'public carnival'.

Cultural criminologists also emphasize that the sheer density of representation of criminal activity in media texts has the effect of blurring the real and the imagined. For example, the assimilation of gangsta rap by commercial ventures manages to package street gang music in ways that are designed to appeal to the young and which at the same time sanitizes the music while retaining a subversive 'criminal' edge (Kubrin, 2005). The cultural criminologists are thus drawn to the emotional dimension of crime, as experienced in the lived experience of those involved in it. They are concerned not just with the risk and excitement associated with joy-riding, for example, but also boredom and exclusion as stimuli to crime. For example, poverty can be experienced as the ultimate humiliation in a consumer society, an intense emotional experience that can lead to those suffering from it to break with restraining influences and enter the world of crime (Hayward, 2003). By looking at the foreground of crime, that is, how engaging in a criminal act makes a person feel, they are adding to our understanding as it is drawn from the background (causes) of crime.

Evaluation of the cultural tradition

Exercise 3.15

(I)(E) 1. Listed below are a number of evaluations of the cultural tradition. Identify which are the strengths and which are the weaknesses and list them in a two-column chart.

- It links together wider social formations, such as values or education, with the experiences of working-class boys.
- The approach offers insights into ways of trying to tackle delinquency.
- It focuses too much on juvenile delinquency and thus neglects more serious adult crime.
- The cultural tradition has helped to shape other sociological theories of crime and delinquency, for example left realism.
- It tends to see adolescents as easily socialized into subcultural values, rather than this being problematic and difficult to accomplish.
- By focusing on 'bad boys', it fails to explore why so many working-class boys become conformist.
- The approach offers a social explanation of delinquency, beyond the psychological.
- It tends to offer a stereotyped view of working-class life.
- It is masculinist and ignores the role of women and girls in working-class subcultures.
- The cultural tradition is open to empirical confirmation by a variety of research methods.
- Cultural criminology operates with a limited view of culture, underplaying different strands in society that feed into a cultural analysis.
- It explores areas of society that would not be investigated, such as street-racing.

(E) 2. Having sorted out the strengths and weaknesses of the cultural tradition, write a conclusion below your chart that weighs up the usefulness of the cultural tradition as an explanation for crime and delinquency.

CONTROL THEORIES

Early control theories

Durkheim (1973 [1895]) saw crime and deviance as inevitable in society, because there will always be those whose desire to satisfy their individual appetites outweighs their commitment to collective rules. Durkheim saw people as 'homo duplex', having both a social side, in which the expression of common sentiments dominates, and an individual side, where selfish needs take first place. Deviance therefore emerges either because of the weakness of integrative forces in society, so that the social side is not supported and nurtured, or because of the weakness of the regulatory forces in society, which fail to keep the egoistic side of human nature in check. It is the latter emphasis that has been influential in the development of control theories.

Early control theorists drew upon this approach to argue that crime and deviance can be expected more in situations where effective control of the individual is weak. For example Reiss (1951) argued that crime and deviance emerge either from a lack of personal control, where individuals are unable to meet their own needs without coming into conflict with the collective prohibitions of society, or from a weakening of social control, where obedience to collective rules is not effectively enforced.

A key early theorist of Control Theory, mainly because his theory of containment was a forerunner of the Risk Theory favoured by postmodern sociologists, was Reckless (see, for example, Reckless, 1967). The key question for Reckless was not 'why do inner-city males commit crime?', but 'why do so many inner-city dwellers continue to conform and obey the law?'. Crime emerges out of the probabilities represented by the balance between containment pressures and the pressure to commit criminal acts. The latter pressure could involve 'push' factors, such as physical or psychological predispositions, and 'pull' factors, such as the opportunity to commit a crime being presented to an individual. Reckless argued that the most common reaction to these factors is not crime but conformity, and that this is because there are enormous inner and outer containment forces that predispose individuals to obey the law. Outer containment is achieved through such factors as the level of identity and reinforcement in a society. For example if individuals strongly identify with the local community they are less likely to commit crimes against that community.

Inner containment involves a whole range of factors, including whether individuals have a reasonable goal orientation that will direct their activities towards lawful actions. For example an individual's goal may be to settle down and raise a family, which will tend to contain any impulse to commit a crime and thus risk being separated from the family. However, where containment pressures are weak, individuals committed to delinquency are likely to emerge.

Item G

Table 3.2 Reasons offered for giving up car theft

Increased responsibilities/maturity	32
Actual or possible custody	14
An accident	5
Motor project	2
Other	4
Total (claiming to have given up)	57

Source: Nee (1993).

Exercise 3.16

① 1. Examine Item G. How many people claimed to have given up car theft because of increased responsibilities/maturity?
① 2. What was the least important reason offered for giving up car theft?

Critique of early Control Theory

Sykes and Matza (1957) argued that there is a tendency in Control Theory to overpredict the degree of commitment to delinquency by individuals, and that what is remarkable is just how conformist most delinquents are. For example most settle into a conformist lifestyle after a certain age. Delinquency is therefore not a characteristic of individuals at all, but rather individuals *drift* into and out of delinquency in an episodic way. The reason why some young people occasionally carry out delinquent acts is partly because they have learned *techniques of neutralization* from the mainstream culture of which they are also part. Learning social rules therefore also involves learning ways in which obedience to them can be suspended through a variety of tactics, for example denying responsibility for an action, or denying that there is a significant victim involved. The latter involves the stigmatization of victims so that they come to be seen as deserving of the delinquent act. Other techniques of neutralization include an appeal to discrimination – that is, that those condemning the delinquent are acting in a discriminatory way – and appealing to a higher loyalty such as the family, friends or an ideology.

The techniques of neutralization used by individuals when they 'drift into deviance' are reinforced by 'official' ideologies-of-neutralization excuses. Thus the courts, politicians and moral entrepreneurs often blame the parents of delinquents or accept that the victims have in part provoked the delinquent act. For example rape victims are often portrayed in court as having 'provoked' the attack through their dress or behaviour. This allows individuals to avoid responsibility for their own delinquent actions by shifting the blame onto others. Young people in the inner cities are therefore prepared for delinquency when they deploy techniques of neutralization, but also when they are desperate enough in their social circumstances to carry out these types of action.

Evaluation of early Control Theory

(I)(E)

Exercise 3.17

For this exercise we would like you to complete the evaluation paragraphs below by inserting key words from the list provided. The first paragraph outlines the strengths of early control theories and the second establishes the weaknesses.

1. Early control theories introduce the . . . . . . that a choice is exercised when an individual commits a deviant or delinquent act. The approach also accepts that even criminal individuals have connections to the . . . . . . of society.
2. Early control theories recognize the importance of the . . . . . . in influencing the decision to commit delinquent acts. Furthermore the approach appreciates the legitimacy of working-class values in their . . . . . . Early control theories are also subject to criticism. A number of key weaknesses can be noted. Firstly, it is not clear why . . . . . . techniques of neutralization are employed by different delinquents. Secondly, the relative importance of peer group pressure and . . . . . . is not made explicit. Thirdly, it remains focused on . . . . . . criminality and tends to assume that middle-class children adopt middle-class values and therefore do not engage in neutralization.

Missing words

- individual choice • peer group • own right • different
- notion • mainstream norms • lower class

Hirschi's Control Theory, 1969

Hirschi took a very different approach from Sykes and Matza in arguing that people are not fundamentally conformist through the internalization of particular beliefs and ideas. Rather he argued that individuals are fundamentally selfish, and when freed from controls that society might impose they are free to make a rational calculation of the costs and benefits of engaging in criminal activity. Hirschi was therefore proposing a much more sociological view of Control Theory that rejected the psychological dimensions of previous theories. For example he argued that social control is achieved by the social bonds of commitment, involvement, belief and attachment. But he did not understand these as some sort of psychological feelings that the individual holds towards others. Rather they are descriptions of the strength of the social links and relationships between individuals in society.

So attachment is not measured by some subjective feeling but by the degree of intimacy of social relations between, for example, parents and children, teachers and pupils. If the degree of intimacy is intense, the subordinate in the relationship is more likely to be (not feel) attached to the superordinate and is therefore more likely to conform (see, for example, Wilson and Herbert, 1978). The importance of social bonds has been shown empirically by Sampson and Laub (1993a) who found that delinquents could be transformed into law-abiders through the establishment of strong social bonds such as stable marriage or employment.

During the 1970s, Box (1981) combined the insights of Labelling Theory (see Chapter 4) with Control Theory to address the issue of why some individuals, subject to the same control conditions as others, do not become involved in delinquent activity. Box distinguishes between being in situations where it is possible to commit deviant acts, and wanting to do so. For example there is the question of deterrence to deviant activity and the individual's subjective assessment of the likelihood of being found out. It is also the case that individuals in a situation of potential deviance may not have the skills or equipment to make the most of the opportunity. Nevertheless, despite the possibility of being discovered, individuals may still choose to commit a deviant act for one or more of four reasons: material gain, thrills, taking control of one's own life or as a confirmation of a gender identity.

① | Exercise 3.18

Listed below are a number of criminal acts. Your task is to decide which of the acts are most likely to be motivated by material gain, thrills, taking control of one's life or as a confirmation of a gender identity. You may decide that some of the acts may be motivated by a combination of these crimogenic impulses, in which case allocate them to the combined row in a chart copied from the example provided. We have only listed a limited range of crimes as we would like you to provide at least one additional example for each of the reasons for crime.

Criminal acts

- Stealing a car
- Handling stolen goods
- Drug dealing
- Graffiti
- Prostitution

- Burglary
- Actual bodily harm
- Fraud
- Shoplifting
- Speeding in a car

Reason for crime	Criminal acts
Material gain	
Thrills	
Taking control over one's life	
Confirmation of a gender identity	
Combined	

During the 1980s and 1990s Control Theory became incorporated into many other approaches, but developments in the theory also continued. For example Bernard (1987) argues that commitment is the most important part of the social bond. What he means by this is that as individuals grow older they are more likely to become involved in activities that connect them to conformity, such as work or marriage. These links to the social bond are the most important factor in determining the extent of delinquent behaviour. The implication of this is that many delinquents will simply grow out of their antisocial behaviour.

Item H

Why do young people grow out of crime?

There is a strong current of thought that suggests that, given the prevalence of offending amongst young people and the relative lack of criminality among older men and women, there must be a process at work whereby young people 'grow out of crime'. The focus for research in this area has been the idea of transition, as young people move from the world of childhood into adulthood. There are various 'markers' of this transition and it is suggested that the accumulation of these marker states is the key to young offenders becoming more responsible and desisting from offending. The markers are:

- getting married or entering into a stable long-term relationship;
- having children;
- graduating from full-time education;
- taking up a 'steady' job.

In modern developed societies, however, these markers have been subject to a time shift, as social conditions vary, either through legislative change or movements in social mores. For example, in Great Britain, the age of getting married and having children has on average been postponed to people's late 20s and 30s, and the government has increasingly raised the age of being involved in education or training until it is effectively 18.

However, there are differences in the patterns of desistance between males and females. It was female offenders in particular for whom these markers seemed to be effective and immediate. For males, gaining these statuses (worker, husband, father, graduate) was not sufficient for desistance. The other factors involved were continuing to live at home, avoiding 'bad company' and specifically other males involved in drug-taking or heavy drinking and having good relationships with their parents. Boys, in other words, take longer to 'grow up' and were more likely to drift in and out of crime as they tried to desist.

Exercise 3.19

Examine Item H and answer the following questions.

1. Identify three factors that cause young people to stop committing crime.
2. Describe the way that desistence from offending varies according to gender.
3. Evaluate the claim that 'here must be a process at work whereby young people "grow out of crime"'.

Item I

Dealing with youth crime

There are two strands to dealing with young people involved in crime: preventing individuals from ever starting to offend, and encouraging and helping those who are trying to stop.

Findings from the research suggest that efforts should focus on:

- strengthening families – e.g. by parent training, family centres and support groups, and specific measures for single parents and step families;
- strengthening schools – e.g. by strategies to prevent truanting,

developing practical measures to improve family-school relationships;

- protecting young people (particularly young men) from the influence of delinquents in their peer group and from high-risk activities such as alcohol and drug abuse;
- harnessing sources of social control within the criminal justice system, families, schools and neighbours;
- preparing young people for fully independent and responsible adulthood.

Source: Graham and Bowling (1995).

Ⓘ Ⓐⁿ
Ⓔ

Exercise 3.20

The authors of Item I offer strategies for dealing with the youth crime problem. Working with other members of your sociology group, discuss each of the solutions. Which do you feel are more likely to reduce youth crime? Are they all possible to implement? Add to the suggestions by offering your own social policy recommendations.

Evaluation of Hirschi's Control Theory

Ⓔ

Exercise 3.21

We have provided below some key strengths of Hirschi's Control Theory, but just one weakness. Try to work out at least three other weaknesses of the theory.

Strengths

1. He focuses on very concrete forms of delinquency.
2. His ideas can be empirically investigated and confirmed.
3. The theory connects to basic assumptions about human nature.
4. He deals with the moment of the actual deviant act.

Weakness

1. The concepts used, such as attachment, are not tightly defined.

Recent developments in Control Theory

Five branches of Control Theory have been developed in the 1980s, 1990s and 2000s.

Power-control Theory

Power-control Theory was developed by Hagan (1989), who argued that those individuals who are more disposed to take risks are much more likely to engage in criminal behaviour, and that this predisposition is influenced by the type of parenting such individuals receive. In particular, it is the power relations between mothers and fathers that determine the degree of risk taking. In patriarchal families, boys are allowed more latitude than girls and are more likely to grow up as risk takers, while in egalitarian families, girls and boys are more likely to be brought up in a similar fashion and engage in less risk taking.

(E)

Exercise 3.22

Work out at least two strengths and two weaknesses of Power-control Theory.

Self-control Theory

Gottfredson and Hirschi (1990) moved beyond the ideas developed by Hirschi in the 1960s to produce Self-control Theory. They reject Hirschi's emphasis on the strength of social bonds as the major constraint on criminal behaviour. The main reason for this is that the social bonds idea does not seem to fit with what criminologists have observed about crime. Moreover they reject the traditional concepts of class and race as explanatory variables because these are so vague as to be meaningless in terms of empirical research. Gottfredson and Hirschi are thus committed to a neopositivistic approach to the study of crime, in which social facts are established by careful research in order to identify the variables associated with criminality. They argue that empirical data suggests that most crime is not planned but undertaken for short-term gratification, usually in response to opportunities presented to the perpetrators. The most telling correlation for Gottfredson and Hirschi (1995) is that between age and crime, in that the vast majority of crime is committed by adolescents and young adults. Moreover those who engage in criminal acts, such as theft when young, characteristically engage in deviant behaviour when older, for example excessive drinking.

Item J

Age and offending

The most common age for starting the following activities is:

- 14 years for truanting and running away from home;
- 15 years for offending and taking cannabis;
- 16 years for taking drugs other than cannabis.

The peak ages for offending are 21 for males and 16 for females (contrasting with the peaks derived from recorded offending of 18 and 15 years respectively).

Self-reported offending by females declines substantially after the mid-teens. By the early 20s, their rate of offending is five times lower than among female juveniles. In contrast, the rate of self-reported offending for males increases with age up to 18 and remains at the same level into the mid-20s. The prevalence of property offending actually increases with age suggesting that, as they grow older, some males switch from relatively risky property offences, such as shoplifting and burglary, to less visible and less detectable forms of property crime, such as fraud and theft from the workplace. However, serious offending decreases for both males and females as they reach their mid-20s, as does frequency of offending.

Source: Graham and Bowling (1995).

Exercise 3.23

Using only the material in Item J, summarize in no more than 50 words the relationship between age and offending.

Criminals therefore lack self-control, not only with regard to their delinquency but also in other areas such as smoking, gambling, and so on. Self-control is defined as invulnerability to the temptations of the moment. The reason why the majority of the population do not systematically engage in criminal activity is because they have been reared in stable family situations where misconduct is punished and lines of behaviour clearly drawn. When parents are unable or unwilling to create a climate of self-control, children are much more likely to grow up without the degree of self-control needed to refrain from delinquent acts. This also explains why relatively few women engage in criminal activity, because women experience closer socialization in their family. However, it is important to recognize that Gottfredson and Hirschi are not arguing that all those with poor self-control will engage in crime. On the contrary, poor self-control leads to a number of different legal and illegal behaviours, and there are other contingent factors that might persuade a person with poor self-control into crime, such as opportunity or the perception that there is little risk of being caught.

This theory corresponds closely with the concerns of the new right (see Chapter 6) and has been supported by empirical studies (for example Grasmick et al., 1993) that have also found that lack of self-control is related to delinquent behaviour. However, unlike many of the new right, Gottfredson and Hirschi do not believe that longer prison sentences can reduce crime significantly, because the poor self-control of criminals means they are focused on short-term satisfaction and tend to disregard prison as a consequence of their actions. However, rehabilitation does not work either, because it tends to be older criminals who become involved in the rehabilitation process, and age itself is likely to reduce their commitment to criminal activities. Nevertheless, the authors are in line with the new right in advocating that unsupervised activities by teenagers should be restricted, that programmes aimed at the socialization of young children would be effective and that support for two-parent families is essential to boost self-control in society.

Ⓘ Ⓐ
Ⓔ

| Exercise 3.24 |

Together with other students, organize a debate on the claim that encouraging two-parent families will reduce the level of crime in society. Select one member of your group to act as chair and a small number of students to argue for and against the claim. It is important that the two teams of debaters first do some research into the opposing arguments. The teams could usefully begin their search by referring to relevant newspaper articles on the internet (for example the *Guardian* or *The Times*).

Evaluation of Gottfredson and Hirschi's Self-Control Theory

Ⓔ

Exercise 3.25

We have listed below some key weaknesses of Gottfredson and Hirschi's Self-control Theory, but only one strength. Try to work out at least three other strengths of the theory.

Strength

1. They seem to explain the concentration of crime in certain areas, while accepting that crime due to lack of self-control can be found in all sectors of society.

Weaknesses

1. It is better at explaining some types of crime than others. For example white-collar criminals often display deferred gratification patterns.
2. While denying the importance of class, the logic of the theory suggests a concentration of criminality among 'social failures', usually to be found in the inner city.
3. They perpetuate the fallacy of autonomy (Currie, 1985), that is, suggesting that the family is somehow isolated from structural forces and government policies that might affect the degree of self-control families are able to instil in their children, for example through the increase in working mothers.
4. It has failed in its attempt to establish clear variables that separate the non-criminal from the criminal (Roshier, 1989).
5. Self-control Theory does not distinguish between the capacity for self-control (the focus of Gottfredson and Hirschi's work) and the desire for self-control. Tittle *et al.* (2004) have argued that the motivational force of the desire to exercise restraint is ignored by Self-control Theory.

Control Theory and Voluntarism

Laub and Sampson (2003) have followed the 'careers' of men who engaged in and desisted from criminal activity over a large number of years. They focused on the social relationships and circumstances that either acted as a brake on criminal engagement or as a spur. While looking at marriage, taking a job or having children, as events that presented opportunities for those men to rethink their engagement with crime, and their tangling with the justice system or other criminals as destabilizing commitments to a less criminal life, the key focus of their work was on the choices that the men made. They argued that there was no inevitability about the processes involved, but that it was the choices that individuals made that were important in criminal or non-criminal outcomes. Thus, there could be no 'profiling' of the criminal, no balancing the number of stabilizing and non-stabilizing factors to come to a conclusion about the likelihood of criminality, because it was the reflection and choices of individuals at these turning points that decided the outcomes.

Differential Coercion Theory

In a nod to Differential Association Theory, Colvin (2000) developed a theory of differential coercion, in which individuals during their life-course experience different levels of coercion. Individuals can be exposed to both physical and psychological coercion and on an interpersonal or institutional level. Where the coercion is strong and/or unpredictable dispositions to criminality build up. There is thus a psychological effect when individuals either experience harsh coercion or cannot predict when punishment is going to occur. Colvin argued that there was a generational effect involved as parents, who themselves had been brought up coercively and were employed in coercive workplaces, used coercive measures in bringing up their own children. Children who experience physical coercion are then more likely to turn to violence as a solution to their larger circumstances and thus engage in violent criminal behaviour.

Life-course Theory

Life-course Theory emerged out of attempts to integrate different aspects of sociocultural theories into a more comprehensive explanation of delinquency. In trying to bring together varying explanations, sociologists began to recognize that they need to look beyond the immediate context of a young delinquent's life and examine their childhood and their adult trajectories. For example, Elliott et al. (1979) found that those who made strong bonds with family and peers in early childhood were most likely not to engage in delinquent behaviour in adolescence, which was in line with the basics of Social Control Theory. However, there were different pathways into delinquency and it was not just those who did not develop strong bonds who ended up in trouble. For some children who did have strong bonds, the appearance of 'strain' in their adolescent life propelled them into antisocial channels.

As sociologists examined the antecedent and subsequent experiences of delinquent youths, two forms of Life-course Theory emerged. The first strand emphasized the continuity of engagement in antisocial behaviour, so that those who developed low self-control in early childhood through inexpert parenting tended to seek out others with low self-control in adolescence and moved into delinquent behaviour, which would be the hallmark of their life into adulthood (Gottfredson and Hirschi, 1990). Other continuity theorists accepted that there were differences in patterns of persistence, distinguishing between early onset and late-onset delinquency, where, in the latter case, it was peer-group interaction that was the key social factor in its development. Furthermore, late-onset delinquents are more likely to move out of delinquent activity as they grow older (Patterson and Yoerger, 1997).

This led to a second strand of theories of life-course that emphasized both the potential for continuity and desistance in the life trajectories of individuals. Moffit (1993, 2006) has distinguished between two groups: those who were 'life-course persistent' and those who were 'adolescent-limited'. Life-course persistent offenders tended to have neurological problems in early childhood, so that they found it difficult to make social connections with families and with others, so that their ability to operate in social environments in a conforming way was limited. In contrast, Moffit argued that most adolescent males engaged in some minor forms of delinquent behaviour, which could be conceived of as strategies to deal with a 'maturity gap'. By this he meant that teenage boys are capable of many adult functions (sexual behaviour, drinking alcohol, etc.), but are limited by social conventions from expressing them. The result is minor defiance of social norms that dissipates as the individuals mature and gain 'legitimate' access to adult activities.

Sampson and Laub (2005), however, carried out a longitudinal study of delinquents which, they argued, demonstrated that desistance from criminality was almost universal, even among those who had been categorized as persistent offenders. They believed that early childhood experiences were not the determining events that had been claimed by persistence theories, but that life-course events such as marriage and the routines that these entailed were strong steers towards prosocial behaviour. However, individuals still had to choose not to engage in criminality as these structural constraints impinged on their lives, and most left criminality behind (though at different ages and under the influence of different events).

Administrative criminology

Administrative criminology was developed during the 1980s by criminologists who were employed by or contracted to the Home Office and therefore closely involved in the development of social policies to combat crime (Jefferson and Shapland, 1994). The approach is critical of 'high' theory in criminology, such as Hirschi's Control Theory, and instead focuses on the manageable prevention of crime. The emphasis is therefore on what is called 'situational' crime prevention, that is, using measures that are relatively cheap and effective, such as closed-circuit television or making residences burglar resistant. While

Control Theory tends to focus on measures to prevent individuals from becoming disposed to commit crime, administrative criminology concentrates on the prevention of crime itself. The key to reducing crime is therefore to reduce the opportunities for crime to be committed by means of more secure premises, greater surveillance and the like (see also pp. 126–7).

Item K

Table 3.3 Ownership of home security devices 2006/7

England & Wales	Percentages	
	Ownership of each security device	
	Victims of burglary/vehicle theft	All households whether victim or not
Home		
Window locks	42	79
Double/deadlocks	40	75
Outdoor sensor/timer lights	18	40
Security chains on door	19	32
Burglar alarm	25	29
Indoor sensor/timer lights	10	24
Window bar/grilles	4	3

Source: Self (2008).

Exercise 3.26

Item K shows some of the measures that can be taken to prevent crime. Examine the item and answer the following questions.

1. What percentage of those who have been a victim of crime has a burglar alarm?
2. Calculate the percentage difference between those who have been a victim of crime and all households which have security chains on doors.
3. Identify two forms of action, other than those in Item K, that members of the public could take to reduce their chances of becoming a victim of crime.

Coleman (1985) has developed a postmodern critique of modernist city architecture by applying the ecological approach of the Chicago School to post-war British public housing projects. She sees crime as a function of the opportunity provided by and the lack of integration in badly designed council estates. Her solutions to the problem of lack of surveillance and access difficulties in modernist housing blocks were widely adopted when tower block estates were revamped in the 1980s and 1990s, including the restoration of garden areas at the front of the blocks and the dismantling of overhead walkways.

However, Coleman's work has been criticized for confusing correlation and causation. The opportunities afforded by the design of urban housing is a factor in, but not the cause of, criminal behaviour. The 'environmental determinism' of Coleman has offered a relatively simple solution to high crime rates, but the results of design changes have not always been consistent. While some estates did show a marked reduction in crime following Coleman's recommended changes, others showed little change at all. Moreover Coleman tends to condemn all modernist attempts to provide better housing for low-income families, but some tower block schemes were relatively successful in terms of the residents' satisfaction with them. While physical factors are important in creating opportunity and setting subtle psychological environments, they cannot be the sole cause of criminal behaviour.

Coleman's work is part of a larger movement towards 'target hardening', which involves measures to make targeted objects more difficult to steal. For example Mayhew *et al.* (1992) have shown that there was a drop in car theft when compulsory steering locks were introduced in Germany and Britain. However, unlike in Germany, in Britain they were not required to be fitted in old cars and so car theft was displaced from new to older cars.

The use of closed-circuit television in city centres as a crime preventative measure illustrates some of the criticisms of administrative criminology. The key issue is whether CCTV actually reduces the crime rate or merely displaces it. Displacement can take many forms, for example geographical displacement, as the criminals move to non-camera locations; temporal displacement, where criminals use darkness more to cover up their activity; and functional displacement, where criminals shift to other forms of crime (Coleman and Norris, 2000). In a metaview of evaluations of the success of CCTV in bringing down crime rates, Coleman and Norris noted that, methodological problems notwithstanding, there was a mixed bag of results. Some studies showed a significant fall-off in criminal offences and no displacement that could be identified, whereas others showed little reduction at all. Moreover, McCahill (2002) argued that the actual practice of CCTV operators, especially in shopping areas, led to exclusionary practices, with young people in particular being targeted for surveillance and action.

(E) | Exercise 3.27

Work out at least two strengths and two weaknesses of administrative criminology.

THE CITY, THE UNDERCLASS AND POSTMODERNISM

A specific aspect of Subcultural Theory is the concept of the underclass. The concept has been utilized most often by realists of both the right and the left (see pp. 174–5, 185–6), but it has also been connected to postmodernist views of society and the development of the postmodern city.

Cities are the main sites of crime in postmodern society. The city is seen by many sociologists as under threat of extinction by the forces of disintegration, disorganization and criminality, both organized criminality, in terms of gangs, and disorganized criminality, such as when urban riots occur. Postmodernist social geographers have argued that the modernist attempt to impose uniformity on urban development arose from a desire to control urban populations. Modernist planners therefore feared diversity and difference, seeing them as symptoms of imminent chaos. Postmodernists argue that the postmodern city should celebrate diversity because complex urban interactions make for successful cities. Therefore planning should focus on small areas within the city, rather than trying to establish grandiose and large-scale changes (see, for example, Krier, 1987). The danger of focusing only on small areas is that ghettoized communities emerge with little connection to the rest of society, leading to the possibility that the underclass that is characteristic of postmodern society might be confined within a section of a city but not contained in it.

Postmodernists see the new underclass as fundamentally different from previous groups of the poor, because the social conditions in which the underclass exists are very different from those in the modern era. In modern societies the poor were incorporated or integrated into mainstream society through the 'discourse of progress', welfare provision and other means. The discourse of progress was a feature of modernity that presupposed that constant improvements would be made to society, with the implication that poverty would be eliminated. This discourse existed as a powerful ideology that served to keep the poor passive in the face of their poverty because of the perceived possibility of an improvement in their economic and social circumstances.

In terms of connectedness, modernity sought to incorporate the poor into mainstream society through a variety of methods. For example they were provided with a basic subsistence income from the time of the Poor Law to the establishment of the welfare state, which served to connect them to the consumption culture of mainstream society. The basic income also provided the poor with the means to gain access to the media, which emphasized the consumerist ethic. The poor in modern societies were also connected to mainstream society through the activities of trade unions and the political parties of the left, which were in part an expression of poor people's interests.

Morrison (1995) argues that in postmodern society the legitimacy of mainstream values has been undermined among the underclass. The crucial parts of this process have been the apparently permanent unemployment of the underclass, which has cut them off from the consumerist values of mainstream society, and the destruction of traditional family forms in the inner city. Using Elias's (1978) theory of the civilizing process, first published in 1938, Morrison argues that the civilizing process has been reversed among the underclass, particularly among black males, whose basis of identity – comprising jobs and family life – has been stripped away from them. Morrison argues that when the fundamental supports for their masculinity are denied, the male underclass may experience feelings of resentment and revenge.

Moreover, under the impact of new right ideas about the culture of dependency, the traditional financial support for these least well-off has been increasingly restricted. The pressure to deliver tax cuts to a mainstream population that is increasingly hostile to welfare provision, and the political imperative to stamp down on welfare 'fraud', have resulted in the financial safety net for the underclass being reduced and in some cases removed. According to some, this may lead to an increase in criminal activity by members of the underclass as they seek to replace lost benefits through illegal means. The problem with this view is that welfare benefits were much less generous in the past than even the reduced levels under postmodernity, and yet the rates of criminal activity among the poorest section of society were not as high.

Morrison goes even further than this, however, in arguing that postmodernity has created a situation in which crimogenic factors predominate in the lives of the underclass. Postmodern society is said to reject all 'metanarratives' and absolute systems of right and wrong. This means that for the underclass, the legitimation of mainstream society is problematic. If social arrangements have no absolute legitimacy, Morrison asks, why should the underclass accept the present 'rules of the game' – the laws and norms of mainstream society – when they have so obviously failed to bring them any benefit? As postmodern society also rejects the 'discourse of progress', there is little hope for the underclass that their condition will be improved through normal political or trade union activity. It is therefore likely that the underclass will turn to illegitimate means of securing some basic 'income', either through the black economy or through crime. Another possible reaction by the underclass to their existential conditions (the basic features of the social world in which they live) is an increase in rage and vengeance on a mainstream society that has apparently rejected them.

These processes are reinforced by global developments that are affecting all cities throughout the world. The move away from Fordist methods of production, in which standardized goods were manufactured by settled communities in a relatively stable urban environment, has given way to post-Fordist manufacturing, where production is constantly changing and shifting as global capital seeks out the most profitable locations for production, creating and discarding urban communities on a global stage. The result is that the modernist formations of production, consumption and exchange, which depended on stability and clear boundaries between social groups, have crumbled before postmodernist formations that create uncertainty and confusion, both in time (individuals can never know how long any specific job will last before it is taken elsewhere) and space (traditional patterns of residence in the city dissolve as the hierarchies of communities based around a particular industry dissipate).

This happens on a global scale, and while some cities adapt well to the demands of postmodern production and become global cities, others decline as their traditional manufacturing base is stripped away (see also p. 135). But the processes that lead to postmodern society also affect all cities in particular ways. One effect is the emergence of an underclass who are unable to find work under post-Fordist manufacturing conditions; but the most potent effect is the loss of traditional uses of space in the city. For example warehouses and churches become homes for the rising affluent of the city, decaying urban areas are revitalized by immigrant communities and previously affluent areas are impoverished when large houses are divided into flats and sublet. Both these effects have been intensified by government policies during the 1980s and 1990s. The sale of public housing to sitting tenants or housing associations has created new forms of ownership and tenancy. Deregulation of urban controls has led to investment in previously rundown areas. Ironically, urban riots in poorer areas of cities may lead to investment into those areas as they are regenerated through injections of state and private capital. The result of these processes is that wealthy and poor live side by side geographically, but a world apart in terms of their life experiences. The possibility that the under-class may spill over into affluent areas may create a fear of them as a criminal class, which will lead to greater demands for their control.

A similar explanation has been put forward by Petras and Davenport (1991), among others, who argue that structural unemployment arising from the deindustrialization that has occurred in Western economies has had a devastating effect on the inner city urban male. It has led to the long-term iso-lation of poor working-class males, which manifests itself in increasing levels of burglary, car stealing and violence (Currie, 1990).

Exercise 3.28

The impact of postmodernity extends beyond the city, transcending physical distances associated with space. This is perhaps evident when we consider the growth in rural crime (see, for example, Webster, 1993). Using the Internet, try to gain data on the growing rural crime problem. Try to find out the extent, trends and nature of rural crime. You should also make notes on any explanations offered to account for the rise in rural crime.

Exam focus

Answer the following questions, using the guidelines provided to assist you with the second one.

1. To what extent do sociological theories of subculture increase our understanding of the relationship between deviance and the social structure?
2. Evaluate the usefulness of the idea of a youth subculture to sociolog-ical explanations of deviance.

Guidelines

The most common mistake that students make when answering this type of question is to write generally about deviance and to ignore or underplay the focus of the question which is the idea of youth subcultures. It might be a good idea to define youth subcultures as a starting point and explore the ways in which the concept has been traditionally used in the sociology of deviance. Take care to establish the theoretical positions of the sociological work you apply to the question. Remember that different perspectives have different viewpoints about the explanatory usefulness of youth subcultures, with some being strongly in favour of them as an explanation for the distribution of deviance and others arguing that they have no explanatory power at all. This difference of opinion should form the basis of the evaluation dimension of your answer. Ensure that you bring in recent material as well as the traditional studies in this area. Write a conclusion that directly addresses the usefulness of the idea.

Important concepts

Deviant subcultures • Biological determinism • Social disorganization • Collective efficacy • Differential association • Social bulimia • Status frustration • Containment • Drift and neutralization • Life-course

Critical thinking

1. Are criminals just 'born bad'? If they are, why should we not just identify them, lock them up and keep them from doing harm to others?
2. Is the neoliberal, free market, put-myself-first ideology of the late twentieth century a key ingredient in developing criminal behaviour? If it is, which groups are most likely to succumb to temptation and use illegal means to get the 'good life'?
3. If deviants can drift in and out of deviance and will eventually grow out of it, should we just focus on making it difficult for them to commit crimes and forget about detecting and arresting them?

Chapter 4

Interactionist Explanations of Crime and Deviance

After studying this chapter, you should:

- understand early and recent developments in Labelling Theory
- know what is meant by the politicization of deviance
- be able to evaluate Labelling Theory
- have a critical understanding of the role of the media and law enforcement agencies in amplifying deviance
- appreciate phenomenological and ethnomethodological views on deviance
- have a grasp of postmodernist views of crime

The existence of different theories that seek to explain crime and deviance has, for interactionist and postmodernist sociologists, far-reaching implications. In modernity, the dominant metanarrative (or all-encompassing explanation of phenomena) is that of science, in which truth can be found through the dispassionate application of scientific procedures. However, if several theories coexist and cannot be proven or disproven, then the discourse of science is called into question. This suggests either that each perspective contains only part of the truth or that the totality of social phenomena cannot be encapsulated in one perspective only. Labelling theorists were the first prominent sociologists of deviance to accept that there could be a variety of discourses concerning crime and deviance and that no one theory could explain all of the phenomena. Indeed labelling theorists argued that in a world of multiple perspectives there can be no such thing as a 'natural crime', but what is defined as crime is the result of social processes, in which certain actions by certain people at certain times come to be labelled as criminal by others.

In postmodern society there are therefore multiple perspectives, none of which, by themselves, can be 'true'. Any explanation can be challenged by another way of looking at the various phenomena. To postmodern theorists, this situation of apparent confusion has also been liberating, in that it has opened up many possibilities for exploration. However, among certain sections of the new right (see pp. 167–76) there has occurred a 'back-to-basics' movement, in which intellectual explanations have been rejected in favour of common-sense views on crime and deviance, where criminology is reduced to a correctional activity (concerned with punishment and control) rather than being one which seeks explanations of and solutions to crime.

LABELLING THEORY

Perhaps the most famous of the theories of crime and deviance is Labelling Theory, associated with the work of Becker (1963), Lemert (1951) and Erikson (1966), among others. The roots of the theory, however, lie in the earlier insight that state intervention in the criminal justice system is itself crimogenic, that is, it causes crime (Tannenbaum, 1938). This insight was developed in various ways and concerned the different activities of the state and its agents when dealing with the law and crime. For example the state shapes the way in which killing is viewed by separating types of killing into legitimate and illegitimate categories (Pfohl, 1985). The activities of the police and law enforcement agencies in differentially arresting and charging different categories of the population engaged in very similar behaviours shapes the perceived patterns of crime in society. Heusenstamm (1975), for example, showed that the use of socially disapproved car-bumper stickers by hitherto law-abiding youths led to an increase in the number of times they were stopped by the police and given tickets for traffic violations. Labelling Theory came to dominate sociological research into deviance during the 1960s, as interest in what Liazos (1972) called 'nuts, sluts and preverts [sic]' developed.

Labelling theorists make a distinction between primary deviance, in which everyone engages but which has few consequences for the individual, and secondary deviance, where the social reaction to deviant actions creates a 'master status' of deviance for some people. Master status is where one aspect of a person's identity dominates the perceptions of others about that person (do

Exercise 4.1 to test your own reactions to labelling). In terms of deviance, 'criminal' is a master status that often influences the way that people perceive an individual. The effect of this labelling process is a self-fulfilling prophecy in which the labelled take on the features of the label. Labellists are not arguing that those labelled do not commit deviant acts, but that they are treated differently once the label has been attached. While it may be possible to reject the label, the most common reaction is to take on the status and behaviour of the label, thus fulfilling the prophecy. For example those who have been imprisoned are likely to find it difficult to obtain a job once freed because of the social reaction to the label, and are therefore more likely to reoffend.

Exercise 4.1

It is 7.00 o'clock on a Saturday evening. You have opted for a 'boring' night in watching the television. At 7.45 your phone rings and you are invited by an old friend to a house party.

You are a bit unsure about going as you have not seen your old friend for three years and you do not expect to know anybody else at the party. Despite your reservations you decide to go. You put on your casual clothes, pick up some drink and catch a bus. At 9.30 you arrive at the party. Your old friend greets you with a kiss. To your surprise your friend has become a transvestite.

The other party guests are:

- a vicar;
- a page three girl;
- a successful barrister;
- a famous TV chat show host;
- someone dying from AIDS;
- an ex-prisoner;
- a heroin addict;
- a schizophrenic;
- a member of a religious cult;
- someone claiming to have been recently abducted by aliens;
- a devoted rave-goer.

(A) 1. What would be your reaction to your old friend?

(A) 2. Your old friend introduces you to all the guests listed above. In each case explain what your perceptions of that guest would be.

(E) 3. Discuss your reactions with other members of your sociology class. To what extent do your responses and that of your colleagues support the idea that a labelling process takes place in society?

The influence of these theories on criminal policy has been immense. The first consequence was a move towards the decriminalization of various victimless crimes, though such steps have often been controversial or unsuccessful. In some areas, such as pornography and gambling, the law has been liberalized. While controversy continues to surround these issues, for example the continuing debate over the ethicality of megacasinos in Britain, by and large they have remained settled over a number of years. Other liberalizing legislation, especially with regard to abortion, has been stable but subject to immense controversy, with challenges from those opposed to abortion in all circumstances and those who argue in favour of further liberalization. Schur and Bedeau (1974) contend that, despite the fact that the police now have a more liberal attitude towards the recreational use of marijuana and that it has been downgraded in law, the criminalization of drugs creates opportunities for further crimes. By this they mean that drug users may turn to criminal activities such as robbery to support their habit. Because drugs are illicit they attract the attention of organized criminals; and because of the lucrative nature of the drug market, the opportunities for police corruption are enhanced.

Exercise 4.2

(An)(E) Draw up an extended version of the chart below and list various arguments for and against the decriminalization of drugs. We have started you off with an argument on each side of the debate.

The decriminalization of drugs

Arguments for decriminalization	Arguments against decriminalization
1. Increases individual freedom and choice.	1. May lead users into more drug related crime.

Labelling theorists have also advocated the deinstitutionalization of most criminals, especially juveniles, arguing that incarceration is more likely to lead to recidivism than other forms of punishment. This was carried out in Massachusetts in the 1970s, where the juvenile detention centres were all but closed in favour of community programmes for offenders. The degree of recidivism only marginally increased, and where alternative action programmes were implemented it fell (Empey, 1982). Such initiatives did not survive the emergence of new right ideologies in the 1980s, which ushered in a much more punitive attitude towards young offenders (see pp. 271–3).

Exercise 4.3

(An)(E) Labelling theorists have also argued against the incarceration of the mentally ill and favour programmes that take mental patients out of institutions and back into the community. Draw up an extended version of the chart below and list at least three arguments for and three arguments against the deinstitutionalization of the mentally ill. We have provided one of each to get you started.

The deinstitutionalization of the mentally ill

Arguments for deinstitutionalization	Arguments against deinstitutionalization
1. Prevents patients from becoming institutionalized.	1. Can prove to be too demanding on carers, e.g. family members.

The amplification of deviance

A particular aspect of labelling was introduced through the work of Wilkins (1964) with the introduction of the 'amplification of deviance' concept. This was used to explain the apparent paradox that action by the media and law enforcement agencies to control illegal activities often results in an increase in the very behaviour that is supposed to be controlled. This is not just a question of copycatting, that is, others copying the behaviour described in the media, but of the ways in which the application of a label by the media or the police can lead to deviant characteristics being incorporated in the mindset of those labelled. The outcome of this incorporation is an intensification of the deviant behaviour, which in turn leads to further investigation by the media and/or police – the classic spiral of deviancy amplification (see Cohen, 1980, for a description of this as it affected mods and rockers). The activities of the police and media create a 'folk devil', that is, a group of people who become demonized in the eyes of the public, who respond with a 'moral panic' – a demand that something be done about the problem.

Exercise 4.4

(I)(A) This exercise is based on an activity idea by O'Donnell and Garrod (1990) on deviancy amplification. Examine the diagram and statements overley. Your task is to decide which statements should appear in which box in the diagram so that you end up with a figure that represents the spiral of deviancy amplification. The

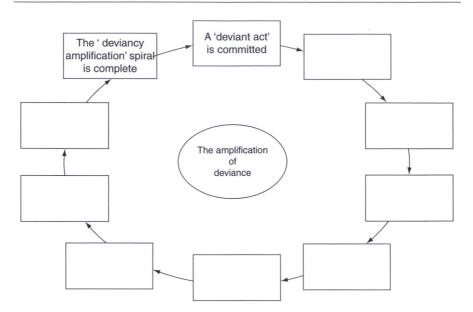

first and last stages have been completed for you. You should be able to gauge how successful you have been with this exercise by referring to Item A, but do not look at it until you have attempted the exercise.

Statements

1. Partly due to the increased police activity, more arrests are made which are reported in the press.
2. The behaviour catches the public attention, which makes it even more 'newsworthy'.
3. The 'deviant group' finds it more difficult to engage in the behaviour without being arrested. People who 'look like' the deviants are increasingly under suspicion. Some deviants live up to the reputation presented by the media.
4. This leads to even more reports in the mass media and demands for 'action' to be taken.
5. Press reports of increasing arrests lead people to talk of 'a major crime wave' sweeping across Britain.
6. Reports of the deviant behaviour, often sensationalized, begin to appear in the mass media.
7. Public interest begins to die, as other news items compete for people's attention. The deviant behaviour is no longer 'big news'.
8. Responding to the calls for action, greater police attention is focused on the act, with officers being taken off other types of investigation.

The issue of amplification is an important one for sociologists because it is related to the validity of statistics and the reality of social phenomena (see Chapter 2). For example some sociologists have argued that there was an increase in Satanic activity in the United States during the 1980s (see, for example, Forsyth and Oliver, 1990). Alexander (1990) disagrees and suggests that the incidence of Satanism remained much the same, but that the phenomenon was socially constructed through media sensationalism to appear as though there had been an increase (see pp. 117–23 for a fuller account of the role of the media in the amplification of deviance)

Ⓘ Ⓐ

Exercise 4.5

In the sociological literature, many of the examples of a moral panic become quickly dated as the issues or groups drop out of public sight once the moral panic has run its course. However, the concept of amplification always has a contemporary resonance. A recent example of a contemporary moral panic is 'knife-related crime'. Despite the fact that some figures suggest that knife crimes are falling, 2008 saw a number of high profile cases in the media, which involved violent attacks, with knives (Jones, 2009).

We would like you to apply the amplification of deviance concept to a recent moral panic (it should be a moral panic concerning deviancy). You might find it useful to construct a diagram similar to the one you completed for Exercise 4.4. Thus you could begin by writing down the deviant act that has come to the media's attention. You could then add a few of the sensationalist headlines that have appeared in newspapers.

The politicization of deviance

By discussing labelling, interactionist theorists had begun to introduce the concept of power into sociological debates on deviance, if only in a 'weak' way. By exploring the power of social agencies to label activities as deviant or normal, they opened the way to a wider consideration of the processes of power as they affect crime and deviance. For example Horowitz and Leibowitz (1968) argued that some deviant groups were moving out of the private realm and into the public arena by organizing politically and seeking to influence public discourse through protest activities. The emergence of militant gay groups such as Outrage is a good example of this development. This extension of the concept of power was taken up in particular by critical criminologists (see Chapter 5) in a much more systematic way.

One aspect of power and deviance that was explored was the power of the police selectively to 'patrol' society. Sampson (1986) carried out a comprehensive survey of the activities of the police and found an 'ecological bias' towards young people in poorer areas. He took into account all the variables that might affect the patterns of policing but still concluded that there were more arrests in poorer areas than could be accounted for with a random distribution of arrests. The suggestion here is that the police tend to concentrate their patrols in the poorer areas because of the perception that such areas will have a higher concentration of lawlessness. The fact that their policing patterns result in a greater number of arrests in poor as opposed to affluent areas tends in itself to be a self-fulfilling prophecy, that is, the police find more crime in those areas because that is where they are looking. This feeds into the official statistics on crime, which appear to 'confirm' the police's view that most crime occurs in these areas (see Chapter 2).

Another aspect of power in relation to deviance can be seen in the social reaction to deviant activity, which is claimed to be a powerful force in the shaping of a deviant identity. However, the social reaction to deviance is very complex. While the social reaction to a particular deviant activity is important, it is unlikely that any effect arising from the application of a label will occur in isolation from other factors. For example Sherman (1992) has found that the likelihood of wife-batterers reoffending once they have been caught and labelled by the police seems to vary according to whether or not the batterer is employed. It is suggested that an employed man's greater chance of loss of employment, of face and of reputation prevent the recurrence of violence against his wife. For the unemployed, who are already removed from the major integrative forces, the consequences of reoffending are less dramatic and they are therefore more likely to assault their wives again.

Developments in Labelling Theory

Gusfield, 1981: labelling and social order

Labelling Theory has been criticized for not taking account of structure and society as a whole, that is, labelling theorists tend to focus on the everyday activities of individuals and groups and ignore the structural conditions, such as inequality and poverty, within which these activities take place. To counter this criticism, some labellists have attempted to place labelling into a wider framework. Gusfield (1981) looked at the implications of labelling in terms of social order. By developing a typology of deviant labels, Gusfield was able to trace the effects of each on social order.

The first two types of deviant reinforce social order. First, *sick deviants* are those who have no control over their actions and are seen as beyond the 'normal'. These might be individuals with particular medical or mental conditions that compel them to act in 'non-normal' ways. These sick deviants act as a definition of abnormal or the 'other'. By representing what is not 'normal' they allow the rest of society to define themselves as 'normal'. This serves to reinforce social order by providing a boundary beyond which is the 'not normal'. Second, *repentant deviants* are those who, having been defined as deviant, are now sorry for their actions. Their remorse about previous deviant acts (and their work with those who still perform the deviant acts) serves to reinforce the social order. This is because their repentance confirms the 'rightness' of the prevailing social order and definitions of 'normal' and 'non-normal'.

The second two types undermine the social order. First, *enemy deviants* are those who not only believe that there is nothing wrong with the way they act, but also that society's rules are wrong and need to be changed. This constitutes a threat to the current order, as they challenge the 'taken-for-granted' assumptions of mainstream society. Second, *cynical deviants* are those who express no remorse about their behaviour and are therefore a threat to the social order because they flout the rules. Gusfield's approach has been criticized as profoundly conservative. By this, critics mean that he accepts the status quo – the best possible social arrangements are those which are already in place. Anyone who challenges this order and its injustices is seen as an 'enemy'.

Melossi, 1985: grounded Labelling Theory

Melossi developed an approach to labelling in which reactions to the application of a label are related to the historical context of the society in which it is applied. The motivations for committing deviant acts therefore have to be understood in the context of the society. Moreover the strength of the reaction of the audience to a label will be affected by the degree of threat the act is seen to represent and the need to do something or nothing about it. The implication of this is that reactions to labels vary according to cultural contexts and to the time in which the act is committed. For example the public attitude towards homosexuality has become more tolerant in Britain over the last 20 years. This is linked to the diminution of the perceived threat that homosexuality poses to 'normal' married life. Where threats are perceived to exist and the necessity to do something about it is great, then reaction to a labelled individual is likely to be hostile. However, it is not clear in Melossi's work how the perception of a threat is to be gauged – that is, how we judge the degree of threat an act poses – or why the intensity of a threat changes over time.

Braithwaite, 1989: crime, shame and reintegration

Braithwaite investigated the ways in which social reaction affects reoffending in a more comprehensive way. He was interested in examining the claims of the labelling theorists that social reaction increases crime and in the conservative criminologists' view (see pp. 286–97) that a strong social reaction, such as increased punishment, decreases crime. He argues that an important aspect of the social control of deviance is the process of shaming, whereby disapproval of offenders is expressed in order to cause them to feel remorse. According to Braithwaite there are two types of shaming. *Disintegrative shaming* has the effect identified by the labelling theorists of making the labelled an outsider, beyond the community and incapable of being absorbed back into it. The rejection of the shamed individual by the mainstream members of the community means that he or she is more likely to join a criminal subculture and carry on with the deviance. *Reintegrative shaming* has the opposite effect. While experiencing the disapproval of the community the offender is not cast out but reabsorbed into the community as a chastened deviant.

Braithwaite thus links the effects of social reaction to the social context in which the offending occurs. Where there are strong communities and individuals are highly interdependent, shaming tends to be reintegrative and, as in Japan, results in low crime rates. However, in diverse societies where communities are weak or in conflict, such as in the United States, shaming tends to be disintegrative and leads to very high rates of criminality.

EVALUATION OF LABELLING THEORY

(I)(E)   Exercise 4.6

Listed below are a number of evaluation points of Labelling Theory. Identify which are the strengths and which are the weaknesses. Record your answers in a two-column table that clearly separates the strengths from the weaknesses. When you record your answers, rank them in order of importance. Justify your ranking to another sociology student.

1. The theory helps to explain differential rates of offending through the activities of the police and the law courts.
2. If deviance is relative, where does it leave actions such as rape and murder?
3. The extent to which the criminal justice system affects whether the labelled continue their criminal careers is unclear (Hirschi, 1975).
4. As a theory it moves beyond the idea that deviance comes from a rule being broken to the idea that deviance emerges from labelling specific cases (and not other, similar cases).

5. There is a tendency to fail to explain the origins of deviant acts. Important structural causes of crime are often neglected.
6. There is a recognition that the nature and extent of deviance is socially constructed.
7. Little empirical support has been found for the process of labelling as traditionally put forward, especially the claim that factors such as race, class and gender are more important in influencing the criminal justice system's view of an offender than factors such as his or her previous record or the type of crime investigated (Gove, 1980).
8. The approach recognizes that the forces of criminal justice are important players in the phenomenon of crime.
9. It draws our attention to the relative nature of deviance.
10. It tends to treat deviants as the passive victims of the social control agencies.

DEVIANCY AMPLIFICATION AND THE MASS MEDIA

An important aspect of power when discussing deviance is the role of the media in creating and sustaining stereotypes of deviants. Some sociologists have attributed a central role to the media in the formation of society's perception of crime. But the evidence for this view is often contradictory and, as Ericson (1991) concludes, any effects are likely to be diverse and situational, that is, embedded in the experiences and social position of the audience of the mass media. But it is also the case, as many sociologists have pointed out, that there is consistent bias in the reporting of crime, especially by the newspapers. In particular sociologists have found that 'crime waves' are constructed by the selective filtering and reporting of street crimes (Fishman, 1978). The factors that influence the ways in which gatekeepers (for example editors, who decide what should appear as 'news') select and present news items are, according to Chermak (1995):

- the seriousness of the offence;
- characteristics of victims and criminals;
- the producers of crime stories;
- the uniqueness of the crime;
- the location and frequency of the crime.

Another important factor in the way that crime is reported by the media is the often close relationship between reporters, editors and the law enforcement agencies. As a prime source of information about crime, the police are in a privileged position to get across their view of crime and ensure that any debate is carried out on their terms (see, for example, Ericson, 1989). As a result, according to Sacco (1995), alternative perspectives about how to deal with crime become marginalized. The effect of this is ideological in that the debate about crime becomes restricted, with traditional law-and-order measures being accepted by many as the most appropriate way of dealing with the crime problem.

One effect of this biased presentation is said to be the amplification of deviance (see pp. 111–13), whereby folk devils are created through media manipulation and a moral panic ensues, ensuring that there is an increase in the amount of deviance reported. However, McRobbie and Thornton (1995) argue that the original formulation of 'moral panics' (see Item A) has been outstripped by developments in society, especially the increasingly complex relationships between a multitude of social groupings, the media and reality, which postmodernists have identified as a crucial feature of postmodern society. They suggest that in the 1960s, when the concept of the moral panic was originally developed, it was feasible for sociologists to write about society as a single entity with a unified social reaction. However, this is not true of 'society' in the 2000s, which has become fragmented and complex.

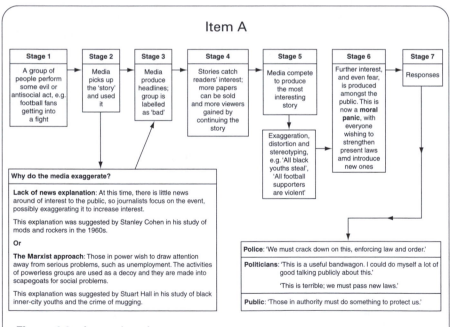

Figure 4.1 A moral panic
Source: Moore (1996b).

Ⓘ
Exercise 4.7

Item A provides a useful diagrammatic map of traditional views of the way the media create moral panics. Using only information from Item A, summarize the social processes involved in the creation of moral panics.

Ⓐ
Exercise 4.8

The following table provides examples of moral panics from the 1950s to the 1980s. We would like you to identify examples of moral panics in the 1990s and 2000s. One is provided for you to start you off.

	Examples of moral panic
1950s	Teddy Boys
1960s	Mods and Rockers
	Permissiveness – drugs, sexual 'freedom' Youth violence – skinheads, football hooliganism Radical trade unionism
1970s	'Muggings' Social security 'scroungers' Punks
1980s	Greenham Common protesters
	AIDS Child abuse Drugs – especially 'crack'
1990s	Video nasties
2000s	Bankers

Whenever a moral panic is proclaimed, the voices that seek to influence the course of the panic are much more disparate and varying than the notion of societal reaction would imply. In particular, new social movements seek to influence the course of debates and may neutralize or accentuate attempts to stigmatize social groups or activities as deviant. In other words, in postmodern society folk devils fight back, employing sophisticated techniques of media manipulation. Many groups, often with hidden interests, become involved in debates about the activities of potentially stigmatized groups. For example Taub and Nelson (1993) show that many 'experts' in the area of Satanic ritual are fundamentalist Christians, with a theological interest in creating a moral panic about the extent and activities of Satanism.

McRobbie and Thornton (1995) argue that in the 1980s and 1990s sociologists interested in moral panic have ironically ignored the experiences of the young. Studies such as Thornton's (1995) suggest that 1990s' subcultures refer back to the history of defiant youth movements in rejecting the label of folk devil and create a discourse which defines their lifestyle as a revolt against normal society. These subcultures also have a complex relationship with the media. It may be in their interest to be defined as a moral panic by the media as it guarantees coverage, therefore extending the range and influence of the subcultural style. More importantly, commercial interests are quick to utilize subcultural styles to make profits. These are likely to be larger when a moral panic is involved.

The structure of the media itself is much more complex than in the 1960s, with the growth of niche markets for magazines, the proliferation of television stations and the rise of new media technologies.

Exercise 4.9

Reproduced below is an adapted extract from an interview analysis by a sociology student carrying out research into dance music cultures. The student carried out a semistructured interview with an ex-raver, whose name was changed for ethical reasons. Read the analysis and answer the questions that follow.

Question asked

There seems to be much coverage of dance music in specialist magazines which I am sure you are aware of, and also in the newspapers. How far do you feel the media have influenced your and the public's view of what is 'in' and what is 'out', and what are your opinions on the coverage of the dance music scene?

Interview analysis

Doug started off the answer with a bold statement of how the job of the media is to tell you what is 'in' and what is 'out'. His tone of voice was fairly negative – this would imply that he was not too keen on the media, which may have added bias to his answer. I would say that this is one of the big strengths that semistructured interviews have over quantitative methods such as self-completion questionnaires, as it would not have been possible for me to pick up on something like the tone of his voice in a self-completion questionnaire due to lack of face-to-face contact...

Another thing Doug picked up on is that the newspapers at the time were giving dance cultures very bad press, what with ecstasy, illegal gatherings etc....An interesting thing that arose from the interview is that when talking about what the press printed Doug's voice had a slight tinge of excitement, implying that he enjoyed the bad press. Even though now not part of this culture and maybe even against the scene, Doug defended the clubbers from the media by saying: 'So it got a real bad press. Society did not like these youths arising in their own sense of expressing freedom and individuality.' ... Could it be then that a reason why the dance culture is so strong with young people is because it entails everything the media despises – drugs, so-called criminal offences, etc. Doug did however finish off by saying that the press did give the dance culture some good press but it was very small. I really did let a lot go in this question as I missed out several key points such as 'selling out' via the press ... and the mainstream created by the media, and why it is that youth cultures relish in media condemnation. I think again that this was due to my lack of interview experience. Also I think that if I were to do this study again I would probably reinterview Doug to fill in the missing gaps. I believe that this would be possible as the semistructured interview technique allowed me to build up rapport and trust with Doug.

Ⓘ 1. The researcher draws our attention to some of the advantages of carrying out semistructured interviews. Identify the advantages he suggests.
Ⓚ 2. What other advantages can you suggest?
Ⓚ 3. What other methods could be used to carry out research into dance music culture?
ⒶⁿⒶ 4. Select one other method and show how it would be specifically useful for studying a phenomenon such as dance music culture

---

The relatively unproblematic relationship between a unified society, the media and a deviant stigmatized social group, which was at the heart of the original formulation of moral panics, has given way to a much more fragmented set of relationships between and within these formations. But McRobbie and Thornton (1995) go further than this and suggest that not only are the concepts of society and the media no longer simple, but they are no longer separable. What they mean by this is that we experience social reality in postmodern society largely as imagery in the media, or 'representations' of the social world. Thus political debates about social policies are often subsumed in media representations of social groups (one-parent families, AIDS victims, and so on), which are open to manipulation and counter-attack through moral panic processes. In particular, groups with a specific interest act to manipulate the media through feeding journalists stories in order to 'manufacture' a moral panic, not on the basis of a one-off news story that dies down naturally, but as a way of keeping their own interests on the public agenda. For example, Haltom and McCann (2004) have demonstrated that businesses which have an interest in restricting legal liability use the media to stir up a panic about 'the litigation crisis' (the notion that people are far too ready to take firms to the courts for any and all reasons) to create a momentum to change the law.

(E)

Exercise 4.10

We would like you to assess the usefulness of the concept of moral panic in understanding the amplification of deviance. You should copy and then complete the following chart by identifying two other strengths and two other weaknesses of the concept. Under the chart, write an overall conclusion that weighs up the relative merits of the concept. It is important that you reflect on both the older and the more recent ideas on moral panics presented in this chapter.

Evaluation of the concept of the moral panic

Strengths	Weaknesses
1. It highlights the media's role in reinforcing stereotypes about 'typical' criminals.	1. There is a tendency to side with the underdog. The deviant is seen as the victim of a biased media.
2. It helps us to understand that deviance is not natural but is socially constructed.	2. The concept tends to be applied to 'colourful' crimes. The overall amplification effect may therefore be overestimated.
3.	3.
4.	4.

The media and fear of crime

In the early part of the twenty-first century, the attention of sociologists was attracted to a seemingly contradictory social development. While recorded crime was decreasing, the public's fear of crime appeared to be increasing (Hope and Sparks, 2000). The fall in recorded criminal activity began in the 1990s in the United States and appeared soon in most developed societies (Blumstein and Wallman, 2000). Sociologists looked to overblown reporting of crime in the media as one of the ways in which a fear of crime can be cultivated in society (the 'cultivation thesis': see Gerbner, 1995). The thesis argues that the fear of crime is manipulated in the media to keep the public compliant with tough 'law-and-order' measures, such as laws against terrorism in the post-9/11 world. Postmodernists see this as part of the disciplinary regime of postmodern governance, in which the media's reporting of crime is framed within a punitive narrative and which marginalizes alternative viewpoints about the crime issue (Cavender, 2004). However, it is very difficult to prove an association between reading or viewing media items about crime and a heightened tendency to fear crime more. Research shows that those who read newspapers that emphasize violent crime are more likely to report in a survey that they are fearful of crime, but this does tell us whether they live in constant fear of crime and change their patterns of behaviour as a result of this fear (Ditton *et al.*, 2004).

PHENOMENOLOGY AND DEVIANCE

Phenomenologists reject official statistics as being socially constructed and focus on the motivations behind crime. They argue that positivistic theories are muddled because many of those who are predicted to commit crime do not do so, and that intermittent criminals go for long periods of time without committing crime, even though the factors that are said by the positivists to cause crime, such as unemployment, class, race, and so on, remain the same. Rather than look for statistical relationships, phenomenologists therefore look for the meanings behind deviant and criminal acts. The important part of this process is to see the act from the point of view of the criminal. Katz (1988) argues that certain situations are exciting to some individuals and can coax them into criminal activity. Different types of crime are seductive for different reasons, but they have the capacity to give excitement to different personalities. Therefore, for Katz, what is important is the 'experiential foreground': the immediate situation that attracts individuals. However, it is not just the excitement of the moment that leads to habitual criminal behaviour but also the establishment of a reputation, such as 'being hard', which allows individuals to transcend their everyday lives and establish notions of superiority over others (usually victims), and also over the system. Inevitably Katz has been criticized for his theory's lack of generalizability as it is impossible to show that all criminals, from the shoplifter to the murderer, share the same motivations and meaning.

ⓀⓊ
ⒶⒺ

Exercise 4.11

Phenomenologists often make use of unstructured interviews to reveal the individual meanings behind deviant actions. We would like you to apply your understanding of this methodological tool by copying and then completing the chart we have started off for you over the page.

Unstructured interviews

Description of method	Perspective	Examples of studies	Sample size	Reliability	Validity	Advantages	Disadvantages
	Phenomenology (anti-positivism)	1. 2. 3.	Generally low	Fairly low		1. In-depth information can be obtained 2. 3. 4. 5.	1. Can suffer from interviewer bias 2. 3. 4. 5.

ETHNOMETHODOLOGISTS AND DEVIANCE

The ethnomethodological approach to deviance stresses the importance of the everyday struggle in making sense of society and the minute-by-minute creation of social order through interactions. Therefore, for ethnomethodologists, deviance is not an objective phenomenon at all, but the result of subjective interpretation. They reject common-sense definitions of deviance in favour of a social construction approach in which crime and deviance is constituted by the audience's perception of an act as criminal or deviant (Pollner, 1976). The implication of this is that there are multiple audiences examining any particular act, some of whom will define the act as deviant, while others will not. For example, what one section of society may see as 'terrorists', another may see as 'freedom fighters'. There is no independent way in which the truth or falsity of these definitions can be tested. It is only common-sense reasoning that assumes there is an objective measure of the deviance or otherwise of an act (see, for example, Hester and Eglin, 1992). However, this is to reduce all judgement to a position of relativism, that is, that there are no standards or criteria by which we can make judgements about right and wrong (see if you agree by doing Exercise 4.12).

ⒾⒶ

Exercise 4.12

The work of contemporary artists such as Damien Hirst and Marcus Harvey has produced a great deal of debate and controversy in the media. Hirst has created work which has involved pickling dead animals, such as sheep and cattle, in formaldehyde. He has also produced paintings of coloured spots. Harvey is perhaps best known for his painting of Myra Hindley, which was created from a child's handprints. Some celebrate their work as inspirational, others damn it as 'sick and deviant'.

Surf the internet to find out more about their work and then support the ethnomethodological claim that 'deviance is in the eye of the beholder'.

POSTMODERN DEVELOPMENTS IN INTERACTIONIST THEORY

In searching for a more general theory of crime and deviance outside the certainties of modernist explanations, some postmodernists have turned to the routine activities of the everyday world as a starting point for explaining criminal and deviant behaviour (see, for example, Reiner, 1993). It is this emphasis on everyday activities that makes this postmodern approach an interactionist one. For a crime to happen in the everyday world there first has to be a legal definition of an act as criminal. This is not always as clear-cut as might be imagined. Interpretations of Acts of Parliament are not always unanimously agreed or obvious. Indeed the definition of an act as criminal is always open to amendment and reinterpretation by the courts during individual cases. Second, there needs to be a motive for the individual to commit (or not to commit) the act that is deemed criminal. Again, this may be difficult for sociologists to determine as individuals may lie about or be unaware of their own motives for carrying out acts.

The third factor that must be explored in a postmodern sociology of crime is the issue of control. This has two dimensions: self-control, in which inadequate socialization is seen as the root cause of the lack of conscience in those who carry out criminal acts; and external control which can include, for example, the concept of deterrence, in which punishment acts as an external control on the activities of potential criminals (see pp. 87–102).

Item B

Boot camps: get tough on young offenders

A pilot scheme for young reoffenders modelled to some extent on the American-style 'boot camps' is planned to come into operation in 1996. Like the 'short, sharp shock' idea introduced by the Conservative Government in the early 1980s, the idea is to deter reoffending by putting certain suitable young offenders, aged 18–21, through a six-month regime of 'deterrents, discipline and training'. The new version places somewhat more emphasis on rehabilitation but there is still a great deal of emphasis placed on discipline and physical training. The inmates will face a longer and more active day than elsewhere in British prisons. Parade drills, assault courses, and heavy manual labour will be used. Short hair and no TV are also the order of the day.

Source: Denscombe (1996).

Exercise 4.13

ⒾⒶ 1. Using information in Item B and the paragraph above, explain how the introduction of 'boot camp' style regimes may control crime.

ⒶⒺ 2. Identify three arguments against the 'get tough policy' described in Item B.

The fourth factor involved in the development of a postmodern theory of crime and deviance is the issue of opportunity, in which the potential perpetrator of a crime has a soft enough target to ensure the success of the crime. It is this aspect that has led many criminologists to focus on target hardening as a way of reducing crime. This can take the form of crime prevention measures, such as home alarm systems, the deployment of closed-circuit TV in city centres, and so on (see pp. 100–2).

Link Exercise 4.1

Study Item K in Chapter 3 (p. 100) and complete the following task and questions.

(A)(E) 1. Item K reproduces data from the 2007/08 British Crime Survey presented in *Social Trends 38*. We would like you to carry out a minisurvey in your area to test the reliability of the British Crime Survey findings. You should work with other sociology students and between you interview 100 people. You need to ask your respondents which of the crime prevention measures mentioned in Item K they have adopted in their own home. When you have completed your survey, convert your results into percentages and compare your findings with the information in Item K.

(E) 2. Why might the findings of the British Crime Survey be considered to be more reliable than your own survey data?

(A) 3. Suggest two reasons why people may join Neighbourhood Watch schemes other than to reduce their own risk of crime. (Hint: think about the notion of community.)

Lastly, postmodernists have drawn upon existential sociology (a branch of sociology that examines all the conditions of our existence, including feelings of irrationality, passion and horror) in emphasizing the emotional dimension as a significant feature of postmodern society. In particular, Denzin (1984) believes that resentment is the most important emotion in postmodern society, and consists of the self-hatred that emerges from the suppression of other emotions such as envy and anger. In postmodern society, where there is a large gap between expectation (fuelled by the media) and achievement those at the subordinate end of social relations, such as the young, women and the sexually stigmatized, are likely to experience resentment, which increases when there is also a feeling of helplessness about improving their circumstances. It is the intensification of resentment in the postmodern condition, caused by the peddling of commodified images, that leads to increased violence towards the self and others. Critics of this approach argue that it is difficult to establish objectively that there has been an 'intensification of resentment'.

Other postmodernists have focused on power as the 'cause' of crime and developed a more dialectical explanation of criminal behaviour (Henry and Milovanovic, 1994). In one sense, these postmodernists deny that there can be a 'cause' of crime in the traditional sociological sense of one factor (for example unemployment) leading to another (for example, theft). Rather the important thing to grasp is that crime is a process that emerges out of the creation of discourse and the exercise of power. Discourses can be seen as ways in which differences between individuals and groups are articulated and expressed, so as to give power to some and subordinate positions to others, in particular circumstances. It is this exercise of power, when it causes pain or hurt, which creates crime.

Crime, then, becomes possible when individuals find themselves in situations where they believe themselves to be free of their obligations to others in a relationship. They operate within discourses that deny others their essential humanity, by establishing differences between the exerciser of power and the recipient, such that the recipient is no longer recognized as possessing the same rights as the exerciser, and the responsibility of the exerciser towards the recipient is denied. The classic phrase utilized by such postmodernists to illustrate the importance of discourse in socially creating crime is 'not my business'. Crime results when usual practices, ideologies and power structures combine to allow individuals to shift responsibility for pain and hurt to others.

KUI

Exercise 4.14

Explain the meaning of the phrase 'not my business'.

Exam focus

1. Evaluate the idea that the extent and the nature of deviance are socially constructed.
2. 'Deviance is not a natural phenomenon, but involves agents of social control defining and labelling individuals and groups.' Assess the sociological evidence and arguments for and against this view.

Important concepts

Master status and labelling • Amplification • Moral panic • Folk devil • Shame and reintegration • Cultivation thesis • Relativism • Intensification of resentment

Critical thinking

1. Is labelling a one-way street or can the criminal justice system use labelling to encourage young people out of crime?
2. Is it all the media's fault that we live in fear of crime, or is it a conspiracy between politicians and the owners of the media to keep us permanently fearful?
3. Can shaming work to promote desistance from crime and how might shaming be implemented in a postmodern society, where 'anything goes'?

Chapter 5

Conflict Explanations of Crime and Deviance

After studying this chapter, you should:

- be able to outline and evaluate different conflict explanations of crime and deviance
- appreciate the way that crime is structurally caused and socially constructed
- be familiar with the relationship between capitalism and crime
- have a knowledge of the function of the law in relation to crime in capitalist societies
- recognize the nature and significance of selective law enforcement in capitalist societies
- understand and be able to explain different types of white-collar crime

Labelling Theory had a large impact on criminology, but a particular group of sociologists, who drew on another sociological tradition in criminology and came to be known as conflict theorists, questioned whether Labelling Theory went far enough. While labelling theorists acknowledged the role of power in the ability to create labels, attach them to people and make them stick, they had little interest in exploring more systematic questions associated with the exercise of political and economic power in society.

Conflict theorists drew their inspiration from the work of Karl Marx (1818–83) and Georg Simmel (1858–1918). The history of early Conflict Theory stretches from the work of Willem Bonger to that of Thorsten Sellin and George B. Vold. Sellin argued that different competing groups are in a situation of cultural conflict over which are the dominant norms in a society. It is the holders of political power who decide which norms of behaviour will prevail and which should be subject to criminalization. Vold took this position to its conclusion by arguing that the rights and wrongs of conflict have little to do with who become known as criminals. It is those who lose who are categorized by the victors as criminals.

After the success of Labelling Theory in drawing attention to the nature of power in creating labels and applying them to stigmatized groups and individuals, the early conflict theorists insisted that there must be an examination of the underlying structural causes of deviance as well as its socially constructed nature. However, the conflict theorists of the 1960s and 1970s went much further than the early ones, who were seen as rather mild in their criticism of the governing groups in society.

STRUCTURAL CAUSES AND THE SOCIAL CONSTRUCTION OF CRIME

The basic ideas of conflict theory can be demonstrated by considering the work of Austin Turk (1969). Turk argued that the status of 'criminal' is not a result of any inherent characteristic, but is given to individuals by the legal authorities, who, however, do not unilaterally impose labels on individuals – the recipients of labels are involved in the process of labelling themselves. Turk argued that people in authority learn roles of domination in which it becomes 'natural' for them to order society as they see it. Conversely those without power learn roles of deference, in which they voluntarily submit to the authority of those in power. The problem is that there is never total agreement between the two groups (the powerful and the powerless) of the definitions of these roles and how each should behave towards the other. As a result the activities of the subordinate groups become subject to the law-making activities of the powerful, and the powerful use the law to control the activities of the powerless and make them conform to the norms of behaviour that the powerful have defined as the 'right' ones.

ⒾⒶ

Exercise 5.1

Trade unions are organizations that work to protect the interests of workers. One of the most potent weapons that trade unions can use to ensure that powerful groups meet their demands is the threat or use of strike action. However, during the 1980s and 1990s a series of Employment and Trade Union Acts in the UK served to reduce trade union power by making strike action more difficult and arguably a less effective weapon than in the past. These Acts provide a good example of the way the powerful use the law to control the activities of the powerless.

We would like you to draw up and complete an extended version of the chart below. Refer to the Internet to read up on the various employment and trade union laws that have been implemented since the 1980s. You should then make a note in your chart of the key aspects of the various laws. We have started this process off for you. You should finish the chart by writing a concluding paragraph that explains how the various employment laws have served to control and reduce the activities and power of trade unions.

Employment and trade union law	Aspects of Acts
1980 Employment Act	Picketing confined to own place of work.
1982 Employment Act	Industrial action has to relate to a 'trade dispute'.
1984 Trade Union Act	Before industrial action can be taken, secret ballots have to be held.
1988 Employment Act	Unions cannot pay members' fines.
1989 Employment Act	
1990 Employment Act	Secondary industrial action unlawful.
1992 Trade Union and Labour Relations (Consolidation) Act	
1993 Trade Union Reform and Employment Rights Act	Union mergers require postal ballots.
1996 Employment Rights Act	
1999 Employment Relations Act	Ballots for union recognition disputes.
2002 Employment Act	
2004 Employment Relations Act	Union learning representatives recognized.

One particular group of conflict theorists describe themselves as 'left idealists', because they come from a left-wing political position and tend to have a more idealistic view of the deviant. An important part of 'left idealist' explanations involves the power of ideology, generated and disseminated by dominant institutions such as the media, to structure the ways in which individuals conduct their lives, such as forming conceptions of proper gender roles, appropriate work ethics, and so on. However, society is composed of individuals with many different characteristics and interests, which do not always conform to the dominant views of capitalist society. As a result, society needs to control potentially difficult population groups, and a strong criminal justice system is developed for the purpose. In this situation the causes of crime are fairly straightforward: the poor commit crime as part of the struggle to live, while the rich commit their own crimes as part of the dictate of capitalist ethics, which demands that individuals accumulate wealth. Spitzer (1976) believes that capitalism generates a surplus population of economic outcasts, mainly the unemployed, who turn to crime to survive. He identifies five types of problem population:

1.   Poor people who steal from the rich.
2.   Those who do not want to work.
3.   Those who retreat into drug-taking.
4.   Those who resist schooling and/or family life.
5.   Those who want to replace capitalism with an alternative form of society.

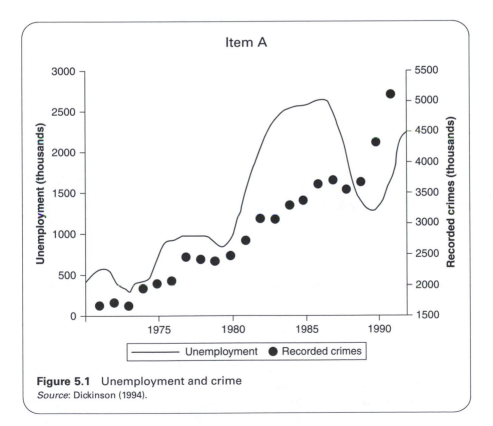

Figure 5.1 Unemployment and crime
Source: Dickinson (1994).

Exercise 5.2

Ⓘ Ⓐ 1. There is a great deal of debate about whether unemployment leads to crime. Use the information in Item A to demonstrate that a link between unemployment and crime does exist.

Ⓐ 2. The author of the work in which Item A appears is careful to point out that it would be wrong to make a simplistic link between unemployment and crime. Suggest two reasons why it would be unwise for sociologists to assume that unemployment automatically leads to crime.

Ⓐ 3. Explain why a high unemployment rate may give rise to each of the five types of problem population identified by Spitzer above.

Those groups who are non-threatening ('social junk' as Spitzer calls them) are likely to be lightly policed, whereas those who go against the status quo will attract a disproportionate amount of law-enforcement activity.

However, the only reason why crime appears to be concentrated among the poor is that the criminal justice agencies arguably operate in a biased fashion to blame the poor and exonerate the rich. Any increase in the crime rate is likely to proceed from increased numbers of police rather than reflecting an actual rise (Scraton, 1985). Focusing on the crimes of the working class performs an ideological function as well. By presenting working-class crime as a social problem for the whole of society, attention is shifted away from middle-class crime, which is seen as relatively unimportant.

Ⓘ Ⓐ
Link Exercise 5.1

Using suitable examples from Chapter 2, write a short paragraph that argues that middle-class crime should not be seen as unimportant. You might want to start your paragraph off in the following way:

It can be argued that middle-class crime is far from unimportant. Marxists draw attention to a number of white-collar crimes that have occurred in the 1980s, 1990s and 2000s. These include...

Quinney (1970a), in his original conflict formulation, argues that crime is the result of reaction by the authorities, who create the definitions of crime and control through the enforcement activities of the state. But, like crime, non-crime is socially constructed. By this Quinney means that very similar actions can be defined as legal or illegal through the political activity of the powerful.

For example the line between tax evasion and tax avoidance is a very fine one and tends to work against the subordinate groups in society, because it is the powerful who determine where the line is drawn. Central to the acceptance of these definitions by the population is the work of the media, which put forward the idea of crime and non-crime in documentary and fictional programmes.

Exercise 5.3

The media are often quick to pick up on stories of social security fraud. Moral panics often ensue and governments react by clamping down on so-called 'dole cheats'. Similar panics and reactions are less likely to ensue from other types of fraud, for example tax fraud.

(An)(A) 1. Give reasons why tax fraud is less likely to be subject to a moral panic than social security fraud.

(A) 2. Apart from economic necessity, suggest one reason for social security fraud.

Chambliss (1975) suggests that capitalist societies inevitably have to strengthen the coercive activities of the criminal justice system against the proletariat. This is because the widening gap in income and wealth between the bourgeoisie and the proletariat that is built into the capitalist system means that tension between the two classes will inevitably increase. An important aspect of this increase will be the criminalization of more sections of the working class, as more and more turn to crime to make a living.

CRIME AND CAPITALISM

Many Marxist criminologists in the 1970s saw capitalism as crimogenic, that is, it is the material conditions of capitalist society that creates crime. 'Left idealists' argued that those caught in criminal activity are not only, in some sense, 'victims' of capitalist laws, but are expressing, in the only way they know, their rejection of the inequalities of capitalism (Quinney, 1970b). Crime was therefore seen as some sort of protest against the prevailing conditions. This was supported by Gordon (1971), who argued that, given the dominant ideologies in capitalist society – greed, individualism and competition – then crime is a rational response by the working class.

Chambliss (1975) examined the functions of crime for capitalist societies, albeit from a more structural Marxist perspective. He suggested that crime is an employment-creating activity in capitalist societies because it not only provides 'employment' for criminals, but also for large numbers of people who are concerned with criminal justice: the police, probation officers, social workers, and so on. Moreover crime is an aspect of false consciousness in that it diverts the attention of the working class from their exploitation by the ruling class and towards the criminals in their own midst. As much of the law is directed at controlling the lower class and protecting the interests of the ruling class, Chambliss also suggested that socialist societies, which experience much less in the way of class struggle, will experience lower levels of crime.

Item B

Table 5.1 Employment in the criminal justice system (thousands)

	1971	1981	1991	1997–98	1998–99
Police service: Police	97	120	127	127	126
Civilian staff	28	38	46	53	53
All police service	125	157	174	180	179
Prison service	17	24	33	41	43
Probation service	–	13	18	17	17

Source: Matheson and Summerfield (2000).

Exercise 5.4

As indicated above, the criminal justice system is a major employer. Item B provides information on employment in the criminal justice system. Study the item and answer the following questions.

1. In 1991, how many people were employed in the police service (including civilians)?
2. Calculate the increase in the number of workers employed in the probation service between 1971 and 1991.
3. Name one group of employees, other than those shown in Item B, who work in the criminal justice system.

Quinney (1975) agreed that capitalism is still crimogenic and that the solution to crime is to move towards a more socialist-based society. However, he rejected the state socialism of communist Russia and argued for the development of democratic socialism as the means of combating crime. He also adapted his earlier position that crime is somehow 'protorevolutionary' to suggest that it is largely a matter of survival, which, while understandable in terms of the material conditions of capitalism, is not sufficient in itself as a means of challenging and changing capitalism. Quinney (1977) also developed a new typology of crime that recognizes the 'crimes of the powerful' as well as those on the margins of society.

Ⓘ Ⓐ

Exercise 5.5

The chart below shows the typology of crime suggested by Quinney. As you can see, Quinney divides crimes of domination and crimes of accommodation into two subdivisions. Your first task is to copy the chart and put the following descriptions into the correct category. When you have done this, you should be able to work out a crime that conforms to each description.

Matching descriptions

1. Crimes against the person.
2. Crimes committed by agents of law and order.
3. Crimes against property.
4. Crimes against the established order.
5. Crimes committed by officials and politicians in pursuance of their duties.

Major categories of Quinney's typology	Subdivisions	Description	Example
Crimes of domination	Crimes of control		
	Crimes of government		
Crimes of accommodation	Predatory crimes		
	Personal crimes		
Crimes of resistance	Resistance crimes		

Other radical criminologists have drawn upon other Marxist traditions, such as the work of Gramsci, to explore the relationship between capitalism and crime. Beckett and Sasson (2000) explore the relationship between inclusionary/exclusionary social policies and the hegemonic strategies of the ruling class in the United States. By adopting an historical approach, they argue that the ruling class in the 1930s and 1940s adopted inclusionary tactics, aimed at incorporating the working class into capitalism by poverty-reducing policies. However, challenges to ruling class hegemony in the 1960s and 1970s, mainly by the anti-Vietnam War and Civil Right movements shifted the ruling class towards more exclusionary strategies. This entailed a move towards a mode of governance called the 'security state' in which a 'new punitiveness' towards criminals became a key element. An example of this harder approach to crime and disorder was the 'three strikes' law in which mandatory tough sentences were automatically imposed at a third conviction for an offence.

CRIME AND THE LAW

The conflict position taken by Chambliss and Seidman (1971) focuses on the relationship between the law and society. They argue that in highly differentiated societies there will be many conflicting norms. The likelihood of any set of norms becoming encapsulated in the law is related to the distribution of power and status in society. Those with the greater amount of power will find that their views are reflected in the law. They also draw attention to the fact that the law is created and administered by bureaucracies that have their own interests in the operation of the law. This basically means that Chambliss and Seidman believed that these bureaucracies are more likely to process those criminals who are least likely to cause problems for the bureaucracies involved. The more powerful the accused, the more problems she or he will cause the legal bureaucracies. The powerful are therefore more likely to escape the criminal justice process. The powerless are not. As a result, laws against the favoured activities of the powerless are more likely to be enforced than laws against the illegal activities of the powerful.

Item C

Table 5.2 Defendants found guilty of indictable fraud offences, 1998–2004

England & Wales	Numbers						
	1998	**1999**	**2000**	**2001**	**2002**	**2003**	**2004**
Obtaining property by deception	11,440	11,480	10,540	9,440	9,350	8,460	7,520
Dishonest representation for obtaining benefit	240	710	1,350	1,950	1,990	1,840	2,460
Making off without payment	1,250	1,440	1,410	1,320	1,300	1,810	1,690
Obtaining services by deception	980	1,030	880	880	830	800	750
False accounting	1,690	1,620	1,160	870	750	650	730
Conspiracy to defraud	470	420	430	450	410	450	520
Other offences	1,130	1,100	1,100	1,000	940	1,030	1,130
All offences	17,200	17,800	16,870	15,910	15,570	15,040	14,800

Source: Babb *et al.* (2006).

Exercise 5.6

1. In the year 2002 how many successful prosecutions were there for:

   (a) benefit fraud?
   (b) false accounting?

2. What was the decline in the number of defendants in obtaining property by deception between 1998 and 2004?

3. Does the evidence presented in the table add weight to Chambliss and Seidman's (1971) contention that the law is enforced selectively?

When looking at capitalist societies, Chambliss (1975) further developed his approach in the Marxist direction. He argues that acts are defined as criminal in direct defence of the interests of the ruling class, while members of this class themselves routinely ignore criminal law with no consequences. In particular, criminal law is employed by the ruling class to defend their material interests in a situation where inequality between the bourgeoisie and the proletariat is growing. The law therefore has a direct control-effect in society. An example of the way that the law can be used by capitalist interests is provided by Graham (1976), who argues that the laws controlling the production and use of amphetamines are weakened by the activities of the pharmaceutical companies, whose profits in part depend on this class of drugs.

Crime and law enforcement

Selective law enforcement refers to the choices the forces of law and order make when policing society. For example, given limited resources the police make choices about where and when to deploy police officers, and when to proceed with legal action and when not (see pp. 27–30). In his social realist theory of crime, Quinney (1970a) argues that selective law enforcement is related to the conceptions of crime that are held by the powerful in society. These elite definitions of crime are important because they find their way into the mass media and thus into personal conceptions of crime. Thus the crime problem in society, as seen by the forces of law and order, is a reflection of the elite's definition of crime. Their conception is therefore real in its consequences and becomes the social reality of crime, rather than just the views of a small segment of society. The effect of all this is that the police choose to implement the law in different ways, depending on who is being policed at the time.

Bauman (1987) argues that in postmodern society the nature of social control has changed from that which prevailed in the conditions of modernity. The crucial development in this respect has been the rejection by society's rulers of the enlightenment project, in which the state and its bureaucracy acted to improve the lot of all citizens. While the state bureaucracy paradoxically continues to expand, its role has been reconceptualized. Rather than the bureaucracy being an agent for the delivery of services that benefit the population, such services have been given over to the market.

The primacy of the market has led, according to Bauman, to two social-control categories being dominant in postmodern society. These are termed the 'seduced' and the 'repressed'. The seduced are those who are attracted by the message of consumption and the market. These are integrated and controlled through the manipulation of consumerist messages and images. The repressed are the new poor, whose consumption is unimportant for the reproduction of capital in postmodern conditions. As peripheral members of consumer society the new poor have to be controlled by more repressive means, such as aggressive policing and regulation. Just as capitalism has turned leisure into an industry, the need for repressive social control of the new poor has led to a crime-control industry, in which members of the seduced group gain the means to consume through manufacturing and selling the technologies of control (Christie, 1993).

The input of the new right into policy during the 1980s was also an important element in changing social control in the 1990s. O'Malley (1991) argues that the effect of criminal policy in the 1980s was to change public attitudes towards crime away from a socialized one and towards a privatized one. That is, the criminal came to be viewed as a rational individual who makes a choice to commit crime, and the public – the potential victims – have to make choices about what they need to do to prevent crime being perpetrated against them. There is a sense in which victim blaming is extended to victims of crime who do not take rational measures to protect themselves from the activities of criminals. Social control is therefore exercised by a strong state that responds to demands for punitive sentencing on an underclass who are seen as responsible for the crime committed in society, while private security firms offer the public devices for protecting life and property.

The rise of new technologies and the consequent increase in the potential for surveillance has led to some pessimistic characterizations of a future surveillance society in the form of the managed society, the suspicious society, the maximum security society, and so on (Dandeker, 1990).

Ⓐ Ⓔ

Exercise 5.7

A good example of the use of surveillance technology to combat crime in Britain is the widespread deployment of closed-circuit television (CCTV) in city centres. Surveillance of this type has attracted both support and criticism from the public, the police and politicians. We would like you to construct a chart like the one below and identify arguments for and against the use of CCTV in city centres. We have provided some examples to get you started.

CCTV in city centres

Arguments for	Arguments against
1. Reduces people's fear of crime	1. Invasion of privacy
2. Provides evidence to convict criminals	2. Very costly
3.	3.
4.	4.

Evaluation of traditional Marxist approaches to crime and deviance

Ⓔ | Exercise 5.8

Listed below are three strengths and three weaknesses of the Marxist views presented so far in this chapter. Suggest two additional strengths and two additional weaknesses of the traditional Marxist views.

Strengths

1. They focus attention on the role of the police and courts in a systematic way.
2. The traditional Marxist views place crime firmly in the context of capitalist relations of production.
3. The ideas emphasize the role of agencies such as the media in definitions of criminal activity.

Weaknesses

1. They tend to focus on situations that are on the margins and therefore not typical of the vast amount of criminal activity.
2. There is a tendency to ignore the fact that the vast majority of crime committed by the working class is also carried out against the working class.
3. It can be argued that the views of the traditional Marxists romanticize the subcultures of criminal groups.

CRITICAL CRIMINOLOGY

The emergence of new or critical criminology in Britain during the early 1970s was in part a reaction to the inadequacies of Labelling Theory and the more traditional Marxist approaches. However, the main theoretical counter point for critical criminology was its objection to the positivistic assumptions of functionalism and the dominant paradigms of criminology. The appearance of the perspective was emphasized by the publication of *The New Criminology* by Taylor *et al.* (1973). The authors make a sustained attack on what they see as the overdetermined theories associated with positivistic criminology. They believe that to reduce the causes of crime to such simple factors as upbringing is to ignore a whole range of contributing factors to the phenomenon of crime. Instead the authors argue that the focus of criminology should be on political, social and economic factors as these shape the form and incidence of criminal activity. From this political economy position, critical criminologists argue that the enforced conditions of capitalism are themselves a major cause of crime.

Moreover Bohm (1982) argues that criminal law is manipulated by the elite to ensure the survival of the capitalist system.

Criminal law is therefore conceptualized as the result of an alliance between business and the state, in which the ethic of individualism glues together the two sets of interests. This ethic makes individuals responsible for their own actions, but denies the importance of social and environmental factors that might influence these actions. The result of this is a dual type of citizenship, in which the powerless are subject to the full rigour of the criminal law while the activities of the powerful are regulated more by the civil law. The powerful are therefore 'beyond incrimination'.

One of the major themes of critical criminology is that deviance is political, and as such is subject to both structural and subjective forces. Whilst critical criminologists recognize the importance of capitalist society as 'crimogenic' – indeed they see the substitution of capitalism with 'socialist diversity' as the only way to a crime-free society – they also wish to avoid the determinism of much of the earlier Marxist approaches to deviance. Taylor *et al.* therefore argue that deviance is a matter of choice, and that it has a political dimension. Their focus on several subcultural groups, such as homosexuals and football hooligans, helps them to explore the voluntaristic and political nature of much deviance.

Item D

A 'fully social theory of deviance'

1. 'The wider origins of the deviant act.' The radical criminologist needs to locate the deviant act within the wider social system – capitalism with its attendant class divisions.

2. 'Immediate origins of the deviant act.' He or she then needs to look at the immediate social context within which an individual chooses to commit an act of deviance.

3. 'The actual act.' Attention needs to be given to what the deviant act means to the individual concerned.

4. 'The immediate origins of social reaction.' He or she then needs to look at the immediate response of other people, such as members of the deviant's family and the police, to the discovery of deviance.

5. 'Wider origins of deviant reaction.' The immediate reaction needs to be located within the wider social system, with particular attention being paid to the question of who has the power to define certain activities as deviant.

6. 'The outcomes of social reaction on the deviant's further action.' While most deviants recognize that there will be a reaction against them, it is important to examine the effects of the labelling process on the deviant.

7. 'The nature of the deviant process as a whole.' Finally these six aspects of the deviant process need to be connected together for there to be a 'fully social theory of deviance'.

Source: Taylor *et al.* (1995).

Exercise 5.9

Taylor *et al.* (1973) argue in the final chapter of their book that a complete or 'fully social theory of deviance' must have seven aspects, as shown in Item C. Read Item C and complete the following tasks. You should record your answers to the tasks in an extended version of the chart below (strand 1 is provided as an example).

1. The seven strands that make up a 'fully social theory of deviance' draw on Labelling Theory, traditional Marxist views and critical criminology. For each strand identify the theoretical influence.
2. For each of the seven strands of a 'fully social theory of deviance', identify whether the strand is concerned with addressing the causes of deviance or its socially constructed nature.
3. Explain how each of the strands identified by Taylor *et al.* can be said to offer a power dimension to the sociological study of deviance.

The new criminology: a 'fully social theory of deviance'

Strand	Theoretical basis	Cause or social construction	Conception of power
1	Traditional Marxism	Cause	Recognition that the crimes of the powerless stem from the inequalities in capitalist society

The application of critical criminology: Pearson (1976)

Pearson is concerned to show that even such actions as 'Pakibashing' can be seen as crypto-political action. Pearson describes a rash of 'Pakibashing' incidents in a Lancashire cotton town as a primitive form of political and economic struggle. It is suggested that the level of unemployment in the town was responsible for the outbreaks, and that white youths were reacting against the apparent substitution of white employees with ethnic minority workers. Pearson also claims that the 'Pakibashers' were seen as folk heroes in a complicit racist conspiracy by the white inhabitants of the town. Tierney (1980) criticizes this approach as accusing the inhabitants of being racist while offering no evidence that they were folk heroes. Nor was the unemployment level (1 per cent) sufficient to confirm that the criminal activities of the 'Pakibashers' was some sort of economic struggle.

Birmingham Centre for Contemporary Cultural Studies (CCCS), 1970s and 1980s

Starting from the position that class conflict is the basic characteristic of capitalist society, the CCCS offers a whole series of studies of youth subcultures, analysing them in terms of their style and the threat that they may or may not pose to dominant ideological forms. For example Clarke *et al.* (1976) argue that the importance of youth subcultures is that they offer alternative conceptions (or identities) to the dominant views of what young people should be like. The CCCS sees the development of a subcultural style as being rich in symbolic meanings that can be decoded by sociologists (Hall and Jefferson, 1976). Youth subcultures therefore offer 'imaginary' solutions to the problems that the young, especially the working-class young, experience in a society of relative affluence. These symbols are therefore proto-political in that they are an unconscious attempt to resolve the contradictions of capitalist society from the position of the subordinate. However, this has been criticized for being a romantic account of working-class subcultures, in which the symbols of youth culture style can be interpreted in many different ways, depending on what the sociologist is trying to show (Rock, 1973).

Hall et al., 1978

In *Policing the Crisis*, Hall (1978) argues that highlighting the existence of deviant activities has been used by the state and the media as a means of deflecting attention away from economic and political crisis in Britain. The economic problems that had beset Britain led to a 'crisis in hegemony', according to Hall. By this he means that the legitimacy of the capitalist society was under threat as the economic system was failing to deliver the goods to the working class.

As a diversionary tactic, the media, in the first instance, but also the forces of social control, seized upon the phenomenon of 'mugging' as a way of refocusing public attention onto a different 'crisis'. Hall is not arguing that mugging had not taken place, but that the reaction of the state and the media had been exaggerated, given the scale of the problem. The aim was to create a 'moral panic' by latching onto deep-seated stereotypes about black people to suggest that mugging is a black deviant activity. The importance of this is that it is much easier for the state to establish legitimacy through consent than through coercion. To establish a folk devil in the popular mind serves to distract attention from the economic and political crisis, and also to bind 'society' together against a common enemy.

Item E

Radical (critical) criminology, the family and crime

- Half of all criminal violence actually occurs within the normal family (Mooney, 2000), therefore it should not be assumed that crime is something 'out there', beyond the sanctuary of the family.
- The family itself is very frequently the cause of crime rather than the reverse. The 'strong' family may well be repressive for both women and children. Violence is used in some families to maintain male authority. The break-up of such families often results in the lowering of violent crime, not its increase. In this context, family break-up can sometimes be seen as a crime prevention strategy, rather than something that produces delinquency.
- The family is often a fundamental and necessary building block of successful organized crime networks. Organized crime needs the security of the strong family. The extended family is also a haven of trust in a divided society, and the needs of the family – over those of the rest of society – are often used by offenders to justify their crime.
- Although community disintegration may well lead to crimes such as vandalism and petty theft, traditional criminologists make the mistake of seeing the family as being somehow separate from the wider structure. Radical criminology claims that crime is the product of the nature of the wider society, which, in the case of certain types of crime, cannot be controlled by family socialization.

Source: adapted from Mooney (2000).

Exercise 5.10

(i) 1. According to Item E, in what way does the radical (critical) approach to the family and crime differ from the approach of traditional criminology?

(A)(An) 2. In what other ways do you think that radical criminology's approach to crime and the family differs from a traditional view of the family?

Evaluation of critical criminology

(I)(A)(E)

Exercise 5.11

Listed below are a number of partly completed sentences outlining the strengths and weaknesses of critical criminology. Complete the statements by selecting appropriate finishing clauses from those offered to you.

Strengths

1. Critical criminology extends the definition of crime to issues concerned with human rights, ...
2. It reasserts the importance of the political economy of crime, ...
3. It unites action and structural approaches to deviance, ...
4. It focuses on the activities of the powerful, ...

Finishing strengths clauses

(a) thereby offering a structuration approach.
(b) such as sexism and racism.
(c) in both rule making and rule breaking aspects.
(d) looking at factors such as the economic arrangements in society.

Weaknesses

1. It offers an incomplete critique of earlier theories, ...
2. By rejecting both biological and psychological factors as partial causes of crime, ...
3. The approach tends to romanticize the deviant as a protorevolutionary, ignoring the harm that is done by many deviant acts, ...
4. There is a tendency for the approach to explain away crime as a social construction and ...

Finishing weaknesses clauses

(a) critical criminologists deny themselves the opportunity to explore many interesting aspects of criminology.
(b) in doing so the reality of crime can be missed.
(c) particularly in working-class communities.
(d) dismissing them rather than showing they are necessarily in error.

Anarchist theory of crime

Anarchist theory is a minor approach to the issue of crime. Tifft (1979) shows an interest in more radical theories of crime and argues for a system of criminal justice that is face-to-face, rather than hierarchical. However, the major contributor in this area is Ferrell (1993). According to the anarchist position, all hierarchies need to be challenged, be they economic – which the Marxists identify as the most important area of domination – or patriarchal or intellectual. Ferrell argues that societies build up hierarchies of credibility, which come to dominate the way that individuals think in society. It is the duty of anarchist criminology to oppose all these hierarchies and expose the taken-for-granted nature of our knowledge. Therefore the anarchist is required to demythologize (or deconstruct) the ideas behind the criminal justice system in capitalist societies. In its place, there should be a plural system in which the essential ambiguity and uncertainty of our knowledge is explicit. This alternative society would be based on a tolerance of difference and would be decentralized, so that justice could be based on individuals and groups negotiating their own solutions to problems, without coercion.

Post-structuralist criticisms of conflict theories

Foucault (1977) rejects the notion that power and control are situated either in the state or in some economically determined class (Henry, 1994). Rather, power is everywhere – in the minute and daily practices in which individuals engage. The law is therefore not created by classes or groups to maintain their power, but by the tension between many legal and non-legal groups, relationships and networks seeking to influence the definition of the law. Crime cannot therefore be seen as some sort of protest against a centralized source of power or just the result of the policing policies of the state, but as present in the everyday activities of individuals, shaped by the discourses that dominate their lives. Therefore the idea that crime can be 'tackled' by the overthrow of capitalism and the introduction of socialism is wrong, because power is more dispersed than conflict theorists would allow.

WHITE-COLLAR AND CORPORATE CRIME

The work of Sutherland (1949) provoked interest in the phenomenon of white-collar crime. As suggested in Chapter 2, Sutherland's definition of white-collar crime is slightly ambiguous and does not distinguish between crimes committed on behalf of an organization and crimes committed by a person in a position of high status within that organization, against the organization. Coleman (1985) describes these as the difference between, respectively, organizational crime and occupational crime (see pp. 150–1). Both of these categories can be seen as 'crimes of the powerful' and they are often intertwined, but the consequences of each are very different. Moreover sociological interest in white-collar crime has grown as new areas of interest have opened up and new definitions have been created. So distinctions have been made between white-collar crime that is individually oriented and crimes committed as part of the 'normal' activities of large corporations.

ⓘⒶ
Link Exercise 5.2

In the light of the information in Chapter 2 on crime statistics, think of two cases of white-collar crime that have been individually orientated and two cases that have been committed as part of the activities of large corporations.

Corporate crime has emerged as a controversial area of sociological investigation. It is of course very difficult to enquire into the activities of powerful individuals, and it is even more difficult when powerful corporations, jealous of their 'industrial' secrets, are involved. Nevertheless some sociologists have argued that the activities of corporations have caused many injuries to, or the death of, employees and members of the public (see, for example, Reasons *et al.*, 1981). These have occurred not just because of negligence by the executives of big corporations, but also because of the everyday pressure on them to cut costs and therefore corners (see Box, 1983, for numerous examples of this). The collapse of the American company Enron in 2001 was a prime example of the harm done to shareholders, pensioners and workers by such corporate activities (Nelken, 2007).

With the growth in international trade, corporate crime has also become global (Coleman, 1985). Such crime can involve a variety of activities, such as international price fixing (where, for example, oil companies operate as a cartel), the illegal discounting of goods and services to overseas subsidiaries, and the dumping of unsafe products in underdeveloped countries where regulations are much laxer. The testing of new but controversial drugs has also been concentrated in countries with less stringent controls over clinical trials (Braithwaite, 1984). Further, the globalization of communications, and especially global financial transactions, has meant that new forms of crime have emerged, ranging from drug money laundering to Internet sales frauds (Croall, 1997). Croall (2001) identifies seven types of white-collar crime, ranging from theft at work to environmental crime.

ⒾⒶ

Exercise 5.12

For each of the types of white-collar crime, provide a definition and an example of an activity that would fall into the category.

Type of white-collar crime	Definition	Example of activity
Theft at work		
Fraud		
Corruption		
Employment offences		
Consumer offences		
Food offences		
Environmental crime		

In the case of occupational crime, where illegal activities are conducted for personal gain, it has been suggested by Weisburd *et al.* (1991) that white-collar crime is taking place much further down the organizational hierarchy than previously. This is because more and more employees are able to gain access to the world of 'paper fraud' through their office computers, and because of the growth in the banking and finance sectors. For example more and more women in 'highly monitored, money-changing' jobs (Daly, 1989) have been caught committing crimes such as embezzlement. However, it would be wrong to focus only on the white-collar criminal statistics, which tend to show much lower middle-class involvement and ignore the really large occupational crimes committed by some top executives. As Braithwaite (1993) shows, this depends on their having social capital in the form of trust and a high organizational position.

This is not to say that occupational crime by subordinates is not a real problem. The cost of activities such as computer sabotage, fraud and 'shrink-age' through shoplifting and employee theft is enormous. According to Buss (1993), theft by employees is the equivalent of about 2 per cent of all sales; but Traub (1996) argues that actual employee theft may be 10 to 15 times greater than this figure. Most employees are aware of the illegal activities of their co-workers but develop taken-for-granted rules about ignoring them (Cole-man, 1994). Levi *et al.* (2007) have estimated that losses from frauds alone were at least £12.98 billion in the UK.

Another area of concern is professional and organized crime, especially the US operations of the Mafia, which is seen as an independent entity that manages illegal goods and services. The work by the conservative American sociologist Bell (1962) in this area foreshadowed the contemporary postmodernist views of organized crime. Bell argues that organized crime once represented a side of the American Dream, in that it offered a route towards social mobility for some immigrants. However, as American society became more organized, controlled and focused on consumption rather than production, so the Mafia became more integrated into mainstream society and concentrated on areas of consumption, for example the leisure indus-try, rather than the production of illegal goods. Organized crime has become 'respectable', blurring the boundaries between the normal and the crimi-nal. Indeed, Lyman and Potter (2004) have argued that these distinctions between organized crime, politics and business were meaningless, as they were central to American political-economic life. A parallel view has been expressed about the Camorra Mafia in Italy – arguing that, as seven of the 32 Mafia leaders arrested have been women, there is more equal opportu-nity in the Mafia than in many parts of legal society. This is contested by South (1997), who asserts that, as crime and business become increasingly intertwined, 'criminal organizations are not renowned as equal-opportunity employers'.

This area of organized crime is therefore of great interest to sociolo-gists, but very difficult to access as members of criminal gangs are unlikely to cooperate in a sociological study of their activities. Sociologists have therefore been forced to rely on more ethnographic techniques such as life histories, biographies, and so on (see, for example, Katz, 1988) or on secondary sources (see, for example, Ruggeiro, 1996). This means that sociologists have found it difficult to produce corroborative evidence for their narrative accounts, and they therefore have to be dealt with very sensitively.

Exercise 5.13

(K)(U)(A) 1. Briefly define and give an example of each of the following concepts:

(a) secondary data

(b) ethnography

(K)(U) 2. With reference to sociological research, assess the strengths and limitations
(A)(E) of one secondary ethnographic technique as a method of studying organized
crime.

In Britain, McIntosh (1975) developed a typology of criminal organizations
that includes two declining modes (the 'picaresque' and 'craft organizations')
and two that are more dominant (the 'project' and the 'business criminal
organization').

(I)(A)

Exercise 5.14

The chart below presents a partly completed summary of the typology of criminal organizations identified by McIntosh. For each of the four forms of criminal
organization we have either offered a description or an example of that type of
organization. Copy the chart and then complete your copy by filling in the blank
boxes so that each of the four types of criminal organization has a description
and an appropriate example.

Type of criminal organization	Description	Example
Picaresque		Pirates
Craft	Where there is an 'apprenticeship' system to learn the tricks of the trade	
Project		The Great Train Robbery
Business	Where stable organizations are developed to pursue crime more efficiently	

Hobbs (1995) argues that, while there are still a large number of small-time criminals, these are increasingly disposable as they have been deskilled through the emergence of large criminal organizations run by 'entrepreneurs'. 'Professional' criminals are therefore more likely to be found within fairly stable organizations, run and managed as businesses, and employing 'craft' criminals on a casual basis for particular 'project' crimes.

However, Chambliss (1978) argues that, as all classes engage in criminality, organized crime is not autonomous but operates in a relationship with the formal economy. Organized crime has thus become 'corporate crime', a form of economic criminality. Moreover there is a symbiotic (each dependent on the other) relationship between organized crime and the bureaucracy of the legal system, in which connections are made between powerful players in both organizations. He suggests that, rather than upset this relationship, the law enforcement agencies focus their activities on less powerful criminals, such as minor drug pushers, where there are few personal and economic relationships.

Globalization and crime

Sociological concern at the end of the twentieth century and the beginning of the twenty-first began to focus on the effects of globalization on criminal activity. An early example of the international dimension to criminal activity was the drug cartels in Colombia and the interweaving of organized crime with the Christian Democrat and Socialist Parties in Italy. In these cases it is difficult to unravel the legal and illegal activities of 'legitimate' and 'illegitimate' organizations. The activities of the drug cartels shape the economy and the politics of Colombia and also have an impact across the world. The activities of organized crime in Italy include the use of large capital resources to support friendly factions within the political parties and the distribution of funds to its members for criminal purposes. The organization therefore has a large number of 'employees' on its payroll, often legally attached to some front organization (see, for example, Hobbs, 1988).

By looking at the global activities of nation-states, criminologists have begun to explore the issue of globalization and crime. Globalization can be defined in several ways, but can be thought of as the ways in which transnational flows and networks of capital and people impinge increasingly on local circumstances. Edward and Gill (2003) argued that new opportunities are created for organized crime with the development of a globalized economy, for example drug and people trafficking, the large-scale smuggling of arms and art, and the illegal movement of money across national borders. Research in these areas is extremely difficult to accomplish and so there are very few 'hard' facts established. At best, global agencies offer estimates of the numbers involved. For example, the US State Department (2004) estimated that between 600,000 and 800,000 people (70 per cent female and 50 per cent minors) were trafficked across national borders, primarily for sexual exploitation and forced labour. Drug smuggling is also global and encompasses rebel political groups, those primarily interested in financial returns and 'adventurers' who enjoy the risk-taking as much as the money (Dorn *et al.*, 2005).

The forces of law and order, nationally based, are in a poor position to combat the activities of the Russian mafia or the Japanese Yakuza. Yet, there has been tremendous pressure to internationalize the forces of law and order, or at least make cross-border cooperation much easier (Newburn and Sparks, 2004), changing an area of activity strongly associated with the nation-state. There has also been a 'militarization' of international responses to transcontinental criminal activity, as terrorist organizations turn to crime to fund their campaigns across the global stage (for example, Iraq and Afghanistan).

On an international level, the twenty-first century has seen the emergence of transnational organized criminal (TOCs) groups, where activities may be global in reach, for example through the Internet. Aning (2007) focuses on the West African base for many TOCs, seeking to establish what allows them to flourish there. He argues that it is a combination of weak governments, often corrupt, and a concentration of poverty that creates fertile conditions for the TOCs, as they are able to penetrate state structures and easily recruit foot soldiers to the gangs. Their main criminal endeavours are based around drug trafficking, computer crime and illegal manufacture of small arms. Gross (2003) agrees that failed or failing states are important in understanding the development of global crime, as they both provide safe havens, out of the reach of global law enforcement activity, and are a source of plundered resources for criminal gangs.

Cybercrime

Another development emerging from globalization is cybercrime (see Chapter 2). In what is a highly significant social development, the internet and computer connectivity have brought many benefits to society, but they have also been accompanied by the appearance of 'e-crimes' or 'hi-tech crime'. Some commentators have argued that this represents a 'new' form of crime and needs new concepts to describe and explain it, in which the virtual environment increases the potential scope of offending and alters the relationship between offender and victim (Capeller, 2001). Above all else, the ability to engage in relationships under anonymous identities creates the potential for a new range of criminal endeavour and is a main reason why cybercrime is so difficult to combat (Joseph, 2003).

Grabosky (2004) classifies cybercrime into three types: conventional crimes committed using computers, such as intellectual property theft; conventional criminal cases in which evidence exists digitally; and attacks on computer networks. He, in contrast to Capeller, emphasizes the continuation of 'old' criminality in a new medium, rather than cybercrime as a new phenomenon (Grabosky, 2001). He also highlights some of the difficulties encountered in combating these crimes when they are committed across national borders. These include determining where the crime is being committed (from the host country or the recipient country), and therefore where jurisdiction lies, and identifying an offender through their virtual identity. There is also the problem of keeping national laws in line with each other and being clear about the nature of the offence. For example, laws that prohibit unauthorized *access* to computers for criminal purposes miss out those who have the legal access but who commit illegal acts using that access. As cybercrime becomes more commonplace, international action is needed to ensure that national, commercial and individual interests are protected from online attacks. International organizations have sought to establish procedures and legal frameworks to do so, such as the Council of Europe's Cybercrime Convention (Broadhurst, 2006). There is another fundamental problem with the policing of cyberspace. Whereas the 'real' world is relatively ordered in time and space, Yar (2005) argues that the virtual is disorganized in time and space and is therefore difficult to police in a routine and systematic way.

In seeking to theorize about cybercrime, sociologists have drawn upon many of the traditional perspectives and concepts, but, as McQuade (2006) reports, there have also been attempts to develop theoretical approaches to cybercrime that are integrated and specific to the technology dimension of the criminal act. Technology-enabled Crime, Policing and Security (TCPS) charts the complex relationship between cybercriminals and the forces of law and order. The focus here is on new forms of crime which are enabled because of the technological dimension. It is from within the criminal class that innovative forms of crime emerge and to which the police are largely reactive to, though also in an innovative and technological way. This leads to new regulations and laws to control the new aspects of the crime, which facilitates the management of the activity by the police and courts. As the innovative use of technology by the criminal becomes controlled, they then have to turn to further innovation or new technologies to keep ahead. Cybercriminals and cyberpolice are therefore engaged in a never-ending and complex interplay of technological, economic and security forces.

Terrorism and crime

With the emergence of globally organized terror groups such as al-Qaeda, sociologists have begun to explore the 'crime-terror continuum' (Makarenko, 2005). This continuum consists of formal and informal alliances between organized crime and terror groups, the adaptation of operational tactics of each type of grouping and the 'Black Hole syndrome', where failed states act as safe havens for organized criminal gangs, terrorist outfits and political warlords, often acting interchangeably or in concert.

Holmes (2007) argued that globalization created a 'borderless world' (Ohmae, 2005), which has made the interconnectedness of organized crime and terror groups more possible. However, he included the corruption of politicians and state bureaucrats as a key development in the global spread of organized crime and terrorism. In addition, he suggested that there was also a fourth player in this web of connections – and that was the personnel of the large corporations, whose activities swing between the licit and the illicit. What is being put forward is the evolution of constantly changing networks of legal and criminal entities that operate sometimes together to pursue their different ends. In including the large corporations in this shifting scenario, Holmes harks back to one of the initial concerns of Sutherland: that corporate crime could be seen as a form of organized crime. However, Holmes carefully maps out the limits of these arguments, pointing out the immense difficulty in carrying out any convincing empirical research in these areas, which leaves much of the evidence at the journalistic rather than the sociological level.

Not all criminologists accept that there is a convergence between organized crime and terrorism (never mind corrupt government officials and the executives of large corporations). Bovenkerk and Chakra (2007) have laid out the problems with assuming such a convergence. In the first place the motivations and ideology of the two groups is very different, with organized criminals focused on financial gain and terrorist groups on political ends. Ultimately, organized crime is a highly conservative business, while terrorist groups are in it to effect radical change. They conclude by arguing that only empirical research can settle the debate between those who argue for convergence and those who disagree – and that, as we have seen, is very difficult to obtain.

State crime and human rights

Kramer (1995) argues that the issue of state criminality has been often ignored by sociologists, mainly because they have tended to accept state definitions of what is criminal. He offers a more global view of the issue of criminal justice, placing the actions of nation-states in the context of international law, especially human rights legislation, and concluding that many actions of the state are themselves illegal. As crimes by states are often hidden and/or complex, the precise frequency and density of such crimes are unknown. However, in far-ranging descriptions of incidences of state crime across the world, Ross (2000) showed that state crimes were not unusual in countries as diverse as the United Kingdom, Israel and Japan. The different crimes committed by these states included military and security crimes, corruption, electoral crime, the abuse of state power and complicity in global drug offences.

Green and Ward (2004) defined 'state crime' as illegal activity perpetrated by state agencies or with their complicity. This includes corruption, state terrorism, abuses of human rights and genocide. State crime may result from the actions or the inactions of the state, or elite groups within the state, against their own citizens or the citizens of other countries (Kauzlarich *et al.*, 2003). It is often very difficult to investigate such crimes as there is no easy agreement that a crime has actually been committed. For example, there are legal disputes over whether the US-led Coalition invasion of Iraq to topple Saddam Hussein was legal under international law. Such debates are infused with political and ideological considerations and sociological positions are not immune from such influences. Michalowski and Kramer (2006) have argued that the invasion of Iraq could be conceptualized as a 'crime of empire', a consequence of the American neoconservative drive under President Bush to establish the United States as a unipolar global power, capable of securing oil supplies and establishing neoliberal economic principles in new areas of the world.

In looking at state crime, there is a temptation to see it as mainly carried out by colonial regimes in the past or by elites in underdeveloped countries in the present (Lenning and Brightman, 2009). Ward (2005) used the imperial regime of Leopold of Belgium in the Congo as an example of the brutality of state crime in the colonial age. He was particularly interested in the processes that led to an 'excess of terror', that is the brutalization of the indigenous population far beyond what would seem to be necessary to achieve the economic gains the colonial regime sought. While colonial excesses have often been explained as irrational actions that are counter-productive in achieving economic ends (Taussig, 2002), Ward used anomie theory and differential association to argue that the brutality did have a rationalist root. Belgian officials were under pressure from the Belgian state to produce large quantities of rubber in difficult circumstances. They were therefore in the classic position of 'strain' where they had to adopt illegitimate means to resolve the strain, which also involved them in discounting the moral cost of such illegal actions as slaughter, rape and mutilation. By associating with other officials who condoned such acts, a culture of excess built up, so that unspeakable acts became common place and morally unchallengeable. By employing other Africans in the colonial police and army, the Belgian officials were able to distance themselves morally from these excesses and blame both the African victims and perpetrators for them.

This process of 'othering' perpetrators and victims in order to absolve the 'real' state criminals has been well documented. Human rights law establishes the legal principle that 'the state is legally responsible for the action of its agents' (Jamieson and McEvoy, 2005). However, those leading states develop a range of strategies to distance themselves from the illegal activities of their agents, including plausible deniability through keeping themselves ignorant of such activities. One of the ways in which this is achieved is by creating operational units (security, counter-insurgency, etc.), whose activities are by their nature hidden, or by ignoring the activities of more shadowy, informal repressive groups such as death squads. In addition, by privatizing security, governments are able to stand at a distance from their actions in violation of human rights. The other side of this othering are the ways in which states seek to define the victims of human rights violations as beyond the usual borders of fairness. This may be done geographically, for example by 'exporting' suspects to countries with fewer legal restrictions on types of interrogation or by creating extra-juridical space such as the American detention facilities in Guantanamo Bay.

Sociologists have therefore been careful to establish that state crimes are carried out in the contemporary world and by all states and not just those in the developing world (Green and Ward, 2005). White (2008), for example, explored the use of depleted uranium (DU) munitions in wars, such as the Gulf Wars, by states, and the legal and illegal ramifications of deployment. The main point made is that DU cannot be contained to a battlefield, but after use spreads through the air to affect the health of civilians as well as combatants who have handled it. If it is shown to have harmful long-term effects, then its use could be defined as a war crime under international law. However, to define this use as a war crime would be highly controversial. The main defence for its use is that it is in the 'national interest' of the user and while there may be some harm done to some people the net result will be long-term gains for the majority. This view allows the state to practise 'denial' in relation to its actions, which may be echoed and supported by the citizens of the offending country (Cohen, 2001). Chancer and McLaughlin (2007) go further and argue that criminology itself may be complicit in this denial of harm as it stays largely silent on the complexities of state crimes. In the case of DU, denial has taken many forms, from outright denial, through the silencing and dismissal of experts, to the shifting of responsibility and blame, amongst others (White, 2008).

While a great deal of sociological attention has been focused on the more hard-edged illegal activities of states, such as mass rape or genocide, the emergence of human rights laws as a framework for judging the actions of states brings in the criteria of 'social harm' as an aspect of state crimes. The concept of 'soft atrocities' is used to describe the consequences of the economic domination and actions of the capitalist West (Farmer, 2005). The argument here is that it is the actions of capitalist states in resisting any policies that might reduce the gap between the richest and the poorest on the planet that leads to a situation where millions suffer from malnutrition, disease, economic displacement and starvation.

Green criminology

Another development in criminology, which has grown out of the focus on corporations and nation-states as criminal enterprises, is the whole area of environmental crime. In part, this development is the outcome of the wider focus that many criminologists have developed in the issue of 'social harm' as the proper focus for criminological investigation (see p. 11) and partly because of the porous nature of criminology's boundaries, so that new perspectives and approaches are incorporated within them. Variously called 'eco-crime' or 'environmental crime', the objects of interest of green criminology are many, but include a number of dimensions of social harm, for example crimes against the environment, against humanity and against non-human animals. They encompass the actions of very powerful institutions such as governments, whose capacity for harm is great, but also the actions of individuals, the accumulation of which can also have detrimental effects to the environment and those who occupy it (both human and non-human).

Specific areas of work covered by green criminologists include:

- 'food crimes', such as adulteration of food, but also the activities of the large supermarket chains in relation to their suppliers and the effects that their policies have on the environment;
- animal rights, from vivisection through animal abuse to the 'labelling' of animals by collaring or computer chip;
- the handling and disposal of radioactive waste, for example, the challenging of legal frameworks and the illegal dumping of waste.

From this list, it can be seen that green criminology has a wider remit than traditional approaches, in that its supporters are often concerned with the moral issues of corporate and individual activities that might be legal, but which do have environmental impact, for example the effects of European directives about fishing that 'manage' fish stocks in potentially harmful ways in the long-term (Beirne and South, 2007).

As green criminology is a relatively recent development, it has not developed a specific set of theories about its areas of interest, but draws upon traditional approaches, as well as the insights of other disciplines such as moral philosophy. However, its main thrust is towards a conflict view of green issues, precisely because it is often concerned with the activities of the powerful. While some criminologists do work with a strictly legalistic definition of green crime (Situ and Emmons, 2000), others adopt a wider conceptualization concerned with social harm (Lynch and Stretesky, 2003).

From the latter perspective emerged one of the key concepts of green criminology, which is the idea of 'environmental justice'. This has a particular focus on environmental hazards to classes of populations and is therefore 'anthropocentric' (focused on the effects on human beings). In this approach, interest is concentrated on the effects of environmental degradation on different classes, genders, ages, indigenous peoples, and so on. An alternative view (called eco-critical criminology in the United States) explores the relationship between human activity and the rest of the biosphere, including plants and animals, and this utilizes the concept of 'ecological justice', bringing the 'rights' of animals and the planet into play. The idea of ecological justice also tends towards a more global view of the problems concerning crime and the environment and more directly confronts the ability of corporations to frame national laws to allow activity that is ecologically harmful. The conflict over the exploitation of oil fields in Alaska is a crucial issue for eco-critical criminology in the early twenty-first century. There is thus a great deal of controversy amongst green criminologists around the notion of 'rights' and the relative balance between those accorded to humans and those which should be given to non-human species (Munroe, 2004).

Explaining white-collar and corporate crime

Hence from a relatively simple beginning, the study of 'middle-class' and 'corporate' crime has mushroomed. As the scope of 'white-collar crime' has widened, sociological explanations from different perspectives have been attempted. For example Passas (1990) has adapted Merton's Strain Theory to explain corporate crime. The strain that enables the white-collar criminal to commit crime in pursuit of profits is conceptualized as economic conditions in which the need to maintain profitability is paramount. For example cost centres in businesses may be under pressure from the central organization to maintain profits in poor trading conditions. One tactic that may be adopted by a cost centre is to cut corners and break the law in order to meet targets.

Control theories have also been applied to corporate crime in an attempt to explain it. These theories focus on the overintegration of the white-collar criminal into the materialist ideologies of modern capitalism. It is claimed that individuals in positions of authority who break the rules do so because they are so committed to achieving the material goals of society that they often get themselves into financial difficulty (Weisburd *et al.*, 1991). Such individuals deploy 'techniques of neutralisation' (Green, 1990) in order to suspend their normal commitment to the law.

More Marxist-inspired studies suggest that capitalism is 'crimogenic' (Box, 1983) in that the pressures of competition virtually compel the personnel of large corporations to commit crimes in order to maintain profitability. The 'real' criminals are those who control the firms because they set the ethos that sustains criminal activity against competitors, the public and consumers. The only thing that can prevent widespread corporate crime is a regulatory state that is prepared to enforce strict sanctions against corporate crime, regardless of the difficulty of proving intention to commit crime in the operations of large organizations. Where controls are weak, such as in the Third World, the predatory and criminal nature of modern capitalism is revealed. So, for example, Pearce and Tombs (1990) argue that businesses are 'amoral calculators' that would commit crimes as a matter of practice if they were not constrained by the threat of sanctions.

However, this approach has been criticized by Nelken (1994b, 2007) for offering an oversimplified view of the controls that affect the behaviour of business people. He argues that the respect of other business people, respect for the law and the activities of competitors can act as powerful incentives to obey the law. There is not an inbuilt tendency to commit crime among the business community. Moreover many organizations that do not face the same competitive pressures as business also engage in fraud and corruption, such as the army, the police and members of the government itself. Nor did the neglect of environmental and safety laws by the state enterprises of communist Eastern Europe suggest that capitalism, of itself, is a major cause of crime (Nelken, 1994b).

Hagan (1994) argues that, just as crimes of the poor are motivated by need, as a result of inequality in society, so the crimes of the wealthy are motivated by greed. Whereas the poor in an unequal society experience a lack of social capital, such as community links, which may lead them into crime, the wealthy experience too much social capital, especially trust, which endows them with the power and freedom from social control to commit large-scale white-collar crimes to their own advantage.

(K)(U)(I)

Exercise 5.15

In this chapter a number of Marxist concepts have been used, some of which are listed below. We would like you to use your knowledge and/or a sociological dictionary to explain the meaning of each of these concepts.

- Bourgeoisie
- Proletariat
- Dominant ideologies

- False consciousness
- Exploitation
- Socialist societies

- Class struggle
- Hegemony
- Discourse

Exam focus

1. Examine the Marxist argument that social class is the most important determinant of a person's criminality.
   Attempt to answer the following question, using the guidelines provided.
2. Evaluate some of the ways in which sociologists have explored the relationship between deviance and power.

Guidelines

The important aspect of this question is the multifaceted relationship between deviance and power. A good response would be to identify and discuss several of these facets in a critical fashion. Examples:

- The relationship between the police and the criminal (see Chapters 2 and 9).
- The relationship between police and the public (see Chapters 2 and 9).
- The societal dimension of power, for example the question of whether or not capitalism is crimogenic (see Chapter 5).
- The power of labelling (see Chapter 4).
- Policing policies (see Chapter 9).
- Corporate crime (see Chapter 5).
- Ruling-class crime (see Chapter 5).
- The criminal justice system (see Chapter 9).

Important concepts

Capitalism as crimogenic • Inclusion/exclusion • Seduction/
repression • Subcultural style • Corporate crime • Globalization
of crime • Militarization • Cybercrime • Social harm
  • Terrorism-crime continuum

Critical thinking

1. In the world of the 'credit crunch' and global recession, should the focus of criminological work shift firmly towards the study of corporate crime? What would be the difficulties that sociologists face in exploring that phenomenon?
2. Are crimes against the environment really criminal acts or just the unintended consequences of human economic activity?
3. What are the implications for civil liberties and human rights of the actions taken by governments to counter international terrorism? Does it matter if our rights are curtailed as long as we are safe?

Chapter 6

Realist Explanations of Crime and Deviance

After studying this chapter, you should:

- have a critical understanding of the origins of and reasons for the emergence of realist explanations
- be able to outline and assess right- and left-realist explanations of crime and deviance
- appreciate that within the right- and left-realist approaches there are a variety of traditions
- be familiar with postmodern views on crime
- have an understanding of Routine Activities Theory and Lifestyles Theory

From the beginnings of criminology, biological explanations such as that of Lombroso (1911) have periodically emerged to attempt to explain crime. In the immediate post-war period the dominance of social democratic explanations of crime tended to push biology into the background. However, by the 1970s, explanations informed by a belief in progress had come under strong attack because of their failure to prevent an increase in the rate of crime. At the heart of the 'enlightenment project' in criminology was the belief that social progress, in terms of rising real incomes and the provision of social benefits, would inevitably lead to a reduction in crime. However, the statistics suggest that the opposite has occurred – that, as prosperity has increased in the post-war era, crime has continued to mushroom. This failure by social democracy to halt the increase has led many criminologists to reassess the power of sociological explanations, and some have turned to biological explanations (more sophisticated than the nineteenth-century ones) to explain the continuation of crime in a society of plenty. For example many criminals have been 'medical-ized', that is, new categories of illness have been formulated to explain criminal behaviour, especially that of juvenile delinquents (see, for example, Box, 1980, on hyperactivity).

Breakthroughs in genetics during the 1980s and 1990s have refocused atten-tion on possible biological causes of crime. Rejecting the crude determinism of the early biological theories, criminologists have looked to sociobio-logical explanations, where biological similarities are seen to be mediated by psychological or social factors (Williams, 2004). However, this has not prevented the examination of brains of executed criminals, or the claim that '90 per cent of over-violent people had brain defects' (Lilley *et al.*, 1995).

Sociobiological explanations focus on the connection between biological predisposition and social factors, especially learning. For example, the connec-tion between low IQ and criminality is not seen as a direct one, but it is argued that low IQ leads to frustration with mainstream activities, the development of low self-esteem and social interaction with others who are similar, so that there is a general drift in the direction of crime and delinquency. The focus here is therefore not on genetic determinants of crime but on the genetic tenden-cies that manifest themselves as inherent responses to environmental influences (Fishbein, 1990).

In particular the work of Mednick, with various colleagues, has been influ-ential in this area (see for example Mednick *et al.*, 1987). Mednick argues that the autonomic nervous system (ANS) of each individual varies in the speed with which it reacts to stimuli, including the fear response. As habit-ual criminals do not learn from their mistakes, it is the slowness of the ANS fear response in such individuals that prevents them from learning conforming behaviour. Technical advances in medical investigations, for example magnetic resonance imaging (MRI scanning) have increased interest in sociobiological explanations, in which the combination of biochemical and environmental factors leads to risk assessments, where biological predispositions are rein-forced by negative social conditions to lead to antisocial behaviours. Some specific biological conditions, such as Attention Deficit Hyperactivity Disor-der (ADHD) have been connected to antisocial or criminal activity, especially drug use (Barkley *et al.*, 2004). However, even where individual factors such as ADHD can be identified as contributing to antisocial behaviour, Piquero *et al.* (2007) argue that they are strongly influenced by social influences and are not the 'cause' of crime. Conversely, some sociobiologists look for protective biological factors that reduce the risk of engaging in antisocial behaviours. For example, Raine (2002) found that young delinquents who did not go on to engage in criminal activity in adult life exhibited higher levels of ANS response than those who did go on to criminality – the obverse of Mednick's findings. In a more radical approach to sociobiological factors, Lynch *et al.* (2006) have suggested that exposure to environmental toxins such as lead and manganese, especially by those in marginal positions, increases the risk of engagement in antisocial and criminal activity, and, in particular, violence.

The reappearance of sociobiological explanations from the 1980s onwards was part of a more general reaction against 'idealist' explanations in favour of more 'realist' explanations of crime and deviance.

Ⓘ Ⓐ
Link Exercise 6.1

Read Item A in Chapter 3 and then write a short paragraph (no more than 100 words) that presents evidence to support the sociobiological explanation of crime and deviance.

Ⓘ Ⓔ
Exercise 6.1

Before considering realist approaches to crime and deviance we would like you to evaluate these ideas that are influenced by biology. Complete the evaluation paragraphs below by selecting the missing words from the list provided. The first paragraph outlines the strengths of biologically inspired theories and the second establishes the weaknesses.

Biological explanations accord with many ... explanations of crime and therefore often strike a chord amongst non-specialists. The approach offers the seductive possibility of identifying ... criminals. It is also of note that increased interest in genetic ... continues to push forward more sophisticated biological views of action.

Biological and sociobiological explanations are open to criticism. Firstly, it can be argued that the explanations are more ... with crimes where there is a biological basis, such as violence, but not so powerful with those far removed from biology, such as fraud. Secondly, one has to ask if biology ... how can the rise in crime be explained? Thirdly, if crime is a consequence of individual biology, then it is possible for criminals to ... their criminality as 'not their fault'. Fourthly, ... has uncomfortable implications for all political and moral positions. For example the notions of evil and good, or the large expense that would be incurred when treating criminals individually.

Missing words

- discoveries • biological determinism • determines • excuse
- effective • commonsense • potential

RIGHT REALISM

The emergence of right realism began in the United States as part of the general dominance of new right ideas in the 1970s and 1980s. In terms of crime and deviance, right realism can be seen as a response to the rise in the underclass associated with the disintegration of inner city communities when 'white flight' – the movement of white Americans from the inner cities to the suburbs – occurred. The right realists were also reacting against idealist conceptions of crime, which explained away crime as a social construction of the law and law enforcement agencies. They argued that crime was a 'real' phenomenon, experienced by people as a thing to fear. However, it was also part of a reaction against the social democratic assumptions of the post-war years, and therefore it rejected any idea of the poor being the 'victims' of wider social arrangements, rather stressing individual responsibility and free will.

Right realism closely follows functionalist assumptions of a consensus in society in which ordinary people are united in the belief that the criminal law is there to protect the lives and property of law-abiding people. The state therefore has a duty to deter criminal activity and severely punish those who break the law. Right realists are therefore concerned with identifying the 'criminal other' and justifying appropriate terms of imprisonment as the legitimate response to criminal activity (see, for example, Zimring and Hawkins, 1990). Some new right theorists are particularly hostile to the idea of social work, or the possibility of rehabilitating criminals (see, for example, Morgan, 1978). There is also a stress on the need for a programme to develop self-discipline among those who might end up as part of the 'yob culture'.

However, the new right do not share a unified perspective and can be divided into broadly libertarian and authoritarian wings. The libertarians, who have had little impact in Britain, have tended to adopt a decriminalization approach to illegal activities that have been termed 'crimes without victims', such as drug taking. They consider that while the state should be strong, it should not intervene in the private affairs of the individual (for an account, see Tame, 1991). The libertarian new right are particularly hostile to traditional sociological explanations, which they see as part of an 'excuse-making industry' that absolves criminals of the consequences of their actions. They see crime as the result of the free will of the individual, who is exercising choice, just like the many poor people who choose not to engage in crime (Bidinotto, 1989).

(E)

Link Exercise 6.2

Look again at your response to Exercise 4.2. In the light of your answers to this exercise, write a concluding paragraph that makes a case either for or against the decriminalization of drugs.

The more authoritarian versions of New Right Theory draw upon traditional conservative values in their approach to criminal activity. They reject the individualism of the libertarians and accept that there are important social values that influence the incidence of crime in society. While the libertarians would reject the category of 'moral crime' to describe crimes without victims, such as drugtaking, homosexuality and prostitution, the authoritarians argue that a strong moral code in society is a major bulwark against crime. So Morgan (1978) argues that it is the cessation of socialization into traditional morality, as a result of the welfare state's reluctance to impose values on individuals, which has been responsible for the rise in crime since 1945. Therefore the only way to combat crime and its detrimental effects on mainly working-class victims is the 're-moralisation of social life' (Marsland, 1988). That is, society must reject relativism (a situation where nothing can be absolutely true) and rediscover the traditional values that civilize a people, such as the nuclear family and sexual abstinence outside marriage. Critics, however, point out that it is far from obvious which moral values act to civilize individuals and that the appeal to traditional values often hides a misogynistic (woman-hating) and homophobic agenda.

Biosocial criminology: Wilson and Herrnstein, 1985

In seeking to explain criminality, Wilson and Herrnstein (1985) investigate why some individuals commit crime and others do not, and why different criminals exhibit different degrees of criminality. They argue that the reason is related to constitutional factors, of which some are biological and not just environmental or social. For example, they cite the work on body types and state that the mesomorphic (robust and muscular) body type is associated with the criminal, and that this predisposition runs in families. They argue that such predispositions influence the extent to which individuals can calculate the rewards associated with immediate and deferred gratification. It tends to be aggressive males with relatively low intelligence who seem to commit crimes in the search for immediate gratification, regardless of the consequences. Moreover the leniency of the criminal justice system in dealing with criminals reinforces the biosocial predispositions of a certain group in society. This population is to be found predominantly in the underclass, created through the dependency culture of the permissive policies of the 1960s and 1970s.

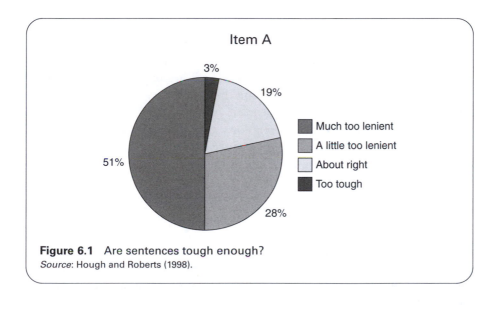

Figure 6.1 Are sentences tough enough?
Source: Hough and Roberts (1998).

Exercise 6.2

One of the issues addressed in the 1996 British Crime Survey (BCS) was the public attitude towards sentencing. As Item A shows, the sample population judged current sentencing policy to be too lenient. This accords with much new right thinking. However, the BCS attributes such attitudes to the interviewees' poor knowledge about crime levels and trends and their limited understanding of the criminal justice system. Study Item A and answer the following questions.

1. What percentage of the interviewees in the 1996 British Crime Survey think that the sentences handed down by the courts were much too lenient?

(A) 2. Give one reason why a tougher system of sentencing might reduce crime.
(E) 3. In general, would you say that sentences handed down by the courts are too tough, about right or too lenient?

(I)(A)

Exercise 6.3

Go onto the internet and find out what is meant by 'dependency culture'.

Wilson and Herrnstein's theory has been criticized for a number of reasons. One of the main criticisms has been the lack of precision of the concepts they employ, such as 'approval of peers'. These are difficult to operationalize because of their lack of definition and thus the theory is impossible to test. Moreover, they use research into identical twins to support their theory, and this is itself open to different interpretations. Gibbs (1985) argues that they use loose labels to describe the crimes with which they are concerned, so that they do not include white-collar crimes, which might serve to disprove the notion of mesomorphic predisposition.

Another criticism has been made by Currie (1991), who argues that the leniency of the courts, which is identified as one of the main reasons for the rise in crime, is not confirmed by the statistics. As the rate of imprisonment in the United States rose in the 1980s, so did the crime rate. Also, by stressing that human nature is a partial cause of crime, Wilson and Herrnstein ignore the existence of different crime rates in different cities of America and throughout the world.

Situational criminology and rational choice theory: Cornish and Clarke, 1986, 2003

Sometimes known as 'administrative criminology' (Young, 1986; pp. 99–102 above) this theory is drawn from classical economics and Hirschi's (1969) Control Theory. It explores the choices that individuals make when they find themselves in situations where the opportunity is presented to engage in criminal acts. It suggests that the final decision depends on the calculations made by the rational individual, balancing the chance of being caught against the advantages that might accrue by engaging in the act. The focus, then, is clearly on the situational aspects of crime and not on the underlying causes, such as culture or criminality. Rather, we would all engage in crime if the benefits outweighed the chance of being caught and punished.

It is important to realize that Rational Choice Theory does not suggest that the individual is always a completely rational calculator in situations of temptation. Cornish and Clarke accept that factors such as morality or a misunderstanding of the facts will affect the decision about whether or not to commit a crime. In addition, Cornish and Clarke (2003) argue that situational crime prevention is not just a question of making targets more secure, but that measures need to be taken to reduce provocations, such as might trigger a crime, and also to remove excuses, such as the plea of ignorance of the law. By including these dimensions, Cornish and Clarke insist that the aim of situational crime prevention is to change in small and subtle ways the behaviour of those who might commit crime. By nearly imperceptible alterations to the physical environment, such as the introduction of 'sleeping policeman', the incidence of crime can be reduced.

Cornish and Clarke (2006) also distinguish between 'involvement' decisions, that is an individual deciding to become involved in ongoing criminal activity and 'event' decisions, which are connected to a specific act of criminality. In the case of the former, they make the logical distinction between decisions of initiation, habituation and desistance, which they suggest are affected by different sets of contingent conditions and therefore need to be studied separately. In the case of event decisions, the process of decision-making by the potential criminal can be studied through the development of 'crime scripts', that is, the step-by-step procedures that lead to the actual act, in which the actor weighs up the risks of getting caught against the possible rewards to be gained.

By emphasizing opportunity, rational choice theorists have looked to situational preventative measures as one way in which crime might be combated, for example by better lighting, the installation of home security systems (see Exercise 6.4), redesigning high-risk areas, and so on (Cook, 1986). However, Cook goes on to suggest that preventative measures may only have the effect of displacing criminal activity to 'softer' targets. Clarke (2005) contrarily argued that preventive measures have a 'diffusion of benefits', that is they have a positive effect even beyond the locations where those measures are sited, so that security cameras in one car park also reduces car theft in adjacent car parks that have no cameras. On the other hand the theory also suggests that there are actually far fewer crimes than the public perceives, and that most people are not at risk of becoming victims of serious crime (Hough and Mayhew, 1985). Based on the 1985 British Crime Survey, Hough and Mayhew argue that the average victim has the same social characteristics as the average criminal (young, male, single and a drinker), terming this the 'moral symmetry' of criminal and victim.

Item B

Table 6.1 Ownership of home security measures among households that were victims of burglary and non-victimized households, 2007/8

Percentages	2007/8 BCS			
	Burglary victim			Not a burglary victim
	Burglary	Burglary with entry	Attempted burglary	
Burglar alarm	25	24	27	30
Double/dead locks	42	38	47	82
Outdoor sensor/timer lights	19	18	22	44
Indoor sensor/timer lights	10	9	11	25
Window locks	40	38	45	87
Window bar/grills	2	2	2	3
Security chains on door	19	17	23	34
Any of these security devices	67	62	74	97

Source: Kershaw *et al.* (2008).

Exercise 6.4

Ownership of security devices dramatically increased in the 1990s and 2000s. Item B provides evidence of the effectiveness of household security measures. Examine the item and answer the following questions.

1. What percentage of households who were not victims of burglary possessed window locks in 2007/08?
2. Using only the information in Item B, support the argument that protecting houses with security devices helps to reduce the risk of burglary. (Hint: compare the security arrangements of the victims of burglary at the time of the incident with those of the non-victims.)

Rational choice theorists are also interested in the levels of sanction required to deter the rational criminal from committing acts of crime. Piliavin *et al.* (1986) argue that increased sanctions do not have the effect of deterring crime because such increases do not get through to the consciousness of individuals who engage in crime. More importantly, the rewards for crime outweigh the perceived penalties. This is the situation in which crime is most likely to be committed.

Item C

Views on legal sanctions

Most offenders accepted that stealing cars was wrong, but typically did not view it as a serious offence. There was some evidence that a few offenders were responsive to the recent attention paid to car theft and now felt that the offence was considered more serious than it had once been.

Most claimed to be fairly immune to the risks of detection – though some 'macho' effect here cannot be discounted. Three-quarters put thoughts of being caught out of their mind, or felt they would not be caught. Nine out of ten claimed they were not deterred by the risk of apprehension anyway.

The thieves' perceptions of likely penalties if they *were* caught appeared unrealistic. Compared to the national picture of how car thieves are dealt with, they *overestimated* the chances of a custodial sentence, and conversely *underestimated* the likelihood of being cautioned. The youngest age group seemed most unrealistic about likely sanctions.

None of those who expected a caution, conditional discharge, probation or community service order reported being deterred. A quarter of those who expected a fine or driving ban saw this as a deterrent, though it is not possible to determine which was the greater threat. Half of those who expected custody felt similarly. When asked about the introduction of the Aggravated Vehicle-Taking Act (which came into force during fieldwork in 1992), over half said it would, or might, deter them.

Nine out of ten of those interviewed claimed they had been chased by the police – though most saw this as yet another occupational hazard. A few thieves welcomed the excitement of a police chase, though a third said that being chased was the worst thing about car crime.

Source: Nee (1993).

Exercise 6.5

In Chapter 3 we reproduced some of the findings of a Home Office study on car theft. Item C presents further information from this study. We would like you to use material from this data source to describe the extent to which car offenders perceive legal sanctions to be a deterrent to 'joy riding'.

James Q. Wilson, 1975

Wilson draws heavily on psychological explanations of crime, especially Behaviourist Theory. While accepting that the individual makes a basic calculation in terms of the rewards of and punishment for criminal behaviour, he argues that conscience is an important aspect of this calculation. However, conscience is not a natural phenomenon but a product of socialization through various agencies such as the family, peer groups, colleagues, and so on. Increasing crime rates are thus a consequence of changes in socialization, the rewards of and punishment for criminal behaviour and demographic trends. For example the changing proportion of young people in a population, who are seen as more likely to be violent, is a factor in changing crime rates. Similarly, changes in the opportunity to commit crime and the effectiveness of social institutions such as the family are important.

Because of the way that Wilson views the causes of crime, he sees only marginal ways in which social policies can affect the incidence of crime. For example, changes in family structure and the effectiveness of child-rearing patterns can only be achieved slowly.

The underclass: Murray, 1990

For Murray, the cause of the increase in crime, and especially violent crime in US and British inner cities, is the welfare dependency culture that has resulted from the welfare policies of successive governments since the Second World War. The provision of safety-net payments to the poor has resulted, according to Murray, in an underclass who have little interest in or incentive to engage in lawful employment, set up their own families or improve their conditions. Rather the underclass accepts a minimum standard of living, legitimately gained, and reject the labour market as a solution to their poverty, opting instead for crime.

Murray also focuses on single women in the underclass, who, he argues, deliberately get pregnant in order to obtain larger benefit payments and public housing. This has resulted in a high illegitimacy rate in both the United States and Britain, with many inner city families being headed by sole females. Because the socialization of their children occurs without a father, it tends to be inadequate.

This underclass engages in a disproportionate amount of violent crime, according to Murray, especially in the case of young men separated from the labour market by welfare dependency. Because the operations of the welfare state deter such men from setting up their own families, they are also denied one of the main ways in which they can construct an identity as a male. In the absence of this, Murray argues, young men turn to violence as an alternative source of male identity.

Critics of Murray argue that the concept of the underclass is an ideological construct designed to segregate a 'deserving poor' from the 'undeserving' in order to cut down the 'burden' of welfare payments to the taxpayer. It concentrates only on one small area of welfare policy and ignores the wider impact of government policy on other sections of the poor, such as pensioners, the disabled, and so on (see Frank Field in Murray, 1990). The 'real' focus of the thesis of the underclass should therefore be the welfare state in general, not just the presumed criminal activities of the underclass, for which there is no real empirical evidence.

Evaluation of right realism

(E)

Exercise 6.6

Listed below are some of the key weaknesses of right realism. We have also listed two of the strengths of this theory – your task is to suggest three additional strengths.

Weaknesses

1. The approach tends to engage in victim-blaming, and especially stigmatizes single mothers.
2. Right realism has a stereotypical view of life in single parent families, seeing them all as somehow inadequate.
3. Rational choice theories focus only on the immediate situation of the individual and ignore the wider forces that might influence his or her decisions, such as morality, conformity and social organization.

4. Rational Choice Theory overemphasizes the degree to which decisions are made on calculative grounds.
5. Right realists have a very narrow view of the 'costs' of crime, seeing these only in terms of the cost to propertied individuals or the taxpayer.

Strengths

1. Right realists draw our attention to the problems of the statusless young male in society, whose masculine identity is threatened.
2. Rational Choice Theory draws attention to issues of deterrence and prevention on a practical level.

LEFT REALISM

Left realism emerged in Britain in part as a reaction against the Conservative government's law and order stance in the 1980s (Young, 1988). It was also an academic reaction to the deviancy amplification school and left idealist approaches that took the side of the criminal.

Left realists take the side of the consumer, in particular the poor and disadvantaged who are disproportionately the victims of crime but have the least resources to combat it or gain compensation if they suffer from it (Jones *et al.*, 1986). The central belief of the left realists is that criminology should be true to the reality of crime, neither glamourizing nor marginalizing it, but treating it as an activity that harms others, especially members of the working class.

There is a shift in focus away from a preoccupation with the criminal to a recognition that there are four actors involved in crime: the forces of the criminal justice system (especially the police), the public, the criminal and the victim (see for example Young, 1994; Item D). The relationship between these actors varies according to time, crime and contingency (the immediate circumstances). Moreover left realists accept that biology is part of criminality. They do not accept crude biological determinism, but do believe that the young are likely to be more aggressive and that males are more violent than women. However, while biology may be a factor, the basis of macho and violent behaviour is to be found in the social arena, including the patriarchal values of society.

Item D

By means of the 'square of crime', left realists claim to offer a complete theory of crime that stresses the interconnections between the victim, the offender, the agents of informal social control (the public) and the state (agencies of formal social control). Young and Matthews (1992) offer the idea of the square of crime as a useful way of conceptualizing how crime is socially constructed. There are four 'actors' involved in the social construction of a crime and it is then interplay between these agencies that produces a social category that we call crime. By focusing on the complex processes of interaction between victim and offender, the state and the public, criminologists can avoid the worst of biological determinism and the arbitrariness of much Labelling Theory. As each type of crime will operate with a different set of combinations between these four players (for example 'victimless crimes' will have little input from the unknowing victim), then the distinctive characteristics can be established. It is clear for example that the relationship between offender and victim in corporate crime is of a different order to that in street crime and is therefore likely to produce different attitudes towards each type of crime. By establishing what is distinctive about the types of crime, government should be able to deliver more effective policies towards crime in general and crimes specifically.

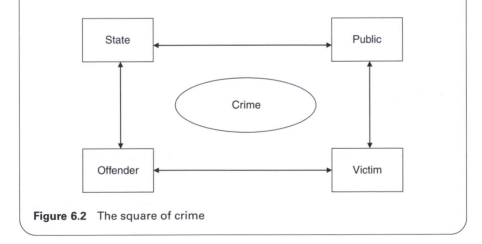

Figure 6.2 The square of crime

①Ⓐ

Exercise 6.7

Study Item D, and using the item and your own knowledge, explain the interplay that exists between the various elements of the 'square of crime' in the case of street crimes and corporate crimes. This is a difficult exercise and you may need to seek help from your teacher or lecturer. Let us start you off with a quick example. In the case of street crime the victim might be related to the offender in the sense that he or she belongs to the same social class and lives in the same neighbourhood.

The causes of crime

Marginalization

Crime, according to left realists, occurs disproportionately among the lower working class and certain ethnic minorities because they are more likely to be marginalized from the material rewards of society. In some respects this is related to the concept of anomie, associated with Durkheim (1960) and Merton (1938), but it is important to recognize that left realists do not just accept one cause of crime, but stress that there are a number of causes that vary according to time, space (geographical location) and social group. Marginalization is likely to be greatest when unemployment is high. However, in the present climate, when a generation has grown up assuming that unemployment reflects the failure of the social system rather than being a fairly ordinary state of affairs, the feeling of marginalization among the unemployed is likely to be intense. But this does not lead to an immediate increase in crime. The feeling of marginalization builds up slowly rather than exploding into criminal activity.

Relative deprivation

Left realists reject the idea that crime is related only to absolute poverty or just exists among the poor. On the contrary, crime can occur in any part of the social structure, as a result of individuals or groups feeling deprived when they compare their circumstances with those of other comparable groups (Lea, 1992). Absolute poverty is rejected as the sole cause of crime, because when the poor commit property crimes they tend to steal not necessities but luxuries (Burney, 1990). However, relative deprivation offers a powerful explanation because it focuses on individuals in all parts of the social structure who feel aggrieved with their share of material goods, and they therefore turn to illegal tactics to redress the perceived unfairness. The decision to engage in crime is a moral choice in certain conditions, so that sociologists can determine that the majority of the poor are honest and that the rich do commit crimes. Crime is not just determined by social conditions such as poverty.

Relative deprivation is used to explain not just material crimes such as theft, but also the occurrence of other forms of criminal activity. For example, when individuals feel they have suffered an injustice due to relative deprivation and no redress is possible, then other forms of deviant or criminal activity, such as drug taking, may be turned to in frustration.

Subculture

While left realists acknowledge the importance of subcultural factors (see Chapter 3), such as the lack of opportunity in working-class areas and the fatalistic culture this sometimes engenders, they also recognize that other features of the subculture may be important. In particular, Young (1994) argues that the working-class subculture has a macho definition of masculinity that stresses danger and risk-taking, and that this contributes to certain types of crime in the community, ranging from public order incidents to wife beating. American left realists such as Currie (1985) also argue that certain aspects of subcultural life, for example the absence of jobs and lack of variety in family forms, are connected to potential criminal behaviour. This should not be used as an excuse, however, for stereotyping the single-parent, jobless family as 'criminal', but it is a realistic attempt to address and resolve factors that, for some members of subcultural groups, are connected to crime.

Though the ultimate aim of some left realists may be the transformation of society into a socialist one, they are not content to wait for this before tackling the problem of crime. Given that it is the working class who suffer most from crime, left realists are concerned to modify the impact and reduce the fear of crime. However, given their hostility towards the capitalist state, they prefer to focus on the community as the level at which to tackle crime. In so doing they are in line with the reformist traditions of the working class and aim to empower them to make their situation better. In particular they suggest that the formation of local community groups to act as defenders of the community is an important way forward (see for example Einstadter, 1984). Lack of jobs and low pay are also issues that need to be addressed if crime is to be combated effectively (Currie, 1985). Left realists have also been involved in suggesting practical schemes to help the victims of crime, for example victim support schemes and victim–offender mediation programmes (Matthews, 1992). A further measure advocated by left realists is for ordinary people to become more involved in structures of power such as the magistrates courts, so that their voices can be heard (Taylor, 1981).

Evaluation of left realism

(I)(E) 1. You will see below a number of evaluation statements relating to the left realist approach to crime and deviance. Separate the strengths from the weaknesses and list them in a two-column chart.

Evaluation statements

(a) There are clear policies that can act as alternatives to crude control by the state.

(b) Left realism barely acknowledges the existence of white-collar crime and does not explore it in a meaningful way.

(c) There is a focus on masculinity and subcultural features as contributing to criminal behaviour.

(d) Left realists have created a category of the 'criminal', who is different from the rest of the population in some way, and they have therefore reverted to a simplistic social control model of crime.

(e) Left realism recognizes the importance of control agencies other than the state, such as social services and the factory inspectorate.

(f) It tends to assume that there is a clear difference between victims and offenders in the working class (Ruggiero, 1992).

(g) Left realists are somewhat idealistic about the chance of communities being able or allowed to police themselves.

(h) There is an appreciation of the reality of crime, as it affects all sections of the population.

(i) There is nothing new about left realism, it is just an amalgam of other theories such as anomie and situational control theories (Downes and Rock, 2007).

(E) 2. Now that you are familiar with the strengths and weaknesses of left realism and right realism we would like you to write under your chart a brief conclusion that establishes why you favour either the right realist or the left realist approach to crime.

POSTMODERN DEVELOPMENTS FROM REALISM

Many of the ideas of realism have been drawn upon by postmodernists when looking at the issue of crime. In particular postmodernists have developed the idea of identity as a way of looking at the phenomenon of crime. They also accept that crude control of the population by the state is not possible in the fragmented conditions of post-modernity, and therefore a more sophisticated analysis of social control is needed. Four main lines of analysis have been developed:

- constitutive criminology;
- discipline in postmodern societies;
- left realism and the underclass;
- sociology of crime and disrepute.

Constitutive criminology

This line of postmodernist thought proposes a 'constitutive criminology', that is, one that recognizes both the freedom and the constraints under which individuals operate. This entails the recognition that individuals are 'constituted', that is, they interact with the social world in order to produce the 'reality' of crime. These interactions may be of a 'legal' or an 'illegal' nature. This reality can be deconstructed and then reconstructed to form less 'criminal' realities. Human beings are therefore both self-interested and cooperate with others – their lives are a process, consisting of a biography (their past), a potential (their future) and the contingent present moment (the 'now'), which exists in social and biological circumstances that are often beyond the control of the individual. The biological circumstances are characteristics such as skin colour, gender, innate factors, and so on. The social circumstances consist of discourses and structures.

Discourses can be viewed as 'ways of talking' (statements that define the 'reality' of the social world). Discourses allow structures (or patterns of behaviour) to be formed, by providing continuity between the interactions of agents carrying out their individual actions. This triad of 'agency, discourse, structure' is discursive, that is, each is constantly being constituted and reconstituted by the actions of others in a process. One does not cause the other, rather they exist in relation to each other. It is from the interactions of individuals with others, in the context of existing and emergent discourses and structures, that crime emerges (Henry and Milovanovic, 1994).

Discipline in postmodern societies

Drawing on the work of Foucault (1977), it can be argued that society is entering a phase in which new technologies are able to regulate and control the body and its movements by means of heightened surveillance. The body has thus become the locus of power in postmodern society. In the same way that Foucault used the public execution of a regicide (the murderer of a king or queen) as a way of dramatizing the nature of power in preindustrial society, electronic tagging can be used as a metaphor for the way that individuals are treated as objects in postmodern society. Society has therefore moved from the disciplinary technique of public torture to the disciplinary technique of self-surveillance. That is, rather than the body being abused physically, new forms of punishment stress the way that the body is trained and supervised through the manipulation of the body by 'micropower'.

The transition from public execution to this new form of disciplinary power is exemplified by the move towards imprisonment as the main form of control in society. In the nineteenth and early twentieth centuries the purpose of prison was to allow experts, through observation, to make 'normalizing judgements' (evaluation of an individual's behaviour against a standard), so that the techniques of discipline – work, exercise, training – would produce docile citizens. In order to achieve this, total control of an individual's body in time and space was necessary – hence prison.

Ⓐ

Exercise 6.9

Draw up an extended version of the chart below and set out what you consider to be the main aims of imprisonment today. We have started the chart off for you by identifying two aims. You should provide a description of these and suggest at least two further aims, with descriptions. You might find Chapter 9 useful here.

Aims of imprisonment

Aim	Description
1. Deterrence	
2. Rehabilitation	

But the 'disciplinary society' is marked not just by the development of imprisonment as a disciplinary technique, but also by the 'swarming' of techniques to the everyday life of the whole of society, in what Foucault called 'No-power'. This means that at every point in their lives individuals are subject to the same techniques and normalizing judgements as prisoners, because the techniques fan out into everyday life. For example schools begin to monitor parents, social security officials vet the lives of the poor and computers are used to track consumers' purchases. In postmodern society, then, the gaze of accountability focuses on individuals' lifestyles – what they do, when they do it, how they do it. An example of the perceived normality of this increased surveillance is the widespread public acceptance of drug and alcohol testing in a whole variety of settings from athletics to the workplace. As Hanson (1993) argues, testing is a ritual – a 'disciplinary drill' – that causes docility among those subjected to it.

This process was reinforced in the 1980s by the moral panic about the nature of society as generated by the new right. This moral panic was itself a response to the collapse of traditional modernist certainties such as the family, separate gender identities, jobs for life, and so on. It was built on a romantic attachment to a mythological past of order and certainty (Denzin, 1991), not just in terms of crime but lifestyle as well. This moral panic constructed a vision of the ideal citizen (hard-working, religious, and so on) with a particular and worthy lifestyle. The effect of this was to extend the attempt to regulate individuals beyond the traditional criminal concerns and into lifestyle issues, such as drugs (both legal and illegal), illegitimacy, disease, and so on.

The main way in which society responded to this moral panic was to extend the microtechniques of surveillance into everyday situations. The emergence of new controlling bureaucracies (home-based probation services), new technologies (tagging equipment – see Exercise 6.10) and disciplinary rituals (the requirement to report once a week to the probation officer) meant that an individual, once intertwined with these bureaucracies, could be controlled and trained. For Foucault, then, disciplinary power was not triumphalist and 'in-your-face', rather it was modest and everyday, based on suspicion and minor procedures.

But 'disciplinary society' involves not just surveillance (which would be quite expensive to maintain if all 'offenders' had an individual looking over them), but self-surveillance. As Corbett and Marx (1991) have shown, much of the home surveillance of convicted offenders is computerized, with automatic phone calls and recorded responses. This system relies on offenders agreeing to the anonymous control to which they are being subjected. The offenders thus become agents in their own surveillance, a form of participatory monitoring. Offenders act as if they are being monitored by a real person – and thus engage in self-surveillance.

Item E

Electronic monitoring: key points

- During the second year of the trials, magistrates and judges made 375 curfew orders – more than four times as many as in the first year of the trials. This was due to increased use at the original courts and the introduction of this sentence in new courts. However, compared with most other disposals, curfew orders remain comparatively rare.
- One area (Greater Manchester) produced most of the orders – over two-thirds of those made in the second year. Once case-loads are taken into account, the rate of use was very similar for Norfolk (between 13 and 14 per 1000 cases) and approximately double the rate of use in Berkshire.
- The most common offences for which offenders received curfew orders in the second year were theft and handling, burglary, and driving whilst disqualified. Just under half of those tagged had previously been in prison, while three-quarters had received other community penalties in the past. More than four of every five orders made were imposed by magistrates on adult offenders and four out of five were successfully completed.
- Curfew orders tended to be used as a severe form of community penalty – effectively 'in competition' with community service orders, combination orders and custody.
- The average cost of a curfew order with electronic monitoring, if used over the whole of England and Wales, was estimated to be less than that for a probation order, but more than a community service order.

Source: Mortimer and May (1998).

Exercise 6.10

A good example of the use of home surveillance is electronic tagging to enforce curfew orders. In 1998 the Home Office reported the findings of three localities that were conducting trials on the use of electronic monitoring as a sentence. The summary findings are reproduced in Item E. Study the item and answer the following questions.

(K)(U) 1. Briefly explain what is meant by a curfew order.
(I) 2. According to Item E, what are the most common offences for which offenders receive curfew orders?
(I) 3. If it were to be used throughout England and Wales, would the average cost of a curfew order with electronic monitoring be more or less than the cost of a community service order?

Developing the work of Foucault, some criminologists have argued for the existence of 'spatial governmentality' in twenty-first century post-industrial cities (Beckett and Herbert, 2008). They highlight the changes in the use of space in the city, as it becomes increasingly privatized and public spaces contract. This is exemplified by the domination of the shopping mall in the post-industrial city. Access to privatized spaces is restricted through architectural forms, the use of gates and walls and through legal ordinance, such as park exclusion laws, that can remove an individual or group for trivial reasons. Such developments are categorized as 'post-disciplinary techniques'. These are post-disciplinary because they are not aimed at the micromanagement of the individual's behaviour, but rather the management of populations, so that potential criminals are excluded from the privatized spaces. The intention is not to arrest criminals and punish them, but prevent them from engaging in problematic behaviour on the 'home turf' of privatized areas, such as shopping malls, gated communities and the like. However, it is important to recognize that modernist, more coercive techniques of control continue to exist in the post-industrial city. Areas of marginalized populations continue to be heavily policed and access to restricted spaces is often controlled by guards, with the ever present threat of force to ensure compliance.

Left realism and the underclass

The concept of an underclass is, according to Gardinier (1995), part of the legitimation of increasing surveillance in society through the emergence of a 'crime control model', designed to get tough with crime. This model is a dual one, in that prisons are seen as one way in which the underclass can be removed both from society and from the unemployment count, but community sentences are seen as a cheaper way of dealing with the increase in crime. Christie (1993) argues that prison is the main way in which industrialized societies attempt to deal with the dangerous underclass. But the increased use of prison means increased costs and therefore decarceration (the use of non-custodial punishment) is also used to control this population. Thus the Criminal Justice Act 1991 established a continuum of punishment from custodial sentences to community service orders. From the left realist perspective, this measure has the potential to be progressive if the community sentences are genuinely connected to the community rather than being imposed cheap labour. Christie suggests that repoliticized communities could begin to develop types of community sentences that reintegrate the criminal into the community.

Item F

Table 6.2 Offenders sentenced for indictable offences, by type of offence and type of sentence, 2006

England & Wales	Discharge	Fine	Community sentence	Fully suspended sentence	Immediate custody	Other	Percentages All sentenced (= 100%) (thousands)
Theft and handling stolen goods	20	13	37	6	20	4	98.6
Drug offences	17	34	23	5	19	2	39.5
Violence against the person	7	5	41	13	29	4	41.9
Burglary	4	2	44	8	41	2	22.7
Fraud and forgery	16	13	36	9	24	2	18.3
Criminal damage	21	11	48	3	10	6	12.5
Motoring	3	26	28	13	28	1	6.1
Robbery	–	–	35	4	59	1	8.2
Sexual offences	3	3	27	6	57	3	4.9
Other offences	8	34	22	5	19	11	50.0
All indictable offences	13	17	34	7	24	4	302.5

Source: Self (2008).

Exercise 6.11

Study Item F and answer the following questions.
1. For which type of offence are you most likely to get an immediate custodial sentence?
2. In 2006, what was the most commonly used sentence?
3. Give one example of a community sentence issued by the courts.

Sociology of crime and disrepute

Social developments in the last quarter of the twentieth century have led some sociologists to suggest that traditional theories of crime and deviance, for example the sociocultural and interactionist approaches, are now so out of date as to be non-explanatory. The importance of a changed context for the commissioning of crime is that it changes the way in which some areas of society handle disrepute. Disrepute is a status associated with criminal activity, which can lead either to social disapproval by the majority of the community or to a sense of excitement and a rediscovered status within a disadvantaged and disorganized community. In particular, the new sociology of crime and disrepute points to the developments in globalization, changes in the labour market and developments in the relationships of identity, especially in gender and ethnicity, as fundamentally affecting the form and nature of crime in the postmodern world.

In particular Hagan (1994) suggests that the combination of the dual labour market – in which there is a core of highly skilled workers and a periphery of casual workers – and the global economy is having a devastating effect on the social fabric of Western societies, especially the United States. The net effect of these structural changes has been the loss of jobs in the core US labour market (Revenga, 1992). Any growth in the labour market has tended to be in low-wage temporary jobs. The result is increasing inequality in the United States.

The connection between these structural changes and the causes of increased crime are the processes of capital disinvestment and recapitalization (investing in new forms of capital – often illegal forms). Hagan argues that the effect of these structural changes is a loss of social capital (Coleman, 1990). Social capital means the existence of well-integrated family and community networks, often reflected in feelings of security and safety, for example women being able to go out at night without the fear of being attacked. The way that work has come to be organized to meet global pressures has led to a loss of this social capital, and therefore societal groups are unable to increase their actions to achieve community and individual goals.

In particular, Hagan (1994) points to three processes of capital disinvestment that are important in understanding the increase in crime. The first is residential segregation, in which the housing market is highly differentiated according to ethnicity (Massey and Denton, 1993). As job losses tend to be concentrated in areas where there is a high ethnic concentration, the disinvestment process disproportionately affects ethnic minorities. The second is race-linked inequality. The evidence suggests that, over a whole range of issues, black people suffer disproportionately from the changes resulting from globalization, ranging from the largest growth in unemployment to a decline in the real minimum wage (Bound and Freeman, 1992). The third process is the concentration of poverty. According to Wacquant and Wilson (1989), as working families and businesses move out of the traditional ghettos, there develop 'territorial enclaves of extreme poverty', where 40 per cent or more of the inhabitants live in poverty. As a result of this concentration the inhabitants of the hyperghetto have a loose 'labour market attachment' (Wilson, 1991). This is reinforced by the lack of mobility by individual families and the poverty of the rest of the ghetto, which acts as a constraint on the ability of individuals to reintegrate themselves into the labour market.

The effect of all three processes of social capital disinvestment is that people look for alternative solutions to their situation, including reinvestment in forms of social capital that diverge from the traditional ones. This process of recapitalization in deviant activity, the existence of which is supported by ethnographic and quantitative analysis, has been mainly focused on the issue of drugs. Because deviant service industries such as the drug market cannot be supplied by legal means, they come to be seen by those with loose links to the official labour market as offering a new opportunity. Because the inhabitants of the ghetto have little to gain from investing in the usual avenues of school and jobs (because the schools are poor and there are few jobs with family or friendship connections) they reinvest in drug dealing and petty crime (see Padilla, 1992, for an ethnographic account).

OTHER REALIST APPROACHES

While the realist debate has been dominated by the differences between the new right and the left realists, other realist approaches were developed during the 1980s that drew on older traditions such as the Chicago School (see Chapter 3). What united them with the right realists and left realists was their insistence on looking at the real phenomenon of crime, the opportunities that society presents for the committing of crime and the factors behind the decision to commit a crime. Three main approaches have been developed here.

Routine activities theory

Developed by Cohen and Felson (1979), routine activities theory draws on the ecological tradition of the Chicago School as well as the assumptions of the new right. Its focus is on everyday, routine activities that are required for the basic necessities of life, such as going to work, shopping for food, and so on. It is argued that if these routine activities are disrupted by social change, then social disorganization could result. For example, since the Second World War routine activities have taken place further away from home and this has provided people with more opportunities to commit crime.

For a crime to be committed there have to be three elements. First, there has to be a motivated offender (the target of much sociological research). Second, there must be no capable guardian, that is, someone who is able to prevent the crime from being committed. Third, there has to be a suitable target, that is, something worth the risks involved in committing the crime. An example of how social change influences these three elements is the increase in female employment over the last 50 years – this has increased the number of suitable targets (houses) that are left without guardians. It is likely that in these circumstances house burglary will increase. But the theory covers a whole range of other factors that influence the rate of crime, ranging from the availability of goods that are worth stealing, to the growth of car ownership (allowing escape) to the ubiquitous telephone, which aids the reporting of crime. Each of these has a differential effect on the commissioning of crime and the possibility of detection.

Because people's routine activities vary, their exposure to the risk of crime also varies. Moreover the concentration of crime in certain locations (because guardians are fewer and hence there is a concentration of targets) creates 'hot spots' that can be geographically determined by social mapping (Roncek and Maier, 1991). The hot spots are concentrated in predictable areas of the city – the disorganized inner-city areas. In addition, a target's suitability for attack in these areas depends on other contingent factors (Felson, 2002), such as value (the worth of the target to the offender), inertia (how realistic is it to remove things from the target), visibility (how far the target is within sight of the offender) and access (how easy it is to gain appropriate access).

This focus on choice, routine and opportunity has led some criminologists to advocate a strong shift in emphasis for the criminological enterprise. Rather than focus on the causes of crime, which entail a consideration of social and cultural factors at a distance from the criminal and their actions, the proper focus for a 'crime science', they argue, is to establish how crimes are committed and subsequently how they can be combated (Clarke 2004). This would tie criminology into police and security industries much more closely and reduce the sociological aspects of criminology through concentrating on the economics, geography and planning dimensions of crime.

International terrorism and crime

Since the events of 9/11 and the destruction of the World Trade Center in New York through terrorist activity, sociologists have turned their attention to the phenomenon of terrorism and its relationship with crime. Terrorism is distinguished from other forms of violence in that it is designed to create a climate of fear by random violent attacks on innocent civilians and is seen as being outside the parameters of 'normal' dissident activity (Wilkinson, 2006). The significance of the attack on 9/11 was that it indicated that terrorism was now a global phenomenon and not restricted to domestic dissidents committing acts of terrorism in order to promote change within a particular society. It is the growth of international terrorism that has fascinated sociologists of crime, as they considered the appearance of globalization and how this impacted on crime.

The criminological response to this was twofold. Firstly, sociologists began to trace the development of terrorism from a usually internal problem to a situation where terrorism had a global reach. Sociologists such as Hamm (2007) have argued that this represented a 'privatization of terrorism'. After 1945, terrorist activity was in the main low-level and state-sponsored, that is terrorist tactics were supported by state agencies in 'cold' conflicts with usually neighbouring countries, in the pursuit of state-determined political or ideological ends. An example of this is the support that the Soviet Union gave to anti-colonial groups that might from time to time engage in terrorist type activity. Low-level domestic terrorism continues to exist, for example in the activities of the Order, a neo-Nazi group in the United States. However, terrorist groups and movements have developed that are independent of state-sponsorship, or at least are not beholden to any state for supplies and logistical support. The emergence of al-Qaeda as a disparate collection of cells, unified by an overarching ideology and commitment to terrorist acts, is the classic example of this global development.

The result of this privatization is that terrorist groups increasingly turned to criminal activities to fund their more political and ideological work and to provide the material and training that they needed. This led to the second response of sociologists. They began to examine the links between terrorism and crime in a search for ways in which the secretive nature of terrorist activity might be penetrated and policies developed by anti-terrorist agencies to combat such groups. While most terrorist groups have used robbery and theft as a source of funds throughout their history, it is the scale and the extent of criminal engagement that allows for the privatization of terror. Many terrorist groups have used kidnapping or extortion as a way of gaining funds, but, more importantly, the global nature of terrorism has led such groups to engage in global criminal activity, such as money laundering, drug smuggling and sex trafficking. However, Hamm (2007) argues that this reliance on crime as a source of support is also a potential opportunity for anti-terrorist agencies to break up terrorist cells. By employing Routine Activities Theory, sociologists can establish what factors thwarted criminal activities by terrorist groups and apply these lessons more generally and through the development of transnational policing, as states have to become more cooperative if they are to subvert the international criminal activities of terrorist groups such as money laundering.

Sociologists have also looked at governmental responses to the growth of international terrorism and especially the use of the phrase 'the war on terror' by governments to describe their approach to the problem. The fundamental issue here is the relationship between human rights and the actions that governments take against terror networks. Welch (2003) argues that the idea of a war on terror is part of the construction by governments of a 'narrative of fear', in which a moral panic is created, through news management, that establishes al-Qaeda for example as a folk devil. This climate of fear is more intense than is needed if the actuarial risk of a citizen's likely victimization in a terrorist attack is calculated. The reason why governments need citizens to be fearful is that they wish to pass legislation that might contravene human rights legislation, or at the very least pose ethical challenges. Both the US and the UK have passed laws that increase the powers of surveillance over the population, for example in relation to email interception.

As governments engage in activities that are legally contested, such as the detention of suspected terrorists in Guantanamo Bay under President Bush (closed down under President Obama), they become embroiled in what Cohen (2001) calls strategies of denial. This might take the form of literal denial, where a government or its agents deny that the event has taken place at all, or interpretive denial, where it is conceded that the event has happened but it has been misunderstood or misrepresented. An example of this is in Afghanistan, where the targets for bombs are Taliban terrorists according to the Americans or innocent bystanders according to the Taliban. Hajjar (2004) draws upon a further level of denial called implicatory denial, which is where the event is conceded, but its significance is different from popular understandings, in order to explain the reaction of the US government to mistreatment of prisoners in Guantanamo. Here, a few individuals, acting outside of standing orders, are blamed rather than the system of detention itself.

Item G

The Patriot Act (2001)	The Homeland Security Act (2002)
The Patriot Act (2001) was developed in the USA as anti-terrorism legislation in response to the 9/11 attacks.	The Homeland Security Act (2002) created the new department of Homeland Security in the USA.

- The Act expands the surveillance and investigative powers of law enforcement agencies.
- The Act provides additional search and surveillance powers to law enforcement and intelligence agencies, including monitoring phone calls and accessing people's Internet Service Provider records.
- Finally, the Patriot Act offers a new search warrant that allows security services and the police to enter private property without the occupier's knowledge or consent and without notification that such a search has been carried out.

- This new department has responsibility for all issues in relation to immigration.
- It introduced new powers for the US intelligence services to search for data relating to individuals and groups and set limits on the data that can be released under the Freedom of Information Act.
- The Act revised 'open meeting' laws to allow government advisory committees to discuss anti-terror measures and related issues of national security, and offered new powers to government agencies to declare national health emergencies.

Source: Best (2006).

Exercise 6.12

(An)(A) 1. What are the implications, if any, of these Acts for basic human rights in the United States?

(E) 2. If these Acts do impact upon human rights, does it matter? Construct a sociological case either for or against the view that it does matter.

One outcome of the Patriot Act that has been of specific interest to socio-logists is Project Carnivore. This is essentially a spyware program (part of the Dragonware suite of programs) that can reconstruct email messages, web pages or any other data streams. It is used primarily to trace digital infor-mation that is indicative of a particular offence and the offender(s) behind it (Marx, 2002). Ventura *et al.* (2005) argue that Carnivore represents a pow-erful tool for social control and draw upon Foucauldian notions to suggest that it is used to establish discipline. They argue that Carnivore is not just about tracking down terrorists, but is a 'means of correct training'. It is Panoptican-like in that it has the potential to track down the smallest digi-tal flows, while remaining unseen itself. In operating at this invisible level of surveillance, it encourages a system of self-surveillance in which citizens are moulded into 'docile bodies' – the objective of governance in the twenty-first century.

Lifestyles theory

Using the notion of risk, Hindelang *et al.* (1978) explain why some individuals are more prone than others to be victims of crime. Their interest was spurred by the growth of victimization surveys (see Chapters 2 and 9), which showed that crime was much more pervasive than the official crime figures suggested. They argue that individuals' work and leisure patterns, which the authors call lifestyles, lead to differential exposure to criminal activity. They further argue that there are three elements to a person's life-style. First there is a rational aspect, in which choices are made to engage in activities that present more or less risk of coming up against illegal activity. So choosing to go to a rave exposes a person to drug taking more than if that person had chosen to go to a classical concert. Second, social position is important, because in general those higher up the social scale tend to have a lower risk of becoming vic-tims, mainly because of the locations in which they spend their time. Third, social role is important because there are certain expectations associated with them. In particular, the young are likely to socialize in areas and at times that present the greatest risk of victimization. The importance of this theory is that it includes an element of choice. Individuals can make decisions that increase or reduce the amount of risk they face on account of their social roles or social status.

Exam focus

1. To what extent is the 'new criminology' a valuable addition to our understanding of crime?

Attempt to answer this question in one hour under exam conditions (that is, without any books or notes). To do this you first need to revise your work, so plan carefully.

2. 'The idea that the working class are stigmatized as criminals through the workings of the police and the criminal justice system is not the full story. The working class are in reality engaged in higher levels of crime.' Discuss.

You need to be able to identify the theoretical position from which this statement comes. Once you have established that this is a realist approach, you should decide whether it is more associated with left realism or right realism, or whether you can draw on both when answering the question. Ensure that you address all the dimensions mentioned in the question. This requires you to be familiar with a wide range of issues in the sociology of deviance. Wherever possible you should cite appropriate studies to support the points you make. You will also need to come to a conclusion about whether you think the evidence suggests that there is a genuinely high rate of crime among the working class.

Important concepts

Sociobiology • Victimless crimes • Dependency culture • Rational choice • Square of crime • Underclass • Discourse • Disciplinary society • Disrepute • Routine activities

Critical thinking

1. Are there sufficient overlaps between right and left realism that might provide a more unified theory of crime?
2. How convincing do you find the Foucauldian tradition in explaining crime? Does it resonate with your own life experiences or is it too rarefied?
3. How far do your own 'routine activities' expose you to the risk of crime? What might you do to reduce any risk that you face?

Chapter 7

Crime, Deviance and Ethnicity

After studying this chapter, you should:

- be familiar with statistical data on ethnicity and crime and appreciate the limitations of this data
- have an understanding of early and recent theoretical positions regarding ethnicity and crime
- be able to evaluate a range of approaches to ethnicity and crime
- recognize patterns of victimization amongst ethnic groups

At every stage of the criminal justice system in the United States black people are disproportionately represented – for example, according to the FBI (2006) *Uniform Crime* statistics, blacks accounted for 28 per cent of all those arrested in 2006. In terms of imprisonment, black Americans are much more likely to be in prison than white Americans: while blacks make up just 13.4 per cent of the US population, in 2007 there were 3,138 black male sentenced prisoners per 100,000 black males in the United States, compared to 1,259 Hispanic male sentenced prisoners per 100,000 Hispanic males and 481 white male sentenced prisoners per 100,000 white males (FBI, 2006). It is also the case that the majority of victims of black crime are black themselves. The over-representation of blacks in the prison population in the USA is mirrored in Britain, where the black prison numbers per thousand population are four times higher than whites and about seven times higher than South Asians. In 2002, 15 per cent of all prisoners in the UK were black. This is in contrast with the under-representation of South Asians in prison (Hearnden and Hough, 2004). This difference suggests that no general notion of racism can be used to explain black imprisonment, as South Asians are as much the object of racism as the black population (explore this further in Exercises 7.1, 7.2 and 7.3).

Item A

Table 7.1   The prison population by ethnicity and gender, 2006

England & Wales	Percentages		
	Males	**Females**	**All**
White	*80.8*	*82.7*	*80.9*
Mixed	*2.7*	*4.1*	*2.8*
Asian or Asian British	*4.9*	*2.0*	*4.8*
Black or Black British	*10.6*	*10.0*	*10.6*
Chinese or Other ethnic group	*0.2*	*0.4*	*0.2*
Total (= 100%) (thousands)	62.7	3.4	66.2

Source: Self (2008).

Exercise 7.1

1. With reference to Item A, provide one example of an ethnic group within the Asian or Asian British category.
2. According to Item A, which ethnic group is least likely to be incarcerated?
3. Making use of the information in Item A, support the claim that blacks are over-represented and Asians under-represented in the prison population.

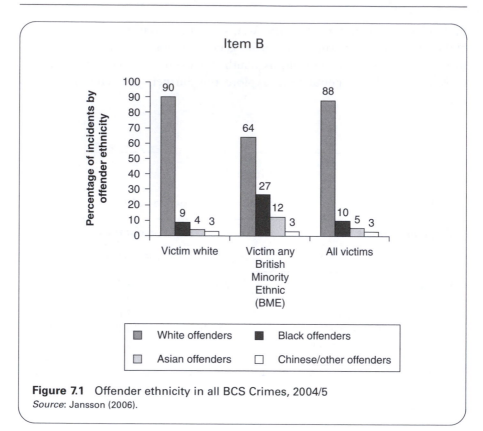

Figure 7.1 Offender ethnicity in all BCS Crimes, 2004/5
Source: Jansson (2006).

Exercise 7.2

Little is known about ethnic offenders before they reach prison, and much of what is known is based upon self-reported offending through the British Crime Survey. Some of the findings of the 2004/5 BCS are presented in Item B. Carefully examine the item and answer the following questions.

1. What does Item B show to be the most common type of ethnic relationship between offenders and victims?
2. What percentage of Chinese offenders admitted to an incident involving another British minority ethnic person?
3. Item B suggests that black and white people have higher rates of offending, while South Asian groups have significantly lower rates. Using only the information in Item B, provide statistical evidence to support this conclusion.

Item C

Asian involvement in urban gangs

Sociologist interest in urban gangs has often had an ethnic dimension, with most attention being focused on West Indian or Afro-Caribbean gangs, such as the Yardies. When looking at South Asian populations, sociologists have tended to lean to the stereotype that South Asians are more quiescent, docile, less engaged with criminality and more likely to be a victim than a perpetrator of crime. This stereotype has been challenged, partly as a result of urban unrest, which saw young South Asians on the streets in Bradford, Burnley, etc., and partly because of the growth of a more militant form of Islam, in which young South Asians in particular are vocal in counteracting what they perceive as the Islamophobia of British political discourse.

During the 1990s, there was believed to have been an upsurge in South Asian offending, especially amongst those of Bangladeshi and Pakistani descent, although the prison figures also showed that the number of South Asian prisoners was roughly commensurate with their distribution in the population as a whole. However, this increase in South Asian offending was not necessarily linked to an increase in criminality amongst those populations generally, but was a by-product of the age structure of those populations. Crucially, the Pakistani and Bangladeshi originated groups have a demographic profile weighted significantly towards the young, with nearly half of these groups being in the 0–15 age bracket. As offending is highly related to age, with young people much more likely to engage in criminal actions than older populations, this means that there should be a 'natural' increase in offending amongst these groups. The picture was not totally clear however as, in the 1990s, statistics were not kept on individual BME groups and so the more affluent and law-abiding Indian community was included in the figures for South Asian populations.

This view that there was an upsurge in criminality amongst these groups has also been challenged. One point of attack is that these populations have always been skewed towards the young and therefore, if crime is mainly a phenomenon of age, then we would have had high levels of criminal behaviour for some time, and not just as an 'upsurge'. As an alternative explanation for any increase in criminality amongst South Asian groups, we should instead look to the different values and behaviour of young South Asians as they find their own way of living in Britain, with some becoming less tied into their parents' culture and others seeking a reaffirmation of that culture, but in peculiarly British ways. We do know that boys in particular, who have weaker social bonds to family, religion and community, whatever their ethnicity, are more likely to engage in deviant activity, and it is perhaps this process that we are seeing.

Exercise 7.3

You will now appreciate that official statistics and self-reported data show that South Asians are less likely to commit crime than other ethnic groups. Moore (1996a) attempts to explain the relative lack of Asian involvement in crime in terms of economic and cultural factors. However, Moore does recognize that a limited increase in Asian crime may occur as the number of young Asians in the population increases. We would like to draw your attention to the possibility of a growing Asian crime problem by referring you to Item C. Read the item and answer the following questions.

(K)(U) 1. What do sociologists mean by the term 'stereotype'?

(K)(U) 2. Using Item C and other sources, explain how the emergence of South Asian
(An)(E) criminality can be explained in terms of the age structure of the ethnic population, police practices, changes in cultural identity, economic deprivation and racial discrimination. We would also like you to evaluate each of the suggested explanations in terms of their strengths and weaknesses. Record your responses to this exercise in a chart copied from the one below.

Explaining a possible upsurge in Asian criminality

Determining factor	Explanation	Evaluation
Age structure of the ethnic population		
Police practices		
Changes in cultural identity		
Economic deprivation		
Racial discrimination		

STATISTICS AND COMMON SENSE

One of the consequences of this statistical association between black people and crime is that common sense assumptions about criminals tend to focus on the ethnicity of perpetrators of crime to the extent that there is a generally held view that the majority of street crime is committed by black Afro-Caribbean or Afro-American males. For example Allan and Steffensmeier (1989) argue that factors such as lack of access to the labour market are strongly associated with high rates of arrest of young people and that there is a stronger correlation between unemployment and arrests in areas of high ethnic concentration.

There is also a whole range of evidence to suggest that there are high murder rates in areas of the United States with a high concentration of poor families. Because areas of concentrated poverty also tend to be racially segregated, this also means that African Americans suffer proportionately higher levels of homicide (see, for example, Lowry *et al.*, 1988), in the main, at the hands of other African Americans.

Item D

Homicide rates in the USA in 2005 declined to levels last seen in the late 1960s:

- the homicide rate nearly doubled from the mid-1960s to the late 1970s;
- in 1980, it peaked at 10.2 per 100,000 population and subsequently fell off to 7.9 per 100,000 in 1984;
- it rose again in the late 1980s and early 1990s to another peak in 1991 of 9.8 per 100,000;
- from 1992 to 2000, the rate declined sharply. Since then, the rate has been stable.

The demographic characteristics of homicide victims and offenders differ from the general population. Based on data for the years 1976–2005:

- Blacks are disproportionately represented as both homicide victims and offenders. The victimization rates for blacks were 6 times higher than those for whites. The offending rates for blacks were more than 7 times higher the rates for whites.
- Males represent 77 per cent of homicide victims and nearly 90 per cent of offenders. The victimization rates for males were 3 times higher than the rates for females. The offending rates for males were 8 times higher than the rates for females.
- Approximately one-third of murder victims and almost half the offenders are under the age of 25. For both victims and offenders, the rate per 100,000 peaks in the 18–24 year-old age group.

Source: FBI (2006).

Exercise 7.4

ⓘ 1. What evidence is presented in Item D to suggest that homicide is mainly a young black social problem?
ⓘ 2. Identify the trend in homicides between the 1950s and the 2000s.
Ⓐ 3. How might sociologists account for the disproportionate appearance of certain sections of the African-American population as both offenders and victims of murder?

In Britain the statistical relationship between ethnicity and crime is very complex. In the 1970s the police argued that ethnic minorities were not engaged in a disproportionate amount of crime, but by the 1980s the Metropolitan Police were suggesting that there was a correlation between the concentration of ethnic minorities and the rate of robbery (Holdaway, 1996). Bowling and Phillips (2002) argued that this was because of ongoing conflict between the police and black communities that led to both the police focusing on collecting statistics about 'black crime' and the media creating links between the images of black men and criminality. However, this statistical connection can be strongly criticized, for example by applying the view of Morris (1976) that arrest rates, upon which these correlations are based, are not the same as the crime rate. Also, reliance on a victim's identification of the 'race' of an offender is not a safe way of conducting victimization studies, as this is influenced by media images and the 'sociological effect'. That is, as sociological 'knowledge' about the connection between ethnicity and crime becomes generally known, a commonsense assumption grows that crime is linked to ethnicity. Finally, collapsing sections of ethnic minority populations, such as the old and young, into one category of location might hide an active but small group engaged in criminal activity. This means that a very small number of (usually young) individuals may be committing most of the crimes in an area that just happens to have a concentration of ethnic minorities. More complex statistical calculations indicate that, when factors such as socioeconomic status and differential police activity are taken into account, there are still higher levels of arrest for assault and robbery among ethnic minorities, and especially black youths (Stevens and Willis, 1979).

However, other sociologists have rejected the idea that ethnic minorities are more 'criminal' than other groups in society. Instead they argue that ethnic minorities are over-represented in the criminal statistics because of the activities of the law enforcement agencies. Research has established that the police tend to stop and search young black males more than other social groups (see for example Reiner, 1985). Nor can the recruitment of more ethnic minority police officers necessarily change this – as Cashmore (1991) argues, this is more about the practicalities of policing the black underclass than any indication of integration. The result of hard policing in black areas is the criminalization of black youth and their being stereotyped as necessarily involved in criminal activity (for example see Keith, 1993).

Holdaway (1996) shows that participant observation and observational studies of police culture demonstrate the pervasiveness of negative views of ethnic minorities among lower-rank officers. However, the stereotypes employed are not static but change over time. Thus references to immigrants in the context of ethnic minority populations have diminished and opposition to racial comment has become more common during the 1980s and 1990s.

(K)(U)
(A)(E)

Exercise 7.5

For Exercise 4.11 we instructed you to conduct a methodological task relating to unstructured interviews. This type of exercise is important as you are more likely to enhance your performance on theory and methods questions if you reinforce your understanding of methodology across a range of topics. Bearing this in mind, we would like you to carry out a similar exercise on observational research. You need to complete a chart copied from the one over the page, based on your understanding of the observational methods used in sociology.

Observational research

Descriptions of method (remember there are different types of observational research)	Perspective	Examples of studies in the area of crime	Sample size	Reliability	Validity	Advantages	Disadvantages
		1. Patrick (1973)				1. Possible to build up trust with those studied.	1. If done overtly behaviour can be changed.
		2.				2.	2.
		3.				3.	3.
		4.				4.	4.
		5.				5.	5.

Another dimension of crime statistics and ethnicity is that ethnic minorities are often the victims of crime. In Britain, the British Crime Surveys (see for example Mayhew *et al.*, 1993) indicate that the fear of crime is high in areas with large concentrations of ethnic minorities. For ethnic minorities, crime with a racial motivation is a distinct concern, and the British Asian population feels particularly vulnerable to racial attack (carry out Exercise 7.6 to develop your understanding of the complexities here). However, victim surveys show a much more complicated pattern of victimization than a simple ethnic-majority/ethnic-minority split. For example small-scale surveys of localities indicate that there are exceptions to the greater victimization of blacks. Jefferson and Walker (1993) show that in some areas of Leeds whites are subjected to more victimization than blacks. The pattern of racial violence is even more complicated, with surveys showing that the Chinese and Jewish populations are often vulnerable to racial attack, and the isolated Asian shopkeeper in a predominantly white area is as likely to be a victim of 'racial terrorism' as those in areas with a high ethnic concentration (Gordon, 1986). The involvement of right-wing groups such as the British National Party in racial violence is well documented and paralleled throughout Europe (Oakley, 1993).

Item E

Table 7.2 Number of racist incidents recorded by the police (to nearest 1000)

Year	1996–7	2004–5
Number of incidents	13,000	58,000

Source: Home Office (2006).

Exercise 7.6

Examine Item E and suggest two reasons why the number of racist incidents recorded by the police has increased so dramatically.

There are great methodological difficulties in defining and therefore measuring the extent of racial violence in Britain. Problems include identifying the motivation of an attacker, defining ethnicity in different ways, the different methods and processes involved in the recording of incidents by the police, and so on. Nevertheless certain patterns do emerge from the national data. The majority of racial attacks are perpetrated by young white males, but Ray *et al.* (2004) in a study of racist attackers argued that the perpetrators did not conform to stereotypes associated with 'hate crimes'. In particular, victims were not chosen just on the basis of their ethnic category in some random manner, but were rather known to the attacker, though usually not well. However, the racist attackers did not come in the main from mixed areas, but were concentrated in deprived working-class areas that were predominantly white. The victims of racist crimes (abuse and not just violence) are also evenly balanced between men and women, but women are more likely to be multiple victims, that is, to suffer repeatedly from racial harassment. Most verbal assaults are not reported to the police, especially as the clear-up rate for such offences is low (Docking and Tuffin, 2005). The Macpherson Report into the death of Stephen Lawrence and the police investigation that ensued highlighted the problem of 'institutional racism' in the police service and triggered a number of policies to ensure equal treatment to ethnic minority victims of crime (Webster, 2007).

EXPLANATIONS OF BLACK CRIMINALITY

Traditional approaches to ethnicity and crime

The link between 'race' and criminal violence was first explored by Shaw and McKay (1931), who linked delinquency to areas of social disorganization (see pp. 61–3). Racial minorities in the United States are therefore linked to violent crime because they are more likely to live in areas of social disorganization. This finding has been supported by Messner (1983), who argues that the high rate of violence among ethnic minorities is linked to the economic deprivation they suffer. As they become frustrated with their lack of opportunity, they turn to aggressive behaviour as a release. However, Liska and Bellair (1995) argue that this is to ignore the effect of crime rates on the ethnic composition of neighbourhoods. They suggest that it is precisely a reputation for violence that has caused those who can afford it to move away from such neighbourhoods, leaving the economically deprived, often black, population behind.

Merton's (1938) Economic Strain Theory can also be utilized to address the link between criminal behaviour and racial minorities. Again, Messner (1983) shows that the high rate of violence among ethnic minorities in the United States is connected to the economic deprivation that is disproportionately experienced by that section of the population. That is, economic deprivation among ethnic minorities leads to frustration, which in turn leads to violence.

Economic deprivation by ethnic group

Item F

Table 7.3 Position of children within the distribution of household disposable income: by ethnic group, 2004/5

United Kingdom	Percentages				
	Bottom fifth	Next fifth	Middle fifth	Next fifth	Top fifth
White	23	24	22	18	14
Mixed	31	33	20	9	7
Asian or Asian British	45	27	11	7	9
Indian	34	22	15	11	18
Pakistani/Bangladeshi	55	31	8	4	2
Black or Black British	32	22	19	15	12
Black Caribbean	23	25	21	18	13
Black African/Other Black	41	20	16	11	11
Chinese or Other ethnic group	37	21	21	11	10

Source: Self and Zealey (2007).

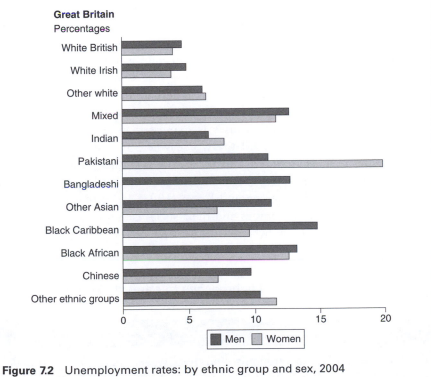

Figure 7.2 Unemployment rates: by ethnic group and sex, 2004
Source: Babb *et al.* (2006).

⬚⬚ Exercise 7.7 ⬚⬚

ⒾⒶ 1. To what extent does the information in Item F support the view that eco-
Ⓔ   nomic deprivation is concentrated among the ethnic minority population in
       Britain?
Ⓐ 2. Apart from the indicators of deprivation shown in Item F, identify one other
      measure that could be used to indicate economic deprivation.

Subcultural theory (see Chapter 3) suggests that some subcultures, of which
ethnic subcultures are a major example, are more susceptible to violence than
others, either because they are more tolerant of violence or because the subcultures themselves encourage it (for example, see Luckenbill and Doyle, 1989).
As we have seen, Liska and Bellair (1995) go further and suggest that crime
levels influence individual decisions about where to live, which in turn affects
the degree of ethnic concentration in different areas. Those who can afford
to move away from areas with more criminal activity do so. Wilson (1987)
argues that those with sufficient resources to move are disproportionately
white, which intensifies the ethnic concentration in the areas they are leaving. The effect of this is to create criminal subcultures that are predominantly
composed of ethnic minorities.

Black crime is therefore seen as a reaction to the social and economic
inequality that black Americans in particular experience. Blau and Blau (1982)
argue that the frustration this causes is expressed in acts such as physical
violence and homicide, made all the worse where it is based on ascriptive
characteristics such as ethnicity. This is because it clashes with the American
Dream, where all men and women of talent are supposed to be able to rise
up the social hierarchy. Peterson and Krivo (1993) argue that the residential
segregation of black communities and their social isolation from mainstream
America leads to aggression, which is the prime cause of the high rate of black
homicide.

Evaluation of the traditional approaches to ethnicity and crime

Ⓔ ⬚⬚ Exercise 7.8 ⬚⬚

Listed below are three strengths and two weaknesses of the traditional
approaches to ethnicity and crime. To provide a thorough evaluation of these

approaches we would like you to suggest one other strength and two other weaknesses.

Strengths

1. They relate the extent of crime to the real social and economic conditions faced by ethnic minorities.
2. They have placed ethnic minority frustration in the context of prevailing ideologies.
3. A connection is made between the rate of criminal activity and the subcultures of the areas in which high levels of crime are recorded.

Weaknesses

1. They take the recorded level of crime to represent the real level of crime in society.
2. Traditional approaches do not explain why all the ethnic minority inhabitants of socially and economically disorganized areas do not behave in the same criminal way.

Left realism, ethnicity and crime

Left realist sociologists (see Chapter 6) start from the basis that they have to deal with the 'real' phenomenon of crime and therefore have to address directly the association between ethnic minorities and criminal behaviour. However, they reject the simplistic view that the higher crime rate among black ethnic minorities reflects the racism of the police and criminal justice system alone. This would be, they argue, to reject any link between deprivation and crime. They have therefore drawn upon the concepts of marginalization, relative deprivation and subculture when looking at ethnicity and crime.

Marginalization

Simpson (1991) argues that the increase in poverty in the United States during the 1980s and 1990s has disproportionately affected lone parent families, of whom one-third are black. This economic marginalization is said to be a major factor in the violent behaviour of young black men, especially in areas of high social disorganization. However Gibbs and Merighi (1994) argue that young black males are marginalized by their ethnicity and their age as well as their socioeconomic status. This marginalization is due to 'hypersegregated housing' and their experiences in the education system and the labour market. This results in the development of identities that recast the sexual, social and economic formulations of mainstream society.

Taylor (1989) argues that this is particularly true of young blacks who do not have a male in their family to act as a traditional role model for masculine identity. They tend to have neither a strong ethnic nor a strong gender identity and feel anger and frustration at their marginal economic situation. With neither the skills nor the educational qualifications to fulfil the traditional masculine role as provider, they develop pseudomasculine identities that seek confirmation through hustling on the street, and then they drift into more serious forms of criminal activity. On the street, activities such as drugs dealing provide young blacks with an income (Brunswick, 1988) and possessing a gun, according to Fingerhut *et al.* (1992), supports a masculine identity that is rooted in 'getting the job done' no matter how dangerous. In the United States, Bourgois (1996) has charted how young Puerto Ricans are deprived of the traditional route to establishing patriarchal respect through work and turn to crime and deviance, such as involvement in drugs and sexual permissiveness, in their search for respect.

Relative deprivation

Lea and Young (1982) argue that the relative deprivation (see pp. 173–4) felt by many black youths is an important factor in their engagement in criminal activity, but this cannot, of itself, explain the rising crime rate of young black males in the 1980s. They suggest that the police, with their prejudiced culture, responded to this real rise in the rate of black offending by intensifying the policing of black communities, thus further increasing the arrest figures for young black males. Thus relative deprivation, exacerbated by the increase in youth unemployment during the 1980s, began a process of criminalization for large sections of the black population.

Culture and subculture

Sellin (1938) argued that, when the cultures of two communities conflict, crime is likely to be the outcome. This 'primary culture conflict' is most obvious when the norms of conduct in an immigrant community offend against the laws (the 'legitimized conduct norms') of the dominant group in the host society, for example Islam allows men to have a number of wives but in Britain bigamy is against the law.

Curtis (1975) argues that there is a 'subculture of violence' in black communities that accounts for the higher levels of violence they experience. This subculture is linked to the economic discrimination and racism that black people encounter in society. Messner and Golden (1992) assert that, where racial discrimination runs deep, the incidence of violence among white communities as well as black is likely to be high. However, Lea and Young (1984) stress that there needs to be a much more sophisticated understanding of the role of subculture in criminal behaviour. They argue that there is not just one subculture emerging from the experiences of ethnic minority immigrants who have settled in the urban areas of Britain, but many. The immigrant communities bring with them many different cultures and histories, and third-generation ethnic minorities react to the culture of their parents and that of the white community in differing ways.

Bursik and Grasmick (1993) consider that the lack of community structures in areas of social disorganization restricts the opportunity for young blacks to participate in organized leisure-time activities. As a result there is a large amount of unsupervised teenage activity, and this is correlated with high levels of robbery and personal violence. Where funding has been provided for leisure-time activities, gangs have been more integrated into community life, with a consequent drop in illegal gang activity.

The use of the word 'gang' in relation to young ethnic subculture is highly controversial in the UK. American researchers seem more at ease with describing groups of young people engaged in semi-legal or illegal activity as gangs, but, in Europe, sociologists have been more wary in the way that they deploy the term. This is at least partly because they are concerned that the labelling of such groups as 'gangs' may contribute to their marginalization and increase their commitment to criminality (Hallsworth and Young, 2004). Add to this the association that is often made between gangs and certain ethnic groups and the term is even more problematic. By emphasizing the ethnic dimension, sociologists and journalists are in danger of stigmatizing minority ethnic groups, when gangs appear in communities regardless of ethnic composition. Indeed, gangs tend to reflect the ethnic composition of the communities they inhabit and if that community is ethnically diverse, so are the gang members (Aldridge *et al.*, 2008).

Evaluation of left realist approaches to ethnicity and crime

(E)   **Exercise 7.9**

Listed below are four key strengths of left realist views on ethnicity and crime, but just one weakness. To achieve a balanced evaluation we would like you to suggest three other weaknesses.

Strengths

1. The approach embeds the analysis of crime in the culture and structure of local communities.
2. Left realists recognize the operation of wider economic social forces that act upon ethnic minorities in high crime areas.
3. Left realism accepts that the racial discrimination experienced by ethnic minorities has a real effect on behaviour.
4. Left realists offer community solutions to the problem of crime.

Weakness

1. Left realists do not address the issue of why different members of ethnic minority groups may acquire different masculine identities.

Social construction approaches

A different approach to ethnicity and crime has been taken by interactionist sociologists (see Chapter 4), who focus on the way that the criminal statistics have been socially constructed to over-represent the ethnic minorities. There are three main aspects to the labelling of ethnic minorities as 'criminal':

- bias among the public in the reporting of crime;
- police bias;
- judicial bias.

Public bias in the reporting of crime

There has been some debate among sociologists about the propensity for crimes committed by blacks to be reported to the police more often than those committed by whites. However, the patterns suggested by the statistics are hard to disentangle and are fraught with problems. For example it is not always clear what is meant by 'non-white'. If the public categorize a glimpsed perpetrator as non-white, do they mean Asian, Mediterranean, or what? In about 40 per cent of the crimes reported to the police the victim cannot describe the criminal at all. Visible crimes such as 'street crime' are more likely to be committed by blacks, and are therefore more likely to appear in the statistics according to ethnicity. Nevertheless the proportion of reported black offenders is higher than their distribution in the general population. Shah and Pease (1992) show that when victims recall a crime there is no difference in the time lapse of recall if the offender is black or white.

Police bias

Since the 1960s sociological research has consistently shown that, in both the United States and Britain, relations between the police and ethnic minorities are based on suspicion and mistrust. This is partly to do with the stereotypical attitudes that exist in the police force (Black and Reiss, 1967) and partly to do with police officers' fears that encounters with ethnic minorities may lead to violence, which causes the police to deal with all black suspects in a stereotypical way (Skolnick, 1966). As a result, even blacks of high social status find themselves in hostile encounters with the police (Hagan and Albonetti, 1982).

In their encounters with the public the police expect some form of respect, and a respectful attitude is a crucial factor in their decision to proceed with an arrest or not (Sykes and Clark, 1975). The hostility and suspicion with which many young ethnic minority males view the police means that their chance of being processed in the criminal justice system is much higher than it is for more 'contrite', respectful, white males (Smith and Visher, 1982). There is some evidence to suggest that this is also true of ethnic minority women when they come into contact with the police, in that when they fail to conform to expectations of gender behaviour they forfeit the 'chivalry' that is seen to be part of the gender structure and become subject to harassment. This is particularly true of ethnic minority female prostitutes (Horowitz and Pottieger, 1991).

Police patrols are an important part of the reason why a disproportionate number of ethnic minorities are caught up in the criminal justice system. Waddington *et al.* (2004) argue that in Reading and Slough, where they investigated stop and search figures, the number of black people involved was not disproportionate to the distribution of ethnic groups at the time and place of a particular search – but this raises the issue of why the police chose those times and places. Based on prior experience, stereotyped views of criminality and reports from the public, the police build up profiles of 'good' and 'bad' neighbourhoods, and areas that are defined as criminally troublesome become subject to more extensive patrolling. Ethnic concentration is one factor in defining these areas, and once an area has been designated as 'more criminal' a process of 'ecological contamination' takes place (Smith, 1986) whereby everyone in the area, regardless of their behaviour, becomes subject to suspicion by the police. On the other hand, the disproportionate use of strip and search powers on black people when they arrive at a police station led Newburn *et al.* (2004) to suggest that racism may play a part in the everyday decisions of police officers.

In summary, there is no simple relationship between being stopped by the police and ethnic background. The limited evidence available suggests that housing area is a mediating factor in the frequency with which this takes place, so that complex patterns emerge in different localities (Holdaway, 1996).

Item G

Police initiated contact

There are also ethnic differences in encounters initiated by the police. According to the 2004/5 BCS more people from black ethnic groups (25 per cent) had been approached by the police during the previous year than whites (22 per cent), Asians (22 per cent) and Chinese and other (14 per cent). The differences between the ethnic groups have narrowed since the 1990s. Police-initiated encounters can be divided into three main categories. Mixed and black, compared with other ethnic groups, were more likely to be:

- stopped while in a vehicle or on foot;
- investigated (e.g. questioned about an offence, have house searched, be arrested);
- asked for documents or a statement.

In 2006–7, Ministry of Justice figures on 'stop and account' searches showed that members of the public were stopped 1.87 million times. This official figure also confirms that stop and account actions involve black people two and a half times more often than white people. When stopped, however, black people were seven times more likely to be searched than white people and three and a half times more likely to be arrested due to the stop and account action. However, this is not uniform around the country. In West Mercia (including Birmingham) police authority the figure is five times more likely and, in Lincolnshire, the reverse is the case, with white people more likely to be stopped. For Asians, there are no differences in their chances of being stopped compared to the general population.

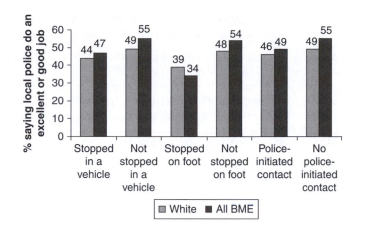

Figure 7.3 Ratings of the local police by type of contact and ethnicity, BCS 2004–5
Source: Jansson (2006).

The police used their powers to stop members of the public in the street and demand they account for themselves on nearly 2 million occasions in the year 2006–7, according to Ministry of Justice figures published yesterday.

The statistics, issued for the first time, reveal the scale of police use of 'stop and account' powers. They show that black people are two and a half times more likely than white people to be questioned by the police on the street. The figures for Asian people do not show such differences compared to the whole population.

The data shows that black people are still seven times more likely to be stopped and searched – as opposed to stop and account; and three and a half times more likely to be arrested.

This figure varies around the country, with black people five times more likely to be stopped than white people by the Gwent and West Mercia police, while in Durham and Lincolnshire black people are less likely to be stopped. (Travis, 2008)

Exercise 7.10

Item G is derived from a Home Office report (BCS) on different ethnic groups' experience of contact with the police and a newspaper account of Ministry of

Justice statistics. The data show that the likelihood of being stopped varies according to ethnicity. Study Item G and answer the following questions.

① 1. What evidence is offered in Item G to suggest that blacks are more likely to experience police stops than Asians and whites?

① 2. What changes have occurred, if any, in the chances of black people being stopped by the police and made to account for themselves?

(An) 3. Give a reason why there might be differences between the two sets of figures. (Hint: look at the sources.)

(An)(A) 4. Suggest reasons why the figures in West Mercia for 2006–7 are much higher than for those in Lincolnshire.

Judicial bias

Once caught up in the judicial system, ethnic minority defendants are likely to be less favourably treated than white defendants. For example in the United States it is suggested that ethnic minority defendants are less likely than whites to be offered good plea bargains (where a defendant admits guilt in return for a less serious charge being levelled), and therefore usually proceed to a contested trial (for example, see Zatz, 1985). They are then left with the very difficult choice between pleading guilty or pleading not guilty – the latter plea is often seen as evidence of lack of remorse and can lead to harsher punishment if the defendant is found guilty (Hagan, 1994).

In the case of Britain, data from the 1970s suggests that ethnic minority youths are much more likely than white youths to be prosecuted when caught (Landau and Nathan, 1983). However, the data is relatively old and does not tell us about current practices. Landau and Nathan argue that, while a previous record is an important factor in the decision to prosecute, direct discrimination also occurs. However, when all arrests, not just those of juveniles, are included in the figures the discrimination effect all but disappears. Once prosecuted, black and South Asian defendants are more likely to be tried in a crown court than in a magistrates court (Brown and Hullin, 1992), though this may be the result of being charged with different crimes from their white counterparts. A higher proportion of blacks is remanded in custody rather than released on bail (Walker, 1989). Similarly, with sentencing, though the patterns are complex, it seems that blacks are likely to receive longer custodial sentences than whites (Smith, 1997), and blacks are six times more likely than whites or South Asians to end up in prison (explore this further in Exercise 7.11).

Item H

Equal opportunities and the law

A study of 3,300 cases at five West Midlands' courts published in December 1992 revealed that blacks have a significantly higher chance than whites of going to prison from Crown Courts. The study, 'A Question of Judgement', was published by the Commission for Racial Equality and was conducted by Dr Roger Hood, director of the Centre for Criminological Research at Oxford University. After taking into account a number of key factors related to sentencing, the study shows that blacks still had a 5 to 8 per cent greater chance of being sent to jail than whites. This overall figure, though, masks a much bigger discrepancy in sentencing that occurred in a few of the courts. At Birmingham Crown Court there was found to be no difference in the sentencing of blacks and whites. But, at Dudley Crown Court, black offenders stood a 23 per cent greater chance than whites of being sent to prison.

The disparity was most in evidence for the less serious offences. It is in these cases that judges have the most discretion in the length of sentence they give. It is worth noting that the Race Relations Act which outlaws racial discrimination does not apply to judges. The study also found that black offenders, in addition, faced a form of indirect racial discrimination because they were less likely than whites to enter a plea of guilty. By pleading not-guilty defendants forfeit the unofficial 'discount' – in the West Midlands it is one-third of the sentence – that goes with a plea of guilty.

Source: Denscombe (1993).

Exercise 7.11

Using information gathered from Item H and elsewhere, evaluate the view that the judicial system in Britain is racist.

Smith (1997) concludes that, although there is some evidence of discrimination at different stages of the criminal justice process, the proportion of blacks at the beginning of the process is roughly the same as at the end. This suggests that no cumulative discriminatory effect is occurring, but that the 'difference in the rate of arrest and imprisonment between black and white people arises from a difference in the rate of offending' (ibid.). Moreover as South Asians are also subject to racism but do not appear to be disproportionately represented in the system, there is no evidence of generalized racism – rather it is black people who are the object of bias in the criminal justice system. Yet, Shute *et al.* (2005) found that lower proportions of ethnic minorities than might have been expected reported that they perceived they had been subject to racial bias in the judicial process.

Evaluation of social construction approaches to ethnicity and crime

Ⓘ Ⓔ

Exercise 7.12

Complete the evaluation paragraphs below by selecting the missing words from the list provided. The first paragraph outlines the strengths of the social construction approaches and the second establishes the weaknesses.

The social constructionist approach to ethnicity and crime has certain strengths. Firstly, it focuses attention on the ... of the law enforcement agencies. Secondly, it identifies elements of ... in the way that the criminal justice system operates. Thirdly, it emphasizes the ... between the police and ethnic minorities as the source of ...

Social constructionists are subject to criticism though. Such approaches tend to ... ethnic minorities from responsibility for their criminal behaviour. Furthermore their arguments ... criminal behaviour solely to that which is defined as such by the criminal justice system. The approach also tends to ignore wider ... processes that might affect the crime levels.

Missing words

- criminalization • social and economic • racism • reduce
- absolve • interaction • behaviour

COMBINED APPROACHES

Other sociologists have attempted to bring together a consideration of the causes of crime at the societal and individual levels (see pp. 83), with the idea that crime is in part socially constructed through the activities of the state and the law enforcement agencies (see pp. 267–82). However, these combined approaches also draw on other traditions, such as sociocultural approaches (see Chapter 3). The main approaches are:

- critical criminology;
- the underclass and ethnicity;
- sociology of crime and disrepute;

▪ masculinities and black youth;
▪ globalization, ethnicity and new forms of crime.

Critical criminology

We have already seen how there is a popular conception that black males are disproportionately involved in street crime and that this view is held not only by the general public but by the police, the media and political commentators. Critical criminologists argue that this assumption is linked to the process of immigration, in which recent immigrants to urban areas are seen as inevitably drawn into a culture of criminality (Gilroy, 1987a). The all-pervasive nature of the imagery of the black criminal transforms this idea into an ideology, which in turn influences the policing decisions of the forces of law and order. The discriminatory practices of the police become legitimated by reference to the ideology of the black criminal. This 'institutionalized racism' is, according to the critical criminologists, rife in the agencies of the criminal justice system.

Critical criminologists are also concerned with the structural situation of ethnic minorities and how this may cause them to turn to crime. They argue that ethnic communities are marginalized from mainstream society because of their economic circumstances. The poverty in areas with a high ethnic minority concentration is a major cause of crime in these areas. As this poverty intensifies, due to the economic crisis created by the operation of the capitalist economy, it is likely that ethnic minorities will become increasingly detached from mainstream society.

However, critical criminologists argue that this marginalization also has an ideological basis. It is part of the strategy of capitalism to ensure a continued supply of subservient and cheap workers. By drawing on neocolonial ideas (ideas based on Britain's imperial past, when Britain had a mission to 'civilize' 'native' populations), black people are constantly reconstructed as being in an 'inferior' position to that enjoyed by the dominant white population. This has the effect of fractionalizing (dividing into parts) the working class (Miles, 1982) into black and white sections.

The ethnic minorities can then be deployed as a reserve army of labour, to be taken into employment or dispensed with as economic conditions dictate. As a result of this they become even more economically marginalized. The irony is that this system is then used to divide ethnic minority workers from the white working class by offering white workers a reason why their economic circumstances are also deteriorating. It becomes part of the 'hegemonic consciousness' of the white working class that black workers are 'taking their jobs' (Gilroy, 1987b).

The effect of these economic and ideological processes is to divide the black and white working class, both materially (ethnic minority workers are likely to be worse off than their white counterparts) and ideologically (ethnic minority workers are seen as different from white workers). Part of the construction of this difference between the white and black populations is society's perception of the 'criminality' of black youth. Believing that blacks are by nature more likely to commit crimes is part of a 'new racism' in which ethnic groups become defined as the 'other', that is, the counterpoint to which 'British' identity is constructed. Hence an implicit contrast is constructed between the law-abiding nature of the 'host', usually white, community and the law-breaking nature of the ethnic minority 'other'. By conceptualizing ethnic minorities as the 'other', a scapegoat is created that diverts attention from the economic and social uncertainties of the age.

(E)

Exercise 7.13

By now you will have come to appreciate the importance of evaluating theoretical ideas in terms of their strengths and weaknesses. Below we have provided an evaluation paragraph that sets out some of the weaknesses of the critical criminology perspective as it applies to ethnicity and crime. We have also started a paragraph that identifies one of the strengths of critical criminology. We would like you to complete the strengths paragraph by identifying two other positive aspects of the theoretical views of the critical criminologists.

'The ideas of critical criminologists can be criticized on a number of counts. Some might argue that their views operate at a high level of abstraction. Furthermore, it can be said that critical criminologists play down the experiences of black victims of crime. Finally, it can be argued that the approach tends to idealize black communities and stereotype white communities as inevitably racist'.

However a number of strengths can also be identified. For example critical criminology stresses the importance of ideological and social structures in the issue of crime and ethnicity. Further strengths are...

The underclass and ethnicity

The concept of the underclass has been used in the United States in particular to describe the largely Hispanic and African–American inhabitants of inner city ghettos. They have been conceptualized as a distinct section of society because they are argued to have little chance of social mobility or employment in the formal economy. The underclass thus exists as a marginalized and separate segment of society, far removed from the mainstream. There is little male employment and few skills that are useful in postmodern society, and therefore the underclass has the potential to be permanently excluded from the main body of society. As a consequence the forces of social order view this group as high risk and likely to develop a culture that supports violence and criminal activity.

The concept has been applied to ethnic communities in the United States by the black sociologist William Julius Wilson (1987). Wilson accepts that there has been a significant increase in lone-parent families and illegitimate births among black inner-city dwellers, but rejects the new right argument that this is a consequence of generous welfare payments. On the contrary, benefits in the United States declined in value during the period with the greatest increase in illegitimate births. Wilson also rejects the simplistic view that the involvement of blacks in violent crime is a result of the racism experienced by many young blacks. Rather he argues that there has been a process of 'historic discrimination' in which, over generations, black people have been cut off from opportunity and legitimate work. Rather than a culture of poverty in the black communities there is a culture of subordination to and exclusion from mainstream society, and this will be difficult to eradicate through short-term policies.

The concept of the underclass has been further developed by Sampson and Wilson (1993), who use both structural and cultural factors to explain the high levels of crime among the underclass. They argue that in postmodern society there is a 'concentration effect' whereby the members of the underclass are increasingly forced into socially disorganized communities, characterized by severe family instability and poverty. These disorganized communities support a culture that is violent and conducive to criminal activity because members of the underclass are forced to seek a living through illegitimate means.

A further consequence of the apparently permanent concentration of the underclass in specific urban locations and disorganized communities is that the agents of social order tend to control the underclass more closely than other sections of the population (see for example Sampson and Laub, 1992). The underclass become stigmatized as a population that needs to be disciplined and controlled rather than being treated as individuals who may or may not commit crimes. The underclass is therefore stereotyped as a permanently dangerous class, with little chance of individual members escaping from the structural and cultural constraints to which they are subject.

Wilson (1987) suggests that the extreme disadvantage in some urban areas creates a distinct social situation that is far removed from mainstream society. He also argues that because of racial segregation it is mainly blacks who make up such communities. Sociologists have pursued this approach when investigating whether such communities experience higher levels of certain types of crime, for example drug taking or violence. In the main it has been found that they do (see, for example, Anderson, 1990).

Working from Wilson's structural perspective, Krivo and Peterson (1996) have empirically tested the view that extremely disadvantaged neighbourhoods experience unusually high levels of crime. Unlike their predecessors they were able to compare predominantly black and predominantly white neighbourhoods, and as a result they were able to investigate the importance of ethnicity as a causal factor. They argue that the conditions that exist in these neighbourhoods encourage criminal activity and that there are few social control mechanisms. They suggest that the inhabitants are socialized into crime by witnessing criminal acts in the absence of alternative role models to act as a counterforce. There is also a spiral of violence as residents seek to defend their lives and property by employing violent means themselves (Massey, 1995).

There is also a lack of social control agencies, such as the Church and even the police at times. Families do not form networks that can act to deter youngsters from becoming involved in crime, nor does the community have the resources to set up more formal crime prevention groups. Most of all, the lack of employment closes the avenue to mainstream society and many inhabitants have too much time on their hands. Krivo and Peterson (1996) argue that it is primarily these structural conditions and not ethnicity that is the main cause of greater criminality. They found unusually high levels of violent crime in extremely disadvantaged areas, but not of property crime. They suggest that this is because there is much less to steal in these areas. Furthermore these results hold regardless of whether the area in question is mainly white or mainly black. This supports Sampson and Wilson's (1995) view that crime has nothing to do with ethnicity, but is structurally located.

Sociology of crime and disrepute

An alternative approach to the issue of ethnicity and crime has drawn upon newer theoretical traditions, while retaining some links with the old. The sociology of crime and disrepute (see Chapter 6) focuses on global processes that destroy the industrial base of certain cities and have a disproportionate effect on ethnic groups in certain locations. For example, as the populations of some North American cities decline as a result of the global redistribution of Fordist (mass production) industry, the ethnic population in deprived urban areas is becoming more concentrated. Another effect is for an increase in crime to accompany this ethnic concentration. For example this occurred in Detroit between 1950 and 1970, where the population fell by a half but the ethnic proportion increased fourfold and the murder rate tenfold. Even allowing for changing patterns of crime in the United States as a whole, this indicates a concentration of certain types of criminal activity in such locations. These processes have had the effect, according to Hagan (1994), of producing concentrations of ethnic minorities in areas with poor employment prospects. This lack of social capital (that is, community bonds – see pp. 87–8) results in the disorganization of communities and the search by ethnic minorities for ways to recapitalize through deviant activity.

One of the main illegal activities in which ethnic minorities have engaged is the drug trade (see Exercise 7.14 for some of the difficulties in researching this issue). As a consequence the law enforcement agencies, especially when there is a political imperative to come down hard on drugs, have focused on ethnic minority areas (Jackson, 1992). The result is that, while in the United States the arrest rate for whites on drug offences since the 1970s has remained fairly steady, ethnic minority groups grew at 15–20 per cent a year between 1980 and 1985 (Blumstein, 1993). Sampson and Laub (1993b) conclude that race and drugs are now so closely intertwined (as well as class) that it is very difficult to untangle them. The 'drug problem' has become a 'race problem'.

Item I

Methodological problems in conducting research into crime: the case of interviewing

One of the advantages of interviewing people involved in a particular activity that the sociologist might be interested in, is that interviewees can 'speak for themselves' and so we can gain an insight into their world. However, when that world includes illegal activity then a number of problems appear with the interview as a strategy. For example, if a sociologist was interested in people whose lifestyle involves the taking of illegal drugs, then how does the sociologist gain entry into that world. There are a number of different dimensions to research into 'drug cultures': how it is sustained; how users are supplied; engagements with the authorities, including the police; relationships with the non-drug world, such as work; the effects on individual lives of addiction to heroin or crack cocaine; etc. However, if the sociologist has no experience of drug culture him or herself, then it might be difficult to gain access to it.

One of the ways that this might be done is through rehabilitation agencies, where drug users who are trying to come off their habits might be willing to speak to an impartial researcher. From that beginning a process of 'snowball sampling' might take place as one user introduces the researcher to another and so on. However, this does raise issues of representativeness and the reliability of any findings. But more importantly, engaging in a world such as the drug culture raises enormous ethical issues. There is an element of seduction for the researcher, who must be trained to preserve a professional detachment from the activity of drug-taking while gaining the drug-taker's trust. There are also responsibilities that the researcher has towards the interviewee, to ensure his or her safety. For example, by encouraging contact with other users (through the snowball technique) there may be a danger that the reforming addict may be tempted into old habits.

Exercise 7.14

Study Item I and answer the following questions.

1. Identify one difficulty that sociologists face when researching drug addicts.
2. Explain what is meant by 'representativeness'.
3. Which sampling method was used in item I to investigate drug users?
4. Identify one ethical consideration that has to be taken into account when working with drug addicts.
5. It can be inferred from Item I that one of the aims of any study would be to examine the extent to which crack (or heroin) had changed the lives of the interviewees. Rewrite this aim so that it takes the form of a research hypothesis.

Masculinities and black youth

In the United States, the Afro-American male has historically been subjugated to a dominant white male masculinity, in which blackness has been conceptualized as threatening and in need of suppression. Therefore black males have been subject not just to physical oppression but to psychological pressure, which has limited the arenas in which they can assert their masculinity. While blacks have succeeded in legitimate ventures such as entertainment and sport, they have also turned to deviant and criminal pursuits, especially drug trafficking (Jefferson, 1997). These illegal activities are often related to repressed aspects of white masculine identity and involve an exaggeration of black sexual prowess, an emphasis on toughness and the body.

The long-term effect of racism has been the emasculation of black males, who have limited positive male images to draw upon and emulate. As economic pressures on black youth increased in the 1980s, there developed a dualistic consciousness, in which resistance to white hegemony was tied to a misogynistic (woman hating) and homophobic attitude that divided the black community (Staples, 1989).

Globalization, ethnicity and 'new' forms of crime

As the 'flows' of migrants increase in an intensifying globalized world, Bosworth *et al.* (2008) argue that criminology needs to re-evaluate how it approaches issues of ethnicity and crime. They suggest that there are strong forces at work, such as the 'globalization of fear', that lead to a fear of the globally mobile classes, who are often distinguished by their ethnicity. The globally mobile are stigmatized by labels such as 'asylum seekers', 'illegal aliens' and even traffickers and terrorists. However, they suggest that traditional approaches to crime and ethnicity, by focusing on difference (the differential offending and victim rates between the British ethnic minority and whites), leads to a narrow conception of the ways that ethnicity and criminality intersect. For example, they show that 'racial profiling' does not just decide who gets stopped and searched on the street, but also influences who can enter and settle in the UK.

Globalization is producing a new 'global underclass' often located in the underdeveloped world and looking to move across borders for economic advantage (Pickering and Weber, 2006). In seeking to make those moves, they often cross the border into criminality, through illegal entry, overstaying their visa permits, and so on. The result is often 'neutralization', as they spend time in holding camps, or marginalization, as they work the grey economy. The processes of exclusion (and inclusion) that they are subjected to are highly racialized (as well as gendered and classed). The combination of worry about terrorist attack post-9/11, and the depiction of asylum seekers and refugees as 'scroungers', leads to a situation where migrants are located within a discourse of the 'criminality of the other'. Hughes (2006) argues that this results in the 'criminalization of migration', in which highly visible ethnic groups are portrayed as a criminal fifth column.

POSTMODERN APPROACHES TO ETHNICITY AND CRIME

Postmodernists are critical of all modernist theories of crime for their neglect of the poor, women and ethnic minorities. Arrigo and Young (1996) argue that, even when modernist theorists paid attention to the position of marginalized groups, they did so in a way that effectively disenfranchised them. Arrigo and Young suggest that modernist theories tend to privilege the idea of sameness amongst criminals, as opposed to the emphasis on difference put forward by the postmodernists. This focus on the essential similarity between criminals, regardless of class, ethnicity or gender stems from the modernist belief in the metanarrative, that is, that there is only one explanation. By rejecting the idea that there is a single all-embracing truth, the postmodernists claim, they open up theoretical space to listen to marginalized groups' experiences and expressions of crime. At the centre of the marginalization of ethnic minorities by modernist theories of crime is the language (concepts, ideas and preconceptions) used to construct them. This language is so steeped in the tradition of masculine and dominant ethnic group imagery and assumptions that marginal groups are reduced to having 'essential' characteristics, which stereotype them and take away their voice.

By employing topology theory, which draws heavily on the work of Lacan (1981), postmodernists attempt to bring into theoretical prominence the attitudes and opinions of those groups who have been denied a voice by modernist sociology (see, for example, Arrigo, 1995). Postmodernists are therefore concerned to allow alternative narratives to surface that include the dominant signifiers (the words or symbols that represent the key beliefs and ideas of a person or group) of the ethnic minorities. The dominant signifiers of modernist criminological discourse (ways of speaking), such as 'criminal career' or 'techniques of neutralization', have squeezed out alternative discourses, such as the experience of ethnic minorities themselves in understanding and experiencing crime. Thus while both white and black communities in the United States used signifiers such as 'fairness' and 'justice' when responding to the acquittal of the police officers in the Rodney King case (the beating of King by the officers had been captured on video) the response of each group was very different. For the black community, the acquittal was placed in the context of their historical experience of the criminal justice system in the United States, which has not always served black people well. This was not part of the dominant discourse that framed the reaction of the white community.

VICTIMOLOGY

The rates of crime committed against Afro-Caribbeans and South Asians have been shown to be higher than those against the white population (Fitzgerald and Hale, 1996). This is particularly so for crimes against households and the person. However, analysis of the statistics shows that the differentials are related to the places where the majority of ethnic minorities live and their daily routines. Moreover, as most victims are relatively young, the age profile of the ethnic minority population is also a factor in the higher rates. Nearly half of all offences that have involved personal contact have been committed by blacks against blacks.

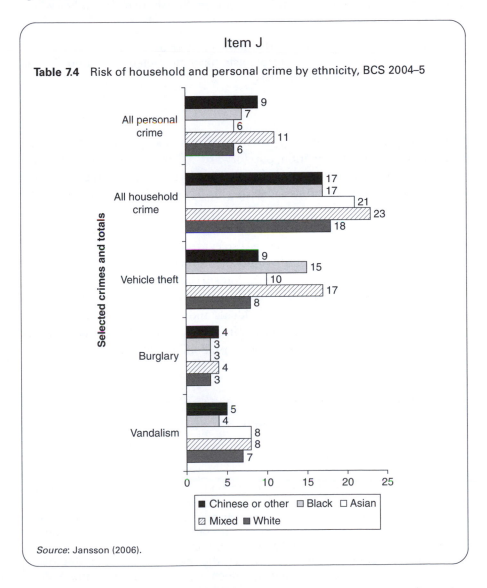

Item J

Table 7.4   Risk of household and personal crime by ethnicity, BCS 2004–5

Source: Jansson (2006).

The categories used in this bar chart are the 2001 Census categories used by the BCS. They are collapsed down from a finer classification of ethnic groups, so that, for example, 'whites' includes 'British Irish' and 'other white' within it.

Ⓘ 1. Briefly describe the patterns of risk shown in Item J.
Ⓐ 2. Identify two ways in which sociologists have attempted to account for the apparent ethnic differences in risk.

Hall (1985) has found that black women are more likely to be attacked than white women. The explanation put forward is that the economic circumstances of black women mean they are more likely to use public transport and work unsocial hours, thus increasing their vulnerability to opportunistic attack.

While the higher rate of crimes against ethnic minorities can be partly explained by area of residence, there is also evidence that many ethnic minority victims are the subjects of racially motivated attack. Though it is difficult to prove racial motivation, and victimization surveys are not good at capturing repeated victimization over time, there is some evidence that repeated harassment of targeted ethnic minority individuals and families does go on, and has a limiting effect on the lives of those affected (Smith, 1997). This is particularly true for ethnic minorities living in predominantly white areas (Virdee, 1997).

Item K

Racially motivated crime

It is estimated that there were 179,000 racially motivated crimes in England and Wales, based on BCS interviews in 2004/5. This compares with a total of 206,000 incidents reported by the 2003/4 and 2002/3 BCS, representing a marked fall in the number of racially motivated crimes. In terms of risk of becoming a victim of racially motivated crime, white people have a lower risk of becoming victims than people in any of the BME groups, but the risk does not vary between the BME groups.

Table 7.5 Estimated numbers of racially motivated crimes of violence, BCS 2004/5

	White	Mixed	Asian	Black	Chinese or other
Common assault	47,300	2,000	26,800	5,000	3,800
Wounding	20,300	500	1,500	1,200	1,100
Robbery	7,700	900	300	800	3,200

Source: Jansson (2006).

Exercise 7.16

Read Item K and answer the following questions.

1. What do you understand by the term 'racially motivated'?
2. How many black people were estimated to have been wounded as a result of a racially motivated attack?
3. Examine Table 7.4. What was the difference between the Mixed and the Chinese or other categories' experience of a racial common assault?
4. Why do you think these are estimated figures?
5. Suggest two reasons why the number of *reported* racial incidents may be less than the *actual* number.

Exam focus

1. 'Members of ethnic minorities are over-represented in crime statistics.' Discuss and evaluate this point of view.
2. 'Globalization has increased the criminalization of members of black and Asian ethnic groups.' To what extent does the sociological evidence support or undermine this claim?

Important concepts

- Stereotyping • Hate crimes • Institutional racism • Marginalization
- Neocolonialism • Reserve army of labour • Racial profile
- Criminalization of migration

Critical thinking

1. Do the changes in the way that British ethnic minority groups have been classified over the years mean that it is impossible to chart trends in their experiences in the criminal justice system?
2. How convincing do you find the concept of a global underclass that is highly racialized? Do the members of any such underclass have sufficiently similar experiences to constitute a class?
3. Have the police changed in their attitudes towards BEM individuals following the Macpherson Report? Are the police no longer institutionally racist?

Chapter 8

Crime, Deviance and Gender

After studying this chapter, you should:

- have a critical understanding of statistical data on gender and crime
- be able to explain female involvement in crime
- be able to outline and evaluate theories that propose that women are less criminally inclined
- be familiar with debates on masculinities and crime
- understand and be able to assess social constructionist approaches to gender and crime
- appreciate how crime and the fear of crime affect the lives of women
- be familiar with debates and explanations of sexual and domestic violence

Interest in female crime rose in parallel with the rise of feminism, especially in the 1970s. Just as feminism has since split into varying strands and traditions, feminist criminologists have adopted different theoretical and social policy positions on the phenomenon of female crime. For example Adamson *et al.* (1988) have identified liberal, socialist, radical and black feminisms. This splitting of the feminist movement has led to different positions on whether there is such a thing as a unified 'feminist criminology'. Smart (1981) suggests that it is difficult to talk about a single feminist criminology because of the divisions within the movement, while Brown (1990) argues that there is such a thing, because all strands agree on a number of key issues. Feminist criminologists tend both to put female crime at the centre of their studies and to adopt a non-scientific approach to their studies.

TYPES OF FEMINISM

Liberal feminism

The central ideas behind liberal feminism are drawn from the Enlightenment with its stress on the rights of individuals and their freedom to pursue their own happiness to the best of their ability. In terms of gender relationships, liberal feminism is concerned to establish a level playing field in terms of law, so that women are accorded the same rights as men. Therefore, where there is discrimination in law, the liberal feminists seek to redress it through political means. Sociologically, liberal feminism challenges the idea that differences between the sexes are somehow 'natural', arguing rather that they are socially constructed through a variety of agencies, including the family, the media, religion, etc. In concentrating on legal redress and the role of socialization in forming gender identities, liberal feminism has been criticized for ignoring divisions between women, such as those of ethnicity and class, and therefore of not addressing the major reasons for women's oppression – the patriarchal nature of society.

Marxist feminism

Drawing on the work of Karl Marx and Marxist sociologists, the focus of Marxist feminism is on the capitalist system and the benefits that the system derives from gender divisions. Women are seen as doubly oppressed under capitalism. As workers, they are subject to the same unequal economic and power relationships that men experience and yet are paid less for doing the same work. In addition, they serve the interests of capitalism as domestic workers and mothers, both providing a safe haven for the oppressed male and reproducing the next generation of workers. They therefore privilege class inequality over gender inequality. They argue that only by overthrowing the capitalism system, with its multiple oppressions, can women truly be free. It is this focus on class rather than gender that has led to Marxist feminism being criticized by other feminists who believe that gender divisions pre-date the class divisions found in capitalism.

Radical feminism

In contrast to the Marxist view, radical feminists see gender divisions as the fundamental fissure in any society, so that patriarchy is the basis of social organization – a position where women are suppressed and controlled by men. This control is not just a symbolic control, but a real physical one, in which women's bodies are shaped and moulded to fit men's interest in issues of reproduction and sexuality. Its most violent manifestation is in the act of rape. Radical feminists therefore argue for a more separatist approach to gender relations, with men and women having their own spheres of autonomy in which to be truly free. Criticism of this approach centres around the idea that all women in all times and places are subject to the power of men – this is argued to be a form of biological determinism, where women's biology is their destiny. It therefore ignores both the many changes in the position of women in time and differences in the position of groups of women within a society.

Socialist feminism

This approach tries to bring together the insights of both Marxist and radical versions of feminism, arguing for a dual-system explanation of women's inequality. They propose that within capitalist societies there are two related systems of oppression for women. On the one hand there is capitalist exploitation and on the other a system of patriarchy in which women lose out to men. The interweaving of these two systems is the context within which women live their lives, and, if women are to become equals, both systems need to be addressed and dealt with. Therein lies the problem for socialist feminism, in that it is imprecise about the nature of that interweaving and indeed that the exact relationship between the two is contingent, that is will change from time to time and even from place to place.

Black feminism

The starting point of black feminism is that previous theories have ignored the particular lived experience of ethnic minority women and produced a feminism that speaks mainly to white (and often middle-class) women. In so criticizing, they suggest that there is a third system of oppression to be addressed in any approach to women's position in society and that is racism. Unless racism is also tackled alongside capitalism and patriarchy, then any feminist 'revolution' will be incomplete. However, black feminists have been accused of doing what they accuse other feminists of doing, which is to conflate the experiences of many different ethnic women under the umbrella of 'black'. The lived experience of women of South Asian background is likely to be very different from those who have a black or mixed heritage.

Postmodernist feminism

This last point forms the starting point of a postmodernist feminism that rejects all feminist 'metanarratives' to focus on the contingent nature of postmodern societies. They conceptualize postmodernity as slightly chaotic, disorganized and fragmented, so that there can be no 'woman's voice'. They reject the concepts of capitalism and patriarchy as having no meaning in a world that is characterized by diversity and difference. Instead, postmodernists focus on plurality, arguing that there are many femininities and masculinities, and not just a single category of men or women. Within each of the femininities there are complex interplays between sexual identity, class, ethnicity, age and sexuality that make up a mosaic of difference. Critics argue that this is to abandon any chance of examining gender oppression as a shared experience for all women and reduces feminism to the merely incidental.

But the debate between feminists about crime goes further than this, with Smart (1990) rejecting the idea that feminists should engage with criminology at all, because as an established discipline it has its own taken-for-granted concepts and methodologies that should be deconstructed rather than accepted. Moreover those who believe that feminists should engage with criminology have differing policy aims. Some, such as Heidensohn (1986), argue for differential treatment of men and women by the criminal justice system because of male and female offenders' cultural differences. Others, such as Carlen (1990), propose decarceration for most female offenders, because imprisonment is an inappropriate punishment for the types of crime in which women engage.

Inherent in the feminist enterprise in criminology is the danger that differences between male and female offenders might be explained by biological factors alone, ignoring social and cultural ones. This is why Carlen (1992) goes on to stress that there is no single cause of criminality and that female crime is intertwined with factors such as ethnicity and social class. Moreover postmodernist feminists such as Young (1994) argue that it is only by engaging with criminology that one can deconstruct the 'master narratives' of a male-dominated discipline and remove the unhelpful binaries (conforming/criminal, male/female) within which feminists have worked.

Exercise 8.1

To familiarize yourself with the different feminisms, complete the following exercise. Read the above section and then complete a copy of the chart below by:

(I) 1. summarizing the key ideas of the different feminist theories;
(I)(E) 2. identifying key criticisms of the different feminisms;
(A) 3. suggesting areas in the field of crime and deviance that the different feminists theories may be concerned with studying or theorizing about.

We have made some entries in the chart for you.

Type of feminism	Outline of key ideas	Criticisms	Likely areas of interest in crime and deviance
Liberal feminism			Equal treatment for women in the criminal justice system
Marxist feminism			
Radical feminism			Domestic and sexual violence
Socialist feminism			
Black feminism			
Postfeminism			

Item A

Reasons for the traditional lack of interest in female crime

Heidensohn, in *Women and Crime*, has suggested the following reasons:

1. **Vicarious identification** Most studies of crime have traditionally been conducted by male sociologists and have been, in particular, studies of street gangs and similar groups. Heidensohn suggests that these sorts of study provided a form of vicarious identification by middle-class sociologists with the lifestyle and activities of these groups.
2. **Precluded** Most female sociologists have been precluded from doing studies of male street gangs, and most male sociologists have been precluded from studying working-class female crime.
3. **Male domination of sociology** Most sociologists have traditionally been male and most studies have been of males, by males, reflecting male interests, as indicated above.
4. **Low recorded levels of female crime** The very low levels of recorded female crime mean that this area has not been seen as significant or worthy of study.
5. **Malestream theories** The theories of crime and deviance developed by sociologists have been male-based, starting from assumptions about the world from a male perspective. The questions and explanations have been framed in such a way that women have been excluded from the central areas of study and relegated to marginal roles.

6. **Social class** Theories of deviance have been primarily based upon social class; other variables, such as gender and race, have not, until recently, been studied in detail.

Source: Moore (1994).

Exercise 8.2

① It has been argued that a number of sociological approaches to deviance have marginalized the issue of female crime (see for example Leonard, 1995). Using only the information in Item A, explain in no more than 100 words why female crime has been a neglected area of study.

STATISTICS, GENDER AND CRIME

The statistics on crime and gender reveal a number of differences between male and female offending. To begin with, the statistics show a remarkable consistency throughout Europe, with men more likely than women to figure in the official statistics by roughly a factor of four (Silvestri and Crowther-Dowey, 2008). In particular, men are more likely than women to be involved in serious crime (Hindelang, 1978). This is also true of the United States (Chesney-Lind, 1997). However, the participation of women in different types of crime does vary according to culture and over time. It is important to recognize that women figure in all types of crime and are not confined to certain types. However, the statistics show that women are more likely to be involved in property crimes and other petty offences, such as drunkenness, than in crimes against the person.

Item B

Table 8.1 Ratio of male and female offenders found guilty or cautioned for selected offence groupings, 1993

	Offence	Ratio
Over 20:1	Sexual offences	75:1
	Taking and driving away motor vehicles	33:1

	Burglary	23:1
	Motoring offences (indictable)	20.6:1
5–20:1	Offences under the Public Order Act 1986	17:1
	Criminal damage (summary/less than £2,000)	16.5:1
	Drunkenness	16.5:1
	Robbery	13.5:1
	Criminal damage (indictable/over £2,000)	9.4:1
	Drug offences	9.4:1
	Common assault (summary)	7.0:1
	Violence against the person (indictable)	5.7:1
	Assault on constable	5.5:1
Under 5:1	Theft and handling stolen goods	2.8:1
	Fraud and forgery	2.8:1
Under 1:1	TV licence evasion	0.5:1
Women form majority	Offence by prostitute	0.01:1

Source: Croall (1998).

Exercise 8.3

Study and answer the following questions.

(I)(A) 1. Give an example of a summary offence.
(I)(A) 2. Give an example of an indictable offence.
(An) 3. What patterns can be identified in Item B about the relationship between gender and offending?

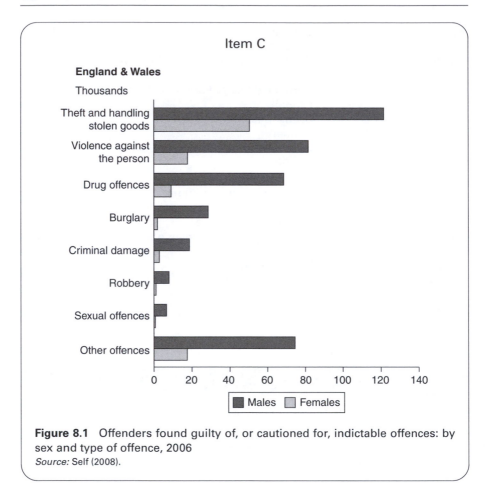

Item C

England & Wales

Thousands

Figure 8.1 Offenders found guilty of, or cautioned for, indictable offences: by sex and type of offence, 2006
Source: Self (2008).

Exercise 8.4

Item C presents data on the types of crime that men and women commit. Study the item and answer the following questions.

1. What are the differences in the patterns of crime between men and women?
2. How might sociologists seek to explain these differences? Describe at least three alternative explanations.

(An)(E) 3. Which of the explanations offered do you find most convincing and why?

Secondly, while it is generally accepted that female crime rates are rising, there is much debate among criminologists as to whether they are rising faster than the rates for men and what the cause of the rise might be. For example Adler (1975) argues that there has been an increase in aggressive criminal acts by women, and that this is connected to changes in gender roles. Adler suggests that there is little difference in the potentiality for crime between men and women, only the opportunities and control differ. The 'achievement' of the women's liberation movement has been to begin to equalize the male and female criminal activity rates. This is disputed by Chesney-Lind and Shelden (1992), who suggest that the rise of the violent female criminal is a myth, spurred by the backlash against women's recent gains in the labour market and society as a whole. Worrall (2004) argues that, while there has been an increase in the numbers of women convicted for violent crime, this has largely been due to a shift in perception by the police and the courts, who are more likely to define bad behaviour by young women as criminal rather than a welfare issue as they previously had done.

The 'search for equivalence' between male and female offenders has led to an increasing focus in the twenty-first century on women who commit acts of violence, either domestically or in public spaces, and on female sex abusers. The emergence of the 'mean girl', binge drinking and fighting on the streets, has been a constant fascination for the media (Chesney-Lynd, 2006). However, Chesney-Lind argues that the large increase in arrests of women for violent behaviour is not reflected in the self-report studies, rather, this increase is the result of a self-fulfilling prophecy, as the police and judiciary respond to media panics about the mean girl.

Others argue that feminism has emancipated women to the extent that they are now more likely to commit crime than previously (Austin, 1981). Simon (1975) considers that increased employment opportunities for women have allowed them to engage in white-collar crimes such as larceny. This is the 'sisters in crime' argument, which lays the responsibility for increased female crime at the door of the women's liberation movement. However, it seems to be minor property crimes such as pilfering and shoplifting that have increased most, rather than white-collar crimes (Steffensmeier and Allan, 1991).

Naffine (1987) argues that, on the contrary, it is the marginal position of most women in the economy that has caused the rise in crime. She suggests that confinement in the 'pink-collar ghetto' of low wages and no real opportunities has led women to commit petty property crimes as a rational response to their marginalization. However, there is a problem with the statistics in that the number of women involved is so small that the statistics are susceptible to large swings in response to, for example, different methods of recording crime. Carlen (1988) has reviewed the evidence for marginalization as the major cause of female crime and concludes that there are some situations in which economic factors are important in the decision to commit crime. Factors such as poverty limit women's choices and therefore increase the likelihood of their engaging in criminal activity. Abuse during childhood and drug taking are other factors.

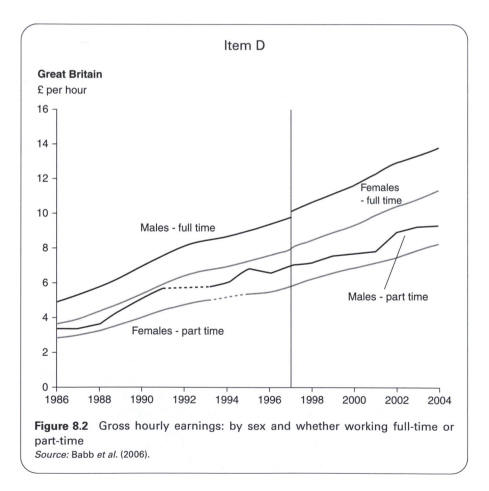

Item D

Great Britain
£ per hour

Males - full time

Females - full time

Males - part time

Females - part time

Figure 8.2 Gross hourly earnings: by sex and whether working full-time or part-time
Source: Babb *et al.* (2006).

Exercise 8.5

ⓘⒶ 1. Explain how the information in Item D lends support to those who argue that women are economically marginalized.

Ⓐ 2. Give two reasons why women are more likely than men to be part of the 'low-paid' workforce.

Thirdly, it should not be thought that women are an undifferentiated category with regard to crime. The concentration of African Americans in areas of high poverty has had consequences for many minority women which do not affect the general population. For example Fagan (1993) argues that the processes of capital disinvestment in urban areas inhabited by African Americans has disproportionately affected black women, especially those who are heads of lone-parent families. With the need to generate income when sources of legitimate employment are limited, and with a dearth of young black men in these areas due to death or incarceration, traditional barriers to female involvement in the illegal drug trade have been weakened, leading to an increase in participation by minority women.

The study of black female offenders is shown by Rice (1990) to be the other 'dark figure' of crime. She argues that black females have fallen between a black criminology that focuses on men and a feminist criminology that studies white women. While feminists have challenged stereotypical views of women, they have done little to undermine the racial stereotyping of their black sisters. By ignoring the different cultural and socialization experiences of black women, feminists have universalized gender differences and ignored the importance of ethnicity. Postfeminists have emphasized the importance of there being many different ways in which femininity can be constructed, rather than the 'ideal liberated woman' implied by much feminist work. Rice shows that the experiences of black women are substantially different from those of white women; for example they are more likely to head a lone-parent family and to be socialized as strong and independent, characteristics that are traditionally associated with the male.

Finally, self-report and victimization studies show that women are often the victims of crime, or live their lives in fear of it. Many feminist writers describe a climate of fear for women in public spaces, in which hegemonic masculinity acts to deter women from using these spaces (see for example Valentine, 1989). But it is also argued that public spaces may have different meanings for different women, depending on their use, construction, their inhabitants, and so on. For example Wilson (1991) argues that the public spaces devoted to shopping contribute to a sense of well-being for many women and are not seen as particularly threatening.

Item E

Fear in the city

Despite figures which show that women are more at risk of violence within the home than of attack in public spaces, the fear of assault, particularly sexual assault, remains high for women. (*The British Crime Survey* (1994) showed that 25 per cent of all female respondents were very worried about rape.) This restricts the activities of many women, who may stay in after dark, not go out unaccompanied, or ensure that they avoid certain places or people altogether.

One in four of the women we spoke to in our survey in Manchester and Sheffield said that they would avoid certain places in the city centre for reasons associated with fear or anxiety over their personal safety and 13 per cent of women who used public transport regularly said that they would not use it at night.

The advice which official agencies give to women in order to promote awareness of their personal safety emphasizes the restriction of movement and the curtailment of women's activities. A Safe City Committee publication of 1988 points out:

> All too often the public response to crime has been to require the vulnerable to curtail their right to participate. Women are warned not to go out at night or to have their husbands, fathers or boyfriend accompany them. Clearly public safety is an equality issue.

Women who do not take this advice can be considered responsible for their own victimization – as a number of highly publicized court cases have shown. Judges have suggested in court that women who have been raped had not taken enough care over their personal safety – being in the wrong places at night or indulging in dangerous activities such as hitch-hiking or walking home alone.

Some writers (Pain 1991; Valentine 1989, 1992) have tried to document exactly where it is that women feel unsafe and to improve the conditions in these places to lessen their fear and improve safety for women. These writers and practitioners have looked at improved street lighting, cutting down shrubbery, attracting people into places at all times of the day and night and promoting 'natural' surveillance of people and property. They have noted too, that it is often in public spaces such as multi-storey car-parks and transport interchanges that women anticipate being at risk, and they have put pressure on public authorities to improve access to and design of these buildings.

Other writers have emphasized the social nature of the restriction and control of women. Kelly (1988) and Gardner (1990) have written of a continuum of violence against women – that men routinely intrude into women's lives, talking to women they do not know, asking personal questions or generally assuming that women want to talk to them. This has implications for the way women feel in public spaces. In a social setting where women can be routinely harassed or made to feel uncomfortable on the street, for example by men who catcall or whistle after them, women may come to feel that they are at risk of more dangerous or violent interventions.

Brooks Gardner interviewed women about their experiences in public spaces and found that women adopt many different strategies to attempt to avoid unwarranted and unwanted contact. One woman would always place a shopping bag on the seat opposite her in cafés, so that it would look as though she were not alone, as she found that men would sit next to her and strike up conversations when they believed her to be alone. Another woman routinely carried a man's coat and hat in her car to deter potential interest from men.

In our research these types of fears and strategies to reduce fear were also discussed. Doreen, who worked in Manchester city centre told us:

> Manchester is now a city where you are always sort of looking around. You can't go and sit and relax in your lunch hour. You're wondering who is going to come and sit next to you ... because I've been pestered when I've been in the Gardens on my own. Even at lunch time.

> *Source*: Evans (1997).

Exercise 8.6

Read Item E and answer the following questions.

(I)(A) 1. What evidence is offered in Item E to support the feminist view that a climate of fear exists for women in public places?

(K)(U) 2. Briefly define and give an example of hegemonic masculinity.

(I)(A) 3. Item E indicates that public authorities can adopt various measures to reduce

(I)(A) women's risk and fear of crime. Identify one such measure and briefly explain how it might reduce women's risk and fear of crime.

Many surveys have found that the general level of fear in public spaces, whether experienced by men or women, is rising (see for example Crawford *et al.*, 1990) and this has led to the creation of private police forces, the use of CCTV in city centres and other public spaces, and so on. This sense of unease afflicts many during their everyday activities, for example when they enter a railway station, an underpass, and so on, and is manifest in the reluctance of grown men to intervene in situations where youngsters, nearly always male, are engaging in threatening behaviour towards more vulnerable groups. This 'loss of civility' is therefore felt by all, but it is females who are subject to the more serious fear of rape and assault in public spaces. Moreover there is an underlying assumption that public space is primarily for men. Danger to women arises not only from the antics of rowdy young men, but from predominantly male police officers who seek to control these antics.

THEORIES THAT PROPOSE THAT WOMEN ARE LESS CRIMINALLY INCLINED

One reaction to the official statistics has been to seek to explain why the rate for women is less than that for men and to look for reasons why women engage less in criminal activity. There are many different approaches to this issue:

- individualistic explanations;
- traditional approaches to female crime;
- structural feminist explanations;
- patriarchy.

Individualistic explanations

Early theories of female crime tended to focus on biological or psychological explanations. Some feminists argue that very early theorists such as Lombroso (1920) and Freud (see Klein, 1973) suggested that deviant women are those who are most like or wish to be men and that crime is therefore biologically caused. However, the interpretation of Lombroso's work has been a subject of some dispute among feminists. Brown (1990) argues that Lombroso has been misinterpreted and that what he was actually arguing was that the biological predisposition of women is towards conformity, not crime. Women who break the law are not of a 'criminal nature', but, in Lombroso's words, 'occasional offenders', and it is not women but men who are predisposed to criminality.

Even more recent theorists have relied on dubious physiological interpretation. For example Pollack (1950) argued that women are inherently deceitful because of their role in the sexual act, where they are able to hide their emotional commitment. For Pollack 'anatomy is destiny', so that although women are vengeful, ironically they are treated chivalrously by the courts. Because of their inherently vengeful and deceitful nature women are more likely to commit certain types of crime than others. The emergence of PMT (premenstrual tension) as a defence in the 1980s can be seen as an aspect of biologism as a cause of female crime (Luckhaus, 1985). The connection between the menstrual cycle and crime has been taken up by those who see female crimes such as shoplifting or infanticide as irrational acts because by nature women are not inclined towards crime (Kendall, 1991). Nevertheless the law does recognize that post-natal depression may be offered as a partial defence in cases of infanticide (Wilczynski and Morris, 1993).

Exercise 8.7

Listed below are two strengths and three weaknesses of individualistic approaches to gender and crime.

(E) 1. Work out one further strength.
(I)(E) 2. Evaluate the individualistic explanations on a theoretical level. We would like you to do this by explaining how any other two sociological theories reject the arguments of the approach. This part of the exercise should be done when you have finished reading this chapter.

Strengths

1. It can be argued that biologism is misrepresented by feminist critiques and that some biological approaches do concede that environmental and social factors influence conformity and criminality.
2. It can be argued that biologists and psychologists are genuinely searching for a 'universal' explanation of crime.

Weaknesses

1. Some people suggest that biological and psychological explanations are ideology dressed up as science.
2. Individualistic explanations focus on how female crime is determined by women's irrational nature, but assumes that male crime is a rational, voluntaristic activity.
3. The fact that female crime is usually reduced to a sexual disorder of one sort or another means that the female body is subjected to the criminological gaze.

Traditional approaches to female crime

Early sociological approaches to crime were concerned with the development of a universal theory of crime, that is, one that can explain all incidences of crime in society. While crime has been statistically concentrated among male working-class youths, the acknowledgement, from the time of Sutherland (1942) onwards, that crime is also committed by the middle class and by women has posed problems for the development of a universal explanation. In particular, women's less frequent engagement in criminal acts and the different crimes in which they engage have posed serious problems for traditional explanations.

Sutherland (see pp. 64–5) rejected biological explanations of female criminality precisely because males and females come from the same genetic pool. Nor did he believe that materialist explanations that locate cause in the economic situation of the criminal were acceptable, because not all poor people commit crime. He did not believe that the criminal statistics described the real rate and nature of criminal activity, which was much more widespread in society than the statistics suggested. However, Sutherland had some difficulty in theorizing the crimes of women until the sociological concept of 'sex role' was developed by Parsons (1942). This enabled Sutherland to argue that girls and boys are differentially supervised by their parents and that lesbianism could be explained by differential association with other lesbians. Feminist critics have argued that this argument is trite and homophobic rather than a properly considered theory (Allen, 1995). However, other feminists argue that Sutherland was right in recognizing that criminal behaviour is learned and not biologically determined, and this recognition highlights the fact that women are differentially treated in society, for example in not being allowed the same freedoms (Leonard, 1982).

Subsequent theorists have tended to focus on male delinquency, especially lower-class subcultural activity, with their sociological fascination for the study of gangs. When female delinquents are considered they are seen as just an adjunct of males. The lack of female delinquency is explained by the respective roles of men and women, in which the primary aim of females is to attach themselves to a man, and therefore women are less likely to suffer the status frustration that young males experience in their more public roles (Cohen, 1955). Similarly Cloward and Ohlin (1960) place women firmly outside the mainstream male culture, arguing that as women are not the main breadwinners they are not subject to the same strains as men and therefore do not commit as much crime.

In Hirschi's Control Theory (see for example Hirschi, 1969), the position of women is not investigated directly. However, Naffine (1987) argues that the concept of conformity is used differently by Hirschi depending upon whether women or men are being addressed. When men conform to social norms, it is seen as a positive development that prevents engagement in deviant activity, but when women conform it is seen as the result of their passive nature, thus turning a positive into a negative phenomenon. Others adapt Control Theory to a consideration of the lack of female crime by showing that daughters are subject to much more supervision and control than boys in the domestic arena. This control, however, is not based on 'male' sanctions that involve coercion and physical control, but on much more subtle shaming strategies, which effectively result in women policing themselves (Hagan, 1989). Carlen (1988) therefore suggests that women engage in crime when they are no longer subjected to 'male' controls (for example when they leave home) and reject the 'gender deal'.

When female delinquency is directly addressed the focus tends to be on female sexuality, either in terms of promiscuousness or in terms of the search for a stable relationship. For example Reiss (1960) argues that when young women engage in promiscuous behaviour that leads to pregnancy or sexually transmitted diseases they lose social prestige, and this is often a cause of criminal behaviour. On the other hand the desire to attract a mate might also cause young women to shoplift clothes, make-up, and so on.

(E)

Exercise 8.8

Listed below are three strengths and three weaknesses of traditional approaches to female crime. Suggest two other strengths and two other weaknesses.

Strengths

1. They dismissed biological accounts of female criminality.
2. They looked to sociocultural factors and the situational location of women to explain female crime.
3. The traditional views acknowledge the differential life experiences of men and women when examining patterns of gendered criminality.

Weaknesses

1. They tend to seek to explain female criminality in terms that are traditional to the study of male crime.
2. They draw upon sexist concepts in seeking to explain female crime.
3. It can be argued that traditional approaches are patronizing in their view of female crime, seeing it as less important than male crime.

Structural feminist explanations

With the emergence of feminism, sociologists began to look at female crime in a different way. Though they drew upon traditional explanations such as Control Theory (see Chapter 3), they eliminated the sexist assumptions that lay behind 'malestream' approaches to female crime. Two structural factors have been employed by feminists when seeking to explain why women are less criminally inclined.

Differential socialization into different value systems

Cohen (1955) suggests in his Status Frustration Theory that young women who turn to delinquent sexual behaviour are frustrated by the sexual double standard that is applied to them and boys.

Steffensmeier and Allan (1991) argue that women are less likely than men to commit crime because they follow a different moral development path, and this makes it more difficult for them to commit a crime. Female interaction is characterized by compassion and empathy, and thus engagement in crime, especially violent crime, is difficult for women. What these authors are suggesting is that moral boundaries are different for men and women, with a consequent effect on their social (or antisocial) behaviour. However, Messerschmidt (1997) contends that this is to make violent crime by females only explicable as an 'aberration', as essentially masculine behaviour rather than violent women expressing an authentic form of being female. He argues that this results in a lack of serious sociological investigation into female crime as it reduces the image of the violent female to a male conceptualization of 'machismo'. Instead sociologists should be seeking to develop a theory of violent female crime that is not dependent on masculinity.

Studies of female gang members in the United States have found that for many delinquent girls the family is not a place of refuge but a locus of abuse, both physical and sexual (see for example Chesney-Lind and Shelden, 1992). The gang therefore becomes the family substitute – the place where identity is given and safety is found. The security provided by all-girl gangs has also been found to exist in mixed gender gangs, but here girls are often subordinate, based on the belief in male superiority (Campbell, 1991). There is also a strong element of sexuality in this relationship, with the female gang members being seen by the males as sexually available.

Teenage gangs therefore reflect the gendered power relations in society at large. However, Messerschmidt (1997) argues that female gang members are not passive actors in this process but actively construct their own femininity in different ways – with some girls emphasizing serial monogamy and others 'stringing the boys along'. In terms of the crimes committed by male and female gang members, the need to make fast money leads the males into robbery and the females into prostitution. Female gang members are thus using the 'street' to celebrate the 'body as an instrument of pleasure rather than an instrument of labour' (Gilroy, 1990, quoted in Messerschmidt, 1997).

However, it is difficult to generalize about 'girl gangs' (as opposed to females who are adjuncts of male gangs), as they differ from each other markedly, in terms of both location and through time (Nurge, 2002). As a result, studies come to different conclusions about the engagement of girls in gangs in violent activity. While it can be established that girl gang members are more violent than non-members, there is no consensus that girl gangs members are equally as violent as males (Coughlin and Venkatesh, 2003). Indeed Miller (2001) argues that many (not all) girl gang members use their gender to avoid risky violent behaviour, knowing that this will reduce their status in the hierarchy of the gang.

Item F

Violent women

There has been increasing public concern about girl gangs and the rise of violence among young women.

The consensus among sociologists, however, is that a massive increase in violence perpetrated by women is not realistic. Most women cautioned, or convicted by the courts, are guilty of minor offences such as theft, fraud and forgery, and not for crimes of violence.

Official statistics however do show an increase in the number of women jailed for offences involving violence. While the numbers involved are small, it is young women in particular who appear in the statistics. Overall there has been a steady growth in both cautions and prison sentences for women convicted of violent crime, often associated with disorder or fighting on the street after drinking sessions, but also connected to robbery. However, these incidences of violence are not gang-related in the main, but are often committed by young women with many social problems in their lives such as a history of being abused or being in violent domestic relationships.

It is sensible to be cautious about the statistics as the increase in violent female offenders comes from a very low base. Violent disorder is still the preserve of young males, not females, and, while the gap may be decreasing, it is not by a great amount. Where females are engaging in violence, it is often in a domestic setting or involving disputes over men, rather than being calculated assaults.

Exercise 8.9

Read Item F, which provides information on violent female crime, then answer the following questions.

(I)(K)(U) 1. Outline the reasons suggested in Item F and other sources for female involvement in 'girl gangs' and violent offending.

(I)(E) 2. What evidence is offered in Item F to suggest that sociologists should be cautious about talking of a major rise in violent offending among young women?

Social control

Early work by feminists on criminology utilized traditional approaches such as subcultural theory (see Chapter 3), but these approaches were of limited use because they had been generated with males in mind (see for example Leonard, 1982). The feminist empiricist perspective, which emerged subsequently and sought to explore scientifically the reasons for female delinquency and crime, moved beyond those traditional approaches (Naffine, 1995). For example Richards and Tittle (1981) explore the way in which men and women differentially calculate their chance of arrest if they engage in a criminal act. Women have a greater awareness of the risk of arrest, which is argued to act as a disincentive.

Heidensohn (1985) has developed a wider view of Control Theory and the way that social control factors lead women to conform. For example she suggests that women in the family are controlled by the expectation that they will bear the main responsibility for child-care and domestic duties. This is reinforced by the assumptions of the agents of the state such as health visitors, who tend to consult the woman of the family when domestic matters are involved. Moreover male violence at home and on the street also acts to control women, giving them less opportunity to engage in criminal behaviour.

Hagan (1989) introduced his Power Control Theory to explain why women are less inclined to commit crime. He argues that the way that patriarchal families structure gender relations makes female involvement in delinquency less likely. He shows that, in our society, males have greater freedom to engage in risk-taking activities and that female children are more controlled in the family than males.

Ⓘ Ⓔ

Exercise 8.10

Examine the following evaluations of the structural feminist approaches. Work out which are the strengths and which are the weaknesses. Make a note of your answers in a two-column table that separates the strengths from the weaknesses. When you note down your answers, rank them in order of importance. Justify your ranking to another sociology student.

1. Such theories are deterministic, in that they assume that certain factors always lead to conformity or criminality.
2. There is some attempt to deal with women in their own right, albeit at a low level and often as an afterthought.
3. It can be argued that studies in this area are androcentric, that is, they measure female crime in terms of how it compares with male crime and experiences.
4. They are an improvement on individualistic explanations as they recognize that criminality is shaped by social factors.
5. The approach does not adequately explain why women are more conformist than men.
6. There is acknowledgment of the importance of domestic and wider social circumstances in influencing female criminality.

Patriarchy

One of the main ways in which radical feminists of the 1970s and 1980s attempted to explain the distribution of female crime was by deploying the concept of patriarchy. This builds upon other theoretical developments at that time, which focused on the issue of power, especially class power. Feminists refocused this concern on the power of males in society. For example Messerschmidt (1986) argues that women tend to commit 'powerless' crime such as prostitution because of their situation in a patriarchal society. Also, some feminists argue that the criminal justice system is so dominated by male assumptions and agendas as to oppress the women who are processed by it. For example 'family law' is seen as male-defined and operating to the detriment of women (Dobash and Dobash, 1992). This results in the silencing of women's voices – as victims of crime, as offenders, and as victims of the law and the criminal justice system (Edwards, 1989).

WOMEN COMMIT DIFFERENT TYPES OF CRIME FROM MEN

One of the enduring problems for feminist criminology has been the statistical phenomenon that some crimes are committed mainly by women and others mainly by men. In rejecting universal theories of crime that seek to explain all criminal acts, some feminists have turned to examining why some crimes are committed more by women than by men. The difficulty for feminism is that this presumes there is something about the female constitution that predisposes women to particular types of crime. Some feminists have argued that feminists need to reintroduce the issue of the body into the consideration of crime, but not in the manner of the crude biologism of earlier years (Gatens, 1983). Rather they should examine why the way that the male body is configured in society leads to a certain type of masculine behaviour that is often criminal. This would have the effect of not allowing men to absolve themselves of responsibility for their oppression of women by claiming it is all down to some sort of cultural conditioning. While much female crime is small scale, for example shoplifting, more serious crimes are committed by women, including infanticide. Feminists have to address these crimes if they are to explain female crime. Feminist explanations have focused on the economic constraints and fear of stigmatization that accompany infanticide cases, where the mothers are often young women who have concealed their pregnancy and the birth of the baby (Wallace, 1986).

POSTMODERNISM, MASCULINITIES AND CRIME

Aware of the danger that concentrating only on female crime may marginalize the contribution of feminism to an understanding of crime, some feminist sociologists have turned to the issue of gender identity. Utilizing concepts drawn from postmodernism, some feminists have looked at the construction of male identities and their connection with criminal and violent behaviour. Indeed Campbell (1993) concludes that the problem of crime is the problem of men, because it is men who construct identities based on coercion and risk-taking.

Messerschmidt (1993) developed a typology of masculinity construction, and considers that the way in which gender is constructed in society allows men greater access than women to legitimate and illegitimate opportunities. Thus men commit the majority of the crimes of both the powerful and the powerless, but women are mainly found only among the powerless. Because masculinity is based on access to power and resources in three locations – the street, the home and the workplace – the opportunity for men to carry out criminal acts in these areas is enhanced. This is true irrespective of whether or not they actually have access to power and resources – only the resulting crime will be different.

As women's identities are traditionally based more on the home and they have less power and fewer resources than men, the types of crime they are able to commit are much more limited. This can be seen in Campbell's (1993) study of a deprived housing estate, where loss of the traditional manifestations of the masculine identity in a time of high unemployment – notably being the breadwinner – increased men's involvement in alternative forms of masculine expression – often illegal. It was the women of the estate who tried to keep a sense of social solidarity alive in a situation where violence was often inflicted on other members of the same community.

While all males are located within general structures that encourage the formation of 'hegemonic masculinities' (Connell, 2002), middle-class and working-class boys inhabit different structural locations and have differing relationships to structures such as schools, which leads to the development of oppositional masculinities. Here, hegemonic masculinity refers to the way in which the imbalance of social power in society creates an assumption of superiority among men in their relationships with women at all levels of the social structure. Oppositional masculinity refers to the ways in which men construct their identities in opposition to the dominant structural forms in society. For white middle-class boys, then, hegemonic masculinity is to do with a well-paid career in a respectable profession (Messerschmidt, 1994). As schools are experienced as constraining institutions, as well as enabling, some white middle-class boys construct an oppositional masculinity. The locus of this opposition tends to be outside the school, and takes the form of minor mischief and high-spirited behaviour. These are expressions of independence, adventure and control, which are suppressed in schools.

For white working-class boys, schools do not offer the same route to hegemonic masculinity and they are therefore likely to construct an oppositional masculinity within the school as well as outside it. As Willis (1977) has shown, within the school this masculinity takes the form of confrontation with the authorities over issues such as smoking and school uniform. Outside school, oppositional masculinity may be constructed in criminal ways. One element of this identity construction is violence, and in particular violence against racial and sexual minorities, for example 'Paki- or gay-bashing' (Harry, 1992; Whitehead, 2005). Mullins *et al.* (2004) argue that, as boys grow up, conflict between men is based on their need to defend a masculine reputation amongst their peers. Furthermore there are different oppositional masculinities among the white working class. For example Sullivan (1989) shows that white working-class boys who obtain adult work through their fathers become far less involved in property theft than those who do not, although they share their racist and homophobic attitudes.

Kersten (1996) argues that the increase in rape in Australia is linked to a crisis in masculinity, caused by the loss of the traditional male dominance in the labour market. This has forced many men into positions of subordination and dependence. For some of these men, rape has become a way of 'accomplishing masculinity', that is, reasserting their hegemonic masculinity when they are no longer the main providers for the family. However, Kersten does not explain why only some of the men in this position resort to violence against women.

The concept of 'hegemonic masculinity' has been criticized on a number of fronts (Hood-Williams, 2001) as presenting only the negative and not the positive attributes of 'being male'. Despite the appearance of other forms of masculinity in the theory of hegemonic masculinity, it is argued that the concept offers a fixed state for masculinity, rather than a fluid state of being, open to contestation and change. Moreover, even within a 'traditional' view of masculinity, variations appear, for example take the contrast between David Beckham and Mike Tyson. Nevertheless, Connell and Messerschmidt (2005) argue that the idea of hegemonic masculinity, not necessarily as a widespread form of masculinity, does go some way to explain why some men are more involved in crime.

(E)

Exercise 8.11

Evaluate the above views on masculinity and crime in terms of their strengths and weaknesses. You should try to come up with at least two strengths and two weaknesses.

FEMALE CRIMINAL ACTIVITY IS UNDERESTIMATED OR FOCUSES ON PARTICULAR CRIMES

A further response to official statistics that indicate women commit less crime than men is to argue that the official statistics do not show the reality of female criminality, in terms of both the extent of female crime in society and the types of crime that women commit. In seeking to explain the underestimation and skewing of the statistics, several approaches have been taken:

- the socially constructed nature of deviance;
- the invisibility of female crime;
- police and judicial bias.

The socially constructed nature of deviance

The ways in which female criminal activities are labelled by the social control agencies are important in explaining why some types of female crime are high-lighted and others are played down. In particular, crimes committed by women that seem to be against female 'nature' attract particular attention from the media and agents of social control, precisely because they seem 'unfeminine' (see Katz, 1987, on female armed robbers). Feminist androgynous (neither male nor female) approaches to criminality argue that there are many similarities between male and female criminals, and any difference is a result of the way in which society differentially 'polices' men and women.

The androgynous approach emphasizes that the patterns of female and male crime do not differ significantly (Heidensohn, 1985). Indeed, self-report studies show that there are few differences between boys and girls in terms of general antisocial behaviour, though boys were more likely to have reported having attacked someone than the girls (Armstrong *et al.*, 2005). Nor do the motives differ significantly, with economic rationality being an important part of the decision to commit crime. It is the economic reality of women's reduced access to resources that produces different patterns of offending. For example, Pantazis and Gordon (1997) argue that the increase in the female prison population may be accounted for by an increase in lone-parent females being unable to pay the fine for not having a TV licence. The lone parent makes a rational economic decision not to pay the fine in order to buy necessities such as food for the family.

The invisibility of female crime

Much female crime, by its nature, lacks a public face. For example prostitution is either hidden behind closed doors or restricted to certain areas of the city or town, so that the majority of the public are unlikely to come into daily contact with it. As it is a 'crime without a victim', prostitution is under-reported in comparison with its incidence. However, prostitution is not dealt with leniently by the police and the legal system. While the police do accommodate some prostitution – that is, as long as it remains contained and peaceful it is largely left alone – when prostitutes are confronted by the police they complain of harassment and entrapment (McLeod, 1982).

Item G

Reasons women give for becoming prostitutes

- prostitution is a rational response to inadequate social security benefits and provides a basic standard of living, not provided by the state;
- lack of alternative employment, either because they are poorly qualified or there are limited opportunities for female work in the locality;
- prostitution is seen by some women as an alternative community and social support network, when faced with single parenthood and poverty;

- where the alternative is homelessness some women will turn to prostitution as a solution to a specific housing crisis in their lives;
- as a way of earning a living, prostitution allows some women some power over their own lives, setting them free from either abusive male relationships, community care homes or from state benefit dependence.

Source: Adapted from Phoenix (1998).

Exercise 8.12

Drawing on the material in Item G, write a short paragraph of no more than 100 words that explains how women's involvement in prostitution is bound up with poverty.

Police and judicial bias

Some feminists have used the concept of chivalry (Morris, 1987) to describe the different police cautioning rates for men and women. Though it is difficult to quantify this, given the uncertain nature of the official statistics on cautioning, the police do seem to have a more lenient attitude towards women. However, Harris (1992) argues that the situation is more complicated in that the 'demeanour' of women who come into contact with the police is only one factor affecting the outcome. The seriousness of the crime and evidence of recidivism (committing the same crime time and again) are also important, as well as the age and respectability of the women concerned. Gregory (1986) considers that, far from chivalry, the more favourable treatment of women is due to paternalism, that is, treating women as if they were children rather than adults. However, this situation may be complicated by ethnic factors: Player (1989) found that black women are treated significantly worse than white women. Furthermore women are not necessarily treated favourably when dealt with by female officers. For example Worrall (1990) has found that female officers have a more censorious attitude than their male counterparts towards female offenders.

The treatment of women offenders by the courts has been the subject of intense study, although the issues are so complex that it is not clear that women are always treated more leniently than men by the courts. Some have argued that there is no leniency at all, but rather that women before the courts are less likely to be persistent offenders or be charged with serious offences (see for example Farrington and Morris, 1983). However, others, such as Allen (1987), argue that even women charged with more serious offences are dealt with more leniently by the courts. Hedderman and Hough (1994) claim that female offenders are much less likely than male offenders to receive a custodial sentence for nearly all indictable offences.

Item H

The sentencing of women

- The sentencing of women shoplifters was characterized by an avoidance of the fine. As a result, many women received a discharge but others received community penalties.
- Women shoplifters were less likely than comparable men to receive a prison sentence.
- Men and women stood an equal chance of going to prison for a first violent offence. However, among repeat offenders, women were less likely to receive a custodial sentence.

- Women first offenders were significantly less likely than equivalent men to receive a prison sentence for a drug offence, but recidivists were equally likely to go to prison.
- Among first and repeat offenders, women convicted of violence and drug offences were always more likely to be discharged and men more likely to be fined. Again, this seems to be a consequence of a reluctance to fine women rather than a policy of leniency.

- Overall, the results show that sentencers exhibit a general reluctance to fine women. This can result in greater leniency (a discharge) or severity (a community penalty) – the results concerning use of custody are less clear-cut.

- The number of women in prison in 2001 was more than 4,000 – a rise of 200 per cent over the previous ten years. This is the highest level since 1901. Nearly 2 in five (39 per cent) of female prisoners have been sentenced for drug-related offences.

Sources: Denscombe (2002); Hedderman and Dowds (1997).

Ⓘ Ⓐ Ⓔ

Exercise 8.13

Item H provides a summary of the key findings of a Home Office study on the sentencing of shoplifters, violent offenders and drug offenders. Read the item and assess the extent to which the conclusions of this study support the idea that the criminal justice system treats female offenders more leniently than male offenders.

What does seem to be the case is that judges' sentencing decisions are influenced by stereotypical views of the lifestyles of those in front of them. In particular, women who are seen as having a 'normal' home background are more likely to receive lighter sentences (see for example Eaton, 1986). Moreover, Young (1990), in a study of Greenham Common women who came before the courts, shows that a range of factors influenced the sentencing of these women, including the desire to deny them the chance to generate propaganda. Heidensohn (2006) argues that one danger of women being seen and treated differently by the courts is 'double deviance and double jeopardy'. She means that women caught up in the criminal justice system can come to be seen as deviant for being a criminal and also deviant from the way that women are supposed to behave. As a result, they may be penalized twice over, through direct punishment by the courts and by more informal sanctions in the family and community who seek to control the 'deviant's behaviour' more closely.

In terms of penology (see Chapter 9), policy in Canada has been strongly influenced by feminist ideas that culminated in the report, *Creating Choices* (Task Force on Federally Sentenced Women, 1990). This argued for the creation of a correctional model that would be sensitive to women's needs and experiences and be based on the notions of empowerment, choice and responsibility. New ways of organizing female prisons have been introduced that aim to reintegrate women into society through female-friendly therapy and the fostering of independence and responsibility through the involvement of community and business organizations. It is hoped that encouraging women to take responsibility for their past actions will empower them to take responsibility for their future actions. The physical manifestation of these changes is less intrusive security, small airy units and access to the land, all within a less obviously secure area.

Critics of this approach argue that it treats women as an undifferentiated category when there is a clear difference between women who are in prison and women who are not, in that the latter are free (Hannah-Moffat, 1995). There is also a tendency to deny the differences in class, ethnicity and sexual orientation that exist among female prisoners. Critics argue that characterizing female incarceration as caring and therapeutic, as opposed to the discipline and security that reign in male prisons, is to reproduce gender stereotypes. Carlen and Worrall (2004) argue that there has been a process of 'carceral clawback', where reform programmes that seek to support women prisoners' needs have been repressed as the traditional functions of prison are emphasized. Finally, the fact that security is less intrusive does not make it any less of a prison, and the prison authorities still have a whole range of disciplinary measures to fall back on, for example solitary confinement.

(I)(A)(E)

Exercise 8.14

Listed below are a number of partly completed evaluation statements relating to the strengths and weaknesses of the social constructionist views on gender and crime. Complete the statements by selecting the missing words from the list provided.

Strengths

1. They draw attention to the ......
2. The approach demands that female crime ......
3. Social constructionists focus on the ...... that treat female offenders differently from men.

Missing words

- social processes
- be taken seriously
- social construction of female crime

Weaknesses

1. They seem to deny any difference between . . . . . . for men and women.
2. They treat women as a . . . . . , when there are many divisions between them.
3. The approach justifies the . . . . . . of male and female offenders who commit the same crime.

Missing words

- offending rates
- differential treatment
- unified group

WOMEN AS THE VICTIMS OF CRIME

Croall (1992) argues that women are the prime victims of white-collar crime for a number of reasons. For example women are subject to health hazards because of the nature of their work, which is often low paid and conducted in hazardous conditions. Similarly it is female workers who in the main face sexual harassment from those in power at work, to the extent of sexual assault. Women are also victims as consumers, especially because of the activities of the slimming and cosmetic industries, and most of all by the contraceptive industry (Clarke, 1990).

Victimization surveys also reveal that women are more likely than men to fear becoming the victims of crime. However, this seems to contradict the finding that more crimes are committed in public places of entertainment, which are visited more by males than by females, than in the domestic sphere, where women are more likely to be found (Zedner, 1997). It seems at first glance that women are over-reacting to the risk of becoming a victim. However, most victimization surveys have focused on the perceived threat to personal safety, which even in these surveys is likely to be under-reported. The evidence suggests that it is male crime, especially crimes of violence, that women fear most. It should be remembered that men also fear male crime, but women's greater fear of crime may be a rational response to their greater personal experience of crime in the form of domestic violence, which often goes unreported (Stanko, 1988).

Ⓘ   Link Exercise 8.1

Re-examine Item N in Chapter 2 (p. 48). Identify and describe the way in which females worry about male crimes.

Women's fear of crime affects their lifestyles in many ways as they seek to avoid situations in which they might become victims. Fear of crime is therefore not just based on formal risk assessment in some general sense, but is related to objective factors such as poor lighting and time of night, or more subjective factors such as a sense of change and uncertainty. Therefore many women engage in avoidance behaviours, in order to minimize the risk, for example going home early from social events. For Crawford *et al.* (1990), this amounts to a 'virtual curfew'.

Ⓘ

Link Exercise 8.2

Look again at Item E in this chapter (pp. 242–3). Identify some of the types of avoidance behaviour that women adopt because of their fear of crime and their desire to reduce unwanted contact.

Sexual violence

Criminology has tended to include the phenomenon of sexual violence within the category of all criminal violence. Hence, sexual violence has been attributed with the same factors that engender all acts of violence, such as ignorance, poverty or alcohol-induced rage. As such, sexual violence tends to be associated with the poorer classes, where such factors predominate (Pavarini, 1994). However, feminist sociologists have shown that sexual and domestic violence occur in all social classes and are not confined to those on the margins of society (see for example Hamuer and Maynard, 1987). As a result attention has switched from 'problem families' to 'ordinary' families as sources of sexual and domestic violence. Feminists have argued that the issue should be viewed from both women's and men's points of view if an understanding of the phenomenon is to be reached.

Social reaction to sexual violence or violence between intimates has been found by sociologists to vary according to whether the perpetrator is male or female. Lees (1989) shows that men who have killed their partners tend to see it as a 'crime of passion', having been provoked into violence by the female partner's nagging or promiscuity. On the other hand female killers of their partners have often been subjected to long periods of violence and abuse prior to the murder, and tend to wait until the partner is asleep or drunk before committing the act, therefore signifying premeditation.

In the case of rape, most explanations have focused on social psychological explanations, that is, why some men rape in some situations. For example Felson (1993) argues that rapists look on others (male and female) as existing for their subjective sexual pleasure. While they prefer consensual sex, when this is denied they resort to rape, as in prison. A fuller sociological account is provided by Sanday (1981), who asserts that because in some societies rape is directed at more independent women, it serves to act as a warning to all women. Other explanations focus on 'cultures of masculinity' as the background to acts of rape, in which the rapist seeks signs of consent (Levi, 1997). This suggests that some male rapists offer consent as a defence in the belief that their victims had been 'asking for it' and were unable to resist their masculine charm.

The reaction of the courts to women seeking redress from sexual violence often depends on the 'master' status of the woman, that is, whether she is labelled a 'madonna' or a 'whore' (Heidensohn, 1985). The past sexual history of the complainant becomes the major component of the rape case, in an attempt to establish the existence of consent by citing previous sexual promiscuity.

Another aspect of the debate among feminists on sexual violence has been the representation of the women involved in such cases. The main focus has been on the extension of the concept of sexual violence into more and more areas of female–male relationships. In particular the idea of 'date rape' has been the subject of much discussion. Radical feminists have extended the notion of rape to include verbal coercion and any behaviour that the victim feels is violative (Roiphe, 1994). Notwithstanding the legal difficulties of accepting a definition that relies on the subjective view of one of the participants in a sexual act, some feminists have rejected the extension because it is based on 'victim feminism', that is, portraying the female as a person without sexuality or free will in sexual situations (Paglia, 1992).

Domestic violence

Domestic violence remained largely invisible until the mid-1980s because of the reluctance of the police to define it as assault (see for example Edwards, 1986). In this, the police were responding to the dominant ideology of the time, which defined what happened in the family as a private matter and husbands were assumed to have the right to chastise their wives (Faragher, 1985). Successive surveys have revealed a bleak picture of rape and domestic violence, which varies according to the timescale asked about in the surveys.

It should not be presumed that women are the only object of domestic violence. For example Straus and Gelles (1990) have found that men are as likely as women to be victims of domestic violence. Indeed, the extent of domestic violence against males (either by male or female partners) is likely to be under-reported, as victims respond to violent events in the context of what it means to be 'masculine' (Finney, 2006). However Archer (1994) argues that violence by women is largely a matter of self-defence against male threats, and Mirrlees-Black (1995) has found that in Britain females are more likely than males to be the main target of domestic violence.

The main reason why women fail to report violent assaults on themselves is that the assailant is known to them. The combination of pressure from family and friends, and apprehension about how the police will respond, keeps the level of reporting low (Stanko, 1985). The treatment by the police, especially male officers, of the victims of domestic violence tends to depend on their assessment of how 'deserving' the victim is (Hanmer *et al.*, 1989). This leads to a process of 'secondary victimization', in which the female defendant is transformed into the 'accused' as her sexual and domestic past is exposed to public scrutiny (Young, 1991). Dobash and Dobash (1992) also argue that the courts have traditionally treated violent male partners leniently.

However, developments in the 1990s and 2000s seem to suggest that the police are taking domestic violence more seriously; and Ferraro (1993) shows that perpetrators are now far more likely to be arrested. This is the result of a Home Office circular in 1986, which stressed the importance of preventing further violence from taking place once the police had left the scene (Home Office, 1986).

Sociobiological explanations of domestic violence focus on the evolutionary benefits of domestic violence. For example Burgess and Draper (1989) argue that violence towards a stepchild can be explained by the lack of a common gene. Daly and Wilson (1994) have looked at male violence towards women and found a complex interplay of biological and social factors. They believe that men have undergone evolutionary pressure to engage in risk taking, which when located within the social context of a male's 'reputation' as defender of his female's virtue, can lead to domestic violence as the male 'proves' he cannot be pushed around.

Other sociological accounts have focused on a subculture of violence in areas where self-esteem is low and therefore apparently trivial incidents may be blown out of proportion (Wolfgang and Ferracutti, 1982). Feminist accounts of male violence stress the construction of masculinity in a patriarchal society that is designed to keep women in their place (see for example Newburn and Stanko, 1994). These accounts have been criticized for being vague about the role of class and ethnicity in the construction of this masculinity, and for being unable to explain the variation in machismo from society to society.

Item I

Violence in Families

The issue of domestic violence by females is controversial. Females are generally perceived to be law-abiding, dependable in a crisis, 'naturally' calm and able to defuse anger and hostility in others while suppressing it in themselves. It is thus not surprising that society finds the notion of violent women disturbing.

There are those today who are still dubious about the use of the term 'domestic violence' ... arguing that the perpetrators of domestic violence are seen to be almost exclusively men who are acting out their 'natural' traits – aggression, physical strength and violence. It is automatically accepted that the male partner is the perpetrator and the female is the victim. This perception has resulted in certain radical feminists arguing that only *women* can be victims, not men. The denial of men as victims of domestic violence has caused some to argue for a change in the way we describe such a phenomenon. Perhaps 'domestic abuse' is a better term, because disputes of this nature are of no universal type or form; the term covers physical abuse, emotional abuse, verbal abuse, psychological abuse and sexual abuse. Evidence suggests that both females and males are capable of those five forms of assault. The findings of a study conducted at Leicester Royal Infirmary in 1992 concluded that almost equal numbers of men and women were being assaulted in their homes, and that assaulted men received more serious injuries than women, lost consciousness more often and required admission to hospital on more occasions.

The British Crime Survey for the year 2000 reported the following:

- Domestic violence accounted for one in four incidents of violence reported to the BCS.
- Domestic violence represented 10 per cent of the violent incidents reported by men.
- Domestic violence represented 40 per cent of the violent incidents reported by women.
- Studies suggest that one in four adult women will experience domestic violence at some point.
- Men also experience abuse within their relationships, but they are less likely to report being hurt, frightened or upset by what has happened. They are also less likely to be subjected to a repeated pattern of abuse.
- It is estimated that an incident of domestic violence occurs within the UK every 6 to 20 seconds every day, 365 days a year.

Source: Adapted from Luckhurst (2003).

Exercise 8.15

(E) 1. What are the arguments for and against using the concept of 'domestic violence' rather than 'domestic abuse'?

(I)(A) 2. What problems can you identify with the Leicester Royal Infirmary research that might make it a less valid piece of research about the nature and extent of domestic violence?

(I) 3. What are the differing chances of men and women experiencing violent incidents in the home?

(A) 4. Suggest reasons why female on male violence in the home has been under-reported?

(E) 5. 'Men subject to domestic violence stay with the family for mainly financial reasons.' Assess the case for and against such a point of view.

Exam focus

1. 'The invisibility of women is notable when looking at crime. Sociologists have tended to ignore the extent to which women actually do commit crime.' Evaluate this point of view.
2. How far do the evidence and the arguments support the view that female crime is significantly under-represented in official statistics?

Important concepts

Domestic violence • Deconstruction • Chivalry thesis • Hegemonic masculinity • Loss of civility • Gender deal • Patriarchy • Carceral clawback • Secondary victimization

Critical thinking

1. Should all women be classed together in the same category? Are the differences between different groups of women sufficient to make the idea of a 'common experience' unlikely?
2. How would you define 'hegemonic masculinity'? How important do you think that the concept of masculinity is in influencing men's behaviour towards criminality?
3. Should women be treated equally within the prison system, or should a different kind of custodial experience be established for female offenders?

Chapter 9

Criminal Justice and the Victims of Crime

After studying this chapter, you should:

- be familiar with issues surrounding the role of the police and policing
- be familiar with Marxist and postmodernist approaches to the law
- be aware of feminist and postmodernist views on the workings of the criminal justice system
- understand traditional and recent theoretical views on the role of prisons and punishment in society
- have gained further knowledge on victimology

Sociologists have, over the years, become interested in all aspects of the criminal justice system. The experiences of those caught up in this system differ according to their social characteristics and such factors as where they live. Teasing out and explaining the patterns of this differential experience have been of interest to successive generations of sociologists. The police have been a constant topic of sociological research, but the focus has been extended to more general areas, such as the role of law and of the concept of justice. Another theme that sociologists have addressed is the way that the courts, the prisons and other systems of punishment operate, both in practical ways and more theoretically. Finally, there has been renewed sociological interest in victims of crime.

POLICING

One of the earliest American approaches to the study of the police was to view them as a bureaucracy and examine their operations in this light. For example

Chambliss and Seidman (1971) argue that as a bureaucracy the police have a vast amount of discretion, with little accountability in the criminal justice system. As a result the police often act with brutality, not because they are by nature brutal but because they see their job as catching criminals by whatever means possible. They therefore have little respect for the due process of the law and there are few consequences when they ignore it.

Sociological interest in the British police began in the 1960s with Banton's (1964) study of the informal norms and values of the police force and the ways that these act to produce a system of 'under-enforcement', as the police seek to keep the peace rather than just catch and convict. Using ethnographic techniques, sociologists have examined 'cop culture', showing that it is multifaceted and varies with the location and rank of the police officers. For example Reus-Ianni (1983) demonstrates the conflict of culture between 'street cops' and the police managers. However, there are certain similarities, including a service ethic and a tendency to turn a blind eye to racism (Holdaway, 1991). The practice of the cop culture is to define who is likely to cause trouble and who, like them, has middle-class values. The world is therefore divided into the rough and the respectable (Reiner, 1992). Part of the reason for the development of a cop culture that is highly traditional in terms of its attitudes to outsiders is that recruitment to the police has been relatively homogeneous. Most police officers in the 1960s were white, heterosexual and male (Sullivan, 2006). More recent work (Loader and Mulcahy, 2003) argues that, as more minority ethnic, gay and most prominently women have been recruited, cop culture has fragmented, creating space for other voices to be heard and more inclusionary practices to develop.

In the 1970s the focus moved, especially in the United States, to the cost-effectiveness of the police force in controlling crime. The uncomfortable consensus that emerged was that increased numbers of police do not lead to increased clear-up rates, and that this is so irrespective of whether 'rapid response' or 'community policing' strategies are adopted. Most detection is carried by the public rather than the police themselves, and the public are dissatisfied with the performance of the police in those criminal activities that are most feared (Skolnick and Bayley, 1986).

In 2001, Garland argued that there had been a fundamental shift in the way that the authorities and the public approached issues of crime and control and suggested that a new 'culture of control' had emerged. He examined a number of attitudinal changes in both US and UK societies that established a basic principle that 'above all the public must be protected' (from crime and criminals). This was signalled by the re-emergence of the victim as the central character of the criminal justice system and an emphasis on increased security for the public whether by public bodies such as the police or through the commercialization of crime control, as exemplified by the huge increase in private security apparatus, such as burglar alarms or gated communities. One of the main results of these shifts is 'mass incarceration', as more and more criminals are sentenced to custodial terms in prison.

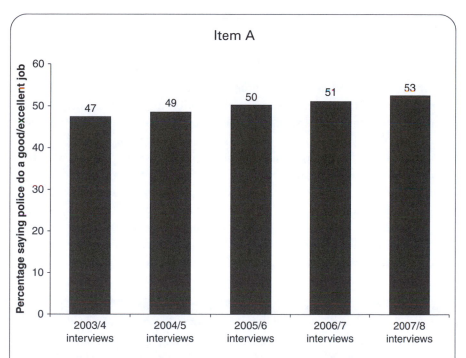

Figure 9.1 Trends in confidence in the local police, BCS 2003/4 to 2007/8

Factors strongly associated with confidence in the local police

After controlling for all other factors, the analysis found that the following factors were strongly associated with perceiving the local police to be doing a good or excellent job:

- believing that the local police are dealing with the things that matter to communities;
- thinking that the local police treat everyone fairly and with respect;
- thinking that the level of crime in the local area had stayed the same or decreased in the previous two years;
- being very or fairly satisfied with the way the police handled the matter after initiating some form of contact with them.

Source: Kershaw *et al.* (2008).

Exercise 9.1

Item A presents findings from various British Crime Surveys on satisfaction with local police performance.

(I) 1. Examine the Item and describe the trend in satisfaction shown with the police.
(E) 2. Which of the four factors identified would you think was most important in influencing levels of satisfaction and give reasons for your choice.

Community policing has been a source of some controversy in Britain and the United States. While it remains a popular option among the general public, Bennett (1994) has argued that by bolting on community police actions, such police–community consultation can raise opposition from the 'cop culture', which defines traditional policing in terms of control, not consultation. However, the alternative – 'paramilitary' policing – can lead to an amplification of crime, as the deployment of large numbers of police encourages conflict rather than dissipates it (Jefferson, 1993). Jones and Newburn (2007) argue that this is an oversimplification of police attitudes, suggesting that it was the opposition of senior police officers to more aggressive police tactics that prevented the adoption of 'zero-tolerance policing' in the UK.

(I)(E)

Exercise 9.2

Table 9.1 shows Kinsey *et al.*'s (1986) summary of community and military policing. You should appreciate that most policing in Britain falls between these two extreme styles. Evaluate these two contrasting policing strategies by identifying what you would consider to be the pros and cons of the different styles. We have provided an example chart for you to copy and use to record your answers (your chart will need to be longer than the one shown). You will see that the evaluation process has been started for you.

Table 9.1 Community and military policing

Subject	Consensus policing	Military policing
The public	Supports the police	Fears/is in conflict with the police
Information from the public	Large amount relevant to crime detection, and specific	Small amount, low-grade and general

Information from the public	Large amount relevant to crime detection, and specific	Small amount, low-grade and general
Mode of gathering information	Public-initiated; low use of police surveillance technology	Police-initiated; extensive use of surveillance technology
Police profile	Low profile; integrated with community; police officers as citizens	High profile; police as outsiders, marginalized; use of force and special militarized units
Targeting by the police	Of specific offenders	Of social groups/ stereotyped populations
Style of police intervention	Individual, consensual, reactive	Generalized, coercive, proactive
Ideal typical example	English village	Northern Ireland

Source: Kinsey *et al.* (1986).

	Consensus policing		Military policing	
Pros		**Cons**	**Pros**	**Cons**
1. Likely to receive help and support from the public.				1. Creates hostility.

These facts have been acknowledged by administrative criminologists (see pp. 99–102). Clarke and Hough (1984) suggest that, in the area of serious crime, increased policing could make a difference. However, the bulk of crime is small scale and opportunistic, and would not be affected significantly by increasing the number of police on the beat. The main purpose, then, in adopting more proactive police strategies is to increase the profile of the police and improve the public's sense of security (see for example Bennett, 1991). As the main aid to detection is evidence by the public, administrative criminologists give high marks to schemes such as Neighbourhood Watch and improved home security.

However, there is some evidence to suggest that strategies such as zero tolerance may reduce crime to some extent. In the case of New York, Skogan (1990) argues that by controlling small-scale crimes an impact can be made on more serious offences. By focusing on 'hot spots' of criminal activity, the incidence of crime can be reduced through the application of problem-oriented policing that focuses on addressing problems in a detailed and scientific way. It is not in itself a policing tactic of controlling criminals, but rather an approach that encourages innovative prevention of crime through microscopic analysis of a problem. Problem-oriented policing is associated with an analysis of factors, such as repeat victimization and prolific offenders, as well as the 'hot spots' of crime (Tilley, 2003). However, Lowman (1992) counters that this merely displaces crime to less patrolled areas, as in the control of prostitution; and Bullock and Tilley (2003) suggest that few police officers have the skills to engage successfully with problem-solving approaches. In the light of these difficulties, the idea of 'intelligence-led policing' has gained ground, in which crime detection is aided by the collection of intelligence in areas of high risk and public anxiety about crime is allayed through high visibility policing (Dalgleish and Myhill, 2004). It is distinctive in that the police gather intelligence from a wide range of overt and covert sources, not for purposes of case-specific trials, but as means of targeting the more prolific or dangerous criminals (Ratcliffe, 2008).

Item B

Zero tolerance policing

An aspect of the 'militarization' of policing is the use of language which invokes authority and 'macho' responses in the listener. Such a term is 'zero tolerance', which conjures up images of steadfastness in the face of the wave of crime. It was a term developed in New York in 1994, when a new police commissioner, Warren Bratton, took over control of the 'fight against crime'. It was a time of particular lawlessness in New York and there was a public sense that 'something must be done' to re-establish some form of law and order on the New York streets. Commissioner Bratton's strategy (called 'quality of life policing' and not 'zero tolerance' – see Newburn and Jones, 2007) was two-pronged. His main thrust was to reorganize the police force so that corruption was eliminated and police officers were placed back on the streets and not in their cars. The second prong was based on the idea of 'broken windows theory' which argued that low levels of criminal disruption, such as begging, incivilities, drunkenness, etc., created a cultural climate within which crime thrived. By getting his officers to enforce the law against fare-dodging on the subway (endemic at the time), there were spin offs in the larger field of crime. Thus, checking out fare-evaders and patting them down (searching them) had the side effect of reducing gun carrying on the subway, as there was more likelihood that carriers would get caught.

Bratton argued that this was not really a 'zero-tolerance' policy at all, but more a systematic attempt to ensure good policing at the level of the street – what has been called 'confident policing'. The effect of all this was that the crime statistics did fall (Zimring, 2006). However, by showing that what might be seen as minor infractions such as graffiti would be acted upon, Bratton argued that he had drawn a line in the sand as to what would be tolerated in a civilized society.

Critics of the approach suggested that the policy adopted was in reality a short-term fix and it would need to be shown that there was a permanent and sustained drop in criminality to prove the policy worked. These critics argue that the construction of the criminal statistics can be manipulated by politicians. Longer-term approaches such as community partnership schemes would need to be developed if the benefits of zero tolerance were going to be long-lasting.

Exercise 9.3

Read Item B and answer the following questions.

Ⓐ 1. According to Item B, 'the construction of the criminal statistics can be manipulated by politicians'. Identify two ways in which recorded crime statistics can be manipulated.

Ⓐⁿ 2. In no more than 100 words, summarize the policing strategy of zero tolerance, as outlined in Item B.

Ⓘ Ⓐ 3. Item B claims that policing strategy alone cannot combat crime. Using information in the item and other sources, support this claim.

Therefore sociological attention has shifted away from just the study of the police towards the concept of 'policing' and the ways in which the forces of social control, including the police, seek to protect a specific social order through surveillance and sanctions (Shearing, 1992). This surveillance is not only carried out by the police but by many other agencies, including the transport police, the army in Northern Ireland and private security organizations, and by technological means such as CCTV in city centres.

It is fairly well established that the objects of this surveillance are those at the lower end of the social hierarchy, who have been described as 'police property' (Cray, 1972). The police themselves acknowledge that these groups of people represent their main work by describing them in derogatory terms – a practice reciprocated by the groups themselves in their descriptions of the police. This underclass (see Chapters 6 and 8) is therefore the focus of the majority of police activity (Morgan *et al.*, 1990).

In the conditions of postmodernity the police react to the underclass as a group tainted with criminality, rather than as a section of society that can contain both law-abiding and law-breaking individuals. This stigmatization of the underclass as inherently criminal leads to resistance among them, for example, to the stop-and-search powers of the police, which are seen as racist and targeted at a particular section of society. In turn this resistance leads the police into coercive responses that expose the iron fist behind the velvet glove of the civilized state.

ⒾⒶ
ⓀⓊ
Ⓔ

Link Exercise 9.1

Re-examine Item G in Chapter 7 (pp. 214–15). Use the information there and elsewhere to assess the extent to which police stops can be seen as racist and targeted at particular sections of society.

Another development in postmodern societies is the use of profiles in policing as a way of identifying high-risk individuals such as drug couriers and hijackers. These profiles consist of defined behaviours that it is argued distinguish ordinary people from potential criminals in specific settings. They also allow the police to target particular individuals for intense surveillance or questioning (Cloud, 1985).

New right criminologists, such as Wilson and Kelling (1982), agree that the primary function of the police is social control rather than the detection of crime. However, they consider that the amount of crime and the degree of orderliness in a community are connected. By providing a community with a sense of security, locals are able to maintain informal control mechanisms that in the long term reduce the incidence of crime. The implication of Wilson and Kelling's approach is that there should be no decriminalization of 'crimes without victims', because deviant behaviour such as drunkenness and pornography can undermine a community's sense of order and willingness to participate in informal crime-control activities. Neither measures aimed at alleviating poverty nor heavy policing can be as effective as the traditional police function of maintaining long-term order.

ⓀⓊⒶ

Exercise 9.4

Briefly define and give an example of each of the following concepts:

1. Informal social control.
2. Formal social control.

Another feature of social control that has been subject to some discussion by sociologists is what is termed the 'privatization of policing'. This is a complex process that includes the massive growth in the number of private security firms, especially in the United States. The majority of private policing is concerned with profit, that is, security personnel are employed to prevent losses (South, 1988). To combat employee theft, corporations rely increasingly on technology to 'police' the actions of their workers. An example of this is POS (point-of-sale technology), which records unusual activity at tills. But it also encompasses the growth in self-policing agencies such as Community Relations Offices, Neighbourhood Watch, CCTV, and so on, which are examples of early reporting and increased surveillance. In the twenty-first century the boundaries between public and private policing have become more blurred with the development of 'extended policing role partnerships', with groups such as local authority wardens and Police Community Support Officers, which exist in formal relationships with the police force (Crisp and Ward, 2008). This growth of 'plural policing' has been attributed in part to financial pressures, the disappearance of secondary control agents, such as park keepers, and an increased demand from the public for more security (Crawford, 2003).

Johnston (1992) distinguishes between 'responsible citizenship', which is activity coordinated or sanctioned by the state, and 'autonomous citizenship', where self-policing groups have little contact with official organizations. Research on Neighbourhood Watch schemes (see for example McConville and Shepherd, 1992) suggests that they have little impact on either the incidence of crime or the fear of crime in the middle-class areas in which they tend to operate. More informal methods of responsible citizenship such as looking out for neighbours' property when they are away are also concentrated in middle-class areas.

Autonomous citizenship is associated with vigilantism, of which the best known examples are the Guardian Angels patrols in the US subway systems. Kenney (1987) argues that the presence of the Angels has caused a fear of crime where no 'crime problem' actually exists. Beck (1992) contends that autonomous citizenship results in a new stratification of risk in which the rich are able to afford protection from crime while the poor cannot. Shearing and Stenning (1983) argue that there is a 'new feudalism', in which large parts of social life are policed by private corporations. Also implied is an integration of social control into the fabric of everyday life, in which members of the local community are simultaneously the watchers and the watched – the disciplinary society of Foucault (1977). But as Marx (1988) argues, private policing and corporate intrusion into private lives may be acceptable in a maximum security society, but such activities raise ethical and political questions in a liberal society.

(A)

Exercise 9.5

Identify two ethical and two political issues arising from private policing.

There is now considerable evidence to suggest that policing has very little impact on the levels of crime in society. Studies suggest that increasing the number of police officers, response rates and community patrols may reassure the public, but they make little difference to the capture and conviction of criminals (see for example Bayley, 1994). This has been accepted to some extent by the managers of the police themselves, who are seeking new ways of involving the public in law enforcement activity. Nevertheless the police retain a prominent place in the public's affection and continue to dominate popular culture, especially television (Sparks, 1992). They retain what Loader (1997) has described as 'symbolic power' – the belief that the police can do something about crime as an important part of the public's world-view. They have come to symbolize a world of order in a time of uncertainty. The police thus have a powerful hold on the public imagination, which constrains the ways in which they can change in order to meet the challenges of the postmodern world. There is also a 'police voice', which frames our understanding of criminal events and also conveys information to the public on the dominant forms of risk and insecurity in society.

In the United Kingdom and in the United States, the phenomenon of terrorist attacks on the World Trade Center and the London Underground has intensified debates over the nature and severity of policing and the social policies and legal framework within which the police operate. Despite the New Labour mantra of 'tough on crime and tough on the causes of crime', some sociologists such as Nellis (2004) detect a new punitiveness in the approaches to crime of post-9/11 governments, in which the focus is just being tough on crime. Policies cited to support this view include electronic tagging, the increased use of CCTV, ASBOs (anti-social behaviour orders) and automatic sentencing.

THE LAW

As early as the 1950s conflict theorists grew interested in the use of the law by powerful groups as a resource to maintain and extend that group's power. The law was therefore seen as a weapon that could be used to criminalize the actions of less powerful groups who might challenge the power and privilege of the most powerful. Vold (1958) has argued that as groups in society come into conflict with each other, they struggle to obtain control over police power and the law-making process. The aim of this control is to criminalize the behaviour of those groups who do not have such control in order to weaken their ability to gain power in society.

Austin Turk (1982), another conflict theorist, asserts that control by the powerful is only partly established through the use of the law. He accepts that by controlling legal images the powerful in society can exercise a subtle form of social control, through their establishment of the formal laws of society and control of the law-enforcement process. However, there is also the issue of 'control of living time'. By this, Turk means the establishment of a normative social order that is accepted by subordinate groups as natural. Here Turk is adding the notion of social change to his view of social order. As members of the 'old order' die out, the rules of the new society become accepted as the norm and serve to secure the power of those in authority.

Marxists argue that the law is a tool of the ruling class in that the definitions of crime in society serve the interests of the ruling class and encapsulate the rights of property rather than human rights. The effect of this is that those without property have no defence in the law, but are subject to its sanctions. Conversely the activities of the ruling class are exempted from the sanctions of criminal law (Michalowski and Bohlander, 1976). Moreover the belief of the proletariat in the just working of the law has the effect that they police themselves. Law is therefore seen as part of the set of institutions that establish a hegemonic culture. This is necessary if workers are to accept the legitimacy of the capitalist state and the discipline of the factory.

A development in Marxist theory during the 1980s and 1990s was the rise of a 'law-and-order ideology', which advocates the harsher punishment of criminals in order to halt the apparent or real rise in the rate of crime. Marxists such as Cavadino and Dignan (1992) argue that the loss of belief in full employment means that the fear of unemployment no longer operates to discipline the workforce and has been replaced by the fear of crime. This involves the creation of an 'enemy within', such as 'dole scroungers' and criminals, who became reconstituted as the 'other'. This leads to demands for the harsher treatment of those who commit crimes. This development coincided with the rise of new right ideologies that combine economic liberalism with authoritarianism on social issues (Scraton, 1987). In order to contain the social unrest created by new right economic policies, a new punitiveness has to be developed.

Lee (2007) takes this view of the fear of crime further, in exploring the paradox of high levels of fear of crime coexisting in the early twenty-first century with falling levels of crime, as recorded by the criminal statistics (Simmons and Dodd, 2003). He has argued that there are two aspects of crime that need to be considered in the context of the governance of crime. On the one hand, governments seek to control the levels of crime and the activities of criminals directly through the operation of the police and courts. On the other hand the fear of crime is used as a 'technology of governance' to reduce crime indirectly by encouraging citizens to manage their own behaviour in order to avoid risks of being made a victim of crime. Here, Lee is being influenced by Foucauldian notions of discipline and governance (see pp. 181–5). This tactic has been explicitly adopted by the Home Office at times: 'An element of fear can be considered helpful in persuading people to guard against victimization' (Home Office Standing Conference on Crime Prevention 1989, quoted by Lee, 2007, p. 140). One effect of this tactic is to produce a fearing subject (the citizen going about her or his lawful business) and the feared object (the stereotyped criminal classes of whom the former is fearful). It is through the fearing subjects managing their own behaviour that the activities of the feared object can be reduced.

With the coming to power of a Labour Government in 1997, the focus shifted towards what is called the antisocial behaviour and respect agendas. The main focus of these initiatives was low-level nuisance behaviour that was thought to lead often to more serious criminal activity. The logic was that, by cracking down on day-to-day irritants, Labour would be seen to be dealing with the crime that most affected people's lives. The central device for controlling (usually young people's) behaviour was the ASBO, or Anti-Social Behaviour Order. Individuals given an ASBO are forbidden to carry out specific activities such as entering particular areas, otherwise they will be arrested. Powers given to the police to deal with low-level disruption have gradually increased in the twenty-first century, to include powers such as dispersal orders to prevent gatherings of groups where trouble has previously occurred. The impact of these agendas is difficult to assess. Morgan (2006) has argued that the main effect has been to allow the police to 'fast-track' young people into custody, rather than increase respect for each other on the street.

Exercise 9.6

'ASBOs have become a badge of honour.'

Ⓘ 1. What do you think is meant by this statement?
Ⓐⁿ 2. Of ASBO breaches, 62 per cent result in the offender being given a custodial sentence. Does this affect the argument that they are a badge of honour?

Some postmodernists take a constitutive approach to the law. That is, they do not see the relationship between the law and society as one where the latter causes the former. Hence they reject the idea that the law has merely been created by powerful social groups in order to preserve their power and privileges. Nor do they accept that the law constitutes the centre of social control and that the process only moves one way, with the law acting to control the actions of individuals. Rather they suggest that in part the law constitutes social relations, and in part social relations make up the law. In other words the law does shape non-legal social relations, but non-legal social relations – made up in part of rules and procedures – penetrate the law and become part of it (Moore, 1973). Therefore law and society are not separate entities, but are interwoven with each other in a seamless web. The law is therefore part of state power, which, as Foucault (1977) argues, is diffused through the social fabric as part of the 'surveillance society'. The law is thus not a fixed body of knowledge, procedures or rules, but an uneasy outcome of the relationships between legal agencies and other social formations (Fitzpatrick, 1984).

Exercise 9.7

We would like you to evaluate the Marxist approach to the law by carrying out the following tasks.

(E) 1. Copy the evaluation chart below and complete it by entering two additional strengths and weaknesses of the Marxist approach.
(I)(E) 2. Underneath your chart, write a postmodernist critique of the Marxist approach to the law. To do this you need to draw on the postmodernist views outlined above.

Evaluation of the Marxist approach to the law

Strengths	Weaknesses
1. The approach has a strong power dimension.	1. The approach is ideologically driven.
2.	2.
3.	3.

THE COURTS AND THE CRIMINAL JUSTICE SYSTEM

Carol Smart (1989) sees the judicial process as inherently 'androcentric', that is, focused on male rather than female concerns. When women go to the courts for justice, they subject women's demands to 'patriarchal domination', that is, they are subject to the decisions of the mainly male judges. This has the effect of deradicalizing their search for equality. By this Smart means that when women demand legal equality there are uncomfortable consequences for men. By having recourse to the courts, the challenge their demands may make to male power is softened, because they are subject to the 'male gaze' of the judiciary. Women would therefore be better off not going to the law for help.

Item C

Judges

In 1991 there were 1,736 full-time and part-time judges. Of these 92 were women and six were from ethnic minorities.

A report by the Law Society in March 1991 argued that the current method of selecting judges in Britain leads to a racial and sexual bias in which the judges are predominantly white and male. Unless the system is changed, argues the Law Society, there is every likelihood that future generations of judges will continue to be white and male. The selection procedure at present relies heavily on comments by judges and other senior lawyers on the candidate's suitability for a post in the judiciary. This weights the system in favour of the views of the existing judges and senior lawyers and effectively loads the system against the selection of women and ethnic minorities. Indeed, the Law Society has warned the Lord Chancellor that the current appointments system may be illegal under the 1976 Race Relations Act in the way its reliance on 'word of mouth' selection operates to reduce the chances of 'outsiders' from getting appointed.

The Law Society report rejects the idea that the profile of judges reflects the make-up of the pool of senior lawyers from whose ranks the judges are selected. Of practising barristers, 21 per cent are women and 6 per cent are from ethnic minorities. Even these proportions are not reflected in the current judiciary.

Table 9.2 The make-up of the judiciary, 1991

Judges	Total	Women	Ethnic minorities
House of Lords	10	0	0
Court of Appeal	27	2	0
High Court	83	2	0
Circuit judges	429	19	1
Recorders	744	42	3
Assistant recorders	443	27	2

Source: Denscombe (1992).

Exercise 9.8

ⓘⒶ 1. Drawing on evidence in Item C, support the argument that the judiciary is a male-dominated profession.

ⓘⒶ 2. Suggest one implication of the information in Item C for women going to the courts for justice.

ⓘ 3. According to Table 9.2, how many circuit judges were from ethnic minority backgrounds in 1991?

ⓘ 4. With reference to Item C, why might the selection system for judges be considered to be illegal under the 1976 Race Relations Act?

ⓘⒶ 5. Apart from the reasons suggested in Item C, identify one other explanation that might account for the low numbers of women and ethnic minorities in the judicial system.

Postmodernists suggest that the criminal justice system (enforcement agencies such as the police and courts, legislative agencies and penal agencies such as the probation service and the prisons) has changed in response to wider changes in society, which together are characterized as postmodernity. In particular the emergence of the 'risk society' (Beck, 1992) has been cited as having an important effect on all social organizations, and specifically on the criminal justice system. The idea of a 'risk society' does not imply that individuals face greater risks now than in the past, but that the idea of risk has come to play an important part in the way that individuals and institutions seek to manage the way in which they live. For example, with the absence of generalized war in the Western democracies since the 1940s, it would be difficult to argue that the risk of death by gunshot had increased. However, individuals may still perceive that their risk of being shot by an individual gunman (and they are nearly always male) may have increased, or, more importantly, this may affect the ways in which institutions organize activities to meet these perceived threats. As Ericson (1994) suggests, the institutions of criminal law use discourses of risk to calculate and manage their activities, which in turn affects the ways in which operatives think and behave. But the converse is also true. As Kasperson and Kasperson (1996) argue, the public also make assessments (mainly based on media reporting of risk events) of the efficiency of the criminal law institutions in dealing with risk, and therefore with the level of trust that is given to them.

The risk society is constituted through fear, rational calculation and insurance. What this means is that modern hierarchical societies that are constituted through status, inequality and integration are replaced by societies in which the distribution, management and control of risk is central in shaping social arrangements. For example risks affect different groups in society differentially, but they do cut across the traditional modernist boundaries of class and property, which become blurred and no longer form the basis of social action. In terms of crime and deviance, the emphasis in the risk society shifts from 'deviance/control/order' to 'knowledge/risk/security' (Ericson and Carriere, 1994). In such circumstances the criminal justice system becomes less concerned with the control of individual deviants, and more with the classification of populations into identifiable categories of risk. For example members of the underclass are seen not as individuals with a capacity for criminal behaviour, but as a category of those who are likely to pose a high risk to others and themselves in terms of crime.

The interrelationships between various institutions in postmodern society are central to the way in which the criminal justice agencies seek to manage risk. For example the police increasingly act upon crime only when it is connected to other agencies concerned with risk, especially the insurance industry. Property theft is therefore 'actioned' by the police in order to meet the requirements of insurance claims. If the sums are so small that no insurance is involved, then the thefts are less likely to be investigated. The police are also transformed from the guardians of the community to advisers on risk for other institutions and social groups. Their activities are also increasingly focused on areas of risk, which are subject to greater surveillance, through, for example, CCTV, the patrolling of high crime areas and the increasing use of covert surveillance technologies. The agencies of insurance are themselves part of the surveillance society, in which individuals engage in the 'coproduction' of their own social control. By calculating risk and managing it through insurance mechanisms, individuals practise surveillance over their own activities (Defert, 1991).

PRISONS, INCARCERATION AND DECARCERATION

Exercise 9.9

Read the following edited extracts from Denscombe (1998, 2002, 2003), then answer the questions below.

Since 1997, the number of people in prison has steadily increased and Britain's prisons are struggling to accommodate the increasing numbers. One of the reasons for the increase is the impact of stiffer sentencing policies following the heavier sentencing provisions of the Crime (Sentences) Act. In 2002, the number of prisoners in England and Wales reached an all-time record of 72,500 and Home Office projections indicate that it could hit 100,000 before the end of the decade. The rate of growth is rapid. In the early 1990s there were 48,000 inmates which means that there has been a 50 per cent increase over a period of just ten years.

1. What was the record number of people in English and Welsh prisons in 2002?
2. Identify two aspects of the Crime (Sentences) Act referred to in the extract. (If you get stuck on this question try searching the Internet for the answers.)

Traditional approaches to prisons tend to see imprisonment as a tool for controlling crime that is in line with the increasing moderation associated with the development of complex societies (Durkheim, 1960). Marxists on the other hand relate the development of prisons to the issue of labour in capitalist society. For Rusche and Kirchheimer (1968), prisons are a source of labour, with convicts acting as a reserve army of labour. Later Marxists such as Melossi and Pavarini (1981) argue that the relationship is more complex. They believe there is a correspondence (or similarity) between the factory and the prison, as the idea of discipline is central to the operations of both types of organization. Prisons and factories have common requirements if they are to be efficient, in that the lower inmates or workers have to accept restrictions on time and space if security or profits are to be achieved.

The work of Foucault (1977) has been an important influence on the sociological understanding of the role of prisons in modern and postmodern societies. Foucault is critical of the liberal reading of prisons as a better form of punishment than the more public and brutal punishments of previous eras. This view has become associated with Spierenburg (1984), who draws on Elias's (1978) notion of the 'civilizing process' to suggest that the move towards imprisonment rather than execution was part of the increasing sensibility of society. Foucault, on the other hand, argues that prisons were just one of the ways in which new forms of domination appeared in modern society, which was essentially a 'disciplinary society'. The power of the disciplinary society was exercised through a variety of means, but involved the objectification (treating people as objects with certain characteristics rather than as individual human beings) and classification of people and activities. The development of prisons, and specifically different types of 'incarcerative institutions' (institutions that govern the whole life of inmates, such as asylums, men's and women's prisons, prisons for the criminally insane, and so on), were therefore not some great improvement on past arrangements, but a more sophisticated way of ensuring compliance through surveillance.

This has led some sociologists to suggest that any attempt to provide new policies to deal with crime and deviance are merely more subtle ways of increasing oppression and recasting repressive practices in less obvious ways. Cohen (1985), for example, argues that decarceration policies such as halfway houses and parole have done little to change the way in which societies see the punishment of criminal activity. Instead they act to blur the boundaries between formal and informal control. Penal reform is therefore seen as a 'technology of power' that makes social control increasingly difficult to attain as the traditional boundaries of time and space ('going to prison', a sentence spent in a confined space) dissolve.

Postmodernists more generally justify prisons in terms of preventative custody, that is, the point of imprisonment is not to punish or reform the inmates, but to protect the rest of society from dangerous individuals. This leads to the development of basic provision prisons, especially in the privatized sector, with little educational or recreational facilities on offer.

However, on the broader level of deviancy control rather than control of crime, Cohen (1979) argues that there has been a transformation in the way that society views institutions such as asylums and reformatories. They have become organizations of last resort, rather than the main way in which society controls deviants and criminals. The social policy of moving inmates out of institutions and into the community is termed a policy of decarceration. This movement towards community punishment is based on the argument that prisons are ineffective or even dangerous, because they strengthen the criminal's commitment to crime. Community-based alternatives, for example community sentence orders, are also seen as cheaper and more humane than the traditional incarceration system. Moreover there has been growth in the ideology of the community, which argues that, as the sources of much crime are in community institutions such as the family and school, solutions should be found within the context of the community.

Cohen is critical of these arguments because he believes they have been asserted rather than tested, and that the effectiveness of community solutions is suspect. He argues that they may lead to the neglect of deviants, or to a more subtle form of coercion being applied to them. Echoing what is often cited as a feature of postmodern society, Cohen believes that there has been a blurring of the boundaries between formal and informal control, so that 'half-way houses' may be institutions where delinquents can experience some sense of freedom, but they are also subject to similar sets of rules that exist in prisons. They can also act as preventative institutions – places where those identified as likely to offend again can be taken and 'treated'. While this 'screening' of potential deviants has always gone on (for example through informal cautioning by the police), the existence of community programmes now allows deviants to be diverted into semiformal control programmes. According to Cohen, this allows new deviant populations, as well as the traditional ones, to be processed in more sophisticated ways. In Cohen's words, community-based-punishment 'widens the net' by bringing new populations into contact with crime prevention and 'thins the mesh' by intensifying the degree to which the system of crime control interferes in the lives of those it touches. This results in a 'punitive city' in which more and more activities are subject to surveillance by and interference from the criminal justice system.

ⒾⓀ
ⓊⒺ

Exercise 9.10

Referring to material in this chapter and other sources, identify five arguments for and five against community punishment and list them in an extended version of the chart below (we have provided one of each to start you off).

Arguments for and against community punishment

For	Against
1. A cheaper alternative to prisons.	1. May be less likely than custodial sentences to deter offenders from engaging in crime.
2.	2.
3.	3.
4.	4.
5.	5.

This approach has been criticized by Bottoms (1983), mainly on the ground that the type of punishment described by Cohen is a relatively minor and declining part of the criminal justice system. The most frequent form of punishment imposed by the courts is the fine. Bottoms argues that the aim of fining criminals is not so much to discipline them into changing their behaviour, but to symbolize their blameworthiness for their wrong-doing. According to Bottoms, rather than the 'disciplinary society' supported by Cohen, we live in a 'juridical society', in which there is increasing indirect control of groups, not increasing control of the individual.

JUSTICE AND PUNISHMENT

The traditional Marxist approach to punishment was established by Rusche and Kirchheimer (1968 [1939]). They argued that the severity or leniency of punishment in society is related to the scarcity or otherwise of labour. When the value of labour is high, then punishment is relatively light, so that labour shortages will not be made worse by the incarceration of large numbers of workers. Moreover they argued for the principle of 'lesser eligibility', that is, conditions in prison should be worse than those outside the prison. This has been criticized as an oversimplification of the relationship between the economy and punishment.

Cohen (1996) argues that there is a 'new punitiveness' in the public attitude towards crime. This is a consequence not just of the increase in crime, but also of the political parties and ideologues using crime waves for their own ends. Crime waves are presented by the media and the agencies of law and order as the intensification of a particular type of criminal activity in order to demand that something be done about that activity (see pp. 117–24). This has led not only to the adoption of military discourse such as the 'war against crime', but also, Cohen argues, to the adoption of military techniques by the forces of law and order throughout the world. The killing of street urchins in Rio De Janeiro by off-duty police death squads is just one extreme example of this process. More mundane is the use of 'Star Wars' technology to track cars in the 'fight against crime'.

This 'new punitiveness' is exemplified by a number of characteristics that have informed policy in many Western societies, such as New Labour's slogan of 'tough on crime and tough on the causes of crime'. The political competition to be hard on crime is based on a public perception that crime is rising and constitutes the major threat in society. This perception exists regardless of whether crimes rates are going up or down. Other assumptions of the new punitiveness are that 'prison works' (see below) and that it is the individual who is responsible for his or her own actions in relation to crime. Similarly, it is a public perception that the criminal justice system favours the criminal not the victim, and the new punitiveness proposes a reversal of this priority.

Sociologists such as Braithwaite (1989) argue that the criminal justice system needs to be geared more towards maximizing the shame felt by the criminal. The procedures and ceremonies of the courts and the activities of the media should be harnessed to induce a sense of shame in those convicted. In this sense there would be a new punitiveness. However, Braithwaite goes on to argue that the actual punishment imposed should as far as possible seek to reintegrate the offender into society. This needs to be done because of an insight of Labelling Theory – that the efforts of society to control criminal behaviour (for example by imprisonment) often leads to an intensification of criminality in the individual. This is partly through opportunities to learn how to be a criminal that imprisonment presents ('prisons as the universities of crime') and partly to an internalization of the criminal label.

An alternative to prison of 'restorative justice' has emerged (Van Ness and Strong, 2007) from peacemaking criminology to try and counterbalance this tendency. Peacemaking Theory emerged from the work of Pepinsky and Quinney (1991) and was opposed both to criminalization and victimization. With its emphasis on non-violence, the approach stressed the need to restore a sense of justice amongst all participants in the criminal justice system, and this was to be achieved through conflict resolution processes rather than incarceration. Criminal justice was therefore seen as a moral process rather than a strictly juridical one and one in which power in society was challenged. By stressing that all people in society are connected, the theory argued that the 'war on crime' resulted in 'negative peace', while only by establishing a 'positive peace' between those involved in criminal events can crime be eliminated (Fuller and Wozniak, 2006). The theory was not just an interpretive approach as the peacemaking theorists also argued that the inequalities of class, race and gender needed to be addressed if a positive peace and a situation of social justice were to be established. The policies advocated by this theory operate at international, national and local levels and include such initiatives as truth commissions, community reconciliation programmes, witnessing for peace, in which groups actively engage with opponents' viewpoints, and, at an individual level, mediation programmes between criminals and their victims. This is clearly an idealistic approach to criminality and has been criticized for being unrealistic and not easily open to empirical testing (Barak, 2005).

In restorative justice then, the offenders meet with the victims of their actions and through the mediation of the state, a plan of compensation is worked out. The victims have an opportunity to explain the hurt that has been done to them and the offenders can offer apologies and restorative action. In this way, the victims gain some compensation and, as it is the offender's actions that are shamed and not the offender's person, the possibility of reintegration is increased. While the effects of restorative justice seem to be positive, with participants generally recording satisfaction with the outcomes (Van Ness and Strong, 2007), the evidence of a meta-analysis seems to suggest that it works best with low-risk offenders (Bonta *et al.*, 2006). A key issue for victim–offender reconciliation or mediation programmes is whether they are effective in reducing reoffending. While there is limited evidence on recidivism, surveys in the UK and Australia (Maxwell and Morris, 2002) have established that there is a significant reduction in reoffending after restorative programmes. Young (2002) has argued that restorative justice is difficult to apply to corporate crime, because the perpetrator is an institution rather than an identifiable individual. Moreover, the power imbalance between victim and corporation makes meaningful interaction difficult. Dignan (2005) argued that there could be a meaningful resolution of hurt and damage where the corporation engages positively with the process.

Item D

Table 9.3   Attitudes towards prisoners, Britain, 1996 (percentages)

	Strongly agree/ agree	Neither agree nor disagree	Disagree/ strongly disagree	Can't choose/ not answered	All respondents
Life sentences should mean life	87	5	5	4	100
Prisons should try harder to reform prisoners, rather than just punishing them	79	10	7	4	100
Courts should give longer sentences to criminals	61	24	10	6	100
People who get sent to prison have much too easy a time	61	23	10	6	100
Prisoners who behave well should usually be released before the end of their sentence	35	21	40	5	100
Only hardened criminals, or those who are a danger to society, should be sent to prison	31	13	52	4	100

Source: Pulinger and Summerfield (1998).

Exercise 9.11

Item D contains findings from the 1996 British Social Attitudes Survey. Study this data and complete the tasks below.

ⓘⒶⒺ 1. Item D suggests that there is a new punitiveness in the public attitude towards crime. Assess the extent of this.

ⓘⒶⒺ 2. Carry out a small-scale survey in your school or college to test the reliability of the British Social Attitude Survey findings. You should question around 50 people on each of the statements in Item D. Use a five-point scale ranging from 'strongly agree' to 'strongly disagree'. When you have completed your survey, convert your results into percentages and compare your findings with the data in Item D.

There have also been changes in the way that punishment, justice and guilt are perceived in postmodern society. Just as sociology has sought to establish the causes of crime in individual and social circumstances, so society has traditionally looked to concepts such as 'guilt', 'responsibility', 'treatment' and 'rehabilitation' as the basic tools for dealing with crime. Thus criminal justice is concerned to find out who are guilty of crimes and hold them responsible, and to penalize them with an appropriate punishment. However, the emergence of the risk society has altered the ways in which justice and the control of crime are viewed.

Rather than focus on the establishment of individual culpability for a crime, postmodern social control agencies are more concerned with the identification and management of groups of individuals according to the degree of danger they present to others. This management is achieved by classifying groups of people according to calculations of their dangerousness, and is expressed through discourses, or ways of speaking, that identify some groups as more dangerous than others (see p. 128). This means that postmodern societies engage in the rational calculation of risk, just like an actuary might engage in risk assessment for insurance purposes. This situation is therefore called 'actuarial justice' (Feeley and Simon, 1994) and crime is taken as normal – an activity to be regulated rather than eliminated or treated. It does not mean that the individual disappears from postmodernist analysis, but that people are seen not as single entities, but as members of certain subgroups with differing degrees of risk attached to them.

An important aspect of actuarial justice is the development of 'incapacitation theory' in dealing with criminal offenders (Moore et al., 1984). This suggests that crime will not be reduced by changing individual criminals into law-abiding citizens, or by eliminating poverty or whatever, but by ensuring that those who offend cannot reoffend for a given amount of time. This implies that there should be greater use of imprisonment, not as a means of retribution or rehabilitation, but because putting criminals away postpones or reduces the number of subsequent crimes, thus changing the actuarial chance of crime in society. Imprisonment reduces the danger to the rest of society. This reduction of danger is maximized by 'selective incapacitation', where criminals with high-risk profiles are given longer sentences and those who constitute a low risk are given non-custodial sentences.

With regard to the United States, Zedlewski (1987) argues that the increased use of imprisonment is cost effective in the long run, in that putting offenders behind bars saves money in terms of policing and the cost to victims, and that such savings outweigh the cost of keeping them in prison. However Greenberg (1990) is critical of this position, arguing that it is highly ideological and ignores important costs, such as the cost to the individual prisoner, or the benefits that would be gained if the money spent on prisons was spent on other welfare programmes, for example education.

(I)(E)

Exercise 9.12

Drawing on relevant information from this chapter, draw up an extended version of the chart below and complete it by identifying five more arguments for and against imprisonment.

Arguments for and against imprisonment

For	Against
1. Serves to punish the offender.	1. Can be hard for ex-prisoners to reintegrate themselves into society.
2. Acts as a form of retribution.	2. Recidivism tends to be high among ex-prisoners.
3.	3.
4.	4.
5.	5.
6.	6.
7.	7.

Exercise 9.13

(I)(E) Printed below is a questionnaire on Community Service Orders and other forms of sentencing. We would like you to examine this questionnaire and weigh up its good and bad points. To help you assess the quality of the questionnaire, refer to the guidelines on survey design on p. 52. You need to give thought to how successful the questionnaire is at operationalizing the hypothesis and those research aims which you think are measurable with the help of a questionnaire. Record your evaluation of the good points and bad points in a two-column chart.

Questionnaire on Community Service Orders and other forms of sentencing

I am a sociological researcher interested in crime and punishment. I would be very grateful if you could complete this questionnaire to assist my research. You do not have to answer any question which you find irrelevant or offensive.

Thank you.
1. What age group are you in?
   20–29 [ ] 30–39 [ ] 40–49 [ ] 50–59 [ ] 60+ [ ]
2. Are you
   Male [ ] Female [ ]
3. Do you live in a rural or urban area?
   Rural [ ] Urban [ ]
4. If a first time offender burgled a house, which sentence would you consider to be the most appropriate?
   Community Service Order [ ] Imprisonment [ ]
5. There are other sentences used, apart from Community Service and imprisonment, in British courts. Please list those which you are aware of below.
6. To what extent do you agree with the following statements?

   a) Community Service is more effective for the individual offender than most other forms of sentencing.
      Strongly Agree [ ] Agree [ ] Disagree [ ] Strongly Disagree [ ]
   b) Compared to imprisonment, Community Service is a 'soft option'.
      Strongly Agree [ ] Agree [ ] Disagree [ ] Strongly Disagree [ ]
   c) Courts should impose tougher sentences on criminals.
      Strongly Agree [ ] Agree [ ] Disagree [ ] Strong Disagree [ ]
   d) Alternatives to imprisonment would be beneficial to society.
      Strongly Agree [ ] Agree [ ] Disagree [ ] Strongly Disagree [ ]

7. There has been a continuing increase in the British prison population. Do you think this will continue to rise or gradually decline?
   Rise [ ] Decline [ ]

8. How much do you think it costs to keep an offender in prison for one year?
   £1,200 [ ] £17,000 [ ] £24,000 [ ]
9. How much do you think it costs to keep an offender on Community Service for one year?
   £1,200 [ ] £17,000 [ ] £24,000 [ ]
10. What do you think are the main aims of Community Service?
11. What do you think are the main aims of prison sentences?

Thank you for your time. You are most welcome to read my study after its completion.

Rationale

Hypothesis

Community Service Orders are more effective than other forms of sentencing for both the individual offender and society.

Additional research aims

1. To investigate the opinions of individuals involved in the running of Community Service Orders and other forms of sentencing.
2. To examine how Community Service Orders and other forms of sentencing have been discussed and portrayed in the media.
3. To look at previous research and studies on Community Service Orders and other forms of sentencing to compare the findings with my own.
4. To investigate the aims of Community Service Orders and other forms of punishment.

While there has been a constant sociological focus on criminals and prisoners, there has been less attention paid to the other side of the equation, the victims of crime. A side effect of the 'new punitiveness' towards criminals that appeared in the public consciousness over the last quarter of the twentieth century was an increasing awareness of the position of the victims of crime and it is to those that we now turn.

VICTIMIZATION AND VICTIMOLOGY

The term 'victimology' was first used by Mendelsohn in 1940 (Mawby and Walklate, 1994) to indicate a focus on those who had suffered from criminal activity. For example Von Hentig (1948) argued that victims are not passive recipients of criminal action but social actors in their own right, often tacitly conspiring with the perpetrator. This was known as Victim Precipitation Theory and dominated sociological accounts of victims in the last half of the twentieth century. It established the idea that criminal and victim were engaged in a social encounter and therefore should be considered together rather than examining the position of the victim in his or her own right. In its early stages the concept of victimology was deployed in a fairly positivistic and conservative way to emphasize the situation of those who experience crimes of violence on the streets (Karmen, 1990) and identify those who are more prone to victimization than others. The establishment of the Criminal Injuries Compensation Board in 1964, which compensates 'deserving' victims of criminal injury, marked the culmination of this approach. By the 1960s crime was on an upward trend and it became politicized, with the 'victim' as a clear and useful image for political campaigns. Because anyone could become a victim and because the risk of becoming one was increasing, the victim became a powerful political image (Geiss, 1990).

In the beginning, interest in the victim centred on the development of different typologies of victims and the ways in which they are similar to and different from criminals. While the resulting typologies are many and varied (see Fattah, 1997, for example), they all include such categories as 'provoking victims' (those who in some way precipitate their own victimization), 'willing victims' (those who consent to their victimization) and 'impersonal victims' (intangible victims such as governments). These approaches tended to look at more serious crimes, partly because the interaction – for example between a burglar and the victim – is mostly at a distance and so could not be seen as a direct interaction. Though even if the central perpetrator–victim relationship was at a distance, sociologists identified ways in which the victim could 'precipitate' the crime, such as not having secure locks or having expensive goods on full view through the windows. However, when it came to the issue of rape, the idea of victim-precipitation came under strong attack. For example, Amir (1967) identified ways in which women could contribute to the circumstances that led to rape, such as 'drinking alcohol' or having a bad reputation. Feminists seized upon this as an example of malestream sociology and transformed victim-precipitation into victim-blaming (Lamb, 1996).

Ⓘ Ⓐ

Exercise 9.14

Make a copy of the chart below and complete your copy by offering examples of each of the six types of victim, based on the descriptions offered.

Types of victim	Description	Examples
Appropriate victims	Those defined by subcultural norms as being a legitimate target.	
Ideal victims	Those most easily given the status of victim by society.	
Deserving victims	Those whose own behaviour leads them to get their just deserts by becoming a victim.	
Worthless victims	Those perceived by society as not worthy of sympathy because they are social outcasts.	
Reckless victims	Those who do nothing to protect themselves and their property from crime.	
Recidivist victims	Those who are repeatedly victimized over a short period of time.	

In the 1970s, increasing interest in feminism and the development of mass victimization surveys led to a development in victimology that drew the attention of sociologists away from the street and towards the home and the private sphere. The 'discovery' of wife beating and other forms of domestic violence helped to reconceptualize the victim (see pp. 262–4). Instead of victims being seen as subject to public injury, radical victimologists argued for the concept of the victim to be extended to those who were suffering private or hidden injury, not only the victims of domestic violence, but also those who suffered injury at work through the negligence of employers and so on (Quinney, 1972). The victims of corporate crimes have been under-researched by sociologists of crime, partly because of their 'invisibility', their variety and the far-reaching effects of damage done through it (Tombs and Williams, 2008). Moreover, because corporations exercise a great deal of power, they are often able to cast the victims of their actions in an unfavourable light. For example, corporations can present damaged workers as complicit in their victimhood, because they have accepted a degree of risk in their work for the pay offered (Tombs and Whyte, 2007).

In the 1980s the position of the victim became more formalized in the official organizations of control. Victim support gained official recognition and funding during the public sector cost-cutting era of the Thatcher governments. This was partly because of the voluntaristic nature of victim support, but also because it fitted in neatly with the ideological preferences of the 1980s, in that it sought to reintegrate the victim into the community rather than create another branch of the dependency culture so despised by the ideologues of the right. Other support services became part of the everyday practices of the police, for example the provision of 'rape suites' for the victims of rape (Mawby and Walklate, 1994).

For much of the 1990s the focus was on critical victimology (a branch of victimology that is critical of the limited and conservative approach used by most victimologists) and the debate on the extension of the category of victim to include those who suffer human rights abuse. It may seem obvious that those whose human rights are abused are 'victims', but this goes well beyond the traditional conception of a victim as someone who has certain needs in an unfortunate situation. According to the extended definition of victim we all have the potential to be victims if the government ignores our rights. For example, if welfare were to be considered a right rather than a matter of policy and the government decided to curtail welfare provision, then all those who were adversely affected would be victims and presumably eligible for support and compensation. This would also be true if the curtailment was to the subsidy given to mortgage holders through MIRAS. In this sense all MIRAS beneficiaries were 'victims' of the Labour budget of 1997, which restricted the level of relief given to mortgage holders.

This plea for a 'global victimology' (Elias, 1986) has not gone unchallenged. Flynn (1982) argues that to adopt a global definition is to designate everyone as a victim, and it is therefore more productive to focus on the traditional concept of a victim of crime.

A recent debate among sociologists and politicians has concerned the 'fear of crime' and whether the real risk (Holloway and Jefferson, 1997) of being a victim of crime is reflected in this fear of crime or whether it is exaggerated. For example Jones et al. (1986), from a left realist position, argue that the public's perception of the likelihood of victimization is a real one, while the official government position (see for example Hough and Mayhew, 1985) is that the real risk of victimization is less than the public fears. The debate has been triggered by the finding that the most fearful group in society – that is, older women – are least likely to become victims of crime. However, Ferraro (1996) argues that the perceived risk of sexual assault accounts for older women being more fearful and that this fear is realistic. Thus fear of sexual attack operates as a 'master offence', affecting women's perception of risk across all categories of crime. However, it is not just in sexual attacks that older women may be victims. Görgen (2006), in a self-report study of Nursing Home nurses, found that 71 per cent reported witnessing or carrying out an act of abuse on their elderly female and male patients in the previous year.

However, there has been a great deal of criticism of the findings that there are high levels of fear about crime amongst certain groups. The basic problem is that it is difficult to research the 'fear of crime' in a way that systematically and reliably captures the emotion of 'fear' (Goodey, 2005). In addition, it is difficult to establish how significant any such fear is, as Farrall and Gadd (2004) showed that, amongst those who expressed a 'fear' of crime, few had a high and/or sustained level of fear. Rather any expressed fear tended to be sporadic and often muted.

The focus on women as victims of crime has led to the dichotomy of women as victims and men as perpetrators. Newburn and Stanko (1994) argue that this is to neglect men as victims of crime. Though there has been relatively little research in the area, the idea that men suffer as victims as much as women undermines the concept of hegemonic masculinity, in which men are constructed as dominant and powerful rather than vulnerable and fearful. However, the authors point out that considerable violence is carried out against men with a subordinated masculinity, such as ethnic minority and gay men. However, the conceptualization of men as victims has led sociologists to propose a wider study of victimology, in which the gendered dichotomy of oppressor and victim gives way to the study of the ways in which men routinely victimize women and other men.

There are an increasing number of social agents who have an economic interest in maximizing the fear of crime. As the privatization of law enforcement grows and the fear of crime accelerates, a whole new industry is growing up that has a stake in crime. This includes the manufacture of personal and property protection devices, the insurance industry and those who are engaged in the personal safety industry. In order to generate profits these industries have to market their wares, and according to Fattah (1997) they have developed a number of strategies, for example doorstep selling, to build upon the fear of crime and sell their products. In other words, the victim is commodified, that is they have a value in the market place, and as society places greater emphasis on the private management of security rather than the public, individuals are exhorted to protect themselves through the purchase of security equipment. The security market is fuelled by the fear of crime (O'Malley, 2004).

Hughes (1993) suggests that Western societies have become 'cultures of complaint', in which ever more categories of people see themselves victimized by previously accepted or hidden activities. For example immunization has long been accepted as including some risk, but is increasingly being legally challenged by those who are harmed by it. This culture of victimization comes out of the new identity politics associated with postmodern society. As society becomes increasingly fragmented under the impact of global economic and cultural developments, groups emerge who define themselves in terms of a claim to a special identity, which can often take the form of a perceived disadvantage or oppression, such as different forms of sexuality.

Exercise 9.15

In light of what you have just read, summarize in a chart, like the example below, the concerns and views of the various strands of victimology since the 1940s. We would also like you to evaluate the usefulness of the different approaches by considering their strengths and weaknesses.

Phase	Concerns and views	Strengths	Weaknesses
1940s–1960s			
1970s			
1980s			
1990s			
2000s			

Exam focus

1. 'We are all victims now.' Assess sociological contributions to our understanding of this point of view.

Attempt to answer this question on your own and in timed conditions. Although the question is wide-ranging you should ensure that you answer it directly. That is, you should evaluate the sociological contributions you include in your answer by discussing their usefulness or otherwise to the understanding of whether 'we are all victims now'. The material in this chapter provides core knowledge, but, in preparation, you might also wish to consult some of the studies cited in order to extend your knowledge, as well as drawing on relevant material from other chapters in this book. You might also see what the Internet has on victimology (try http://www.victimology.nl/), but ensure that any material is from a reputable source and is clearly sociological.

2. Examine the contribution that sociologists have made to an understanding of the police and policing.

Important concepts

Cop culture • Culture of control • Zero tolerance • Militarization • Privatization of security • New punitiveness • Governance • Restorative justice • Incapacitation theory

Critical thinking

1. Is our society becoming harsher in its attitudes towards criminals and 'others'? What would signify such a move towards a new punitiveness?
2. How representative of the population at large should the judiciary be? Does it matter if they are not?
3. Of the models of policing you have learned about, which do you think has the most chance of reducing the level of crime in society and why?

References

Adamson, M., L. Briskin and M. McPhail (1988) *Feminist Organising for Change: a contemporary woman's movement in Canada* (Toronto: Oxford University Press).

Adler, Freda (1975) *Sisters in Crime* (New York: McGraw-Hill).

Agnew, R. (1985) 'A Revised Strain Theory of Delinquency', *Social Forces*, 64.

Agnew, R. (1992) 'Foundation for a General Strain Theory of Crime and Delinquency', *Criminology*, 30 (1).

Agnew, R. (2001) 'Building on the Foundation of General Strain Theory: specifying the types of strain most likely to lead to crime and delinquency', *Journal of Research in Crime and Delinquency*, 36.

Akers, Ronald L. (1985) *Deviant Behaviour: a social learning approach* (Belmont: Wadsworth).

Aldridge, J., J. Medina and R. Ralphs (2008) 'Gang research in the UK: is it too dangerous?', *Social Science Teacher*, 38, 1.

Alexander, David (1990) 'Giving the Devil More Than His Due', *The Humanist*, 50 (2).

Allan, Emilie and Darrell Steffensmeier (1989) 'Youth, Underemployment and Property Crime: differential effects of job availability and job quality on juvenile and young adult arrest rates', *American Sociological Review*, 54.

Allen, H. (1987) *Justice Unbalanced! Gender, Psychiatry and Judicial Decisions* (Milton Keynes: Open University Press).

Allen, J. (1995) 'Men, Crime and Criminology', in Ngaire Naffine (ed.), *Gender Crime and Feminism* (Aldershot: Dartmouth Publishing).

Allen, J. and P. Patton (eds) (1983) *Beyond Marxism? Interventions After Marx* (Sydney: Intervention Publications).

Amir, M. (1967) 'Victim precipitated forcible rape', *Journal of Criminal Law, Criminology and Police Science*, 58 (4).

Anderson, Digby (1988) *Full Circle: bringing up children in the post-permissive society* (London: Social Affairs Unit).

Anderson, Elijah (1990) *Streetwise: race, class and change in an urban community* (Chicago, Ill.: Chicago University Press).

Anderson, Elijah (1999) *Code of the Street: decency, violence and the moral life of the inner city* (New York: W. W. Norton).

Aning, K. (2007) 'Are There Emerging West African Criminal Networks?: the case of Ghana' *Global Crime*, 8, 3.

Archer, J. (1994) *Male Violence* (London: Routledge).

Armstrong, G. (1994) 'False Leeds', in R. Giullianotti and J. Williams (eds.), *Game without Frontiers: football, identity and modernity* (Aldershot: Arena).

Armstrong, D., J. Hine, S. Hacking, R. Armaos, R. Jones, N. Klessinger and A. France (2005) *Children, Risk and Crime: The On Track Youth Lifestyles Survey* (London: The Home Office).

Arrigo, Bruce (1995) 'The Peripheral Core of Law and Criminology: on postmodern social theory and conceptual integration', *Justice Quarterly*, 12 (3).

Arrigo, Bruce and T. R. Young (1996) *Postmodern Theories of Crime* (Essex, MI: Red Feather Institute) (www.uvm.edu/~dlanger/archives/pomo-crm.htm).

Austin R. L. (1981) 'Liberation and Female Criminality in England and Wales', *British Journal of Criminology*, 21 (4).

Babb, P., H. Butcher J. Church and L. Zealey (eds.) (2006) *Social Trends 36* (Basingstoke: Palgrave Macmillan).

Banton, Michael (1964) *The Policeman in the Community* (London: Tavistock).

Barak, G. (2005) 'A Reciprocal Approach to peacemaking: between adversarialism and mutualism', *Theoretical Criminology*, 9 (2).

Barkley, R. A., M. Fischer, L, Smallish and K. Fletcher (2004), 'Young Adult Follow Up of Hyperactive Children: antisocial activities and drug use', *Journal of Child Psychology and Psychiatry*, 45.

Bart, P. B. and E. G. Moran (eds) (1993) *Violence Against Women: the bloody footprints* (Newbury Park, CA: Sage).

Bartol, C. R. and A. M. Bartol (1989) *Juvenile Delinquency: a systems approach* (Englewood Cliffs, NJ: Prentice-Hall).

Bauman, Zygmunt (1987) *Legislators and Interpreters* (Cambridge: Polity Press).

Baxter, J. and L. Koffman (eds) (1985) *Police: the constitution and the community* (London: Professional Books).

Bayart, J-F., S. Ellis and B. Hibou (1999) *The Criminalisation of the State in Africa* (Bloomington: Indiana University Press).

Bayley, D. (1994) *Police for the Future* (Oxford: Oxford University Press).

Beck, Ulrich (1992) *The Risk Society* (London: Sage).

Becker, Howard S. (1963) *Outsiders: studies in the sociology of deviance* (New York: Free Press).

Beckett, K. and S. Herbert (2008) 'Dealing with Disorder: social control in the post-industrial city' *Theoretical Criminology*, 12 (1).

Beckett, K. and T. Sasson (2000) 'The War on Crime as a Hegemonic Strategy: a neo-Marxian theory of the new punitiveness in U.S. criminal justice policy' in S. Simpson, (ed.) *Of Crime and Criminality* (Thousand Oaks, CA: Pine Forge Press).

Beirne, P. and N. South (2007) *Issues in Green Criminology*, (Cullompton: Willan).

Bell, Daniel (1962) *The End of Ideology* (New York: Free Press).

Bennett, T. (1979) 'The social distribution of criminal labels', *British Journal of Criminology,* 19.

Bennett, T. (1991) 'The Effectiveness of a Police-initiated Fear Reducing Strategy', *British Journal of Criminology,* 31 (1).

Bennett, T. (1994) 'Recent Developments in Community Policing', in M. Stephens and S. Becker (eds), *Police Force, Police Service: care and control in Britain* (London: Macmillan).

Bernard, Thomas J. (1987) 'Structure and Control: reconsidering Hirschi's concept of commitment', *Justice Quarterly,* 4.

Best, S. (2006) 'Sociology and the "War on Terror"', *Sociology Review,* 16 (2).

Bidinotto, James (1989) *Crime and Consequences* (Irvington-on-Hudson: Foundation for Economic Education).

Bilton, Tony, Kevin Bonnett, Philip Jones, Michelle Stanworth, Ken Sheard and Andrew Webster (1987) *Introductory Sociology,* 2nd edn (Basingstoke: Macmillan).

Bilton, Tony, Kevin Bonnett, Philip Jones, Tony Lawson, Davis Skinner Michelle Stanworth and Andrew Webster (2002) *Introductory Sociology,* 4th edn (Basingstoke: Macmillan).

Black, Donald and Albert J. Reiss (1967) 'Patterns of Behaviour in Police-Citizen Transactions', *Studies in Crime and Law Enforcement in Major Metropolitan Areas, Field Surveys 111, Vol 2. President's Commission on Law Enforcement in Major Metropolitan Areas* (Washington, DC: US Government Printing Office).

Blau, Judith R. and Peter M. Blau (1982) 'The Cost of Inequality: metropolitan structure and violent crime', *American Sociological Review,* 47.

Blumstein, Alfred (1993) 'Making Rationality Relevant', *Criminology,* 31.

Blumstein, A. and J. Wallman (eds.) (2000) *The Crime Drop in America* (Cambridge: Cambridge University Press).

Bohm, R. M. (1982) 'Radical Criminology: an explication', *Criminology,* 19.

Bonger, Willem (1969) *Criminality and Economic Conditions* (Bloomington: Indiana University Press) (originally published 1916).

Bonta, J., R. Jesseman, T. Rugge and R. Cormier (2006) 'Restorative Justice and Recidivism: promises made, promises kept?' in D. Sullivan and L. Tiff (eds), *Handbook of Restorative Justice* (New York: Routledge).

Bosworth, M., B. Bowling and M. Lee (2008) 'Globalisation, Ethnicity and Racism: an introduction' *Theoretical Criminology,* 12 (3).

Bottoms, A. E. (1983) 'Some neglected features of modern penal systems', in D. Garland and P. Young (eds), *The Power to Punish* (London: Heinemann).

Bottoms, A. E., A. Claytor and P. Wiles (1992) 'Housing Markets and residential Community Crime Careers: a case study from Sheffield', in David J. Evans, Nicholas R. Fyfe and David T. Herbert (eds), *Crime, Policing and Place: essays in environmental criminology* (London: Routledge).

Boulton, Richard (1990) 'The Cultural Contradictions of Conservatism', *New Art Examiner,* 17.

Bound, John and Richard Freeman (1992) 'What Went Wrong? The Erosion of Relative Earnings and Employment Among Young Black Men in the 1980s', *Quarterly Journal of Economics*, 107.

Bourgois, P. (1996) 'In Search of Masculinity: violence, respect and sexuality among Puerto Rican crack dealers in East Harlem', *British Journal of Criminology*, 36 (3).

Bovenkerk, F. and B. A. Chakra (2007) 'Terrorism and Organised Crime', in L. Holmes *Terrorism, Organised Crime and Corruption* (Cheltenham: Edward Elgar Publishing).

Bowling, B. and C. Phillips (2002) *Racism, Crime and Justice* (London: Longman).

Bowling, G., J. Graham and A. Ross (1994) 'Self-reported offending among young people in England and Wales', in J. Junger-Tas, G. J. Terlouw and M. Klein (eds), *Delinquent Behaviour among Young People in the Western World* (Amsterdam: Kugler).

Box, S. (1980) 'Where have all the Naughty Children Gone?', in National Deviancy Conference (ed.), *Permissiveness and Control* (London: Macmillan).

Box, S. (1981) *Deviance, Reality and Society*, 2nd edn (Eastbourne: Holt, Rinehart & Winston).

Box, Stephen (1983) *Power, Crime and Mystification* (London: Tavistock).

Braithwaite, John (1984) *Corporate Crime in the Pharmaceutical Industry* (London: Routledge).

Braithwaite, John (1989) *Crime, Shame and Reintegration* (Cambridge: Cambridge University Press).

Braithwaite, John (1993) 'Crime and the Average American', *Law and Society Review*, 27.

Broadhurst, R. (2006) 'Developments in the Global Law Enforcement of Cyber-crime' *Policing: an International Journal of Police Strategies and Management*, 29 (3).

Brown, B. (1986) 'Women and Crime: the dark figures of criminology', *Economy and Society*, 15.

Brown, Beverley (1990) 'Reassessing the Critique of Biologism' in Loraine Gelsthorpe and Allison Morris (eds), *Feminist Perspectives in Criminology* (Milton Keynes: Open University Press).

Brown, I. and R. Hullin (1992) 'A Study of Sentencing in the Leeds Magistrates' Courts: the treatment of ethnic minority and white offenders', *British Journal of Criminology*, 32 (1).

Brunswick, A. F. (1988) 'Young Black Males and Substance Use', in J. T. Gibbs (ed.), *Young, Black and Male in America: an endangered species* (Westport, CT: Auburn House).

Bucke, Tom (1997) *Ethnicity and Contacts with the Police: latest findings from the British Crime Survey*, Home Office Research and Statistics Directorate Research Findings no. 59 (London: Home Office).

Bullock, K. and N. Tilley (2003) *Crime Reduction and Problem-oriented Policing* (Cullompton: Willan).

Burchell, G., C. Gordon and P. Miller (eds) (1991) *The Foucault Effect: Studies in Governmentality* (Chicago, IL: University of Chicago Press).

Burgess, R. and P. Draper (1989) 'Biological, Behavioural and Cultural Selection', in L. Ohlin and M. Tonry (eds), *Family Violence* (Chicago, IL: University of Chicago Press).

Burney, Elizabeth (1990) *Putting Street Crime in its Place* (London: Goldsmiths' College).

Burrell, Ian and Lisa Brinkworth (1994) 'Sugar N' Spice But . . . Not At All Nice', *The Sunday Times*, 27 November.

Bursik, Robert and Harold Grasmick (1993) *Neighbourhoods and Crime* (New York: Lexington Books).

Buss, Dale (1993) 'Ways to Curtail Employee Theft', *Nation's Business,* 81.

Campbell, A. (1981) *Girl Delinquents* (Oxford: Blackwell).

Campbell, A. (1991) *The Girls in the Gang* (Cambridge: Basil Blackwell).

Campbell, B. (1993) *Goliath: Britain's Dangerous Places* (London: Virago).

Capeller, W. (2001) 'Not such a neat net: some comments on virtual criminality' *Social & Legal Studies*, 10.

Carlen, P. (1988) *Women, Crime and Poverty* (Milton Keynes: Open University Press).

Carlen, P. (1990) *Alternatives to Women's Imprisonment* (Buckingham: Open University Press).

Carlen, P. (1992) 'Criminal Women and Criminal Justice', in R. Matthews and J. Young, *Issues in Realist Criminology* (London: Sage).

Carlen, P. and A. Worrall (2004) *Analysing Women's Imprisonment* (Cullompton: Willan).

Cashmore, E. Ellis (1991) 'Black Cops Inc.', in E. Cashmore and Eugene McLaughlin (eds), *Out of Order: policing black people* (London: Routledge).

Cashmore, E. Ellis and Eugene McLaughlin (eds) (1991) *Out of Order: policing black people* (London: Routledge).

Cavadino, M. and J. Dignan (1992) *The Penal System: an introduction* (London: Sage).

Cavadino, M. and J. Dignan (2006) *Penal Systems: a comparative approach* (London: Sage).

Cavender, J. G. (2004) 'Media and Crime Policy', *Punishment and Society*, 6 (3).

Chambliss, William J. (1975) 'Towards a Political Economy of Crime', *Theory and Society*, 2.

Chambliss, William J. (1978) *On the Take: from petty crooks to the Presidents* (Bloomington: Indiana University Press).

Chambliss, W. J. and M. Mankoff (eds) (1976) *Whose Law? Whose Order?* (New York: Wiley).

Chambliss, W. J. and R. H. Nagasawa (1969) 'On the Validity of Official Statistics: a comparison of white, black and Japanese high school boys', *Journal of Research in Crime and Delinquency,* 6.

Chambliss, W. and R. T. Seidman (1971) *Law, Order and Power* (Reading, MA: Addison-Wesley).

Chancer, L. and E. McLaughlin (2007) 'Public Criminology: diverse perspectives on theory and policy', *Theoretical Criminology*, 11 (2).

Chermak, S. M. (1995) *Victims in the News: crime and the American news media* (Boulder, CO: Westview Press).

Chesney-Lind, Meda (1997) *The Female Offender: girls, women and crime*, (Thousand Oaks, CA: Sage).

Chesney-Lind, M. (2006) 'Patriarchy, crime and Justice: Feminist Criminology in an era of Backlash', *Feminist Criminology*, 1 (1).

Chesney-Lind, Meda and Randall Shelden (1992) *Girls, Delinquency and Juvenile Justice* (Pacific Grove: Brooks/Cole).

Christie, Nils (1993) *Crime Control as Industry: towards gulags, Western style?* (London: Routledge).

Clarke, J., S. Hall, T. Jefferson and B. Roberts (1976) 'Subcultures, Cultures and Class: a theoretical overview', in S. Hall and T. Jefferson (eds) *Resistance Through Rituals: youth subcultures in post-War Britain* (London: Hutchinson).

Clarke, M. (1990) *Business Crime: its nature and control* (Cambridge: Polity Press).

Clarke, R. V. G. (2004) 'Technology, Criminology and Crime Science', *European Journal on Criminal Policy and Research*, 10.

Clarke, R. V. G. (2005) 'Seven Misconceptions of situational crime prevention', in N. Tilley (ed.) *Handbook of Crime Prevention and Community Safety* (Cullompton: Willan).

Clarke, R. and M. Hough (1984) *Crime and Police Effectiveness* (London: HMSO).

Cloud, Morgan (1985) 'Search and Seizure by the Numbers: the drug courier profile and judicial review of investigative formulas', *Boston University Law Review*, vol. 65.

Cloward, R. A. and L. E. Ohlin (1960) *Delinquency and Opportunity: a theory of delinquent gangs* (Glencoe, IL: Free Press).

Cohen, Albert K. (1955) *Delinquent Boys: the culture of the gang* (New York: Free Press).

Cohen, Lawrence E. and Marcus Felson (1979) 'Social Change and Crime Rate Trends: a routine activities approach', *American Sociological Review*, 44.

Cohen, Stanley (1979) 'The Punitive City: notes on the dispersal of social control', *Contemporary Crises*, vol. 3.

Cohen, Stanley (1980) *Folk Devils and Moral Panics*, 2nd edn (Oxford: Martin Robertson).

Cohen, Stanley (1985) *Visions of Social Control: crime, punishment and classification* (Cambridge: Polity Press).

Cohen, Stanley (1994) 'Social Control and the Politics of Reconstruction', in David Nelken (ed.), *The Futures of Criminology* (London: Sage).

Cohen, Stanley (1996) 'Crime and Politics', *British Journal of Sociology*, 47 (1) (March).

Cohen, S. (2001) *States of Denial: knowing about atrocities and the suffering of others* (Cambridge: Polity Press).

Coleman, A. (1985) *Utopia on Trial* (London: Hilary Shipman).

Coleman, Clive and Jenny Moynihan (1996) *Understanding Crime Data: haunted by the dark figure* (Buckingham: Open University Press).

Coleman, C. and C. Norris (2000) *Introducing Criminology* (Cullompton: Willan).

Coleman, James S. (1990) *Foundations of Social Theory* (Cambridge, MA: Harvard University Press).

Coleman, James W. (1994) *The Criminal Elite* (New York: St Martin's Press).

Coleman, James W. (1985) 'The Criminal Elite: the sociology of white-collar crime', *American Journal of Sociology*, 93.

Colvin, M. (2000) *Crime and Coercion: an integrated theory of chronic criminality* (New York: St Martin's Press).

Connell, R. W. (2002) *Gender* (Cambridge: Polity Press).

Connell, R. and J. Messerschmidt (2005) 'Hegemonic Masculinity: rethinking the concept' *Gender and Society*, 19 (6).

Cook, D. (1997) *Poverty, Crime and Punishment* (London: CPAG).

Cook, Philip J. (1986) 'The Demand and Supply of Criminal Opportunities', in M. Tonry and N. Morris (eds), *Crime and Justice: an annual review of research, Vol. 7* (Chicago, IL: University of Chicago Press).

Corbett, Ronald and Gary T. Marx (1991) 'Critique: No Soul in the New Machine: technofallacies in the electronic monitoring movement', *Justice Quarterly*, 8.

Cornish, D. B. and R. V. G. Clarke (1986) *The Reasoning Criminal: rational choice perspectives on offending* (New York: Springer-Verlag).

Cornish, D. B. and R. V. G. Clarke (2003) 'Opportunities, precipitators and criminal decision', *Crime Prevention Studies*, 16.

Cornish, D. and R. V. G. Clarke (2006) 'The Rational Choice Perspective' in S. Henry and M. Lanier (eds) *The Essential Criminology Reader* (Boulder, CO: Westview Press).

Cottle, S. (2006) *Mediatized Conflict* (Maidenhead: Open University Press).

Coughlin, B. C. and S. A Venkatesh (2003) 'The Urban Street Gang after 1970', *Annual Review of Sociology*, 29.

Cowell, David, Trevor Jones and Jock Young (eds) (1982) *Policing the Riots* (London: Junction Books).

Crawford, A. (2003) 'The Pattern of Policing in the UK: policing beyond the police' in T. Newburn (ed.), *Handbook of Policing* (Cullompton: Willan).

Crawford, Adam, Trevor Jones, J. Lloyd and Jock Young (1990) *The Second Islington Crime Survey* (London: Middlesex Polytechnic).

Cray, E. (1972) *The Enemy in the Streets* (New York: Anchor).

Crisp, Annette and Dave Ward (2008) 'Policing the Community in the 21st Century' in Stout, B., J. Yates and B. Williams (eds), *Applied Criminology* (London: Sage).

Croall, H. (1992) *White-collar Crime* (Buckingham: Open University Press).

Croall, H. (1997) 'Business, Crime and the Community', *International Journal of Risk, Security and Crime Prevention*, 2.

Croall, Hazel (1998) *Crime and Society in Britain* (Harlow: Longman).

Croall, H. (2001) *Understanding White-collar crime* (Buckingham: Open University Press).

Crow, I., P. Richardson, C. Riddington and F. Simon (1989) *Unemployment, Crime and Offenders* (London: Routledge).

Crow, I. and F. Simon (1987) *Unemployment and Magistrates Courts* (London: NACRO).

Currie, E. (1985) *Confronting Crime: an American challenge* (New York: Pantheon).

Currie, Elliott (1990) 'Heavy with Human Tears: free market policy, inequality and social provision in the United States', in Ian Taylor (ed.), *The Social Effects of Free Market Policies* (Hemel Hampstead: Harvester Wheatsheaf).

Currie, E. (1991) 'The Politics of Crime: the American experience', in K. Stenson and D. Cowell (eds), *The Politics of Crime Control* (London: Sage).

Curtis, L. (1975) *Violence, Race and Culture* (Lexington: Lexington Books).

Dalgleish, D. and A. Myhill (2004) *Reassuring the Public: a review of international policing interventions* (London: Home Office).

Daly, Kathleen (1989) 'Gender and Varieties of White-Collar Crime', *Criminology,* 27.

Daly, M. and M. Wilson (1994) 'Evolutionary Psychology of Male Violence', in J. Archer (ed.), *Male Violence* (London: Routledge).

Dandeker, Christopher (1990) *Surveillance, Power and Modernity* (New York: St Martin's Press).

Defert, D. (1991) '"Popular Life" and Insurance Technology', in G. Burchell, C. Gordon and P. Miller (eds), *The Foucault Effect: Studies in Governmentality* (Chicago, IL: University of Chicago Press).

Denscombe, Martyn (1992) *Sociology Update* (Leicester: Olympus Books).

Denscombe, Martyn (1993) *Sociology Update* (Leicester: Olympus Books).

Denscombe, Martyn (1995) *Sociology Update* (Leicester: Olympus Books).

Denscombe, Martyn (1996) *Sociology Update* (Leicester: Olympus Books).

Denscombe, Martyn (1998) *Sociology Update* (Leicester: Olympus Books).

Denscombe, Martyn (2002) *Sociology Update* (Leicester: Olympus Books).

Denscombe, Martyn (2003) *Sociology Update* (Leicester: Olympus Books).

Denzin, Norman K. (1984) *On Understanding Emotion* (San Francisco: Jossey-Bass).

Denzin, Norman K. (1991) *Images of Postmodern Society: social theory and contemporary cinema* (Newbury Park: Sage).

Dickinson, D. (1994) 'Criminal Benefits', *New Statesman and Society,* vol. 14 (January).

Dignan, J. (2005) *Understanding Victims and Restorative Justice* (Maidenhead: Open University Press).

Ditton, J., D. Chadee, S. Farrell, E. Gilchrist and J. Bannister (2004) 'From imitation to intimidation: a note on the curious and changing relationship between the media, crime and fear of crime' *British Journal of Criminology,* 44 (4).

Dobash, R. E. and R. P. Dobash (1992) *Women, Violence and Social Change* (London: Routledge).

Dobash, R. E., R. P. Dobash and L. Noaks (1995) *Gender and Crime* (Cardiff: University of Wales Press).

Docking, M. and Tuffin, R. (2005) *Racist Incidents: Progress since the Lawrence Inquiry* (London: Home Office).

Dorn, N., M. Levi and L. King (2005) *Literature Review on Upper Level Drug Trafficking, Home Office Report 22/05* (London: Home Office).

Downes, D. and K. Hansen (2006) 'Welfare and punishment in comparative perspective' in S. Armstrong and L. McAra (eds) *Perspectives in Punishment* (Oxford: Oxford University Press).

Downes, D. and P. Rock (2007) *Understanding Deviance*, 5th edn (Oxford: Oxford University Press).

Dunning, E., P. Murphy and J. Williams (1988) *The Roots of Football Hooliganism* (London: Routledge).

Durkheim, E. (1960) *The Division of Labour in Society* (Glencoe, IL: Free Press).

Durkheim, E. (1973 [1895]) *Rules of Sociological Method* (New York: Free Press).

Eaton, M. (1986) *Justice for Women?* (Milton Keynes: Open University Press).

Edwards, A. and P. Gill (eds) (2003) *Transnational Organised Crime: perspectives on global security* (London: Routledge).

Edwards, S. (1989) *Policing 'Domestic' Violence* (London: Sage).

Edwards, S. S. M. (1986) *The Police Response to Domestic Violence in London* (London: Polytechnic of Central London).

Edwards, Susan (ed.) (1985) *Gender, Sex and the Law* (London: Croom Helm).

Einstadter, W. J. (1984) 'Citizen Patrols: prevention or control?', *Crime and Social Justice*, 21–2.

Elias, Norbert (1978) *The Civilising Process, Volume 1* (Oxford: Basil Blackwell).

Elias, Robert (1986) *The Politics of Victimization: victims, victimology and human rights* (New York: Oxford University Press).

Elliott, D. S., S. S. Ageton and R. J. Canter (1979) 'An integrated theoretical perspective on delinquent behaviour' *Journal of Research on Crime and Delinquency*, 16.

Elliott, D. S. and S. S. Ageton (1980) 'Reconciling Race and Class Differences in Self-Reported and Official Estimates of Delinquency', *American Sociological Review*, 45.

Elliott, Delbert, David Huizinga and Suzanne Ageton (1985) *Explaining Delinquency and Drug Use* (Beverly Hills, CA: Sage).

Empey, L. T. (1982) *American Delinquency: its meaning and construction*, rev. edn (Homewood, IL: Dorsey).

Enderby, Sarah (1997) 'Battered and Bruised', unpublished A-Level project.

Ericson, Richard V. (1989) 'Patrolling the Facts: secrecy and publicity in police work', *British Journal of Sociology*, 40, pp. 205–26.

Ericson, Richard V. (1991) 'Mass Media, Crime Law and Justice: an institutional approach', *British Journal of Criminology*, 31 (3).

Ericson, Richard (1994) 'The Division of Expert Knowledge in Policing and Security', *British Journal of Sociology*, 45.

Ericson, Richard and Kevin Carriere (1994) 'The Fragmentation of Criminology', in David Nelken *The Futures of Criminology* (London: Sage).

Erikson, K. T. (1966) *Wayward Puritans: a study in sociology of deviance* (New York: John Wiley).

Evans, D., N. R. Fyfe and D. T. Herbert (eds) (1992) *Crime, Policing and Place: essays in environmental criminology* (London: Routledge).

Evans, Karen (1997) 'Men's Towns: women and the urban environment', *Sociology Review*, 6 (3).

Fagan, Jeffrey (1993) 'Drug Selling and Licit Income in Distressed Neighbourhoods: the economic lives of street-level drug users and dealers', in A. Harrell and G. Peterson (eds), *Drugs, Crime and Social Isolation* (Washington, DC: Urban Institute Press).

Faragher, T. (1985) 'The Police Response to Violence Against Women in the Home', in J. Pahl (ed.), *Private Violence and Public Policy* (London: Routledge & Kegan Paul).

Farmer, P. (2005) *Pathologies of Power: health, human rights and the new war on the poor* (Berkeley: California University Press).

Farnworth, M., T. P. Thornberry, M. D. Krohn and A. J. Lizotte (1994) 'Measurement in the Study of Class and Delinquency: integrating theory and research', *Journal of Research in Crime and Delinquency*, 31.

Farrall, S. and D. Gadd (2004) 'The frequency of the fear of crime' *British Journal of Criminology*, 44 (1).

Farrington, D. P. and E. Dowds (1985) 'Disentangling Criminal Behaviour and Police Reaction', in D. Farrington and J. Gunn (eds) *Reactions to Crime: The Public, the Police, Courts and Prisons* (Chichester: John Wiley).

Farrington, D. P. and A. M. Morris (1983) 'Sex, Sentencing and Reconviction', *British Journal of Criminology*, 23 (3).

Farrington, D. and S. Walklate (eds) (1994) *Offenders and Victims: theory and policy* (London: British Society of Criminology).

Fattah, Ezzat A. (1997) *Criminology: past, present and future* (Basingstoke: Macmillan).

FBI (Federal Bureau of Investigation) (2006) *Uniform Crime Reports 2006* (Washington: FBI).

Feeley, Malcolm and Jonathan Simon (1994) 'Actuarial Justice: the emerging new criminal law', in David Nelken (ed.), *The Futures of Criminology* (London: Sage).

Felson, R. (1993) 'Sexual Coercion: a social interactionist approach', in R. Felson and J. Tedeschi (eds) *Aggression and Violence: social interactionist perspectives* (Washington, DC: American Psychological Association).

Felson, (2002) *Crime and Everyday Life*, 3rd edn (Thousand Oaks, CA: Pine Forge Press).

Felson, R. and J. Tedeschi (eds) (1993) *Aggression and Violence: social interactionist perspectives* (Washington, DC: American Psychological Association).

Ferraro, Kenneth (1993) 'Cops, Courts and Women Battering', in P. B. Bart and E. G. Moran (eds) *Violence Against Women: the bloody footprints* (Newbury Park, CA: Sage).

Ferraro, Kenneth (1996) 'Women's Fear of Victimisation: shadow of sexual assault?', *Social Forces,* 75 (2) (December).

Ferrell, Jeff (1993) *Crimes of Style: urban graffiti and the politics of criminality* (New York: Garland).

Ferrell, Jeff (1995) 'Culture, Crime and Cultural Criminology', *Journal of Criminal Justice and Popular Culture,* 3 (2).

Ferrel, Jeff (2005) 'Cultural criminology' in R. A. Wright and J. M. Miller (eds) *Encyclopedia of Criminology, Vol. 1* (New York, Routledge).

Fingerhut, L. A., D. D. Ingram and J. J. Feldman (1992) 'Firearm Homicide among Black Teenage Males in Metropolitan Counties', *Journal of the American Medical Association,* 267.

Finn, G. (1994) 'Football Violence: a social psychological perspective', in R. Giullianotti *et al.* (eds) *Football, violence and social identity* (London: Routledge).

Finney, A. (2006) *Domestic Violence, Sexual Assault and Stalking: findings from the 2004–5 British Crime Survey* (London: Home Office).

Fishbein, D. H. (1990) 'Biological Perspectives in Criminology', *Criminology,* 28.

Fishman, M. (1978) 'Crime Waves as Ideology', *Social Problems,* 25.

Fitzgerald, M. and C. Hale (1996) *Ethnic Minorities: Victimisation and Racial Harassment: findings from the 1988 and 1992 British Crime Surveys* (London: Home Office).

Fitzpatrick, Peter (1984) 'Law and Societies', *Osgoode Hall Law Journal,* 22.

Flynn, E. E. (1982) 'Theory Development in Victimology: an assessment of recent progress and of continuing challenges', in H. J. Schneider (ed.), *The Victim in International Perspective* (Berlin: de Gruyter).

Forsyth, Craig J. and Marion D. Oliver (1990) 'The Theoretical Framing of a Social Problem: some conceptual notes on Satanic cults', *Deviant Behaviour,* 11.

Foucault, Michel (1967) *Madness and Civilisation: a history of insanity in the age of reason* (London: Tavistock).

Foucault, Michel (1972) *The Order of Things: an archaeology of the human sciences* (New York: Random House).

Foucault, Michel (1977) *Discipline and Punish: the birth of the prison* (Harmondsworth: Penguin).

Friday, P. and G. Hage (1976) 'Youth Crime in Postindustrial Societies: an integrated approach', *Criminology,* 14.

Fuller J. R. and J. F. Wozniak (2006) 'Peacemaking criminology: past, present and future' in F. T. Cullen, J. P. Wright and K. R. Blevins (eds) *Taking Stock: the status of criminological theory* (New Brunswick, NJ: Transaction).

Galeotti, M. (ed.) (2005) *Global Crime Today: The Changing Face of Organised Crime* (Oxford: Routledge).

Gardinier, Simon (1995) 'Criminal Justice Act 1991 – management of the underclass and the potentiality of community', in Lesley Noaks, Michael Levi and Mike Maguire (eds), *Contemporary Issues in Criminology* (Cardiff: University of Wales Press).

Gardner, C. B. (1990) 'Safe Conduct: women crime and self in public places', *Social Problems*, 37.

Garland, David (2001) *The Culture of Control: crime and social order in contemporary society* (Oxford: Clarendon).

Garland, D. and P. Young (eds) (1983) *The Power to Punish* (London: Heinemann).

Gartner, R. (1990) 'The Victims of Violence', *American Sociological Review*, 55 (1).

Gatens, M. (1983) 'A Critique of the Sex/Gender Distinction', in J. Allen and P. Patton (eds) *Beyond Marxism? Interventions After Marx* (Sydney: Intervention Publications).

Geiss, G. (1990) 'Crime Victims: practices and prospects', in A. J. Lurigio, W. G. Skogan and R. C. Davis (eds), *Victims of Crime: problems, policies and programs* (Newbury Park, CA: Sage).

Gelsthorpe, L. R. and A. M. Morris (eds) (1990) *Feminist Perspectives in Criminology* (London: Routledge & Kegan Paul).

Genn, H. (1988) 'Multiple Victimisation', in M. Maguire and J. Pointing (eds), *Victims of Crime: a new deal?* (Milton Keynes: Open University Press).

Gerbner, G. (1995) 'Television Violence: the power and the peril', in G. Dines and J. Humez (eds), *Gender, Race and Class in the Media* (Thousand Oaks, CA.: Sage).

Gibbs, Jack P. (1985) 'Review Essay', *Criminology*, 23.

Gibbs, J. T. (ed.) (1988) *Young, Black and Male in America: an endangered species* (Westport, CT: Auburn House).

Gibbs, Jewelle Taylor and Joseph R. Merighi (1994) 'Young Black Males: marginality, masculinity and criminality', in Tim Newburn and Elizabeth A. Stanko (eds), *Just Boys Doing Business* (London: Routledge).

Gilroy, P. (1987a) 'The Myth of Black Criminality', in P. Scraton (ed.), *Law, Order and the Authoritarian State* (Milton Keynes: Open University Press).

Gilroy, P. (1987b) *There Ain't No Black in the Union Jack* (London: Hutchinson).

Gilroy, P. (1990) 'One Nation under a Groove: the cultural politics of "race" and racism in Britain', in D. T. Goldberg (ed.), *Anatomy of Racism* (Minneapolis: University of Minnesota Press).

Glaser, Daniel (1978) *Crime in our Changing Society* (New York: Holt, Rinehart & Winston).

Gold, M. (1966) 'Undetected Delinquent Behaviour', *Journal of Research in Crime and Delinquency*, 3.

Goldberg, D. T. (ed.) (1990) *Anatomy of Racism* (Minneapolis: University of Minnesota Press).

Goodey, J. (2005) *Victims and Victimology: research, policy and practice* (Harlow: Longman).

Gordon, D. M. (1971) 'Class and the Economics of Crime', *Review of Radical Political Economy*, 3.

Gordon, P. (1986) *Racial Violence and Harassment* (London: Runnymede Trust).

Görgen, T. (2006) ' "As if I just didn't exist" – elder abuse and neglect in nursing homes' in A. Wahidin and M. Cain (eds), *Ageing, Crime and Society* (Cullompton: Willan).

Gottfredson, Michael R. and Travis Hirschi (1990) *A General Theory of Crime* (Palo Alto: Stanford University Press).

Gottfredson, Michael R. and Travis Hirschi (1995) 'National Crime Control Policies', *Society*, vol. 32.

Gove, W. R. (1980) *The Labeling of Deviance: evaluating a perspective,* 2nd edn (Beverly Hills, CA: Sage).

Grabosky, P. (2001) 'Virtual Criminality: old wine in new bottles?' *Social & Legal Studies*, 10.

Grabosky, P. (2004) 'The Global Dimension of Cybercrime' *Global Crime*, 6 (1).

Graham, J. M. (1976) 'Amphetamine Politics on Capitol Hill', in W. J. Chambliss and M. Mankoff (eds), *Whose Law? Whose Order?* (New York: Wiley).

Graham, John and Ben Bowling (1995) *Young People and Crime,* Home Office Research and Statistics Directorate Research Findings no. 24 (London: Home Office).

Grasmick, H. G., C. R. Tittle, R. J. Bursik Jr. and B. J. Arneklev (1993) 'Testing the Core Empirical Implications of Gottfredson and Hirschi's General Theory of Crime', *Journal of Research in Crime and Delinquency,* 30.

Green, G. S. (1990) *Occupational Crime* (Chicago, IL: Nelson-Hall).

Green P. and T. Ward (2004) *State Crime: governments, violence and corruption* (London: Pluto Press).

Green P. and T. Ward (2005) 'Introduction', *British Journal of Criminology*, 45.

Greenberg, D. (1990) 'The Cost-Benefit Analysis of Imprisonment', *Social Justice*, 17.

Gregory, J. (1986) 'Sex, Class and Crime: towards a non-sexist criminology', in R. Matthews and J. Young (eds), *Confronting Crime* (London: Sage).

Gross, J. (2003) 'Trouble in Paradise: crime and collapsed states in the age of globalisation', *British Journal of Criminology*, 43

Gusfield, J. (1981) *The Culture of Public Problems: drinking, driving and the symbolic order* (Chicago, IL: University of Chicago Press).

Gusfield, J. (1989) 'Constructing the Ownership of Social Problems: fun and profit in the welfare state', *Social Problems*, 36.

Hagan, John (1977) *The Disreputable Pleasures* (Toronto: McGraw-Hill Ryerson).

Hagan, John (1989) *Structural Criminology* (Cambridge: Polity Press).

Hagan, John (1994) *Crime and Disrepute* (Thousand Oaks: Pine Forge Press).

Hagan, John and Celesta Albonetti (1982) 'Race, Class and the Perception of Criminal Injustice in America', *American Journal of Sociology*, 88.

Hagan, John and Ruth Peterson (eds) (1993) *Crime and Inequality* (Stanford: Stanford University Press).

Hajjar, L. (2004) 'Torture and the Future' *Orfalea Center for Global & International Studies. Paper 5*. repositories.cdlib.org/gis/5 (last accessed: 21 January 2009).

Hall, R. (1985) *Ask Any Woman: a London enquiry into rape and sexual assault: Report of the Women's Safety Survey Conducted by Women Against Rape* (Bristol: Falling Wall Press).

Hall, S., C. Crichter, T. Jefferson, J. Clarke and B. Roberts (1978) *Policing the Crisis: mugging, the state and law and order* (London: Macmillan).

Hall, S. and T. Jefferson (eds) (1976) *Resistance Through Rituals: youth subcultures in post-War Britain* (London: Hutchinson).

Hallsworth, S. and T. Young (2004) 'Getting real about gangs', *Criminal Justice Matters* 55.

Haltom, W. and M. McCann (2004) *Distorting the Law: politics, media and the litigation crisis* (Chicago: Chicago University Press).

Hamm, Mark S. (2007) *Terrorism as Crime* (New York: New York University Press).

Hamuer, J and M. Maynard (eds) (1987) *Women, Violence and Social Control* (London: Macmillan).

Hanmer, J., J. Radford and E. A. Stanko (1989) *Women, Policing and Male Violence* (London: Routledge).

Hannah-Moffat, Kelly (1995) 'Feminine Fortresses: women-centred prisons?', *Prison Journal*, vol. 75.

Hanson, F. Allan (1993) *Testing Testing: social consequences of the examined life* (Berkeley: University of California Press).

Harrell, A. and G. Peterson (eds) (1993) *Drugs, Crime and Social Isolation* (Washington, DC: Urban Institute Press).

Harris, R. (1992) *Crime, Criminal Justice and the Probation Service* (London: Routledge).

Harry, Joseph (1992) 'Conceptualising Anti-Gay Violence', in G. H. Herek and K. T. Berril (eds), *Hate Crimes* (Newbury Park, CA: Sage).

Hartless, J., J. Ditton., G. Nair and S. Phillips (1995) 'More Sinned against than Sinning: a study of young teenagers' experience of crime', *British Journal of Criminology*, 35.

Hayward, K. J. (2003) 'Consumer Culture and Crime in Late Modernity', in C. Sumner (ed.), *The Blackwell Companion to Criminology* (Oxford: Blackwell).

Hearnden, I. and M. Hough (2004) *Race and the Criminal Justice System: an overview to the complete statistics 2002–2003* (London: Home Office).

Hedderman, Carol and Lizanne Dowds (1997) *The Sentencing of Women: a section 95 publication*, Home Office Research and Statistics Directorate Research Findings no. 58 (London: Home Office).

Hedderman, Carol and Mike Hough (1994) 'Does the Criminal Justice System Treat Men and Women Differently?', Home Office Research and Statistics Directorate Research Findings no. 10 (London: Home Office).

Heidensohn, F. M. (1985) *Women and Crime* (New York: New York University Press).

Heidensohn, F. M. (1986) 'Models of Justice: Portia or Persephone? Some thoughts on equality, fairness and gender in the field of criminal justice', *International Journal of the Sociology of Law*, 14.

Heidensohn, F. M. (1991) 'Women and Crime in Europe', in F. M. Heidensohn and M. Farrell (eds), *Crime in Europe* (London: Routledge).

Heidensohn, F. (1994) 'Gender and Crime', in M. Maguire, R. Morgan and R. Reiner (eds), *The Oxford Handbook of Criminology* (Oxford: Clarendon Press).

Heidensohn, F (2006) *Gender and Justice: new concepts and approaches* (Cullompton: Willan).

Heidensohn, F. M. and M. Farrell (1991) (eds) *Crime in Europe* (London: Routledge).

Henry, Stuart (1994) *Social Control* (Aldershot: Dartmouth Publishing Company).

Henry, Stuart and Dragan Milovanovic (1994) 'The Constitution of Constitutive Criminology: a postmodern approach to criminological theory', in David Nelken (ed.), *The Futures of Criminology* (London: Sage).

Herek, G. H. and K. T. Berril (eds) (1992) *Hate Crimes* (Newbury Park, CA: Sage).

Hester, S. and P. Eglin (1992) *A Sociology of Crime* (London: Routledge).

Heusenstamm, F. K. (1975) 'Bumper Stickers and the Cops', in D. J. Steffensmeier and R. M. Terry (eds), *Examining Deviance Experimentally: selected readings* (Port Washington: Alfred).

Hillyard, P. and S. Tombs (2004) 'Beyond Criminology?' in P. Hillyard, C. Pantazis, C. Tombs and D. Gordon (eds) *Beyond Criminology: taking harm seriously* (London: Pluto Press).

Hindelang, Michael (1978) 'Race and Involvement in Common Law Personal Crimes', *American Sociological Review*, 27.

Hindelang, M. J., M. R. Gottfredson and J. Garofalo (1978) *Victims of Personal Crime: An Empirical Foundation for a Theory of Personal Victimization* (Cambridge: Ballinger).

Hindelang, M. J., T. Hirschi and J. G. Weis (1979) 'Correlates of Delinquency: the illusion of discrepancy between self-report and official measures', *American Sociological Review*, 44.

Hirschi, Travis (1969) *Causes of Delinquency* (Berkeley, CA: University of California Press).

Hirschi, Travis (1975) 'Labeling Theory and Juvenile Delinquency: an assessment of the evidence', in W. R. Gove (ed.), *The Labeling of Deviance: evaluating a perspective* (Beverly Hills, CA: Sage).

Hirst, P. Q. (1975) 'Radical Deviancy Theory and Marxism: a reply to Taylor, Walton and Young', in I. Taylor, P. Walton and J. Young (eds), *Critical Criminology* (London: Routledge & Kegan Paul).

Hobbs, D. (1988) *Doing the Business* (Oxford: Clarendon Press).

Hobbs, D. (1995) *Bad Business: Professional Crime in Britain* (Oxford: Oxford University Press).

Holdaway, S. (1983) *Inside the British Police* (Oxford: Blackwell).

Holdaway, S. (1991) *Recruiting a Multi-racial Police Force* (London: HMSO).

Holdaway, S. (1996) *The Racialisation of British Policing* (Basingstoke: Macmillan).

Hollaway, Wendy and Tony Jefferson (1997) 'The Risk Society in an Age of Anxiety', *British Journal of Sociology*, 48 (2).

Holmes, L. (2007) *Terrorism, Organised Crime and Corruption* (Cheltenham: Edward Elgar Publishing).

Home Office (1986) *Home Office Circular 69/1986* (London: HMSO).

Home Office (2006) *Statistics on Race and the Criminal Justice System – 2005* (London: Home Office).

Hood-Williams, J. (2001) 'Gender, Masculinities and Crime; from structures to psyches' *Theoretical Criminology*, 5 (1).

Hope, T. (2005) 'Pretend it doesn't work: the "anti-social" bias in the Maryland scientific methods scale' *European Journal on Criminal Policy and Research*, 11, 3–4.

Hope, T. and R. Sparks (eds.) (2000) *Crime, Risk and Insecurity* (London: Routledge).

Horowitz, I. L. and M. Leibowitz (1968) 'Social Deviance and Political Marginality: towards a redefinition of the relationship between sociology and politics', *Social Problems*, 15 (3).

Horowitz, R. and A. E. Pottieger (1991) 'Gender Bias in Juvenile Justice Handling of Seriously Crime-Involved Youth', *Journal of Crime and Delinquency*, 28.

Hough, M. (1995) *Anxiety about Crime: Home Office Research Study No. 147* (London: Home Office).

Hough, M. and P. Mayhew (1985) *Taking Account of Crime* (London: HMSO).

Hough, Michael and Julian Roberts (1998) *Attitudes to Punishment: findings from the 1996 British Crime Survey*, Home Office Research and Statistics Directorate Research Findings no. 64 (London: Home Office).

Hughes, G. (2006) *The Politics of Crime and Community* (Basingstoke: Palgrave Macmillan).

Hughes, Robert (1993) *The Culture of Complaint* (New York: Oxford University Press).

Jackson, Pamela Irving (1992) 'Minority Group Threat, Social Context and Policing', in A. E. Liska (ed.), *Social Threat and Social Control* (Albany, NY: State University of New York Press).

Jamieson, R. and K. McEvoy (2005) 'State Crime by Proxy and Juridical Othering', *British Journal of Criminology*, 45.

Jansson, K. (2006) *Black Minority Ethnic Groups' Experiences and Perceptions of Crime, Racially Motivated Crime and the Police: findings from the 2004/5 British Crime Survey* (London: Home Office Online Report).

Jefferson, T. (1993) 'Pondering Paramilitarism', *British Journal of Criminology*, 33 (3).

Jefferson, T. (1997) 'Masculinities and Crimes', in Mike Maguire, Rod Morgan and Robert Reiner (eds), *Oxford Handbook of Criminology* (Oxford: Clarendon Press).

Jefferson, T. and J. Shapland (1994) 'Criminal Justice and the Production of Order and Control', *British Journal of Criminology*, 34 (3).

Jefferson, T. and M. Walker (1993) 'Attitudes to the Police of Ethnic Minorities in a Provincial City', *British Journal of Criminology*, 33 (2).

Jeffrey, C. Ray (1965) 'Criminal Behaviour and Learning Theory', *Journal of Criminal Law, Criminology and Police Science, 56.*

Johnson, R. E. (1979) *Juvenile Delinquency and its Origins* (London: Cambridge University Press).

Johnston, L. (1992) *The Rebirth of Private Policing* (London: Routledge).

Jones, M. (2009) 'Moral Panics' *Sociology Review,* 18 (3).

Jones, R. L. (ed.) (1989) *Black Adolescents* (Berkeley, CA: Cobb & Henry Publishers).

Jones, T. and T. Newburn (2007) *Policy Transfer and Criminal Justice* (Buckingham: Open University).

Jones, T., B. Maclean and J. Young (1986) *The Islington Crime Survey: crime, victimisation and policing in inner city London* (Aldershot: Gower).

Jorgenson, Nik, John Bird, Andrea Heyhoe, Bev Russell and Mike Savvas (1997) *Sociology: an Interactive Approach* (London: Collins Educational).

Joseph, J. (2003) 'Cyberstalking: an international perspective' in Y. Jewkes (ed.) *Dot.cons: crime, deviance and identity on the internet* (Cullompton: Willan).

Karmen. A. (1990) *Crime Victims: an introduction to victimology* (Pacific Grove: Brooks Cole).

Kasperson, Roger and Jeanne Kasperson (1996) 'The Social Amplification and Attenuation of Risk', *Annals of the American Academy of Political and Social Science,* 545.

Katz, J. (1987) 'What Makes Crime "News"?', *Media, Culture and Society,* 9.

Katz, J. (1988) *Seductions of Crime: moral and sensual attractions in doing evil* (New York: Basic Books).

Kauzlarich, D., C. Mullins and R. Matthews (2003) 'A Complicity Continuum of State Crime' *Contemporary Justice Review,* 6 (3).

Keith, M. (1993) *Race, Riots and Policing: lore and disorder in a multi-racist society* (London: University College London Press).

Kelly, L. (1988) 'How Women Define their Experiences of Violence', in Kersti Yllo and Michele Bograd (eds) *Feminist Perspectives on Wife Abuse* (Newbury Park, CA: Sage).

Kendall, K. (1991) 'The Politics of Premenstrual Syndrome: implications for feminist justice', *Journal of Human Justice,* 2 (2).

Kenney, D. J. (1987) *Crime, Fear and the New York City Subways* (New York: Praeger).

Kerr, J. (1994) *Understanding Soccer Hooliganism* (London: Routledge).

Kershaw C., S. Nicholas and A. Walker (2008) *Crime in England and Wales 2007/8: Findings from the British Crime Survey and police recorded crime* (London: Home Office).

Kersten, J. (1996) 'Culture, Masculinities and Violence Against Women', *British Journal of Criminology,* 36 (3).

Kimmell, M. S. and M. A. Messner (eds) (1989) *Men's Lives* (New York: Macmillan).

Kinsey, R. (1984) *Merseyside Crime Survey* (Edinburgh: Centre for Criminology, University of Edinburgh).

Kinsey, R. and S. Anderson (1992) *Crime and the Quality of Life: Public Perceptions and Experiences of Crime in Scotland: Findings from the 1988 British Crime Survey,* Scottish Office Central Research Unit (Edinburgh: HMSO).

Kinsey, R., J. Lea and J. Young (1986) *Doing the Fight Against Crime* (Oxford: Basil Blackwell).

Kirby, Mark, Warren Kidd, Francine Koubel, John Barter, Tanya Hope, Alison Kirton, Nick Madry, Paul Manning and Karen Triggs (1997) *Sociology in Perspective* (Oxford: Heinemann).

Klein, D. (1973) 'The Etiology of Female Crime: a review of the literature', *Issues in Criminology,* 8.

Kramer, Ronald, D. (1995) 'Exploring State Criminality: the invasion of Panama', *Journal of Criminal Justice and Popular Culture,* 3 (2).

Krier, R. (1987) 'Tradition-Modernity-Modernism: some necessary explanations', *Architectural Design Profile,* 65.

Krivo, Lauren J. and Ruth D. Peterson (1996) 'Extremely Disadvantaged Neighbourhoods and Urban Crime', *Social Forces,* 75 (2) (December).

Kubrin, C. (2005) 'Ganstas, Thugs and Hustlas: identity and the code of the street in Rap music', *Social Problems,* 52 (3).

Lacan, J. (1981) *The Four Fundamental Concepts of Psychoanalysis* (New York: Norton).

Lamb, L. (1996) *The Trouble with Blaming* (Cambridge, MA: Harvard University Press).

Landau, S. and G. Nathan (1983) 'Selecting Delinquents for Cautioning in the London Metropolitan Area', *British Journal of Criminology,* 23 (2).

Laub, J. and R. Sampson (2003) *Shared Beginnings, Divergent Lives: delinquent boys to age 70* (Cambridge, MA: Harvard University Press).

Lawson, Tony (1986) 'In the Shadow of Science', *Social Studies Review,* 2 (2) (November).

Lea, J. (1992) 'Left Realism: a framework for the analysis of crime', in J. Young and R. Matthews (eds), *Rethinking Criminology: the realist debate* (London: Sage).

Lea, J. and J. Young (1982) 'The Riots In Britain 1981: urban violence and marginalisation', in David Cowell, Trevor Jones and Jock Young (eds), *Policing the Riots* (London: Junction Books).

Lea, J. and J. Young (1984) *What is to be Done About Law and Order?: crisis in the eighties* (London: Penguin).

Lea, J. and J. Young (1993) *What is to be Done About Law and Order?: crisis in the eighties* (London: Pluto Press).

Lee, Murray (2007) *Inventing Fear of Crime: criminology and the politics of anxiety* (Cullompton: Willan).

Lees, S. (1989) 'Blaming the Victom', *New Statesman and Society,* 24 November.

Lemert, Edwin M. (1951) *Social Pathology* (New York: McGraw-Hill).

Lenning, E. and S. Brightman (2009) Oil, Rape and State Crime *Critical Criminology,* 17.

Leonard, Eileen B. (1982) *Women, Crime and Society* (New York: Longman).

Leonard, Madeleine (1995) 'Masculinity, Femininity and Crime', *Sociology Review*, 5 (1).

Levi, Michael (1997) 'Violent Crime', in Mike Maguire, Rod Morgan and Robert Reiner (eds), *Oxford Handbook of Criminology* (Oxford: Clarendon Press).

Levi, M., J. Burrows, J. Fleming and M. Hopkins (2007) *The Nature, Extent and Economic Impact of Fraud in the UK* (London: Association of Chief Police Officers).

Liazos, A. (1972) 'The Poverty of the Sociology of Deviance: nuts, sluts and preverts', *Social Problems*, 20.

Lilley, J. Robert., Francis T. Cullen and Richard A. Ball (1995) *Criminological Theory: causes and consequences* (London: Sage).

Liska, A. E. (ed.) (1992) *Social Threat and Social Control* (Albany, NY: State University of New York Press).

Liska, Allen A. and Paul E. Bellair (1995) 'Violent Crime-rates and Racial Composition', *American Journal of Sociology*, 101 (3) (November).

Loader, Ian (1997) 'Policing and the Social: questions of symbolic power', *British Journal of Sociology*, 48 (1) (March).

Loader, I. and A. Mulcahy (2003) *Policing and the Condition of England: memory, politics and* culture (Oxford: Oxford University Press).

Lombroso, Cesare (1911) *Crime: its causes and remedies* (Boston, MA: Little, Brown).

Lombroso, Cesare (1920) *The Female Offender* (New York: Appleton) (originally published 1903).

Lowman, J. (1992) 'Police Practices and Crime Rates in the Lower World: prostitution in Vancouver', in D. Evans, N. R. Fyfe and D. T. Herbert (eds), *Crime, Policing and Place: essays in environmental criminology* (London: Routledge).

Lowney, Kathleen (1995) 'Teenage Satanism as Oppositional Youth Subculture', *Journal of Contemporary Ethnography*, 23.

Lowry, P., S. Hassig, R. Gunn and J. Mathison (1988) 'Homicide Victims in New Orleans: recent trends', *American Journal of Epidemiology*, 128.

Luckenbill, David F. and Daniel P. Doyle (1989) 'Structural Position and Violence: developing a cultural explanation', *Criminology*, 27.

Luckhaus, Linda (1985) 'A Plea for PMT in the Criminal Law', in Susan Edwards (ed.), *Gender, Sex and the Law* (London: Croom Helm).

Luckhurst, I. (2003) 'Violence in families: male victims' *Sociology Review*, 13 (1).

Lurigio, A. J., W. G. Skogan and R. C. Davis (eds) (1990) *Victims of Crime: problems, policies and programs* (Newbury Park, CA: Sage).

Lyman, and G. Potter (2004) *Organised Crime* 3rd edn (New York: Prentice Hall).

Lynch, M. J., H. Schwendinger and J. Schwendinger (2006) 'The State of Empirical Research in Radical Criminology' in F. T. Cullen, J. P. Wright and K. R. Blevins (eds) *Taking Stock: the status of criminological theory* (New Brunswick, NJ, Transaction Publishing).

Lynch, M. and P. Stretesky (2003) 'The Meaning of Green: contrasting criminological perspectives', *Theoretical Criminology*, 7 (2).

Madood, T., R. Berthoud, J. Lakey, J. Nazroo, P. Smith, S. Virdee and S. Beishon (1997) *Ethnic Minorities in Britain: diversity and disadvantage* (London: Policy Studies Institute).

Madry, Nick and Mark Kirby (1996) *Investigating Work, Unemployment and Leisure* (London: Collins Educational).

Maguire, M. (2002) 'Crime Statistics: The Data Explosion and its Implications', in M. Maguire, R. Morgan and R. Reiner (eds), *The Oxford Handbook of Criminology*, 3rd edn (Oxford: Oxford University Press).

Maguire, M. (2007) 'Crime Data and Statistics' in Maguire, M., R. Morgan and R. Reiner (eds) *Oxford Handbook of Criminology*, 4th edn (Oxford: Oxford University Press).

Maguire, M. and T. John (2006) 'Intelligence Led Policing, Managerialism and Community Engagement: competing priorities and the role of the National Intelligence Model in the UK' *Policing and Society*, 16 (1).

Maguire, M. and J. Pointing (eds) (1988) *Victims of Crime: a new deal?* (Milton Keynes: Open University Press).

Maguire, Mike, Rod Morgan and Robert Reiner (1994) *Oxford Handbook of Criminology* (Oxford: Oxford University Press).

Maguire, Mike, Rod Morgan and Robert Reiner (1997) *Oxford Handbook of Criminology*, 2nd edn (Oxford: Clarendon Press).

Maguire, Mike, Rod Morgan and Robert Reiner (2002) *Oxford Handbook of Criminology*, 3rd edn (Oxford: Clarendon Press).

Maguire, Mike, Rod Morgan and Robert Reiner (2007) *Oxford Handbook of Criminology*, 4th edn (Oxford: Clarendon Press).

Makarenko, T. (2005) 'The crime-terror Continuum: tracing the interplay between transnational organised crime and terrorism' in M. Galeotti (ed.), *Global Crime Today: the changing face of organised crime* (Oxford: Routledge).

Marsh, P., E. Rosse and R. Harre (1978) *The Rules of Disorder* (London: Routledge).

Marsland, David (1988) 'Young People Betrayed', in Digby Anderson (ed.), *Full Circle: bringing up children in the post-permissive society* (London: Social Affairs Unit).

Marx, Gary T. (1988) *Undercover: police surveillance in America* (Los Angeles: University of California Press).

Marx, G. T. (2002) 'Technology and Social Control' in N. Smelser and P. Baltes (eds) *International Encyclopedia of the Social and Behavioral Sciences* (Oxford: Pergamon).

Massey, Douglas (1995) 'Getting Away with Murder: segregation and the making of the underclass', *American Journal of Sociology*, 96.

Massey, Douglas and Nancy Denton (1993) *American Apartheid: segregation?, the making of the underclass* (Cambridge, MA: Harvard University Press).

Matheson, J. and C. Summerfield (eds) (2000) *Social Trends 30* (London: The Stationery Office).

Matthews, R. (1992) 'Replacing "Broken Windows": crime incivility and urban change', in R. Matthews and J. Young (eds), *Issues in Realist Criminology* (London: Sage).

Matthews, Roger (1993) 'Squaring Up to Crime', *Sociology Review,* 2 (3).

Matthews, R. and J. Young (1986) (eds) *Confronting Crime* (London: Sage).

Matthews, R. and J. Young (1992) *Issues in Realist Criminology* (London: Sage).

Matthews, S., L. Brasnett and J. Smith (2006) *Underage Drinking: findings from the 2004 Offending, Crime and Justice Survey,* Findings 277 (London: Home Office).

Mawby, R. I. and S. Walklate (1994) *Critical Victimology* (London: Sage).

Maxwell, G. and A. Morris (2002) 'Restorative Justice and Reconviction', *Contemporary Justice Review,* 5 (2).

Mayhew, Pat, Ronald V. Clarke, A. Sturman and Mike Hough (1992) 'Steering Column Locks and Car Theft', in Ronald V. Clarke (ed.), *Situational Crime Prevention: successful cure studies* (New York: Harrow & Heston).

Mayhew, P., N. A. Maung and C. Mirrlees-Black (1993) *The 1992 British Crime Survey* (London: HMSO).

Mayhew, P. and J. Van Dijk (1997) *Criminal Victimisation in Eleven Industrialised Countries: key findings from the 1996 International Crime Victimisation Surveys* (London: HMSO).

McCahill, M. (2002) *The Surveillance Web: the rise of visual surveillance in an English city* (Cullompton: Willan).

McCarthy, Bill (1996) 'The Attitudes and Actions of Others: tutelage and Sutherland's Theory of Differential Association', *British Journal of Criminology,* 36 (1) (Winter).

McCarthy, B. and J. Hagan (1992) 'Mean Streets: the theoretical significance of situational delinquency among homeless youths', *American Journal of Sociology,* 98.

McConville, M. and D. Shepherd (1992) *Watching Police, Watching Communities* (London: Routledge).

McGaw, D. (1991) 'Governing Metaphors: the war on drugs', *American Journal of Semiotics,* 8.

McIntosh, M. (1975) *The Organisation of Crime* (London: Macmillan).

McKie, Robin (1995) 'America Trembles before a Plague of Murder', *Observer,* 19 February.

McLeod, E. (1982) *Women Working: prostitution now* (London: Croom Helm).

McNeill, Patrick and Charles Townley (eds) (1989) *Fundamentals of Sociology,* 2nd edn (Cheltenham: Stanley Thornes).

McQuade, S. C. (2006) *Understanding and Managing Cybercrime* (Boston: Pearson).

McRobbie, Angela and Sarah L. Thornton (1995) 'Rethinking Moral Panic for Multi-Mediated Social Worlds', *British Journal of Sociology,* 46 (4) (December).

Mednick, S. A., T. E. Moffitt and S. A. Stack (eds) (1987) *The Causes of Crime: new biological approaches* (New York: Cambridge University Press).

Melossi, D. (1985) 'Overcoming the Crisis in Critical Criminology: Towards a Grounded Labelling Theory' *Criminology,* 23.

Melossi, D. and M. Pavarini (1981) *The Prison and the Factory: origins of the penitentiary system* (London: Macmillan).

Merton, Robert K. (1938) 'Social Structure and Anomie', *American Sociological Review,* 3 (October).

Merton, R. K. (1949) *Social Theory and Social Structure* (New York: Free Press).

Messerschmidt, J. W. (1986) *Capitalism, Patriarchy and Crime: towards a socialist feminist criminology* (Totowa: Rowman & Littlefield).

Messerschmidt, J. W. (1993) *Masculinities and Crime* (Lanham: Rowman & Littlefield).

Messerschmidt, J. W. (1994) 'School, Masculinities and Youth Crime', in Tim Newburn and Elizabeth A. Stanko (eds), *Just Boys Doing Business* (London: Routledge).

Messerschmidt, J. W. (1997) *Crime as Structured Action: gender, race, class and crime in the making* (London: Sage).

Messner, Steven F. (1983) 'Regional and Racial Effects on the Urban Homicide rate: the sub-culture of violence re-visited', *American Journal of Sociology,* 88.

Messner, Steven F. and Reid Golden (1992) 'Racial Inequality and Racially Disaggregated Homicide Rates: an assessment of alternative theoretical explanations', *Criminology,* 30 (3).

Messner, Steven F. and R. Rosenfeld (2001) *Crime and the American Dream,* 3rd edn (Belmont: Wadsworth).

Michalowski, Raymond J. and Edward W. Bohlander (1976) 'Repression and Criminal Justice in Capitalist America', *Sociological Inquiry,* 46.

Michalowski, R. and R. Kramer (2006) 'State-corporate Crime and Criminological Inquiry' in G. Geis and H. Pontell (eds) *International Handbook of White Collar Crime* (Dordrecht: Plenum Publishers).

Miles, R. (1982) *Racism and Migrant Labour* (London: Routledge & Kegan Paul).

Miller, J. (2001) *One of the Guys: girls, gangs and gender* (New York: Oxford University Press).

Miller, Walter B. (1962) 'The Impact of a Total-Community Delinquency Control Project', *Social Problems,* 10.

Mirrlees-Black, C. (1995) 'Estimating the Extent of Domestic Violence: findings from the 1992 BCS', *Home Office Research Bulletin,* 37.

Mirrlees-Black, Catriona, Pat Mayhew and Andrew Percy (1996) *The 1996 British Crime Survey: England and Wales,* Home Office Statistical Bulletin issue 19/96 (London: HMSO).

Mirrlees-Black, Catriona and Tracey Budd (1997) *Policing and the public: findings from the 1996 British Crime Survey,* Home Office Research and Statistics Directorate Research Findings, 60 (London: Home Office).

Moffitt, T. E. (1993) Adolescent-limited and life course-persistent antisocial behaviour: a developmental taxonomy *Psychological Review,* 100.

Moffitt, T. E. (2006) 'A review of research on the taxonomy life of life course-persistent versus adolescent-limited antisocial behaviour' in F. T. Cullen, J. P. Wright and K. R. Blevins (eds), *Taking Stock: the status of criminological theory* (New Brunswick, NJ: Transaction Publishing).

Mooney, J. (2000) *Gender, Violence and the Social Order* (Basingstoke: Macmillan).

Moore, Mark H., Susan R. Estrich, Daniel McGillis and William Spelman (1984) *Dangerous Offenders: the elusive target of justice* (Cambridge: Harvard University Press).

Moore, Sally Falk (1973) 'Law and Social Change: the semi-autonomous field as an appropriate subject of study', in S. F. Moore (ed.), *Law as Process* (London: Routledge & Kegan Paul).

Moore, Stephen (1994) *A Level Sociology* (London: Letts Educational).

Moore, Stephen (1996a) *Investigating Crime and Deviance,* 2nd edn (London: Collins Educational).

Moore, Stephen (1996b) *Sociology Alive,* 2nd edn (Cheltenham: Stanley Thornes).

Moore, Stephen with Stephen P. Sinclair (1995) *Sociology: an Introduction* (London: Hodder & Stoughton).

Moore, S. F. (ed.) (1973) *Law as Process* (London: Routledge & Kegan Paul).

Morgan, P. (1978) *Delinquent Fantasies* (London: Maurice Temple Smith).

Morgan, R. (2006) 'With respect to order, the rules of the game have changed: New Labour's dominance of the "law and order" agenda', in T. Newburn and P. Rock (eds), *The Politics of Crime Control* (Oxford: Oxford University Press).

Morgan, R., I. McKenzie and R. Reiner (1990) *Police Powers and Policy: a study of custody officers* (London: ESRC).

Morris, A. (1987) *Women, Crime and Criminal Justice* (Oxford: Blackwell).

Morris, A. M. and L. R. Gelsthorpe (eds) (1981) *Women and Crime* (Cambridge: Institute of Criminology).

Morris, T. P. (1976) 'Commentary by Peter Morris on the Memorandum by the Metropolitan Police, vol. 3 Select Committee on Race and Immigration 1976–77 Session', quoted in Simon Holdaway (1996) *The Racialisation of British Policing* (Basingstoke: Macmillan).

Morrison, Wayne (1995) *Theoretical Criminology: from modernity to postmodernism* (London: Cavendish Publishing).

Mortimer, Ed and Chris May (1998) *Electronic monitoring of curfew orders the second year of the trials,* Home Office Research and Statistics Directorate Research Findings no. 66 (London: Home Office).

Mullins, C. W., R. Wright and B. A. Jacobs (2004) 'Gender, streetlife and criminal retaliation' *Criminology,* 42.

Mungham, G. and G. Pearson (eds.) (1976) *Working Class Youth Culture* (London: Routledge & Kegan Paul).

Munroe, L. (2004) 'Animals, "Nature" and Human Interests', in R. Wright (ed.), *Controversies in Environmental Sociology* (Melbourne: Cambridge University Press).

Murray, C. (1990) *The Emerging British Underclass* (London: IEA Health and Welfare Unit).

Naffine, Ngaire (1987) *Female Crime: the construction of women in criminology* (Boston: Allen & Unwin).

Naffine, Ngaire (1995) *Gender Crime and Feminism* (Aldershot: Dartmouth Publishing).

National Deviancy Conference (ed.) (1980) *Permissiveness and Control* (London: Macmillan).

Nee, Claire (1993) *Car Theft: the offender's perspective,* Home Office Research and Statistics Directorate Research Findings no. 3 (London: Home Office).

Nelken, David (1994a) *The Futures of Criminology* (London: Sage).

Nelken, David (1994b) 'White-Collar Crime', in Mike Maguire, Rod Morgan and Robert Reiner (eds), *Oxford Handbook of Criminology* (Oxford: Oxford University Press).

Nelken, David (2007) 'White-Collar and Corporate Crime', in Mike Maguire, Rod Morgan and Robert Reiner (eds), *Oxford Handbook of Criminology*, 4th edn (Oxford: Oxford University Press).

Nellis, M. (2004) 'They don't even know we're there: the electronic monitoring of offenders in England and Wales', in K. Ball and F. Webster (eds), *The Intensification of Surveillance: crime, terrorism and warfare in the information age* (London: Pluto).

Newburn, Tim (2007) *Criminology* (Cullompton: Willan).

Newburn, T. and T. Jones (2007) 'Symbolizing Crime Control: reflections on zero tolerance', *Theoretical Criminology*, 11 (2).

Newburn, T., M. Shiner and S. Hayman (2004) 'Race, Crime and Injustice: strip search and the treatment of suspects in custody', *British Journal of Criminology*, 44.

Newburn, T. and R. Sparks (2004) *Criminal Justice and Political Cultures* (Cullompton, Devon: Willan).

Newburn, Tim and Elizabeth A. Stanko (1994) *Just Boys Doing Business* (London: Routledge).

Newburn, Tim and Elizabeth A. Stanko (1994) 'When Men are Victims', in Tim Newburn and Elizabeth A. Stanko (eds), *Just Boys Doing Business* (London: Routledge).

Noaks, Lesley, Michael Levi and Mike Maguire (1995) *Contemporary Issues in Criminology* (Cardiff: University of Wales Press).

Nurge, D. (2002) 'Liberating yet limiting: the paradox of female gang membership', in L. Kontos, D. Brotherton, and L. Barrios (eds), *Alternative Perspectives on Gangs and the Community* (New York: Columbia University Press).

Oakley, R. (1993) *Racial Violence and Harassment in Europe* (Brussels: Council of Europe).

O'Donnell, M. (1997) *Introduction to Sociology*, 4th edn (Walton-on-Thames: Nelson).

O'Donnell, Mike and Joan Garrod (1990) *Sociology in Practice* (Walton-on-Thames: Nelson).

Ohmae, K. (2005) *The Borderless World: power and strategy in the interlinked economy* (New York: HarperBusiness).

O'Malley, Pat (1991) 'After Discipline? Crime Prevention, the strong state and the free market', paper presented at the Law and Society Association Annual Conference, Amsterdam, cited in Stanley Cohen (1994) 'Social Control and the Politics of Reconstruction', in David Nelken (ed.), *The Futures of Criminology* (London: Sage).

O'Malley, P. (2004) *Risk, Uncertainty and Government* (London: Glasshouse Press).

O'Sullivan, S. (2006) 'Cops on the Box: the media and policing' *Sociology Review* 16, 1.

Padilla, Felix (1992) *The Gang as an American Enterprise* (New Brunswick: Rutgers University Press).

Paglia, C. (1992) *Sex, Art and American Culture* (New York: Vintage).

Pahl, J. (ed.) (1985) *Private Violence and Public Policy* (London: Routledge & Kegan Paul).

Pain, R. (1991) 'Space, Sexual Violence and Social Control: Integrating Geographical and Feminist Analyses of Women's Fear of Crime', *Progress in Human Geography*, 15.

Pantazis, C. and Gordon, D. (1997) 'Television Licence Evasion and the Criminalisation of Female Poverty', *Howard Journal of Criminal Justice*, 36 (2).

Park, R. and W. E. Burgess (1927) *The Urban Community* (Chicago, IL: Chicago University Press).

Parsons, Talcott (1942) 'Age and Sex in the Social Structure of the United States', *American Sociological Review*, 7.

Passas, Nikos (1990) 'Anomie and Corporate Deviance', *Contemporary Crises*, 14.

Patterson, G. R. and K. Yoerger (1997) 'A Developmental Model for Late-onset delinquency' in D. W. Osgood (ed.) *Motivation and Delinquency* (Lincoln, NE: University of Nebraska Press).

Patrick, James (1973) *A Glasgow Gang Observed* (London: Eyre Methuen).

Pavarini, Massimo (1994) 'Is Criminology Worth Saving?', in David Nelken (ed.), *The Futures of Criminology* (London: Sage).

Pearce, F. and S. Tombs (1990) 'Ideology, Hegemony and Empiricism; compliance theories of regulation', *British Journal of Criminology*, 30.

Pearson, G. (1976) 'Cotton Town: a case study and its history', in G. Mungham and G. Pearson (eds), *Working Class Youth Culture* (London: Routledge & Kegan Paul).

Pence, Ken (1995) Rate Your Risk at (www.Nashville.Net/~police.risk).

Pepinsky, H. E. and R. Quinney (1991) *Criminology as Peacemaking* (Bloomington, IN: Indiana University Press).

Peterson, Ruth D. and Lauren J. Krivo (1993) 'Racial Segregation and Black Urban Homicide', *Social Forces*, 71 (4).

Petras, J. and C. Davenport (1991) 'Crime and the Development of Capitalism', *Crime, Law and Social Change*, 16.

Pfohl, S. J. (1985) *Images of Deviance and Social Control: a sociological history* (New York: McGraw-Hill).

Phoenix, J. (1998) *Making Sense of Prostitution* (London: Macmillan).

Pickering, S. and L. Weber (2006) *Borders, Mobility and Technologies of Control* (Amsterdam: Springer).

Pilcher, Jane (1993) ' "I'm Not a Feminist, But…": understanding feminism', *Sociology Review*, 3 (2).

Pilcher, Jane (1998) 'Hormones or Hegemonic Masculinity?: Explaining gender and gender inequalities', *Sociology Review,* 7 (3).

Piliavin, I., R. Gartner, C. Thornton and R. L. Matsueda (1986) 'Crime, Deterrence and Rational Choice', *American Sociological Review,* 51.

Piquero, A., D. Farrington and A. Blumstein (2007) *Key Issues in Criminal Career Research* (Cambridge: Cambridge University Press).

Player, E. (1989) 'Women and Crime in the City', in D. Downes (ed.), *Crime in the City* (London: Macmillan).

Pollack, O. (1950) *The Criminality of Women* (Philadelphia: University of Pennsylvania Press).

Pollner, M. (1976) 'Mundane Reasoning', *Philosophy of Social Sciences,* 4 (1).

Povey, David, Julian Prime and Paul Taylor (1998) *Notifiable Offences: England and Wales 1997,* Home Office Statistical Bulletin issue 7/98, April (London: Home Office).

Pratt, T. C., F. T. Cullen, K. R. Blevins, L. E. Daigle and T. D. Madensen (2006) 'The empirical status of deterrence theory: a meta-analysis' in F. T. Cullen, J. P. Wright and K. R. Blevins (eds), *Taking Stock: the status of criminological theory* (New Brunswick, NJ: Transaction Publishing).

Pulinger, J. and C. Summerfield (1998) *Social Trends 28* (London: The Stationery Office).

Quinney, Richard (1970a) *The Social Reality of Crime* (Boston, MA: Little, Brown).

Quinney, Richard (1970b) *The Problem of Crime* (New York: Dodd, Mead).

Quinney, Richard (1972) 'Who is the Victim?', *Criminology,* November.

Quinney, Richard (1975) *Critique of the Legal Order: crime control in capitalist society* (Boston, MA: Little, Brown).

Quinney, Richard (1977) *Class, State and Crime: on the theory and practice of criminal justice* (New York: McKay).

Raine, A. (2002) 'The Biological Basis of Crime' in J. Q. Wilson and J. Petersilia (eds) *Crime: public policies for crime control* (Oakland, CA: ICS Press).

Randall, Colin (1998) 'Parties Scramble to Claim Credit for Drop in Crime', *Daily Telegraph,* 8 April.

Ratcliffe, J. H. (2008) 'Intelligence-led Policing' in R. Wortley and L. Mazerolle (eds) *Environmental Criminology and Crime Analysis* (Cullompton: Willan).

Ray, L. and D. Smith (2001) 'Racist Offenders and the Politics of "hate crime"' *Law and Critique,* 12 (3).

Ray, L., D. Smith and L. Wastell (2004) 'Shame, Rage and Racist Violence', *British Journal of Criminology,* 44.

Reasons, C., L. Ross and C. Paterson (1981) *Assault on the Worker: occupational health and safety in Canada* (Toronto: Butterworths).

Reckless, Walter C. (1967) *The Crime Problem,* 4th edn (New York: Meredith).

Reiner, Robert (1985) 'The Police and Race Relations', in J. Baxter and L. Koffman (eds), *Police: the constitution and the community* (London: Professional Books).

Reiner, Robert (1992) *The Politics of the Police* (Sussex: Wheatsheaf).

Reiner, Robert (1993) 'Policing a Postmodern Society', *Modern Law Review*, 55.

Reiner, R. (2007) *Law and order: an honest citizen's guide to crime and control* (Cambridge: Polity Press).

Reiss, A. J. (1951) 'Delinquency as a Failure of Personal and Social Controls', *American Sociological Review*, 16.

Reiss, Albert J. (1960) 'Sex Offences: the marginal status of the adolescent', *Law and Contemporary Problems*, 25.

Reiss, Albert J. (1986) 'Why Are Communities Important in Understanding Crime?', in Albert J. Reiss and Michael Tonry (eds), *Communities and Crime* (Chicago, IL: University of Chicago Press).

Reiss, Albert J. and Michael Tonry (eds) (1986) *Communities and Crime* (Chicago, IL: University of Chicago Press).

Reus-Ianni, E. (1983) *The Two Cultures of Policing* (New Brunswick: Transaction).

Revenga, Ana (1992) 'Exporting Jobs? The Impact of Import Competition on Employment and Wages in U.S. Manufacturing', *Quarterly Journal of Economics*, 107, pp. 255–82.

Rice, Marcia (1990) 'Challenging Orthodoxies in Feminist Theory', in L. R. Gelsthorpe and A. M. Morris (eds), *Feminist Perspectives in Criminology* (London: Routledge & Kegan Paul).

Richards, Pamlea and Charles Tittle (1981) 'Gender and Perceived Chances of Arrest', *Social Forces*, 59.

Rock, P. (1973) *Deviant Behaviour* (London: Hutchinson).

Roiphe, K. (1994) *The Morning After: sex, fear and feminism on campus* (New York: Little, Brown).

Roncek, Dennis and Pamela A. Maier (1991) 'Bars, Blocks and Crimes Revisited: linking the theory of routine activities to the empiricism of "hot spots"', *Criminology*, 29.

Roshier, B. (1989) *Controlling Crime* (Milton Keynes: Open University Press).

Ross, J. I. (2000) *Varieties of State Crime and its Control* (Monsey, NY: Criminal Justice Press).

Ruggeiro, V. (1992) 'Realist Criminology: a critique', in J. Young and R. Matthews (eds), *Rethinking Criminology: the realist debate* (London: Sage).

Ruggeiro, V. (1996) *Organized and Corporate Crime in Europe* (Aldershot: Dartmouth).

Rusche, G. and O. Kirchheimer (1968) *Punishment and Social Structure* (New York: Russell and Russell).

Rutter, M. (2007) *Genes and Behaviour* (Malden, MA: Wiley-Blackwell).

Sacco, Vincent (1995) 'Media Constructions of Crime', *Annals of the American Academy of Political and Social Science*, 539.

Sampson, Robert J. (1986) 'Effects of Socioeconomic Context on Official Reaction to Juvenile Delinquency', *American Sociological Review*, 51.

Sampson, Robert J. (2006) 'Collective Efficacy: lessons learned and directions for future inquiry' in F. T Cullen, J. P. Wright and K. R. Blevins (eds), *Taking Stock: the status of criminological theory* (New Brunswick, NJ: Transaction Publishing).

Sampson, Robert J. and W. Byron Groves (1989) 'Community Structure and Crime: testing social-disorganisation theory', *American Journal of Sociology*, 94 (4) (January).

Sampson, Robert J. and John H. Laub (1992) 'Crime and Deviance in the life-course', *Annual Review of Sociology*, 18.

Sampson, Robert J. and John H. Laub (1993a) *Crime in the Making: pathways and turning points through life* (Cambridge, MA: Harvard University Press).

Sampson, Robert J. and John H. Laub (1993b) 'Structural Variations in Juvenile Court Processing: inequality, the underclass and social control', *Law and Society Review*, 27.

Sampson, Robert J. and John H. Laub (2005) 'A life-course view of the development of crime', *Annals of the American Academy of Political and Social Science*, 602.

Sampson, Robert J. and William Julius Wilson (1993) 'Towards a Theory of Race, Crime and Urban Inequality', in John Hagan and Ruth Peterson (eds), *Crime and Inequality* (Stanford: Stanford University Press).

Sampson, Robert J. and William Julius Wilson (1995) 'Race, Crime and Urban Inequality', in John Hagan and Ruth D. Peterson (eds), *Crime and Inequality* (Stanford: Stanford University Press).

Sanday, P. (1981) 'The Socio-Cultural Context of Rape: a cross-cultural study', *Journal of Social Issues*, 37 (4).

Sanderson, J. (1994) *Criminology: Textbook*, 5th edn (London: Holborn Law Tutors).

Schneider, H. J. (ed.) (1982) *The Victim in International Perspective* (Berlin: de Gruyter).

Schur, E. M. and H. A. Bedau (1974) *Victimless Crimes: two sides of a controversy* (Englewood Cliffs, NJ: Prentice-Hall).

Schwendinger, Herman and Julia S. Schwendinger (1985) *Adolescent Subcultures and Delinquency* (New York: Praeger).

Scraton, P. (1985) *The State of the Police: is law and order out of control?* (London: Pluto).

Scraton, P. (ed.) (1987) *Law, Order and the Authoritarian State* (Milton Keynes: Open University Press).

Self, A. (ed.) (2008) *Social Trends 38* (Basingstoke: Palgrave Macmillan).

Self, A. and L. Zealey (eds) (2007) *Social Trends 37* (Basingstoke: Palgrave Macmillan).

Sellin, Thorstein (1938) *Culture, Conflict and Crime* (New York: Social Science Research Council).

Shah, R. and K. Pease (1992) 'Crime, Race and Reporting to the Police', *The Howard Journal*, 31 (3).

Shaw, Clifford R. and Henry D. McKay (1931) *Social Factors in Juvenile Delinquency* (Washington, DC: Government Printing Office).

Shaw, Clifford R. and Henry D. McKay (1942) *Juvenile Delinquency in Urban Areas* (Chicago, Ill.: University of Chicago Press).

Shearing, Clifford D. (1992) 'The Relation Between Public and Private Policing', in M. Tonry and N. Morris (eds), *Modern Policing* (Chicago, IL: Chicago University Press).

Shearing, Clifford D. and Philip C. Stenning, (1983) 'Private Security: implications for social control', *Social Problems,* 30.

Sheley, Joseph (ed.) (1991) *Criminology* (Belmont: Wadsworth).

Sherman, L. (1992) 'Attacking Crime: policing and crime control', in M. Tonry and N. Morris (eds), *Modern Policing* (Chicago: University of Chicago Press).

Shute, S., R. Hood and F. Seemungal (2005) *A Fair Hearing?: Ethnic minorities in criminal courts* (Cullompton: Willan).

Silvestri, Merissa and Chris Crowther-Dowey (2008) *Gender and Crime* (London: Sage).

Simmons, J. and T. Dodd (2003) *Crime in England and Wales 2002/2003: Home Office Statistical Bulletin* (London: Home Office).

Simon, Rita J. (1975) *Women and Crime* (Lexington, MA: D.C. Heath).

Simon, D. R. and D. S. Eitzen (1993) *Elite Deviance* (Needham Heights, MA: Allyn & Bacon).

Simpson, Sally (1991) 'Caste, Class and Violent Crime: explaining difference in female offending', *Criminology,* 29.

Situ, Y. and D. Emmons (2000) *Environmental Crime: the criminal justice system's role in protecting the environment* (Thousand Oaks: Sage).

Skogan, W. (1990) *Disorder and Decline: crime and the spiral of decay in American neighbourhoods* (New York: Free Press).

Skolnick, Jerome (1966) *Justice without Trial* (New York: Wiley).

Skolnick, J. and D. Bayley (1986) *The New Blue Line* (New York: Free Press).

Smart, C. (1981) 'Response to Greenwood', in A. M. Morris and L. R. Gelsthorpe (eds), *Women and Crime* (Cambridge: Institute of Criminology).

Smart, Carol (1989) *Feminism and the Power of Law* (London: Routledge).

Smart, Carol (1990) 'Feminist Approaches to Criminology, or Postmodern Woman Meets Atavistic Man', in L. R. Gelsthorpe and A. M. Morris (eds), *Feminist Perspectives in Criminology* (London: Routledge & Kegan Paul).

Smith, David J. (1997) 'Ethnic Origins, Crime and Criminal Justice', in Mike Maguire, Rod Morgan and Robert Reiner (eds), *Oxford Handbook of Criminology* (Oxford: Clarendon Press).

Smith, D. J. (1983) *Police and People in London: A Survey of Londoners* (London: Policy Studies Institute).

Smith, Douglas (1986) The Neighbourhood Context of Police Behaviour', in Albert J. Reiss and Michael Tonry (eds), *Communities and Cities* (Chicago, IL: University of Chicago Press).

Smith, Douglas and Christy Visher (1982) 'Street Level Justice: situational determinants of police arrest decisions', *Social Problems,* 29.

Social Focus on Ethnic Minorities (1996) (London: The Stationery Office).

Social Trends (1994) vol. 24 (London: The Stationery Office).

Social Trends (1997) vol. 27 (London: The Stationery Office).

Social Trends (1998) vol. 28 (London: The Stationery Office).

South, Nigel (1988) *Policing for Profit* (London: Sage).

South, Nigel (1997) 'New Directions in the Study of Criminal Organization', *Sociology Review,* 7 (1).

Sparks, R. (1992) *Television and the Drama of Crime: moral tales and the place of crime in public life* (Buckingham: Open University Press).

Spierenburg, P. (1984) *The Spectacle of Suffering* (Cambridge: Cambridge University Press).

Spiro, Melford E. (1968) 'Culture and Personality', in *International Encyclopedia of the Social Sciences Volume 3* (New York: Macmillan and Free Press).

Spitzer, Steven (1976) 'Towards a Marxian Theory of Deviance', *Social Problems,* 22 (5).

Stanko, E. (1985) *Intimate Intrusions* (London: Routledge & Kegan Paul).

Stanko, E. (1988) 'Hidden Violence Against Women', in M. Maguire and J. Pointing (eds), *Victims of Crime: a new deal?* (Milton Keynes: Open University Press).

Staples, R. (1989) 'Masculinity and Race: the dual dilemma of black men', in M. S. Kimmell and M. A. Messner (eds), *Men's Lives* (New York: Macmillan).

Stark, Rodney (1987) 'Deviant Places: a theory of the ecology of crime', *Criminology,* 25.

Steffensmeier, Darrell and Emilie Allan (1991) 'Gender, Age and Crime', in Joseph Sheley (ed.), *Criminology* (Belmont: Wadsworth).

Steffensmeier, Darrell J. and R. M. Terry (eds) (1975) *Examining Deviance Experimentally: selected readings* (Port Washington: Alfred).

Stenson, K. and D. Cowell (eds) (1991) *The Politics of Crime Control* (London: Sage).

Stephens, M. and S. Becker (eds) (1994) *Police Force, Police Service: care and control in Britain* (London: Macmillan).

Stevens, P. and C. Willis (1979) *Race, Crime and Arrests* (London: Home Office).

Straus, M. and M. Gelles (1990) *Physical Violence in American Families* (New Brunswick, NJ: Transaction).

Strossen, Nadine (1992) 'Academic and Artistic Freedom', *Academe,* 78.

Sugrue, Bill (1995) 'Interpretation and Application', *Sociology Review,* 4 (4).

Sullivan, M. (1989) *Getting Paid: youth crime and work in the inner city* (Ithaca: NY: Cornell University Press).

Sullivan, P. (2006) *101 Synoptic Links to Crime and Deviance* (Northumberland: Lindisfarne Press).

Sumner, Colin (1994) *The Sociology of Deviance: an obituary* (Buckingham: Open University Press).

Sutherland, Edwin H. (1942) *On Analysing Crime* (Chicago, IL: University of Chicago Press).

Sutherland, Edwin H. (1949) *White Collar Crime* (New York: Dryden Press).

Sykes, C. J. (1992) *A Nation of Victims: the decay of the American character* (New York: St Martin's Press).

Sykes, Gresham and David Matza (1957) 'Techniques of Neutralisation: a theory of delinquency', *American Sociological Review,* 22.

Sykes, Richard and John Clark (1975) 'A Theory of Deference Exchange in Police Civilian Encounters', *American Journal of Sociology*, 81.

Tame, C. R. (1991) 'Freedom, Responsibility and Justice: the criminology of the New Right', in K. Stenson and D. Cowell (eds), *The Politics of Crime Control* (London: Sage).

Tannenbaum, F. (1938) *Crime and the Community* (New York: Columbia University Press).

Task Force on Federally Sentenced Women (1990) *Creating Choices: Report of the Task Force on Federally Sentenced Women* (Ottawa: Correctional Service of Canada).

Taub, Diane and Lawrence Nelson (1993) 'Satanism in Contemporary America: establishment or underground?', *Sociological Quarterly*, 34.

Taussig, M. (2002) 'Culture of terror – Space of Death: Roger Casement's Putumayo Report and the explanation of torture' in A. L. Hinton (ed.), *Genocide: an anthropological reader* (Oxford: Blackwell).

Taylor, I. (1981) *Law and Order: arguments for socialism* (London: Macmillan).

Taylor, I. (1987) 'British Soccer after Bradford', *Sociology of Sport Journal*, 4.

Taylor, Ian (ed.) (1990) *The Social Effects of Free Market Policies* (Hemel Hampstead: Harvester Wheatsheaf).

Taylor, Ian (1995) 'Critical Criminology and the Free Market', in Lesley Noaks, Michael Levi and Mike Maguire (eds), *Contemporary Issues in Criminology* (Cardiff: University of Wales Press).

Taylor, Ian (1997) 'Running on Empty', *Social Science Teacher*, 27 (1).

Taylor, Ian, Paul Walton and Jock Young (1973) *The New Criminology: for a social theory of deviance* (London: Routledge & Kegan Paul).

Taylor, I., P. Walton and J. Young (eds) (1975) *Critical Criminology* (London: Routledge & Kegan Paul).

Taylor, P., J. Richardson, A. Yeo, I. Marsh, K. Trobe and A. Pilkington (1995) *Sociology in Focus* (Ormskirk: Causeway Press).

Taylor, R. L. (1989) 'Black Youth Role Models and the Social Construction of Identity', in R. L. Jones (ed.), *Black Adolescents* (Berkeley, CA: Cobb & Henry).

Thornton, S. L. (1995) *Club Culture: music, media and subcultural capital* (Oxford: Polity Press).

Tierney, J. (1980) 'Political Deviance: a critical commentary on a case study', *Sociological Review*, 36 (1) (February).

Tifft, Larry L. (1979) 'The Coming Redefinitions of Crime: an anarchist perspective', *Social Problems*, 26.

Tilley, N. (2003) 'Community Policing, problem-oriented policing and intelligence-led policing', in T. Newburn (ed.) *Handbook of Policing* (Cullompton: Willan).

Tittle, C. R., D. A. Ward and H. G. Grasmick (2004) 'Capacity for self-control and individuals' interest in exercising self-control' *Journal of Quantitative Criminology*, 20.

Tombs, S. and D. Whyte (2007) *Safety Crimes* (Cullompton: Willan).

Tombs, Steve and Brian Williams (2008) 'Corporate Crime and its Victims', in Stout, B., J. Yates and B. Williams (eds), *Applied Criminology* (London: Sage).

Tonry, M. (1995) *Malign Neglect: race, crime and punishment in America* (Oxford: Oxford University Press).

Tonry, M. and N. Morris (eds) (1986) *Crime and Justice: an annual review of research Vol. 7* (Chicago, IL: University of Chicago Press).

Tonry, M. and N. Morris (eds) (1992) *Modern Policing* (Chicago, IL: Chicago University Press).

Traub, Stuart (1996) 'Battling Employee Crime: a review of corporate strategies and programs', *Crime and Delinquency,* 42.

Travis, Alan 'Police stop nearly 2m for questioning in year', *The Guardian,* 9 July 2008.

Turk, Austin (1969) *Criminality and the Legal Order* (Chicago, IL: Rand McNally).

Turk, Austin (1982) *Political Criminality: the defiance and defense of authority* (Beverly Hills, CA: Sage).

Uniform Crime Reports (1991) *Crime in the United States, 1990* (Washington, DC: US Government Printing Office).

Unsworth, Katherine (1997) 'A penny spent teaching will save a pound spent punishing', unpublished A-level project.

US Department of State (2004) *Office to Monitor and Combat Trafficking in Persons, Trafficking in Persons Report* (Washington, DC: Department of State).

Valentine, Gill (1989) 'The Geography of Women's Fear', *Arena,* 21.

Valentine, Gill (1992) 'Images of Danger: Women's Sources of Information about the Spatial Distribution of Male Violence', *Arena,* 24.

Van Ness, D. W. and K. H. Strong (2007) *Restorative Justice* (Cincinnati, OH: Anderson).

Ventura, H. E., J. M. Miller and M. Deflem (2005) 'Governmentality and the War on Terror: FBI Project Carnivore and the diffusion of disciplinary power', *Critical Criminology,* 13.

Virdee, S. (1997) 'Racial Management', in T. Madood, R. Berthoud, J. Lakey, J. Nazroo, P. Smith, S. Virdee and S. Beishon (eds), *Ethnic Minorities in Britain: diversity and disadvantage* (London: Policy Studies Institute).

Vold, G. B. (1958) *Theoretical Criminology* (New York: Oxford University Press).

Von Hentig, Hans (1948) *The Criminal and His Victim* (New Haven, CT: Yale University Press).

Wacquant, L. D. and William J. Wilson (1989) 'The Costs of Racial and Class Exclusion in the Inner City', *Annals of the American Academy of Political and Social Science,* 501.

Waddington, P. A. J., K. Stenson and D. Don (2004) 'In Proportion: race and police stop and search', *British Journal of Criminology,* 44.

Walker, M. A. (1989) 'The Court Disposal and Remands of White, Afro-Caribbean and Asian Men London 1983', *British Journal of Criminology,* 29 (4).

Walklate, Sandra (1994) 'Crime Victims: Another "Ology"?', *Sociology Review,* 3 (3).

Wall, D. (2001) *Crime and the Internet* (London: Routledge).

Wallace, A. (1986) *Homicide – the Social Reality* (Australia: NSW Bureau of Crime Statistics and Research Attorney General's Department).

Walmsley, R., L. Howard and S. White (1992) *The National Prison Survey 1991: Main Findings,* Home Office Research Study no. 128 (London: HMSO).

Ward, T. (2005) 'State Crime in the Heart of Darkness', *British Journal of Criminology,* 45.

Warr, M. and M. Stafford (1991) 'The Influence of Delinquent Peers: what they think and what they do', *Criminology,* 29.

Weale, Sally (1995) 'Girlz 'n' the Hood', *Guardian,* 19 September.

Webster, C. (2007) *Understanding Race and Crime* (Maidenhead: Open University Press).

Webster, Fiona (1993) 'The Crime of their Lives', *The Sunday Times,* 13 June.

Weisburd, David, Stanton Wheeler, Elin Waring and Nancy Bode (1991) *Crimes of the Middle Classes: white collar offenders in the Federal Courts* (London: Yale University Press).

Welch, M. (2003) 'Trampling Human Rights in the War on Terror: implications to the sociology of denial', *Critical Criminology,* 12.

White, R. (2008) 'Depleted Uranium, State Crime and the Politics of Knowing', *Theoretical Criminology,* 12 (1).

Whitehead, A, (2005) 'Man to Man Violence: how masculinity may work as a dynamic risk factor', *Howard Journal of Criminal Justice,* 44 (4).

Wilczynski, A. and A. Morris (1993) 'Parents Who Kill Their Children', *Criminal Law Review* (London: Sweet & Maxwell).

Wilkins, L. (1964) *Social Deviance: social policy, action and research* (London: Tavistock).

Wilkinson, P. (2006) 'Terrorism' in M. Gill (ed.), *The Handbook of Security* (Basingstoke: Palgrave Macmillan).

Williams, John (1996a) 'In Focus: Drugs', *Sociology Review,* 6 (1).

Williams, John (1996b) 'Football's Coming Home? From 1966 to 1996', *Sociology Review,* 6 (2).

Williams, John (1998) 'Research Roundup: Crime trends and fear of crime', *Sociology Review,* 7 (4).

Williams, Katherine S. (1997) *Textbook on Criminology,* 3rd edn (London: Blackstone).

Williams, Katherine S. (2004) *Textbook on Criminology,* 5th edn (Oxford: Oxford University Press).

Willis, Paul (1977) *Learning to Labour* (Farnborough: Saxon House).

Wilson, D., A. Patterson, G. Powell and R. Hembury (2006) *Fraud and Technology Crimes: findings from the 2003/04 British Crime Survey, the 2004 Offending, Crime and Justice Survey and Administrative Sources* (London: Home Office).

Wilson, Elisabeth (1991) *The Sphinx in the City: urban life, the control of disorder and women* (London: Virago).

Wilson, H. and G. Herbert (1978) *Parents and Children in the Inner City* (London: Routledge & Kegan Paul).

Wilson, James Q. (1975) *Thinking about Crime*, 2nd edn (New York: Vintage Books).

Wilson, J. Q. and R. J. Herrnstein (1985) *Crime and Human Nature* (New York: Simon & Shuster).

Wilson, J. Q. and G. Kelling (1982) 'Broken Windows', *Atlantic Monthly,* March.

Wilson, William J. (1987) *The Truly Disadvantaged: the inner city, the underclass and public policy* (Chicago, IL: University of Chicago Press).

Wilson, William J. (1991) 'Studying Inner-City Social Dislocations: the challenge of public agenda research', *American Sociological Review,* 56.

Wolfgang, M. (1958) *Patterns in Criminal Homicide* (Philadelphia: University of Pennsylvania Press).

Wolfgang, M. E. and F. Ferracuti (1982) *The Subculture of Violence: towards an integrated theory in criminology* (Beverly Hills, CA: Sage).

Worrall, A. (1990) *Offending Women* (London: Routledge).

Worrall, A. (2004) 'Twisted Sisters, Ladettes and the New Penology: the social construction of violent girls', in C. Alder and A. Worrall (eds) *Girls' Violence: Myths and Realities* (Albany, NY: State of New York University Press).

Wykes, Maggie (1995) 'Passion, Murder and Marriage', in R. E. Dobash, R. P. Dobash and L. Noaks (eds), *Gender and Crime* (Cardiff: University of Wales Press).

Yar, M. (2005) 'The Novelty of 'Cybercrime': an assessment in the light of routine activity theory' *European Journal of Criminology* 2, 4.

Yar. M. (2006) *Cybercrime and Society* (London: Sage).

Young, A. (1990) *Femininity in Dissent* (London: Routledge).

Young, A. (1994) 'Feminism and the Body of Criminology', in D. Farrington and S. Walklate (eds), *Offenders and Victims: theory and policy* (London: British Society of Criminology).

Young, J. (1986) 'The Failure of Criminology: the need for radical realism', in R. Matthews and J. Young (eds), *Confronting Crime* (London: Sage).

Young, J. (1988) *Realist Criminology* (London: Sage).

Young, J. (1991) 'Left Realism: alternative approaches to prevention and control', in Kevin Stenson and David Cowell (eds), *The Politics of Crime Control* (London: Sage).

Young, J. (1994) 'Incessant Chatter: recent paradigms in criminology', in Mike Maguire, Rod Morgan and Robert Reiner (eds), *Oxford Handbook of Criminology* (Oxford: Clarendon Press).

Young, J. (2007) *The Vertigo of Late Modernity* (London: Sage).

Young, J. and R. Matthews (eds) (1992) *Rethinking Criminology: the realist debate* (London: Sage).

Young, R. (2002) 'Testing the Limits of Restorative Justice: the case of corporate victims', in C. Hoyle and R. Young (eds), *New Visions of Crime Victims* (Oxford: Hart Publishing).

Zatz, Marjorie (1985) 'Pleas, Priors and Prison: racial/ethnic differences in sentencing', *Social Science Research,* 14.

Zedlewski, E. W. (1987) *Making Confinement Decisions* (Washington, DC: US Department of Justice).

Zedner, Lucia (1997) 'Victims', in Mike Maguire, Rod Morgan and Robert Reiner (eds), *Oxford Handbook of Criminology* (Oxford: Clarendon Press).

Zimring, F. (2006) *The Great American Crime Decline* (New York: Oxford University Press).

Zimring, F. and G. Hawkins (1990) *The Scale of Imprisonment* (Chicago, IL: University of Chicago Press).

Index